AF657684

THEORETICAL SOCIOLOGY

THEORETICAL SOCIOLOGY

Dr. S.S. Ralhan
Dr. S.R. Lambat

Theoretical Sociology

First Published : 2006

ISBN 81-311-0044-8

Published by :

Ajay Verma
For COMMONWEALTH PUBLISHERS
4831/24, Prahlad Street,
Ansari Road, Darya Ganj,
New Delhi - 110002
Ph. : 23272541, 23257835
Fax : 91- 011- 23257835
e-mail : campusbooks@hotmail.com

Typesetting by :

Arjun Computers
Delhi - 110051

Printed at :
S. P. Printech
Delhi

Bibliography

Althusser, Louis, *For Marx*, Allen Lane The Penguin Press, 1969, and New York, Random House, 1970, p. 25.

Applebaum, Richard P., *Theories of Social Change,* Chicago: Markham, 1970.

Armor, David, "The Evidence on Busing, "*The Public Interest,* no. 28 (Summer 1972): 90–126.

Astin, Alexander W., "Undergraduate Achievement and Institutional "Excellence," *Science,* vol. 161, no. 3842 (August 16, 1968): 661–68.

——, "A Summary of the Major Findings in 'The Second Year of Sesame Street: An Evaluation", Princeton, N. J.: Educational Testing Service, November 1971.

——, "Equal Schools or Equal Students?" *The Public Interest,* no. 4 (Summer 1966).

Ball, Samuel and Gerry Ann Bogatz, "A Summary of the Major Findings in 'The First Year of Sesame Street: An Evaluation'. 'Princeton, N. J. Educational Testing Service, October 1970.

Bandura, Albert and Richard H. Walters, *Adolescent Aggression,* New York; Ronald, 1959.

Barron, Milton, ed., *The Blending American,* Chicago: Quadrangel, 1972.

Barry, H., Margaret K. Becon, and I.L. Child, "A Cross-Cultural Survey of Some Sex Differences in Socialisation." *Journal of Abnormal Psychology,* vol. 55 (1957): 327–32.

Beard, Charles, *An Economic Interpretation of the Constitution of the United States,* New York: Free Press, 1949.

Becker, Howard S., *Outsiders,* New York: Free Press, 1963.

Becker, Howard S., ed., *The Other Side,* New York: Free Press, 1964.

Bell, Daniel, *The Coming of the Post-Industrial Society,* New York: Basic Book, 1973.

Bell, Daniel, *The Coming of the Post-Industrial Society,* New York: Basic Books; 1973.

Bell, Derrick A., Jr., "Racism in American Courts," *California New Law Review,* vol. 61, no. 1 (January 1973): 165–203.

Bellah, Robert N., "American Civil Religion in the 1970s," unpublished paper given at Drew University, March 1973.

Bellah, Robert N., *Beyond Belief,* New York: Harper & Row, 1970.

Berg, Ivar, *Education and Jobs: The Great Training Robbery,* New, York: Praeger, 1970.

Bettelheim, Bruno, *Children of the Dream,* New York: Avon, 1971.

Black, Cyril, *Dynamics of Modernisation,* New York: Harper & Row, 1968.

Bloch, Albert A., and Gilbert Geis, *Man, Crime and Society,* 2nd ed., New York: Random House, 1970.

Brightman, Lehman L., "Mental Genocide", *Inequality in Education,* no. 7 (February 1971): 15–19.

Brinton, Crane, *The Anatomy of Revolution,* New York: Random House, 1965.

Bronfenbrenner, Urie, "Socialisation and Social Class Through Time and Space," in Eleanor Maccoby. Theodore Newcomb, and Eugene L. Hartley, eds., *Readings in Social Psychology,* New York: Holt, Rinehart and Winston, 1958: 400–25.

Bronfenbrenner, Urie, *Two Worlds of Childhood,* New York: Russell Sage Foundation, 1970.

Bruce, Lenny, *How to Talk Dirty and Influence People,* Chicago: Playboy, 1963.

Chambliss, William J., "The Saints and the Roughnecks," Society, vol. 11 (December 11, 1973): 24-31.

Clark, Burton R., "The 'Cooling-out' Function in Higher Education", *American Journal of Sociology,* vol. 65 (May 1060): 567–76.

Cloward, Richard A., and Lloyd E. Ohlin, *Delinquency and Opportunity,* Glencoe, III: Free Press, 1960.

Cohen, Albert K., *Deviance and Control,* Englewood Cliffs, N.J.: Prentice-Hall, 1966.

Cohen, David K., "Public Schools: The Next Decade", *Dissent (*April 1971).

Coleman, James S., *The Adolescent Society.* New York; Free Press, 1961.

Cornish, Sally Woodhull, "Marriage Has Many Futures," *The Futurist* (June 1972): 103.

Covello, Leonard, *The Heart is the Teacher.* New York: McGraw-Hill, 1958.

Cox, Harvey, *The Secular City,* rev. ed., New York: Macmillan, 1966.

Craven, W. Frank, *The American Revolution, A Guide for Independent Study,* Princeton, N.J.: Princeton University Press, 1973.

Current Population Reports, "Literacy in the United States: November 1969," (series P-20, no. 217 (March 10, 1971).

Dahrendorf, Ralf, "*Toward a Theory of Social Conflict,*" in Etzioni-Halevy and Etzioni, 1973.

Davis, Alan J., "Sexual Assaults in the Philadelphia Prison System," in Wallace, 1971.

Demarath III, N.G., "Trends and Anti-Trends in Religious Change," in Eleanor B. Sheldon and Wilbert E. Moore, eds., *Indicators of Social Change,* New York: Russell Sage, 1968.

Demarath III, N.G., *Social Class in American Protestantism,* Chicago: Rand McNally, 1965.

Deutsch, Karl A., "The Growth of Nations: Some Recurrent Patterns of Political and Social Integration," *World Politics,* vol. 5, no. 2 (January 1953): 160 - 95.

Digest of Educational Statistics, Office of Education, Department of Health, Education, and Welfare. Washington, D. C.: Government Printing Office, 1970.

Dollard, John, et al., *Frustration and Aggression,* New Haven, Conn.: Yale University Press, 1939.

Durham, Michael, "For Swedes a Prison Sentence Can Be Fun," *Smithsonian* (September 1973): 46–52.

Durkheim, Emile, *The Division of Labour in Society,* New York: Free Press, 1964.

Durkheim, Emile, *The Elementary Forms of Religious Life* (1912), trans. by Joseph Ward Swain, New York: Free Press, 1965.

Durkheim, Emile, *The Rules of the Sociological Method* (1895), trans, by S.A. Solovay and J.H. Mueller Glencoe, III.: Free Press, 1964.

Edmiston, Susan "How to Write Your Own Marriage Contract," *Ms.* (Spring 1972): 66–74.

Eisenstadt, S.N., *Modernisation: Protest and Change,* Englewood Cliffs, N.J.: Prentice-Hall, 1966.

Eisenstadt, S.N., "Post Traditional Societies and the Continuity and Reconstruction of Tradition," *Daedalus* (Winter 1973): 1 - 27.

Erikson, Kai T., *Wayward Puritans,* New York: Wiley, 1966.

Etzioni-Halevy, E. and A. Etzioni, eds., *Social Change,* New York: Basic Books, 1973.

Farrell, William E., "School Integration Resisted in Cities of North," *The New York Times* (May 13, 1974): 24.

Findley, Warren G. and Miriam M. Bryan, *Ability Grouping, 1970: Status, Impact, and Alternatives*, Atlanta: University of Georgia, Center for Educational Improvement, 1970.

Friendenberg, Edgar Z., "Status and Role in Education", *The Humanist,* September-October 1968.

Friendenberg, Edgar Z., *Coming of Age in America: Growth and Acquiescence*. New York: Vintage, 1965.

Gasset, Jose Ortegay, *The Revolt of the Masses,* New York: Norton, 1957.

Gibbons, Donald, *Society, Crime, and Criminal Careers,* Englewood Cliffs, N.J. Prentice-Hall, 1968.

Glueck Eleanor and Sheldon, *Physique and Delinquency,* New York: Harper & Row, 1956.

Goffman, Erving, *Behaviour in Public Places,* New York: Free Press, 1963A.

Goffman, Erving, *Stigma : Notes on the Management of Spoiled Identity,* Englewood Cliffs, N.J.: Prentice-Hall, 1963B.

Goring, Charles, *The English Convict,* London: His Majesty's Stationery Office, 1913.

Goslin, David A., *The School in Contemporary Society.* Chicago: Scott, Foresman, 1965.

Gove, Walter R., "Societal Reaction as an Explanation of Mental Illness: An Evaluation," *American Sociological Review,* vol. 55 (October 1970): 873-84.

Gracey, Harry L., "Learning the Student Role: Kindergarten as Academic Boot Camp." In Dennis H. Wong and Harry L. Gracey, eds., *Readings in Introductory Sociology,* New York: Macmillan, 1972.

Hansen, W. Lea, and Burton A. Weisbrod, "The Distribution of Costs and Direct Benefits of Public Higher Education: The Case of California," in Harry G. Johnson and Burton A. Weisbrod, eds., *The Daily Economist,* Englewood Cliffs, N. J. : Prentice-Hall, 1969.

Harris, Marvin, *Culture, Man and Nature,* New York: Crowell, 1971.

Havighurst, Robert J., and Bernice Neugarten, *Society and Education,* Boston: Allyn & Bacon, 1968.

History and Class Consciousness: Studies in Marxist Dialectics, translated by Rodney Livingstone, London, Merlin Press, and Cambridge (Mass.) M.I.T. Press, 1971.

Hodgson, Godfrey, "Do Schools Make a Difference?" *The Atlantic,* vol. 213 (March 1973): 35–46.

Hoebel, E. Adamson, *Anthropology,* 4th ed. New York: McGraw-Hill, 1972.

Hollingshead, August B., and Frederich C. Redlich, *Social Class and Mental Illness,* New York : Wiley, 1958.

Holt, John, *How Children Fail.* New York: Pitman, 1964.

Holt, John, *The Underachieving School,* New York Dell, 1972.

Illich, Ivan, *Deschooling Society.* New York: Harper & Row, 1970.

Inkeles, Alex, "The Modernization of Man," in Myron Weiner, ed., *Modernisation,* New York: Basic Books, 1966.

Jackson, Philip W., *Life in Classrooms.* New York: Holt, Rinehart and Winston, 1968.

Jencks, Christopher, *Inequality: A Reassessment of the Effect of Family and Schooling in America.* New York: Basic Books, 1972.

Kagan, Jerome, "The Poor Are Educable," *The New York Times Annual Education Review* (January 16, 1974): 57ff.

Karnow, Stanley, "China-Journal-IV". *The New Republic* (July 28 and August 4. 1973): 9–21.

Kartz, Michael B., *Class, Bureaucracy and Schools: The Illusion of Educational Change in America.* New York: Praeger, 1971.

Katzenbach, Nicholas de B., Chairman, *The Challenge of Crime in a Free Society,* Washington, D.C.: U.S. Government Printing Office, 1967.

Kitsuse, John I., "Societal Reaction to Deviant Behaviour: Problems in Theory and Method," in Becker, 1964.

Knowles, Louis L. and Kenneth Prewitt, eds., *Institutional Racism in America.* Englewood Cliffs, N. J.: Prentice-Hall, 1969.

Kohl, Herbert R., *The Open Classroom: A Practical Guide to a New Way of Teaching.* New York: Vintage, 1969.

Kornhauser, William, *The Politics of Mass Society,* New York: Free Press, 1959.

Kuhn, James W., "The Misuse of Education. The Problem of Schooling for Employment," in Berg, 1970.

Larry L. and Joan M. Constantine, "Where is Marriage Going?" *The Futurist* (April 1970): 44–46.

Lauter, Paul and Florence Howe, "How the School System is Rigged for Failure." in *The Conspiracy of the Young,* New York, World, 1970.

Lewis, Flora, "Western Europe Falters," *The New York Times* (March 4, 1974): 1,7.

Lewontin, R.C., "Evolution—The Concept," *The International Encyclopaedia of the Social Sciences,* New York: Macmillan 1968.

Lombroso, Cesare, in G.L. Ferrero, *Criminal Man,* New York: Putnam, 1911.

Marx, Karl and Friedrich Engels, *The Manifesto of the Communist Party,* New York: International Publishers, 1932.

Merton, Robert K., *Social Theory and Social Structure,* Glencoe, III. : Free Press, 1957.

Miller, Walter B., "Lower-class Culture as a Generating Milieu of Gang Delinquency," *Journal of Sociological Issues,* vol. 14 (1958): 5–19.

Mitford, Jessica, *Kind and Usual Punishment,* New York: Knopf, 1973.

Moore, Barrington, *Social Origins of Dictatorship and Democracy,* Boston: Beacon Press, 1966.

Moore, Wilbert E., *Social Change,* Englewood Cliffs, N.J.: Prentice Hall, 1963.

Morgan, Edmund S., *The Birth of the Republic, 1763-89,* Chicago: University of Chicago Press, 1956.

Morris, Richard B., *The American Revolution Reconsidered,* New York: Harper & Row, 1967.

Myers, Jerome K., and Lee L. Bean, *A Decade Later: A Follow-Up of Social Class and Mental Illness,* New York: Wiley, 1968.

Nisbet, Robert A., *The Social Bond,* New York: Knopf, 1970.

Ophuls, William, "The Scarcity Society," *Harper's* (April 1974): 47 - 52.

Ottenberg, Simon, "Ibo Receptivity to Change," in William R. Bascom and Melville J. Herskovitz, *Continuity and Change in African Cultures,* Chicago: University of Chicago Press, 1959.

Parsons, Talcott, *Societies: Evolutionary and Comparative Perspectives,* Englewood Cliffs, N.J.: Prentice-Hall, 1966.

Parsons, Talcott, *The Social System,* New York: Free Press, 1951.

Rainwater, Lee, "Post-1984 America," *Society,* vol. 9, no. 4 (February 1972): 18 - 27.

Reich, Charles, *The Greening of America,* New York: Random House, 1970.

Reiss, Albert J., Jr., *The Police and the Public,* New Haven, Conn.: Yale University Press, 1971.

Roszak, Theodore, *The Making of a Counterculture,* New York: Doubleday, 1969.

Schur, Edwin M., *Crimes Without Victims,* Englewood Cliffs, N.J.: Prentice-Hall, 1965.

Schwartz, Barry "Deprivation of Privacy as a Functional Prerequisite' in the Case of Prison," *Journal of Criminal Law, Criminology and Police Science,* vol. 63 (1972): 229–39.

Schwartz, Herman "Prisoners' Rights: Some Hopes and Realities," in *A Programme for Prison Reform,* Cambridge, Mass.: The Roscoe Pound-American Trial Lawyers Foundation, 1972.

Schwartz, Richard D., and Jerome H. Skolnick, "Two Studies of Legal Stigma," in Becker, 1964.

Selznick, Philip, "Institutional Vulnerability in Mass Society," *The American Journal of Sociology,* vol. 56 (January 1951): 320 - 31.

Shaw, Clifford R., and Henry D. McKay, *Delinquency Areas,* Chicago: University of Chicago Press, 1929.

Shaw, George Bernard, *Saint Joan* (1924), Baltimore: Penguin, 1951.

Sheldon, William H., with Emil M. Hart and Eugene McDermott, *Varieties of Delinquent Youth,* New York: Harper & Row, 1949.

Srole, Leo, et al., *Mental Health in the Metropolis : The Midtown Manhattan Study,* New York: McGraw-Hill, 1962.

Sutherland, Edwin H., and Donald R. Cressy, *Principles of Criminology,* 6th ed., Philadelphia: Lippincott, 1960.

Sykes, Gresham, *The Society of Captives,* Princeton, N.J.: Princeton University Press, 1958.

"Following Up on Headstart," *The New Republic* (April 1, 1969): 12-13.

"Goals of the Headstart Program," Letter to the Editor, *The New York Times* (July 10, 1971).

"How Head a Head Start?" *The New Republic* (April 26, 1969): 8-9.

PREFACE

Efforts to improve social life were made in Europe in the nineteenth century. Taking its cue from science, sociologists wanted to reform societies on scientific lines. There were two streams of this effort, one was the capitalist stream and the other was the Marxist stream. Emile Durkheim belonged to the first category of sociologists and *Karl Marx* was the vanguard of the communist or the Marxist stream. Comments were made on history and class consciousness. What role played the element of deviance in social control. The institutions of family, education, religion and power politics were analysed and a theoretical frame work of sociological theory had emerged.

The authors are grateful to all the social philosophers of the west from whose works, most of the material has been collected.

Dr. S.S. Ralhan
Dr. S.R. Lambat

Contents

1

Personal Reality, Social Theory and the Tragic Dimension in Science

Gunnar Boalt's work on the *Sociology of Social Research* is a major contribution to a sociology of sociology and it provides substantial testimony to the seriousness with which many sociologists throughout the world today are probing toward a heightened self-awareness. It is not only in its social implications, however, but also in its scientific contribution that Professor Boalt's work is impressive. Indeed, I am tempted to suggest that his is perhaps the first systematic (if partial) theory of the sociology of sociology. Boalt's theory is enhanced by its ample discussion of the formal requirements for testing the theory systematically, by its provocative suggestions of a mathematical model that might further this testing, and, far from least, by its author's sensitivity to the problems and limits of his own theory as well as his full awareness of the way it ranges beyond a sociology of sociology to more general problems of sociological analysis. An appreciation of his work, moreover, cannot fail to be enlivened by its informal dimensions, by its casual, quiet thrusts of wry wit, and the civilised sensibility with which it firmly grasps the distinction between understanding something and having a theory about it.

Gunnar Boalt is a major Swedish sociologist who - with all this implies in a European university-occupies the Chair in Sociology at the University of Stockholm. This biographical remark is not, however, intended as an introductory nicety, or as a way of introducing him to American scholars unfamiliar with

Swedish sociology; rather, and as will be seen shortly, it is mentioned because of its specific relevance to the work he presents here. In particular, it will soon be apparent that, in formulating his theory about the sociology of social research, Professor Boalt has drawn freely and extensively from his own experience, both as a working sociologist and as an academic administrator. His work is enriched by the fact that he knows whereof he speaks; his 'theoretical self' has remained in open communication with his other roles or selves. He has pursued his work here not simply as an intellectual puzzle conducted within the narrow framework of an insulated professional role but also, it seems to me, as an effort at personal orientation disciplined by scholarly requirements.

This observation is, I think, of pointed relevance for the sociology of sociology. For insofar as this continues to develop, it will inevitably be subjected to pressures that aim to transform it into just one other technical specialty, and to make it serve as just one other topic for specialised panels at professional congresses to the extent that the emerging sociology of sociology succumbs to this pressure, it will probably be crippled in its capacity to further sociologists' understanding of their own personal situation, or of their profession as a personal situation. Boalt's work is a paradigm, in this respect as in others, of what a humanely conceived sociology of sociology should be. It is a technically disciplined effort at an understanding of a social role that has special (because personal) values to sociologists, namely, their roles as researchers and teachers.

The development of a sociology of sociology that would avoid a confrontation between the sociologist and himself would, I fear, be the development of a redundant specialisation. It would fail to achieve and to fulfil the only distinctive function that can be performed by a sociology of sociology. The development of a sociology of sociology as just one other technical specialisation would, in effect, be to use this intellectual innovation as a kind of sociological defence mechanism against the potential illuminations of self that such an enterprise inherently possesses.

While this connection between personal meaning and scholarly work is particularly visible in Boalt's work, it is a relationship that is germane to the sociology of sociology precisely because it is not peculiar to Boalt's work. For some appreciable part of any sociological enterprise is activated by the sociologist's effort to explore, to objectify, and to universalise some of his own most deeply personal experiences. Some part of the sociologist's effort to know the social world around him is an effort - more or less deliberate and disguised - to understand himself: his experiences in his social world and his reltionship to it. While this has no bearing on the validity of the resultant knowledge or theory, it does bear on another interest legitimate to the sociology of sociology: the sources, the motives, and the aims of the sociological quest.

In the following, I want to suggest something of the larger significance of a concern about the relation between the personal and the scholarly. I shall begin with the commonplace that all sociologists, however theoretical their bent, seek to explain-tacitly or overtly - some part of the social world. Not all parts of the social world are of equal interest or importance to sociologists, and they focus their attention upon it selectively. Very much under the influence of Talcott Parsons, many American sociologists during the forties and fifties assumed that this selectivity of focus was largely a function of the theory to which the sociologist was committed. 'Facts' were seen as the products of an effort to pursue the inferences of theories and, indeed, as constituted in terms of the conceptual schemes embedded in the structure of theories. From the standpoint of a sociology of sociology, however, we are interested in the *extra*-theoretical sources of theory, and in developing a view that acknowledges social theories as the work product of certain individuals who are seen as having a specific location in a specific social and cultural matrix.

With this as background, I will add that sociologists like others impute 'reality' to certain things in their social world; which is to say, they believe, sometimes with focal and sometimes with only subsidiary awareness, that the world has a certain character, that certain things are truly attributable to it. In what follows, I will suggest that it is not only theories or facts but anything that the sociologist defines as 'real' that will shape his work importantly. For simplicity's sake, I will suggest there are two kinds of things that are imputed to have reality by any sociologist. One consists of 'facts' yielded by previous researches, whether conducted by themselves or others. The second, however, consists of what I will call the 'personally real'. These are aspects of the social world to which sociologists will, like those who are not sociologists, impute reality because of their personal experiences: because of what they have seen, Learn, been told, or read, and which are distinct from 'facts' that have been systematically gathered and scientifically evaluated. Indeed, many elements in personal reality have been developed long before the sociologist was professionally trained or intellectually mature. The personal reality of the sociologist is every bit as real to him as the facts he has acquired through sociological research, although *his own* research - far more than that of others - becomes an especially important component of his personal reality.

Things to which the sociologists imputes reality, whether the factual or the personally real, may play a role in his sociological research in at least two ways, either as elements in his explanatory efforts or as foci around which these efforts develop. Here I want to concentrate in particular on the manner in which the imputedly real often becomes a focus around which certain (but not necessarily all) explanatory efforts converge, or as elements in the explanation. Most specifically, I want to suggest that the imputedly real enters into theory construction by being treated as possessed of a generalisable significance, by being regarded as examples of or cases of a larger set of realities. In other words, sociologists use what they impute to be real as paradigms or, in Stephan Pepper's terms, as a 'root metaphor'; they assume that things which they have researched or with which they have had some personal acquaintance are like other things with which they are unacquainted or have not yet researched.

Social theories or accounting schemes tend, therefore, to be generalised to a set of events that extend beyond the sociologist's facts or personal realities; yet, at the same time, such social theories tend to be influenced, limited or informed by the distinctive characteristics of the things to which sociologist has imputed reality.

To put the matter in another way: for the purpose of theory construction, sociologists treat imputed realities as models of a more extensive set of as yet unobserved events. They tend to assume that sections of the world that they have not yet encountered are similar to the smaller section incorporated in their facts or personal realities. Theory-making thus proceeds in a manner similar to the fable of the blind men and the elephant, each man generalising his theory from and anchoring it in a limited sector of the world to which he imputes reality and on the basis of which he generalises about larger wholes. Theories, therefore, are influenced by the distinctive character of the limited things to which we impute reality and which we use as root metaphors or paradigms. Thus, for example, one reason why Malinowski's theory of magic differed from Radcliffe-Brown's was because the data that each had used differed from the other's, Malinowski focusing on cases of work magic and Radcliffe-Brown on childbirth magic, and because each regarded his limited data as paradigmatic, that is, as exemplary of or essentially akin to other kinds of magic.

Sociologists, of course, are familiar with these dangers, at least *en principe,* and they seek to use systematic sampling as a way of obviating them. Nonetheless, sampling techniques cannot fully avoid the problem, for these only provide a basis for testing a theory subsequent to its formulation. If systematic research entails the use of a systematic sample in order to test inferences from a theory, then, in the nature of the case, the theory must be formulated prior to acquiring a systematic sample. Indeed, the more the sociologist stresses the importance of articulate theory the more this is likely to be the case. The theory will therefore tend to revolve around, and will consequently be skewed or shaped by, the limited facts and personal realities available to the theorist, and in particular by those imputed realities that he treats as paradigms.

Moreover, systematic sampling only constitutes a restraint on unjustified generalisations from 'facts', but does not similarly restrain the influence of 'personal realities'. Since the latter are deemed scientifically irrelevant, it is often assumed that they are scientifically inconsequential-which merely means that the sociologist has here confused the morality of science with its acutal practice. In point of fact, the personally real and problematic often enough becomes the starting point for disciplined inquiry - and, indeed, there is no scientific reason why this should not be the case.

What is personally real to men is real, frequently enough though not always, precisely because it is not personal to them - in the sense of idiosyncratic to or uniquely different for them - but because it is social and collective. Collectively held imputations of reality are, of course, among the most firmly constituted components of personal reality. Yet the personally real does not entirely consists of, or depend upon, collective definitions of social reality but may also derive from recurrent personal experiences-unique to the person or shared by others-in a sector of the social world. What becomes personally real, then, is not such simply because it is also personally real to others, or because these others have communicated their conception of reality. But whether deriving from collective definitions or from recurrent personal experiences, imputed realities are of special importance to the kinds of theories that sociologists formulate: 'facts' are only a special case of imputed realities.

It may therefore be instructive to review some of the things that are a part of Professor Boalt's 'personal reality', and which have formed the foci around which his theory of social research was constructed. We will notice that the personal reality of a Swedish sociologist may differ from that of an American sociologist. It would be naïve in the extreme, however, were we to conclude that this difference explains only the lacunae in Boalt's theory and if we fail to see that it also infuses his theory with certain strengths. It would also be naïve in the extreme were we to use the occasion only to observe how Swedish society affects the personal reality of Swedish sociologists in intellectually consequential ways, but failed to recognise that American society does exactly the same thing to American sociologists, even if in somewhat different ways.

In mentioning some of the elements in Professor Boalt's personal reality, I do not mean to be comprehensive but only exemplary. In the main, I shall focus on those elements that Professor Boalt tacitly tends to assume may be universal, that is, which he tends to treat as paradigmatic, but which I - from my different American personal reality - may not regard as universal. Thus, for example:

'I suppose most researchers reach their apex with their doctor's thesis or shortly afterwards. Once they have finally got a permanent position one of the motives urging them on to a high scientific standard disappears.' It is relevant to note here that Professor Boalt speaks explicitly of 'most' researchers as manifesting this pattern, thereby exemplifying precisely what I mean when I say that personal reality often tends to be taken as paradigmatic, that is, as indicative of the character of a larger sector than one has information about. Professor Boalt's observation above also seems to imply, first, that departments that train professional sociologists set extremely demanding scientific standards for their students and, secondly, that this high standard is expressed and enforced most especially in the preparation of a doctoral dissertation. It is my somewhat different impression, however, that many departments of sociology in the United States, particularly since the rapid expansion of the academic market for doctorates, perhaps since the mid-1950s, have come to stress that a candidate should not take 'too long' to complete his degree and have, therefore, searched for ways of expenditing the preparation of the dissertation. (In some part, it may be that the growing emphasis on the use of 'secondary analysis' as a way of writing dissertations may reflect this pressure to expedite the training of Ph.Ds.).

While this speed-up may not necessarily lead to a general decline in scientific standards-most endorsing an educational speed-up would deny that it does - nonetheless, it would seem to make the dissertation a less demanding task. Certainly, students are now less likely to be reminded that *The Division of Labour in Society* was Emile Durkheim's dissertation! In consequence of the tendency to 'relax' standards for the dissertation, one may at least wonder whether there is not a more general 'relaxation' of the scientific standards communicated to candidates. To teach students appropriate techniques and methodologies in seminars while, at the same time, telling them - as is now often done in the United States - that they must not dally over their dissertations, may be in effect to tell students that they can get by without applying and without internalising high scientific standards.

Many American students that I have known in the last decade take the attitude that their dissertation is a job of work that they must 'get out of the way'; presumably, after they graduate and take up positions elsewhere, they will then do work of importance and high standards. The relevant consideration here, however, is not the factuality but the personal reality of my statements about these patterns of training in some American universities, and my clear conviction that my 'personal reality' differs from Professor Boalt's - or that his differs from mine. Were I to take my own distinctive personal reality and treat it as paradigmatic and problematic, I might go on to propose a theoretical explanation along the following lines: namely, that the degree to which graduate-training centres emphasise scientific values may be a function of the market situation for those with new doctorate degrees. In other words, when there is a very limited and only slowly growing number of academic places for those with doctorates – as in Sweden and other European countries – an insistence on extremely high scientific standards serves to curtail the supply of doctorates and to accommodate to the smaller demand for them. Correspondingly, the reduction of scientific standards may be a way of increasing the supply of doctorates to fill a larger or growing demand for them. So much for out theoretical sketch. The important consideration here is that theory often tends to get constructed around a personal reality that is treated as paradigmatic and problematic. Yet Professor Boalt has been most unreasonable; he has constructed his theory around his personal reality rather than around mine!

Again: 'It is not hard to acquire the scientific values, but it is all the harder to satisfy them. Young research students have no idea of this, and it upsets them when they find that so many of the investigations they come across are full of shortcomings in so many respects.' Two points are worth developing here. First, there is a suggestion that an important part of Professor Boalt's personal reality entails a tacit focus on the researcher as a student. In other words, Swedish educators, like those in different cultures, seem to develop the conviction that an important part of their reality consists of students and of efforts to educate them. It may be, therefore, that of all the people an educator has an opportunity to observe doing research, a relatively large and salient group of them happen to be students. Furthermore, the extent to which a sociologist takes his educational responsibilities seriously, rather than subordinating them to his own research, will shape the extent to which he defines students as part of his personal reality.

In any event, my own personal reality in this respect seems to differ somewhat from Professor Boalt's'; for my part, I seem to find that some academic sociologists take their educational responsibilities to students rather more lightly than is implied by Professor Boalt's conception of the matter, and that some seem to treat their students as 'hired hands', or as paid subordinates. In short, they may treat students not as people to whom they have responsibility as educators, but as research clerks who have an obligation to do as they have been told. And while such academic sociologists may be few in number, since they so violate my own conception of the educational enterprise, even these few loom large in my own personal reality, thus anchoring it at some remove from Professor Boalt's.

That, so far as professors are concerned. Now, insofar as students are concerned, I should also confess that here, too, my personal reality appears different from Professor Boalt's. For my part, I simply would not have described the young research students whom I have known in quite the manner that Professor Boalt did, namely, as upset about the difficulty in realising scientific values. I, instead, see some of them as all too willing to do any tacky piece of work, so long as it is acceptable to their faculty and enables them to acquire a doctorate (the 'union card', as they say), even though they *know* that their work is tacky. Such student expectations are the counterpart of those held by professors who urge them to do almost any kind of study, just so long as they can complete it in short order. Still other students whom I have known - perhaps the better ones - far from being upset when they encounter scientifically deficient work, seem to be delighted; they may see this as confirmation of their own sense of superiority, and as justifying the contempt that they feel for those whose scientific values differ from their own. In short, Professor Boalt's and my personal realities seem to be somewhat different concerning both students and professors.

Indeed, it may well be that Professor Boalt's personal reality does not merely differ from mine with respect to students and professors but, further, that he thinks of men more generally somewhat differently than I do. He tends, I suspect, to think of them as being more highly conscientious, as being disposed to pursue fixed values with tenacious effort, as suffering deeply or as losing self-confidence when unable to achieve these values, and as persevering in the face of difficulty. Professor Boalt thus remarks that typically the researcher 'suffers setbacks [yet] we know that notwithstanding he usually perseveres.'

In other words, I suspect that Professor Boalt's personal reality contains an image of man broadly different from my own, and perhaps from that of many other Americans. I get the impression that Boalt tends to assume generally that men are more reluctant to surrender their high values, even in the face of difficulty, that they are more controlled by a punishing super - ego, that they are men of a Lutheran inwardness struggling within themselves to achieve conformity with high ideals, and who seek a kind of inner rectitude rather than success in the world and validation by others.

My point here, of course, is not that my personal reality is superior to Boalt', not that his is wrong and mine is right. I can well imagine that the opposite might be the case. Not only do I suspect that our personal realities differ, but I further suspect that this has a great to do with the fact that he is, in some large part, a product of Swedish culture and that I, in contrast, am a product of a more pragmatic, more gratification-seeking, and more exchange-oriented American culture. My point, then, is not at all - indeed, most definitely not - that a personal reality acquired in American culture provides a sounder basis for theory construction than one acquired in Swedish culture. My point simply is that these two cultures do generate somewhat different personal realities for those who have lived in them and that these provide different (not superior or inferior) bases for theory construction. In short, my point is that these culturally patterned differences in personal reality are theoretically consequential. In sum, I have the impression – and I know this will come as no surprise to Professor Boalt that his theory about the sociology of social research was formed around his experiences in Swedish culture and society, just as mine would be informed and limited by my experiences in American culture and society, and that, to some extent, both the penetration and the limitations of his theory are related to the personal reality he has acquired in Swedish society more generally, and in the Swedish university more particularly.

Let me develop this by elaborating a bit on my own impressions - in other words, by presenting my personal reality, not the 'facts' - concerning certain relevant aspects of Swedish culture and Swedish sociology derived in part from my reading, and in part from a brief visit in the summer of 1965 which provided me with an opportunity to talk with some Swedish sociologists, including Professor Boalt. Let me reiterate: these are impressions and are very far indeed from being the product of systematic observation.

As I poked about it, I somehow acquired a sense of the Platonic and, more particularly, the Apollonian, character of Swedish culture: the attitude towards sex was, it seemed to me, a far cry from frenzied promiscuity; I saw it, rather, as a disciplined effort to do the 'right' and 'rational' thing – to manage sex intelligently, to control the irrational rationally. I saw a similar Apollonianism in the widespread concern about excess drinking and the fear of drunkenness which, incidentally, was also one of Plato's pet anxieties. Above all, there was the Apollonian sense of Stockholm's public architecture and squares, each building well boundaried, sitting firmly in its own space and well demarcated from others, balanced and orderly. I had the impression that many of the men I met in various walks of lief felt that Reason and Theory were powerful forces and could see and plan much. Indeed, I felt that nowhere in Europe do ordinary men, as well as men of affairs, give a truer or at least a more energetic expression to their belief in a life of reason. I came to feel that what was developing there was Plato's 'second best city', the city of the Laws, permeated (in the Swedish case) by a humane but pervasive superintendence of daily life, by a measured *gravitas* that settles invisibly upon spontaneity, transforming joy into education, movies into theatre, and conversation into discussion.

It seemed to me that Swedish sociology was of one piece with Swedish culture, most particularly with respect to the consensus that was given concerning the importance of using formalised, systematic, and external methodologies. It was my impression that there is no group of sociologists anywhere in the world today who, more than those in Sweden, have a clearer and more agreed-upon view of the standards and values to which good sociology should conform. Swedish sociologists seemed to me to the people of, by, and for a formal methodology. This methodological drive of Swedish sociologists appears to be typically Apollonian; to express a quest for something firm, hard-edged, well-boundaried, and clearly structured.

The culturally shared emphasis, then, among Swedish sociologists, as I gleaned it, is on a self-conscious use of sophisticated methodologies, research designs, experimental techniques, measurement systems, questionnaire technologies, explicitnorms of inference - on all of the devices of formalisation. Aside from the indications of their research reprots, one of the main linguistic clues that I would cite concerning the pervasiveness of this formal conception of research is the repetition of, and the accented reference to, the term 'model'. There is hardly a discussion with Swedish sociologists in which this term is not presented in an invocatory mood, as a pathos-resonating statement on both the method and the objective of social research.

Before developing this point, allow me at once to qualify and to clarify it. In describing the Swedish style of sociology as formal and 'high science'-oriented, I am not saying that this describes the *behaviour* of all Swedish sociologist but, rather, their research culture, their ideology of procedure, their methodological morality.

What must be understood, of course, is that the rules of methodology are always a morality that can be more or less believed in and given more or less conformity. Such rules are often an ideology with which one group of sociologists seeks to influence, control, change, and dominate another group. In the United States, 'high science' methodology is the priestly ideology of a relatively small, somewhat embattled, group who identify themselves as 'methodologists'. Their self-appointed mission is not simply to better their own work, but actively to reform the behaviour of other sociologists whom they regard as misguidedly employing informal, unjustified, and ultimately immoral procedures.

The methodological subculture of American sociologists seems much more varied and differentiated than the Swedish. There are many unregenerate sociological sinners among us who do not heed the message. There are even some who formulate counter-methodological ideologies. Perhaps worst of all, there are those who can live such deviant intellecutal lives guiltlessly, without even experiencing a need for elaborating a counter-ideology. In Sweden, however, the high-science model has a commanding, almost unchallenged place; while many Swedish sociologists, perhaps eapecially among the young, do fail to practise what is preached to them - and this is a central part of Boalt's argument - few do so with an easy conscience. This is very much to the point in attempting to understand the personal reality that has shaped the character of Professor Boalt's theory about social research.

The world of social science is unavoidably a moral world and nowhere more than in its methodologies. But what needs to be stressed here is that men can relate to their moralities, and hence to their methodologies, in rather different ways. What I am suggesting, then, is that many Swedish sociologists, it seemed to me, related to their methodologies in ways that I felt to be discernibly different from the manner in which Americans do. Americans, it seems to me, are somewhat more prone to temper their commitment to morality and methodology by a greater concern for what 'other people think', how other people will react, and by an estimate of what the consequences or outcomes will be. In short, American orientation to methodology and morality seem to be tempered by American sociability and pragmatism.

I am suggesting, then, that there is an interplay between Swedish culture and Swedish sociology which expresses itself most pointedly in swedish methodological morality. I am suggesting that their apparently mores formalistic approach to social research must be seen within a broader set of conventions that regulate the social intercourse of intellectual life more broadly. Here I am especially reminded of certain patterns of conversation that seem to me to characterise Swedish academicians, at least in contrast to Americans, and, most especially, the reluctance of the former to express personal views unless they were very sure of what they were saying. For example, I often found myself asking very broad and open-ended questions - as much to move discussion along as to acquire information - about subjects that I thought were well within the other's personal experience, only to be told that he had no 'information' about the subject. Perhaps a relevant hunch here is that Swedish sociologists may, more than Americans, suppress or exclude their 'personal reality' from their intellectually responsible efforts and that this may be one way in which Boalt's work is not characteristically Swedish. On one occasion, when a person did reply to such an open-ended question, he did so only with evident tension, with the tight clasping and unclasping of hands, and with numerous qualifications. Swedish academicians, including many sociologists among them, seemed to be engaged in an undeclared war against uncertainty, seemed to be reluctant to play with ideas, and reluctant to reward those who could and did. I wondered if this reluctance to play with ideas did not also inhibit the development of new ideas; for if one is morally opposed to talking about the uncertain, it seemed possible that there might also be discomfort and unwillingness even to think about uncertain things. In short, there was, it seemed, a danger that the speculative and creative imagination could become an unintended casualty of such an undeclared war against uncertainty.

A few Swedish sociologists have themselves reacted critically against the distinctively formal and high-science aspirations of Swedish sociology, and I believe that one of the most astute of these is Gunnar Boalt. Most particularly I believe that Boalt's theory of social research is, in some part, a polemic against and perhaps an 'unmasking' of the Swedish emphasis upon formalisation. What I am suggesting, then, is not only that Boalt's theory of social research is a generalisation from his Swedish experience but that it is also a *critique* of it.

It is notable, however, that this last implication of his work became clearly apparent to me only after I had spent time with him in Stockholm and had talked rather extensively with him about his own theories. Indeed, after that experience, I began to suspect that every sustained theoretical analysis emerges out of a matrix of personal reality that is socially derived and socially relevant. It would be most instructive to have and to record personal discussions with all contemporary theorists and to compare their full, ranging, oral commentaries with their lean, antiseptic, published prose. There is, I believe, usually an importance gap between the two, and the oral commentary commonly contains much additional information of value for interpreting the published work, and in particular gives us clues about the personal reality in which it is grounded. If this is correct, then we are surely training our graduate student badly. For, in effect, we are training them to conceal and to obfuscate their deepest intentions and meanings when we teach them to write reports in the usual 'professional' style, an understanding of which requires special training in a kind of intellectual archaeology.

As Boalt and I discovered our common passion for the sociology of sociology, and as we talked at great and animated length about his work, it became clear to me that his sociology of social research focused precisely on (and against) Swedish sociology's penchant for high-science models; it was a polemic against the 'hell' - as he put it - that this inflicts upon their students, and the manner in which this makes them into 'mashed potatoes'.

While the deepest structure of Boalt's work here rests on his tacit critique of Swedish sociology, his is nonetheless a very characteristically Swedish work. In some part, this may be seen in its own thrust toward formal explication and the development of a systematic model. Yet there may be another way in which it manifests kinship with and expresses a personal reality derived from Swedish culture and Swedish sociology. To clarify this, however, it now becomes necessary to say a few words about Boalt's theory itself. The theory goes something like this.

Sociologist have a special, scientific subculture into which they train and socialise their students. Boalt conceives of this culture as a set of regulative ideals concerning research, and indeed much of the discussion in his monograph entails an effort to explicate them systematically : these comprise, for instance, the formulation of the intellectual problem and hypotheses concerning it, securing an appropriate sample, measurement techniques, etc. The decisive consideration for Boalt, however, is that no one can fulfil all of these values in his own research. In some ways and in some degree, even the most talented and most mature of scientist - let alone their students - will always fail. All social scientists, therefore, must learn to cope with failure. The problem of adapting to failure is the pivotal problem in Boalt's entire theory, while the centrality of failure is, perhaps, the pivotal 'personal reality'. The point that Boalt stresses, the point around which all his thinking revolves, is not simply the occasional and idiosyncratic occurrence of failure but, rather, failure seen as a universal experience of all science and indeed (one clearly feels) of all human enterprise. It is the inescapability and universality of failure, not failure as an liberation or as an accident, not failure as marginal to the human enterprise, to which Boalt is drawn with humane fascination. Boalt's sociology of social research is therefore directly expressive of a tragic vision and, indeed, it is, in my view, the only sociology of science that centres on this tragic dimension.

Men make some adaptation to and seek some compensation for these inevitable failures, says Boalt. They may, within their scientific role, shift from an emphasis on sciencific values that are difficult or impossible to fulfil, to an emphasis upon values that they are able to achieve. In short, they may balance their scientific deficiencies and failures with their successes in achieving other scientific values, on which they come to place enhanced importance. This is an intra-role compensation or strategy for adapting to failure. There is, however, another strategy, namely, an inter-role form of compensation. Here, for instance, men who fail as scientists may adapt by increasing their investment in their other roles, in their domestic or familial roles or in their roles as teachers.

In his personal discussion of his theory with me, Boalt also emphasised that there were two kinds of students. There were, first, those who recognised that they must deviate from the high-science rules taught them and there were, secondly, those who could not and did not do so. The latter, suggested Boalt, may be particularly represented among those who fail to complete their dissertations and never get their degree. In other words, scientific success may be contingent on *deviance* from scientific values, as well as conformity to them. The former, or 'deviant', students are those who have greater talent and flexibility in departing from the high-science model and in learning how to get this departure accepted by their professors. To use an analogy, it may be that the student faces a problem similar to that of an unmarried girl still living at home who has become pregnant: she must somehow tell her parents that she is pregnant, without a breakdown in their relationship.

To revert to the suggestion concerning the Swedish 'nature' of Boalt's work, it can be seen how Boalt believes, as part of his personal reality, that there is a set of scientific values that are treated as givens and hypostasised; that is, he postulates that social scientists do in fact commonly use an externalised methodological model which they view as a set of moral imperative rather than only as heuristic benchmarks.

This conception of professors having and demanding conformity to a single, externalised, morally tinged, high-science model seems to me much more distinctly Swedish than American. American sociologists, it appears to me in terms of my own different personal reality, hold a number of different methodological models; they use a variety of different methodological moralities that they claim to be scientifically legitimate. Such variety may, as Boalt himself suggests, be a function of the greater number of professors in American departments. The more 'informal' styles of work in the United States are not simply felt to be compromise adaptations to difficulties in conforming with a single high-science model but are, rather, often deemed legitimate in their own right. Moreover, and this is a distinct point, major American methodologists - such as Paul F. Lazarsfeld - have developed an entirely different conception of what methodology is. In this conception, methodology is not conceived of simply as the formal explication of logically defensible and *a priori* models but, rather, as the inductive codification of successful patterns of work - whatever they may be - which are in fact used by working sociologists.

To put the matter otherwise, it appears as if American sociologists are somewhat less likely to use externalised models and are more likely to use 'paradigms' (in Thomas Kuhn's sense) to guide their work. That is, they identify certain specific and concrete pieces of research as good or outstanding and then use these specific works as guides for their own efforts. It may be that this is an informal style of evaluation relatively more characteristic of Americans. It may also be that an American readiness to utilise specific and concrete researches, as paradigms to guide and evaluate their own work, is not radically different from what Swedish sociologists do. Rather, Americans may have a relatively greater readiness to allow their paradigms to surface into focal awareness while, correspondingly, Swedish sociologists may differ only in their tendency to suppress their orientations to such paradigms and to retain them only in subsidiary awareness. Furthermore, I would hypothesise that one of the functions of such concrete paradigms is precisely to provide a mechanism for accommodating to the difficulty in achieving the high science models or formal methodologies. I would not wish to be understood, however, as suggesting that the only relationship of paradigms to formal methodological models is simply one in which the paradigms reduce tensions that derive from departing from the model. Without elaborating here, I would suggest, rather, that this relationship is a much more complex one in which the paradigm may serve not only to enable men to adjust to failure in achieving high scienctific values, but also subverts and undermines them. At the same time, however, commitment to the model correspondingly undermines a commitment to the paradigm. Each, in short, constitutes a solution to the problems of the other and, moreover, each 'subverts' the other. A paradigm permits the researcher to do somewhat less than a formal model requires, while a model always requires that the researcher do somewhat more than the paradigm indicates.

It is clear that Boalt's theory is not simply a limited theory about social research but has far broader implications; tacitly but importantly, it links up with a more generalised theory of role behaviour and of anomic. Boalt assumes - indeed he emphasises that (i) men have multiple, culturally sanctioned values even in one role and, (2) with the failure to achieve one or some of these values, they may then switch their involvements to other values - which are no less culturally sanctioned. In short, in this aspect of his theory Boalt presents what I would call a theory of 'selective conformity' with, no less than of deviance from, role requirements.

Boalt's theory, then, stresses that a failure to achieve certain legitimate norms may elicit conforming behaviour. Unlike certain American theories, which stress that when man fail they become deviant, this Swedish theorist says that failure may simply lead men to try, try again, to conform; that is, to conform with some other, more readily achievable, socially sanctioned value. Men are seen as loath to violate their values.

Responses to failure, then, are notheld to be confined to withdrawing belief in or activity on behalf of a legitimate value; nor as continuing to behave in conformity with the value but without genuine belief in its ultimate achievement; nor, again, as claiming legitimacy for new patterns of behaviour that are not as yet widely accepted. Boalt's theory makes salient a distinctive addition to the various possible strategies of adapting to failure, namely, selective conformity – i.e., an increasing effort to achieve certain already established values, and a attribution of increased importance to them, with resultant reorganisation of role behaviour.

Boalt's theory thus contributes toward a generalisable model for explaining role change, or variations in role behaviour, within which one may account for both deviant and conforming changes. Stated in other terms, Boalt's work makes it very clear that a theory of deviant behaviour is just a special case of role change; it provides a parsimonious framework within which deviant changes may be linked with conforming role changes. And it not only includes within its purview changes that occur within one role but, also, systematically focuses on the ways in which different roles may be interconnected, and shows how changes in any one of these may induce changes in an altogether different role-set. It thus contributes to a deepening of our understanding concerning inter-role dynamics.

One of the central aspects of Boat's work, then, is its focus upon the consequences of failure; we might say Boalt's theory rests upon an unshakable belief in the reality of failure. One wonders whether corresponding American theories may not differ fundamentally precisely because they are not permeated by such a conviction in the reality of failure but, to the contrary, tend to think of failure as peripheral, marginal, accidental to the human enterprise and, instead, dwell in a world whose 'reality' centres upon success. It may be that European cultures are somewhat ahead of American culture in their understanding of the profound and permeating significance of failure, and that Americans are only in the process of catching up with them. In contrast, it may be that Americans are somewhat more sensitive than Europeans to the 'failure of success', and that we recognise the manner in which continued success, no less than failure, may also induce tensions that promote role and value changes.

Be that as it may, I suspect than Boalt's theory is of particular value to American social scientists because it dwells in a personal reality that makes failure central, that sees the tragic components in science as well as elsewhere, that accepts the necessity of paying for one's achievements and successes with deficiencies and failures elsewhere, that sees scientific values not as a harmoniously intergrated system but as heteronomous and indeed, as conflicting. For instance, Boalt notes that what he calls the 'news values', in other words, the originality of a scientific research, is a central value in the culture of science. He notes, therefore, the possibility that scientists seeking to establish their originality and priority may press their work forward rapidly, to publish before others do, even at the sacrifice of certain other scientific values. Boalt notes, however, that it is not only originality but replication also that is a value of science and he observes that these two values conflict; since a replication cannot be original, there is a tendency not to use one' scarce time in producing replications. Indeed, he observes with characteristic paradox that replications are so rare that they might actually be regarded as a form of originality!

Because of his sensitivity to these conflicts and to the tragic dimension more generally, Boalt provides a welcome contrast to those sociologists of science who tend to focus on the manner in which the various components of science are harmoniously integrated, who assume that there is an identity between the fate of science and the fate of individual scientists, and who miss the manner in which the milestones of science are the tombstones of individaul scientists.

To what is this tragic component in science due? Is it the inevitable outcome of an insurmountable gap between science's great eternal demands and the inevitably limited, smaller talents of individual men? I think not. It is, I believe, only insofar as men cleave compulsively to a culturally prescribed and historically transient definition of what they should be doing scientifically, and only where conformity to these demands is viewed as an absolute moral requirement apart from their own varying individual impulses and talents, that they develop the sense of tragic incompleteness. It is only when men fall spellbound to the demands of cultural prescription, but fail to heed their own inner impulses, to know their own special bents or aptitudes; and fail to grasp that there are many valuable ways they can live and contribute as scientists - and not only one culture - prescribed way - that their lives must be tragic. Men may escape tragedy when they recognise that they need not allow themselves to be assimilated to their cultural masks; when they insists on the difference between themselves and their roles; when they insist that it is they who are the measure, and they who do the measuring - one man with and one against the others - and not one man against the standards of culture and requirements of roles.

To do this, men must accept their own unique talents and varying ambitions as authentic. If they find these are distant from the requirements of their culture and role, they should, at least, face up if not surrender to the difference; they must consider the possibility that their personal impulses and special talents have as much right to be heard as the cultural norms, while all the while accepting the possibility that they may simply be in the wrong business. When ordinary men can do this they need not be inescapably burdened by a sense of their own failure and inadequacy. When great men can do this they will no longer need tacitly to project an inflated image of themselves as gods. When either ordinary or great men can do this, both will recognise the value of their human contribution as sufficient to justify their lives.

Men surmount tragedy, then, when they use themselves up fully; when they use what they have and what they are, whatever they are, and wherever they find themselves, whether this requires them to ignore certain cultural prescriptions or to behave in innovating ways that are uninvited by their roles. The tragic sense does not derive from men's feeling that they must always be less than history and culture demand; it derives, rather, from the sense that they have been less than they needed to be, that they have needlessly betrayed themselves, needlessly forgone fulfilments that would have injured no one - needlessly wasted the possibilities of their lives.

The sociological enterprise, like others becomes edged with a tragic sense, I suspect, precisely because in confining work to the requirements of a demanding and unfulfilable paradigm, sociologists are not using themselves up in their work but are, indeed, sacrificing unexpressed parts of themselves - their playful impulses, their unverified hunches, and speculative imagination - in a wager that this sacrifice is 'best for science'. Whether this is really so, they cannot confirm; but they often need no further confirmation of the pain that this self-confinement causes them.

The more that sociologists commit themselves to a high-science model the more they flirt with this most untestable of metaphysics. My point, of course, is not that there can be a sociology without such a metaphysical wager but, rather, that various wagers are possible. The question is not whether the sociologist must make a bet, but on what. He can bet that the paradigm or model of science presently prescribed is right and trustworthy, and that his own errant impulses are not. In short, he can bet against himself. He can also bet on himself; that is, he can trust his own individuating impulses, unique aptitudes, and all the fainter powers of apprehension – as Gilbert Murray called them – with which these endow him. To say that the sociologist need not make only one kind of bet is not, of course, to say that the number of bets he can make is unlimited. If the basic problem is how to link himself as a person with the requirements of his role as a sociologist there would seem to be, for the sociologists as others, a limited number of solutions.

The culturally standardised role of the sociologist, like any other social role, can be thought of as a 'bridge' - both facilitating and limiting certain tasks, enabling men to 'overcome' certain obstacles, and to get to the 'other side'. But social roles are always unfinished bridges and invariably incomplete; they reach out only part way across the void. It is their incompleteness that is the eternal problem, and thus even those who love and respect the bridge cannot entirely rely upon it to get them safely across.

There are a limited number of attitudes one can adopt toward this situation. For example, some men say: So be it; if this is the way of bridges then we must learn to live with them as they are. They will parade back and forth along the completed section of the bridge, sometimes dangling their feet over the unfinished edge, looking down. Other men say: We must be grateful for whatever we have and, repaying those who built it, we must continue working, each adding his own little plank to the unfinished end; occasionally resting at the edge, they may dangle their feet over it. In both cases, one is bound to have something of a tragic sense, a sad whimsical wish that things were not like that.

But there is another possibility. One thing is certain, a man might feel: the building of this bridge will never be completed, but my life will surely have its end. A man might therefore risk a running leap from the unfinished edge to the shore that he thinks he sees ahead. Perhaps he has seen right and has estimated his own powers correctly. In which event, applause. Perhaps he has badly miscalculated on both counts. In which event, a certain dampness sets in. Maybe he can swim back to safety, even if somewhat less than applauded. In any event, he has found out how far he can see and how well he can jump. Even if he is never heard from again, perhaps those who are still dawdling at the edge will learn something useful.

2

Romanticism and Classicism: Deep Structures in Social Science

The industrialisation of nineteenth-century Europe was uneven, and this meant that the eastward parts of Europe, which underwent industrialisation somewhat later, had to cope with two tasks simultaneously: on the one hand, they had all the problems intrinsic to their own emerging industrialisation; on the other, they also had to fomulate a position about the industrialisation and the rise of the middle class that had appeared earlier in the West. The Germans, therefore, were influenced not only by their own local situation, but were also affected by the earlier experience of the middle classes in *France*. The French experience was widely watched and intensively analysed by the Germans, and it became a pivot around which the Germans developed a reaction to their own cultural situation.

Following the French Revolution, the still nascent middle classes in Germany thus faced two problems at once. First, they sought to modify the social reality of German society and to create a new conception of the emerging social order more fully consistent with their own distinctive interests and assumptions. Secondly, however, many were also disposed to reject the new order that revolutionary France had offered Europe. Germany, then, faced the problem of being unable to live with the old feudal order and of being unable to accept the most visible alternative presented by the French. The subsequent development of German modernisation was to be shaped profoundly by its effort to cope with this quandary.

Romanticism as a Movement for Cultural Revitalisation

Caught within this dilemma, German intellectuals were restive but uncertain of their direction. In the first quarter of the nineteenth century, and perhaps particularly before the War of Liberation, they were therefore unable to mount an offensive against their own 'old regime', or to give full support to the emerging new order. Thus, even though change was felt to be necessary, politics and a political solution were then widely experienced as impossible. Many educated Germans of that period turned therefore to the sphere of culture, to the achievements of intellect and art that were more individually controllable: they fostered a movement for cultural revitalisation instead of a political revolution. Unable to revolutionise society, German intellectuals sought to revolutionise culture. As Madame de Staël remarked, it was not difficult to find Germans who composed the most comprehensive philosophical systems, but it was almost impossible to find Germans who wrote on politics.

Seeking to respond to the German problem while rejecting the French solution, living in a society where feudalism was still relatively strong although visibly decaying, *and* where the middle classes were still weak although manifestly emerging, certain German intellectuals developes an especially uninhibited expression of the powerful movement for cultural revitalisation which they called Romanticism. This social movement had three main cultural expressions: first, the philosophical idealism of Kant, Hegel, Schelling and Fichte; secondly, *historismus* and the new historiography; and third and finally, there was a revolution in art, aesthetics and literary criticism. Each of these parameters conditioned the others and all were institutionally consolidated within the German university; together they became the core culture of the German Mandarins.

Dissatisfied with the condition of Germany, yet unable to accept the future offered by the French, the German Romantics sought to devise an alternative image of the social order that would be neither bourgeois nor feudal, or would at least combine elements of the two. Unable to move forward to the future or to accept the present, the German Romantic image of an alternative social order could be located only in the past, in myth and history. They immersed themselves in the past, however, and to a great extent they *knew* they did so, in order that they might more clearly distinguish the characteristics of the new *present* within which they lived and to gain perspective on it.

The time orientations of the early nineteenth century and, in particular, of the 'systematic' (i.e., post-*Sturm und Drang*) German Romanticists, the Berlin-Jena School, are implicit in the new concepts with which they characterised historical European cultures. Specifically, toward the end of the eighteenth and the beginning of the nineteenth centuries, and in *an effort to clarify the nature of the 'modern',* August and Friedrich Schlegel advanced a distinction between 'Classical' and 'Romantic' cultures, and came to eulogize the latter as the truly modern. Since, however, the Schlegels regarded Romantic culture as distinctively Christian in character, they therefore conceived themselves as living with an enocompassing time-unit that included the Middle Ages, and thus also the literature of the Renaissance and of the Elizabethan periods.

In the Romantic view, therefore, the 'modern' was not marked by the eruption of science and of rationalism but, rather, by certain innovations in the arts and especially in literary culture. This distinction between the Romantic and the Classical, with its focus on artistic and religious components, thus had the effect of redefining the place of science in modern life, and therefore it also redefined the nature of the modern itself. Specifically, it *diminished* the significance that the French had attributed to science as the characterising innovation of the modern epoch. Conversely, we might say that it was out of an anterior impulse to diminish the value attributed to a reifying science that the 'modern' and the 'Romantic' came to be defined in this particular manner. Nineteenth-century Romanticism thus rejected the specifically French Enlightenment conception of the modern as centered on reason/science/technology. Moreover, for them the modern was not therefore critical of or in opposition to religion. In effect, the Romantics were searching for a way to be modern without having to reject religion and the values that associated with religion.

While the distinction between the Classical and the Romantic initially aimed at discerning the differences between the modern and the ancient, it ended by fusing the then contemporaneous present with the Middle Ages, and by bidding the modern to seek a similar glory. Through their idealisation of the Middle Ages, the Romantics could establish a standpoint for criticism of the new German present and, at the same time, they could crystallise an image of a social order that was obviously critical of The French alternative. The distinction between the Romantic and the Classical thereby enabled German Romantics simultaneously to reject both the political backwardness of the German present and the 'irreligion' of the French future.

The German Romantics could now have the best of both possible worlds: linking the modern to the past, they could extol the achievements of German culture, while at the same time calling for its improvement. They could now reject the French alternative and still acknowledge that the German present needed to be transcended. They could pursue 'development' without endorsing 'progress'. They could look forward to renewed greatness without neglecting the past or holding it in contempt.

Moreover, they could also maintain that the mechanism of this development was already in hand. That is, they did not need to wait for a political re-ordering of the social world, for the necessary mechanism was already in existence. This mechanism was a kind of puissant spirituality: it was the *Geist* that was also *Macbt*. The Romantics, then, were the intellectual shamans that sought to summon the German *Geist* to find a distinctive path to the revitalisation of German culture.

Romanticism, then, was not only a philosophical and aesthetic doctrine; it was also a social movement. It was a movement for the revitalisation of German, and indeed of all, culture in post-revolutionary Europe. In the German case, with its special concern for autonomy from French culture, this movement for cultural revitalisation took strongly 'nativistic' or nationalistic forms; and in its emphasis upon the value and depth of the German historical past, it also took strongly 'revivalistic' forms.

Despite this, the Romantic movement cannot be understood simply as an expression of traditionalism and, on the contrary. It had certain strongly *anti*-traditionalistic emphases. For Romanticism was, in another of its aspects, a revolt of intellectual and artistic élites against their own cultural establishments, and against the standards that had been conventionally used to govern their own specialised spheres of cultural activity. Thus, if the *Enlightenment* was the intellectual's critique of society, of religion and of politics, Romanticism was the revolt of an intellectual and an artistic élite against its own internal subculture. In this degree, then, Romanticism was the substitution of aesthetics for politics, of cultural criticism for social criticism; and it was a demand for artistic freedom in place of political freedom.

Romantic Perspectives and Doctrines

Perhaps the most general aspect of Romantic anti-traditionalism was its revolt against the conception that art should be governed by reason, i.e., by a disciplined conformity to certain received and impersonal rules. Romanticism was thus free enterprise in art and literature. It was the artistic equivalent of the bourgeois doctrine of *laissez faire*.

At the spearhead of the Romantics' attack there was a doctrine of unfettered aesthetic individualism that took the form of a polemic against the dominant aesthetic doctrines of Classicism: the unities of time and place; the universality and permanence of the truly beautiful; the objectivity of taste; conformity to the semblances of probability, and to the requirements of decorum; and the avoidance of mixed genres, styles or tones and moods.

The Romantics rebelled on every from against the once-honoured conventions of the artistic community and its classical tradition: they welcomed a *mélange* of times, tones, moods and places in one artistic product, counterpoising it to the classical doctrine of the unities; they affirmed the value of the contingent, the changing and the local, counterpoising this to the doctrines of universality and permanence; they prized inward conviction, counterpoising it to judgements oriented to externalised and objectified standards; they delighted in the exotic, deviant or special case, counterpoising these to the probable or average case; they portrayed the indecorous as a way of conferring reality on an individuality that was to be defined by its departure from, rather than its conformity with, social convention.

As against the established tradition of conveying meaning as some kind of unity, the Romantics countered by affirming the reality of plurality. The world was seen as a mosaic, each tile of which had some unique reality or value in itself. The whole itself was often seen, however, not as a harmonious and integrated entity, but as an incongruous assemblage and as a tensionful conjunction of parts. The Romantic concern with the 'grotesque' was a concern with a conjunction of parts perceived as incongruous and ominous Romanticism rejected received artistic rules and conventional aesthetic doctrines, and, instead, sought a liberation of the imagination and a mobilisation of sentiment to provide the vision and the energy to carry artistic work forward.

The Romantics lived in a twilight world of transition, between an unsatisfactory present and an unworkable past, between decaying feudal tradition and emerging bourgeois reform. Living in a world in which the conventional social maps had lost their effectiveness, but in which acceptable new ones had not yet been formulated, it was to the individual self as the maker of meanings that they turned rather than to the traditional rules. Living in a world where received cultural categories and conventional social identities no longer made social reality meaningful, they came to see reality as possessed of intrinsic vagueness. They saw objects as blending into one another, rather than as well demarcated by clear-cut boundaries. They therefore felt that those who sought to conquer truth by the careful dissections of analytic reason were engaged in a vivisection that could only destroy living reality.

The Romantics experienced the object worked as no longer isomorphic with the neat categories wrought by the classical mind. It was therefore characteristic of Romantic poetry that it commonly loved the imagery of twilight, of a boundary - dissolving moonlight, or of the fleeting moments before dawn, rather than the imagery of the clear, boundary-sharpening light of the classical mind. It was thus that the casual and the irregular, or the wild and the disorderly in nature, was prized by the Romantic aesthetic - particularly if it could be viewed from some safe distance. In this, the Romantics were not above mixing feudal heroics with a dash of bourgeois prudence.

In this twilight social world, a new structure of sentiments was being activated to which the Classical-Aristotelian logic - in which an object was either 'A' or 'not-A' - was no longer felt to correspond. In this breach between the new sentiments and the inadequate old languages provides by classical logic and convention, the Romanticists - and perhaps especially those of the earlier *Sturm and Drang* period - could, at first, only *affirm* dogmatically the truth of their new vision. They could only polemically insist on the vitality and reality of their own inner sentiments - the 'reasons of the heart' - since they at first lacked the rationale of a new language or a new logic.

In the prefigurings of Romanticism, as in the *Sturm und Drang* school, the gap between the new sentiments and a way to talk about them was greatest. The next generation of Romanticists may be called the 'systematic Romantics', however, precisely because they did create new languages, new conceptual schema and a new set of theories to express and communicate their sentiments. The Schlegel brother's very distinction between the Classical and Romantic signified an emerging new language and contributed to a growing self-awareness.

The Romantic breakthrough to a new language of the sentiments and of the imagination took several discernible forms. Among its earliest intellectual achievements were important new aesthetic doctrines, particularly doctrines stressing the importance of symbolism, irony and the grotesque. Another major language breakthrough occurred with the development of a non-Aristotelian logic. This first developed from a more diffuse notion of a 'logic of polarities' into the systematic Hegelian dialectic of the self or *Geist,* which was then 'stood upon its feet' and was developed in turn by Marx into a materialist dialectic of society.

In the twentieth century there emerged, with Freudianism, a systematic psychology of the irrational sentiments. The importance attributed by the Freudians to the unconscious, as well as the assumption that a 'cure' requires an awareness of the hitherto unconscious and its reintegration into the consciousness, are rooted in the Romantic paradigm fundamental to German idealism. The latter's basic problematic revolves on the relationship between a knowing 'Subject' and a known 'Object', and it regarded this very distinction as a false consciousness of the Subject, since the Object, rather than being that which was *not* the Subject, was actually unconsciously created by it. Idealism premised that human Emancipation entailed the Subject's achievement of awareness about its own hitherto unconscious role in shaping the Object, its discovery of *itself* in the Object-other. In short, German idealism clearly foreshadowed Freudianism's concept of the unconsciousness as well as its conception of a therapy.

In contrast to the French revolutionaries, who had largely defeated the old régime with its own cognitive weapons, it remained for the Romantics to begin the serious and systematic reconstruction of the language and images used for talking about man and society. It remained for them to take as central the language of sentiment; although the language of the sentiments was already emerging in France, The *philosophers* had largely continued to employ the rhetoric of Reason during the Enlightenment epoch. Even later, it is perfectly plain from the National Assembly's 'Declaration of the Rights of Man and Citizen' that the public discourse of the Revolution remained far closer, in its images of man and society, to the classical tradition with its conception of eternal natural reason and of unchanging natural law, than it was to the emerging Romantic Age.

The 'modern' only begins to manifest itself when, in answer to the question, 'What is distinctively human?', Romanticism replies not by referring to man's eternal capacity for reason and universal rationality, but, instead, to his creative originality, to his individuated capacity to feel and to dream uniquely. The modern begins to emerge when man is seen, not merely as a creature that can *discover* the world, but also as one who can *create* new meanings and values, and can thus change himself and fundamentally transform his world, rather than unearth, recover or 'mirror' an essentially unchanging world order.

The thing to see is that Romanticism was not only an aesthetic, but that it was a many-faceted and enduring social movement. It was a movement for the revitalisation of European culture in all of its manifestations - artistic, literary, philosophical, religious and even scientific.

Faced with a changing social reality, in which the social structure to be understood as well as the traditional ways of understanding it were both dissolving simultaneously, and faced with the collapse of the conventional hierarchies of value, the Romantics sought to rescue a world of meaning by 'romanticizing'. Which means: by endowing the ordinary, everyday world with the pathos of the extraordinary - by 'idealising' mundane reality. The 'ordinary', the everyday, the lowly, the fleshly and the deviant were to be rescued by viewing them from a perspective that endowed them with new and enhanced value, rather than being routinised, ignored or thingafied. As Novalis said, to romanticise was to see the infinite in the finite - the universe in the grain of sand, in Blake's terms. It was to gaze deeply into the 'blue flower' and to see eternity in it.

There were no longer things that were inherently lowly but only pedestrian *perspectives* on the world. The 'Classical' view of the world had generated excluded enclaves of underprivileged reality, whose neglect it had no hesitation in justifying. The Romantic view believed that the insignificance of things was born of a failure of imagination: reality was now democratised.

Above all, Romanticism rejected bourgeois, vulgar materialism's tendency to 'deaden' the universe and men with it. In the words of Georg Lukàcs, Romanticism was a rejection of 'reification' and, we might add, it expressed a refusal to equate modernity with reification. Romanticism sought a path to a *non*-reifying modernism. If bourgeois reification transformed men into inanimate objects, no different from other passive 'things', Romanticism resonated with an animism of Pantheism that sought to transform even inanimate objects by a dethingafying 'spiritualisation'. To 'romanticise' was thus to endow those parts of the world that had been exposed to a deadening reification with a new enlivening by insisting that *all* things were *loci* of *self*-movement, of potency, and of value. To this extent, Romanticism was profoundly anti-mechanical and *anti*-bourgeois; it was thus by no means exclusively 'reactionary', despite its sponsorship by aristocratic and other Old Régime élites and even though at first expressive of their defensive manoeuvres against the emerging bourgeoisie.

It is clear, then, that our interpretation of Romanticism differs from that of Karl Mannheim, who tended (as did the *later* Lukàcs) to over-emphasize Romanticism's backward-looking conservatism. Insofar as Romanticism rejects a reification of men and provides a basis for a critique of reification, insofar as it expresses a resistance to historically obsolescent and unnecessary rules or limits, then Romanticism is indeed an *emancipatory* standpoint. It provides leverage for the great break-through into a *Subject*-sensitive modernism, as distinct from the *Objectivistic* modernism of the Enlightenment which sought to free reason from superstition that it might better 'mirror' the world. However, insofar as Romanticism seeks to *replace* (rather than complement) Enlightenment objectivism with subject-sensitive modernism, then the latter becomes a *subjectivism* vulnerable to irrationalism and to anti-intellectualism.

All this, by way only of the faintest outline of Romanticism. It is all that space will permit here. This preface completed, we now turn to the relationship between Romanticism and the social sciences.

Positivism and Romanticism in France

Both sociology in France and anthropology in Germany and England, emerged as elements in a Romantically-tinged, European-wide movement for cultural revitalisation.

F. M. H. Markham observes that 'in 1830 there was the first performance of Victor Hugo's *Hernani:* in 1831, that of Hector Berlioz' *Symphonie Fantastique*. Paris experienced an orgy of grandiose and romantic ideas.' Leaving aside Markham's Goethian inclination to see Romanticism as a pathology, he is quite correct in noting that the Saint-Simonians, 'like the rest of their generation. . .were intoxicated by the. . .romantic movement

. . .Henri Lafebvre is also correct in characterising Saint-Simon as belonging to the 'left wing of romanticism.' In a similar vein, we might distinguish Comte from Saint-Simon by conceiving of the former as belonging to the 'right wing' of Romanticism. In what follows, however, I want to focus not on their differential politics but on certain common elements in their Romanticism.

Like the German Romantics, French positivism - particularly in its Comtian version - held constitution making in contempt. It stressed the weakness of reason and the power of sentiment, and, parenthetically, it thus agreed with the Schlegels and other Romantics on the heightened significance to be accorded women as the alleged bearers and guardians of sentiment. In the modern era, 'Women's Liberation' begins with the Romantics. In their conceptions of man and society, both German Romantics and French positivists thus agreed on the unique value of sentiment, as well as on the vulnerability and limitations of reason.

Both also looked to the past for their models of a hierarchical and coherent society. The French positivists, however, were more ambivalent in their attitudes toward the past, since, after all, they, unlike the Germans, lived in a society in which the middle classes had succeeded in making a revolution, even if this was stalemated and threatened during the Restoration. The French positivists thus created a *New* religion of humanity rather than returning, as did some of the German Romanticists, to the venerable Mother Church.

Still, France under the Restoration was a stalemate society in which the middle classes could not go forward, while the returned Royalists could not go back. Saint-Simon and Comte responded to this by creating positivism as a fusion of religion and of science. They wanted to be modern without rejecting religion. The positivists' new 'religion of humanity' was patently such a patchwork compromise; its new priests would be scientists, but its scientists would also be priests. And it aimed at progress, no less than order and love. French positivism was, thus, in the beginning a characteristically Romantic compromise between older images of hierarchical order and the new bourgeois order, spurred on by the conflicts of the Restoration, but subject to the more powerful modernising influences of a French middle class that was far stronger than the German.

It would be utterly wrong, then, to think of positivism and Romanticism as two entirely separate and altogether opposing responses to the crisis of their time. Both, for example, sought to find new bases for social norms and authority, to replace those of their discredited old regimes. The positivists sought to find this new authority in science; for all their critique of the Enlightenment, they carned forward the Enlightenment's effort to emancipate men from reason-shackling superstitions, and it is this which lurked behind their rejection of the non-empirical and metaphysical. The Romanticists also sought a new basis for crumbling authority, but they sought it in the certitudes of inner feeling and artistic imagination.

Both the positivists and Romanticists wanted to be modern without relinquishing religion. The positivists identified the modern with the scientific and they sought to accommodate religion to science by creating a new religion of humanity. The Romanticists identified the modern with the emancipation of the sentiments or feeling, not of reason or science, and defined sentiment as near the core of religion. That Romanticism and positivism were not altogether exclusive may be seen even on the grossest level. Recall that the father of positivism, Saint-Simon himself, made the 'grand' gesture of offering to marry Madame de Staël, the propagandist and interpreter of German Romanticism. Nor would it be amiss to remember Saint-Simon's less illustrious followers, Enfantin and Bazard, whose epistemology stressed the importance of intuition, hypothesis and of the genius that produces these; or Saint-Simonism's search for *la femme libre,* and its agonising over the question of 'free love'. Initially, French positivism was a *blend* of science and of Romanticism; it was an intellectual marriage that Saint-Simon consummated without the benefit of de Staël's consent. It was a blend, however, in which the scientific element was the more focal and dominant. In short, what positivism was in the beginning, and the colourless enterprise that it later evolved into, are two different things.

In its initial structure French positivism was a social movement based upon and attractive to the *new* professions engineering, medicine and science - while German Romanticism was at first largely created by artists and by humanistic scholars of an *older* vintage. Positivism was from the very beginning intricately linked to the emerging new *infra*structure - to the new industrial society whose prophet Saint-Simon was Romanticism, however, was from the very beginning the vocalised *ressentiment* of those in a newly devalued *super*structure. Positivism, in short, was a social movement led by a new technological élite whom the new industrialism had almost immediately advantaged, who had better prospects in bourgeois society, and who could, therefore, be more easily integrated into it. Romanticism, however, was the product of older, culture-creating élites - artists, dramatists, poets, musicians – who at first were squeezed aside and had no place in the new world of business, industry, and science, and who would not be needed widely in this new world until the media of mass communication developed.

But if positivism was a compromise between science and Romanticism, it was a compromise in which its *methodology* was developed under the hegemony of a natural science model, and in which natural science methods became in time progressively dominant. So far as the later development of Western sociology is concerned, the positivists' 'religion of humanity' was defrocked and was gradually secularised as a tool of the Welfare State. The most Romantic and religious components of positivism were thus increasingly subordinated. This is not to say, however, that they disappeared altogether, but only that they were ultimately suppressed or repressed. In other words, the Romantic and religious components in academic sociology lost out as elements in the *focal* awareness of its practitioners; but they did not disappear, as the work of Robert Friedrichs makes clear.

German Social Sciences and Romanticism

In Germany, however, something more nearly like the opposite process occurred. That is, the German social sciences also developed out of a dialectic between Romanticism and science; but here, in Germany, the Romantic component was far more influential than in Western Europe, even if not unchallenged. The power of the Romantic components in Germany may be appraised if it is remembered that the German social sciences matured in the shadow of the triumphant natural sciences in Germany, with their very great public and university prestige. Yet, despite this, the German social sciences were not dominated by a natural science model.

The Romantic influence on German social science was both manifested in and preserved by the German development of a systematic distinction between the human or cultural sciences, on the one hand, and the natural sciences, on the other hand. This distinction was consonant with another that had been persistently produced by German social scientists, that between 'culture' and 'civilisation'. And this, in *its* turn, also resonated a still deeper distinction in German culture between *Geist* and *Natur*.

The distinction between *Geisteswissenschaften* and *Naturwissenschaften* remains important to the contemporary School of Critical Theory at Frankfurt. In *one* of its basic dimensions, Critical Theory is surely rooted in a hermeneutics that seeks to formulate 'interpretations' that enhance 'understanding' of social worlds, rather than to develop 'law' that 'explain' phenomena. And there is little question but that hermeneutics' roots in the modern era are traceable to Romanticism. Indeed, we have it on the authority of the leading modern philosopher of hermeneutics, Hans Georg Gadamer, that 'hermeneutics came to flower in the Romantic era. . .It did so, it might be added, most specifically in the work of the theologian Friedrich Schleiermacher, who was associated with the Schlegels and the Berlin-Jena Romanticists.

In discussing recent developments in the Critical School, it is quite obvious that many Europeans, whether positivists or hermeneuticists, share an understanding of Critical Theory's relation to Romanticism. Thus, Gadamer says of Jürgen Habermas' position: 'I believe this is pure romanticism, and such romanticism creates an artistic abyss between tradition and the reflection which is grounded in historical consciousness. (It is characteristic that Gadamer uses 'romantic' as a dyslogism despite his own indebtedness to it; ever since Hegel, romantics have expressed their sense of distance from others by condemning them as 'romantics'.) This judgement on Critical Theory is shared by Ernst Topitsch, although his own neopositivism is far removed from Gadamer's Heidegerrian phenomenology. Topitsch holds (according to Paul Lorenzen) that 'All Marxists and neo-Hegelians, including the dialectical philosophers and sociologists of the Frankfurt School. . . belong to this group of left Romantics.

If Critical Theory and hermeneutics are in part rooted in Romanticism, they are only the most recent expression of the continuing *creativity* of that infrastructure for social theory. Earlier, the continuing efforts of German social science to work out the relationship between Romanticism and science had manifested itself in the sociology of Max Weber and, still earlier, had found a powerful expression in the work of Karl Marx.

Karl Marx

In this connection, we may be reminded of Marx's aphorism that 'philosophy is the head of emancipation, and the proletariat is the heart'. Certainly, for Marx, reason alone could not liberate the world or the proletariat; reason had to be embodied in and liberated by a theory-correcting *praxis.* For Marx, praxis was not simply a scientific experiment to be conducted in the laboratory. It was a commitment of the whole man, to be expressed in the world and in the course of his everyday life. It was a commitment of his passions as well as of his cognitive faculties, to change the world and, through this, to change himself.

Marx's abiding aim to transcend 'alienation' is a characteristically Romantic effort to mend the split *between* and *within* men, and to reunite sensuous man with national man. In the end, Marx wanted a society in which *all* men's faculties and senses - and not only his intellect - would find a home. Marx, therefore, counterpoised to the Socratic rule - one man, one task - and to medieval organicism, the new vision of a society in which one man could play *many* parts, not simply during his lifetime, but even during a single day, uniting manual and intellectual, aesthetic and cognitive activities.

Like the Romantics, Marx also stressed a pluralism of perspectives. Unlike them, however, he situated this pluralism not in the will or imagination of the individual, but rather in the social location of the individual's group or class. At the same time, however, Marx also sought a universalistic transcendence of pluralism by conceiving of certain social perspectives as entailing a 'false consciousness'. In short, Marx's pluralism of perspectives was counterbalanced by the universalism of human reason.

The very concept of a 'capitalist society', that we owe to Marx, bears witness to his abiding effort to transcend the conflict between Romantic and Classical perspectives. For, in insisting that capitalism was only one *type* of society, Marx is here attempting to combine the Romantics' concern with concrete *uniqueness* and historical individuality with the Classical concern for abstracted universals. Marx's emphasis on *types* of societies is in the nature of a half-way house between the Classical abstraction and the Romantic concrete.

Again, for Marx like the Romantics, the future remains to some degree an emergent: its full character cannot be seen or predicted except insofar as one approaches it. It is therefore useless to attempt to predict it in blueprinted detail. Thus, Marx polimicises against the French socialists, whom he terms 'utopians', and rejects the idea of blueprinting the future. This is consonant with the Romantic component in Marx's politics which insists that political outcomes depend on struggle, on individual commitment and effort, as well as on class solidarity and revolutionary will.

On the other hand, there is also the Classical component in Marx's theory and politics that calls for patient waiting until there is a maturation of the appropriate *objective* conditions for social change. From *this* perspective, then, the revolution for Marx is not waiting in the wings of history, ready to be ushered in at any time through a merely wilful *coup d'état.* Here, then, there is a *rejection* of political Romanticism. Since Marx's time, the history of Marxism has been a cyclical oscillation between these two versions of politics, but this oscillation occurs around a long-range *trend* toward an increasingly romantic politics. This Romantic upsurge in Marxism begins with the Leninist breakthrough in Russia, and continues today in the still more

Romantic strategies of Mao and Ché Guevara. Our discussion of 'The Two Marxisms' and of 'The Red Guard' will develop this further.

When Marx spoke of the 'contradictions of capitalism,' he was giving voice to an essentially Romantic sense of the grotesqueness of modern life, in which incongruous cultural elements cohabit, in which things give birth to their very opposites, in which death comes with life, and things bear the 'seeds of their own destruction'. Here we might note the remark by that authentic fountainhead of Romanticism, Friedrich Schlegel, who observed that 'States disappear; the most powerful often bear within themselves, from their very origin, the germ of their own decay. In this vein, Marx's critique of modern science and technology sees their development as leading to increased misery, suffering, unemployment, and to the reserve army of the unemployed. Under the conditions of a capitalist society, science and technology do not liberate man, says Marx, but rather enslave him, and at the height of these technological triumphs man becomes a tool of his machines. Man becomes a marionette, while the marionettes take on life. Here, Marx is in the tradition of the Romantic enjoyment of the grotesque. Yet something more is involved, for he also sees this grotesque condition from a Hegelian perspective, as something that will give rise to its own negation, and whose own tensions guarantee an ultimate transcendence by a more harmonious order.

In discussing Marx's relation to Romanticism, I have not intended to say and I have not said that he was 'a Romantic'. I have, however, intended to show that there were important *components* of Romanticism in his thought and to suggest that Marxism is to be understood as a whole, then these components must be firmly grasped. It is not amiss to notice that Marx was actually a student of August Schlegel at the University of Bonn, although one should not make too much of this in understanding the *sources* of Marx's Romanticism. Marx is a crucial episode in the effort to accommodate Romanticism and science within the framework of a *social* theory. Essentially similar effort had been earlier made within the framework of

German philosophy, where the culminating formulation had been Hegel's. It was Marx's historical task to formulate the Hegelian synthesis in the idiom of a political economy rather than that of academic philosophy.

On those few occasions that Marx mentions Romanticism directly, there is no doubt that his comments are negative. (This also seems to be true of Nietzsche!) But such negative remarks usually focus on Romanticism as the ideology of the German monarchy, as something reactionary and ineffectual. Marx's critique of 'true' socialism, of its stress on the role of sentiment as a source of social change, converges with his critique of Romanticism as ineffectual. Here Marx's rejection of the sentimentality and political ineffectuality of Romanticism is, in one way, a critique of Romanticism's *feminine* component. (There is little question but that Romanticism placed a particularly *high* value on what were *them* culturally defined as feminine qualities - sentimentality, affective expressivity - and, indeed, was associated with earliest efforts at the liberation of women from male-dominated sexual standards, in the family and in private life generally.) In viewing the Romanticism of his period as lacking in resoluteness and 'hardness', Marx's is in effect rejecting a feminised Romanticism. Conversely, Marx's mission, we might say, was not to reject but to 'masculinise' romanticism; he adopts much the same masculinising mission toward historical Romanticism as Max Weber and Nietzsche later did, and Hegel earlier had.

Hegel's relation to Romanticism has much in common with Marx's. Hegel, like Marx, took the Romantics to task, criticising their effusive expressivity , their lack of a hard-edged clarity and rigorous system, and sought to make philosophy more scientifically serious. Like the Romantics, however, Hegel held that men never achieve anything great without passion, that history develops through struggle and conflict, and, as epitomized by his master-bondsman paradigm, is characterised by ironic reversals. The most fundamentally Romantic aspect of Hegelianism is that what the Hegelian Subject at last discovers in the Object-other is *himself*.

Max Weber

The effort of German social science to accommodate Romanticism and science to one another is renewed and brought to a new development in the sociology of Max Weber. As Weber conceived it, social science was far from the generalising, universalising and externalising social science formulated in the tradition of Comteian Positivism. Rather than stressing its cultural autonomy, Weber's social science conceived of social science as changing, both in fact and with propriety, as historical problems themselves changed. Its starting point was the cultural-value interest of the social scientist and not necessarily a purely technical hypothesis. Weber's social science was thus conceived as responsive to changing cultural perspectives, and thus as a science to which 'eternal youth was granted', rather than as one that grew progressively and continuously with age.

Weber's social science focused on understanding individual events and historically located entities, conceived in their uniquely given individuality, rather than searching for universal generalisations about classes of units or events. For all its comparative method, Weber's concern was primarily with the unique development and destiny of Europe. And it was a comparative method that was to proceed with the use of 'ideal types' that focused on extreme cases rather than on the *average* case, and which were formulated intuitively, rather than through statistical induction.

Such a manifestly Romantic conception of social science also stressed the significance of *verstehen,* of intuition and insight, through which the 'inwardness' of other men would be apprehended, and the importance of the 'mental experiment', through which the consequences of changes in values, ideas, and meanings would be gauged. In other words, Weber's focus was typically Romantic both in its ultimate objective as well as in its methodology.

Here, then, there was no image of the social scientist as a bloodless intellect, isolated from his culture and operating primarily with well-codified procedural rules. Here there was no conception of the social scientist painstakingly moulding his little brick, and modestly adding it to the growing wall of science.

Instead of conceiving of the social scientist as a kind of bricklayer, the Weberian image is much more heroic. There is an image of the dedicate scholar who must find his lonely way without well-charted rules; who must rely on his own inner and very personal resources of empathy and intuition; there is an image of a man whose own unrelenting self-discipline sacrifices his other, science irrelevant passions or political ambitions to his calling and to his culture. This, then, is the protean and recurrent image of the German scholar, where scholarly work is conceived as a form of suffering and entails the 'tormented surmounting of self'.

The creation of a social science is, in Weber's view, seen as contingent ultimately on the exertion of essentially *personal* powers rather than professional skills. Its focal concern is on the quality of a man's inwardness, his sense of responsibility, individual intuition and empathy, rather than on the cumulative resources of the scientific community outside of himself. The Weberian conception of social science thus entailed a systematic application of Romantic premises.

Weber's theory of plural perspectives, of plural values and plural ideal types, comes down to the Romantic assumption that each man makes his own world and fights for it, rather than searching for a more universal map. The unity of the world is, in characteristically Romantic style, not vouchsafed by anything external to the individual but is created, rather, by his own personal and passionate commitment.

Here there is no one overarching order or *logos* in the world that awaits discovery or in which the sociologist, like others, participates. On the contrary, the world is one of cosmic conflict among divergent, heteronomous values. It is a grotesque world, therefore, in which the highest values may and do compete with the lowest, and live alongside of them without being able to command distinction. It is a cosmos in which good and evil are intertwined, and often mutually productive of one another; in which, for example, *Geist* is defenceless without *Macht,* but is, at the same time, perpetually corrupted and threatened by it. It is a grotesque world in which there is no way to choose one's path, except to feel an inner certainty that the path is one's own.

There is nothing more deeply Nietzschean in Weber's perspective than his injunction to fight only for what is one's own. Yet, while Nietzsche was contemptuous of the German state and of German *Kultur,* Weber, in contrast, seems to have been sure that only these were his very own. He thus gave his commitment to the German nation-state as his highest value. And at this point, the tragic is grotesquely mixed with the comic. The story ends in a kind of black humour. Weber's exaltation of the local and the contingent as the very highest value is characteristically Romantic; but it is a Romanticism through which the winds of an invisible grotesqueness had begun to blow.

Toward a Sociology of Anthropological Romanticism

An analysis of the historical development of anthropology in the nineteenth century would similarly reveal the profound impress of the Romantic movement. This will be particularly clear to those familiar with the German development of the concept of 'culture' which, early in the nineteenth century, began to replace the classical doctrine of a 'uniformitarian' human nature with a view that stress the reality and value of a cultural variability that was seen as something more than changes in external stage props or customs that overlay a constant human nature, pursuing essentially similar motives in merely different garb. Similarly, so far as nineteenth-century evolutionary theory in England is concerned, J. W. Burrow stresses that it was 'very largely . . .the outcome of a tension between English positivistic attitudes to science on the one hand and, on the other, a more profound reading of history, coming to a large extent from German romanticism. . .' There is no doubt that the history of anthropology has been and can be further illuminated by exploring its connections with Romanticism.

Rather than pursuing such historical concerns here, however, I should like to change course. Having spoken about the relationship between Romanticism and the social sciences in the past century, I now want to explore briefly some of their present connections. In particular, I want to shift over to a concern with the sociology (rather than the history) of Romanticism in its bearing on the contemporary social sciences.

To suggest just a few of the possibilities here, it may be useful to attempt a brief, impressionistic sketch of some of the current differences between American cultural anthropology and sociology today.

Looking at American anthropology and sociology today, not only as theoretical and research activities, but as modally differentiated occupational subcultures, it seems reasonable to suggest that anthropology, even today, still remains the more Romantic, and sociology the more Classical, discipline. In suggesting this, let me reiterate that I mean to refer not only to differences in their articulated theories and focalised methodologies, but, also, to differences in their infrastructures: in their more inarticulate background assumptions and in their occupational subcultures. It is in this sense that I believe it may be said that anthropology is a much more Romantic discipline than sociology. For example, anthropology is based upon and also prizes a much more diffuse (less role-segmented) involvement in 'field work'. The anthropologist's is a more personal method, both in the intensity of involvement it permits and in the diversity of personal attributes that it requires the anthropologist to use.

The sociologist, however, is commonly seeking to extricate his person from his research, to deny or to reduce their connection, and to depend upon more impersonal and codified rules of work—that is, on a more formalised and externalised methodology. Anthropologists, however, are *less* likely to deny the significance *or the value* of the anthropologist's *person* for the results he produces. One way in which this is often expressed is to say that anthropology retains a greater linkage with the humanities than does sociology, and that it entails a form of creativity more nearly akin to the humanities, while sociology, in its turn, is more usually bent upon the use of a natural science model.

The very activities of the anthropologist require him to go to more exotic and romantic locales; sociology, however, remains, for the most part, a study of the familiar, the everyday, and the commonplace. The anthropologist himself is more likely to surface to public attention as a more highly individuated person, in his dress and in his manner, and he is more readily conceived there, as John Bennett puts it, as a romantic hero. In contrast to the anthropologist, who is still felt to be rather more of a glamorous, adventuresome, and colourful person, the sociologist blends increasingly into the apparatus of the Welfare State and becomes one more species of staff expert and bureaucrat.

The writings of the anthropologist frequently take a less generalised form than those of the sociologist. The anthropologist is more concerned to present concrete ethnographic detail than the sociologist who, instead, is more inclined to elaborate on his abstractions. The anthropologist writes about extraordinary locales that have colour and vividness, in contrast to the sociologist's greater proclivity for the matter-of-fact and the prosaic. The anthropologist persuades and convinces his reader through his presentation of an interlocking set of mosaic details, which establish his intellectual authority because they imply his personal presence in the locale under discussion. To the anthropologist, the concrete detail are often regarded as valuable in their own right; but to the sociologist the concrete details are often stage props subordinated to a more general problem, or to the development of generalisations.

In contrast to anthropology, sociology is a much more Classical discipline which remains based, tacitly if not nominally, on a uniformitarian doctrine of human nature, of a human nature which, being everywhere alike, may therefore be legitimately studied in the convenience of the sociologist's nearby laboratory or by observing his own easily accessible students. Cross-cultural study by sociologists, although increasingly regarded as an ideal, still remains relatively rare.

G. H. Mead and Chicago School Romanticism

In characterising American cultural anthropology as relatively more Romantic than American sociology, I am well aware that anthropology has important Classical and Enlightenment aspects, and, also, that its heightened 'Structuralism' now manifests increasing tendencies to converge with sociology. Conversely, I am also aware that there are certain schools of thought within American *sociology* that are relatively more Romantic and, in fact, sometimes emphatically so. The purest vein of Romanticism in American sociology is, I believe, to be found in the 'Chicago School', which had the most concentrated exposure to the German tradition and was, in fact, established by many (A.W. Small, W.Y. Thomas and R.E. Park) who were directly trained in it. Currently, its leading exponents are Anselm Strauss, Erving Goffman and Howard S. Becker.

I think it notable that much of the focus of their work is not simply on the study of occupations and deviant behaviour, but that these Chicagoans' studies often produce a blending of the two. From this Chicago standpoint, the prostitute is just as much an *occupational* role as it is a manifestation of *deviant* behaviour. More generally, the style of these Chicago sociologists seems to have a greater tolerance of conceptual ambiguity; its conceptual distinctions are usually also deeply embedded in a rich texture of ethnographic detail; in fact, they commonly prefer an anthropologically informed style of fieldwork. In this methodological vein Becker has been an advocate of participant observation and has sought to entrench the method by codifying it, while Strauss (together with B. Glaser) has spoken for the merits of 'data-grounded theory', which is primarily a polemic against deductive, formal styles of sociological theorizing and an argument for inductive theorising - once again revealing the paradoxical but abiding affinity of certain forms of Positivism and Romanticism.

To many of these Chicagoans, the *demi-monde* is not only a fact of life, to be treated like any other, but also provides a *standpoint* for pronouncing a judgement upon respectable society. Indeed, they seem to speak on behalf of the *demi-monde,* and to affirm the authenticity of 'disreputable' life styles. This Chicago standpoint embodies a species of naturalistic Romanticism: it prefers the offbeat, i.e., the extreme case, to the familiar or average case; the evocative ethnographic detail to the dispassionate and dull taxonomy; the sensuously expressive to dry formal analysis; informal, naturalistic observation to formal questionnaires and rigorous laboratory experiments; the standpoint of the hip outsider to that of the square insider. In short, and as the nineteenth-century Romantics might have said, they prefer the standpoint of Bohemians to that of Philistines.

Crucial to this Chicago approach to deviance in particular, and to the social world in general, is the influence of Kenneth Burke's device of 'perspective by incongruity', which is to say of seeing and understanding some part of the social world by looking at it from an unusual or incougruous perspective. Thus, respectable occupations are seen as kin to deviant occupations correspondingly, the pimp is viewed as just another type of salesman. In effect, 'perspective by incongruity' is Kenneth Bruke's pragmatic routinisation of the Romantics' concept of the grotesque - that is, it is the Americanisation of the grotesque.

The strategy of perspective by incongruity has, of course, been most fully applied by Erving Goffman. In Goffman's work, for example, the relationship between psychiatrists and patients, or between priests and parishioners, are held to be akin to the relationship between 'con men' and their 'marks'; the behaviour of children on a carousel becomes a device for understanding the 'serious' world of adults; the stage becomes a model which is not merely casually but systematically exploited for understanding social life in all its complexities. Here, in Goffman's work, perspective by incongruity becomes a central method and as a result, the world as unified hierarchy is shattered and abandoned.

The linkage of this Chicago School of sociology to Romanticism is a complex and authentic one, and indeed it is the closest by far of any important American school of sociology. The major transmission belt for the saturation of the Chicago perspective by Romanticism was the social psychology of George Herbert Mead as developed by Herbert Blumer.

More than any other major figure in modern sociological theory, and more than any of the other founders of the Chicago school, Mead was the most thoroughly in command of the technical details of Romanticism; he was the most deeply appreciative of it's originality and viability, as well as being most knowingly sympathetic with its animating spirit – and this despite the fact that he did not receive his formal training in Germany. As Anselm Strauss says, 'The Romantic writers had a profound influence upon Mead. . .'

The convergences between Mead and the Romantics, to outline them simply and briefly, consist in the following:

(1) They commonly feel that there is so me tensionful *difference* between at least a private component of the self and some other more socially oriented part of the self, which is expressed by Mead's distinction between the 'I' and the 'me'.
(2) They also commonly believe (with the Idealists) that the self and the not-self are bound up together in and constituted by one single process; so that the objects of the experienced world cannot stand apart from 'subjects' who constitute them as objects.
(3) Mead and the Romantics also agree that a crucial aspect in the development of self depends upon its capacity to look back upon the *past,* and to claim certain events in it as its own.
(4) Again, both agree that the forms, no less than the concrete contents of awareness, of self and others, are continually evolving rather than being statically given.
(5) Both, therefore, stress that the self is an evolving and changing process.
(6) Again, both Mead and the Romantics agree that the 'past' has no one fixed significance but varies instead in its relationship to ongoing or contemplated action; one therefore does not discover but rather one reconstructs and creates pasts, seeing them differently at different points in the action process.
(7) Furthermore, but believe that the self is not a passive recipient of outside forms but is, rather, an active and selective agent, changing itself as it acts upon and toward others.
(8) So far as both Mead and the Romantics are concerned, moreover, at the end of an action, the self is always somewhat changed, as is the object world it deals with, and hence.
(9) The future is always somewhat unpredictably emergent from action that is continually seeking to surmount the ambiguities that it confronts.

Mead, then, like the Romantics, rejects an image of the social world as a given, neatly arranged static order; both view it instead as a tensionful, changing, open-ended, loosely stranded somewhat indeterminate and fluid process. Mead's emphasis that a plurality or multiplicity of selves is a *normal* and creative phenomenon may be regarded as an effort to transcend the fragmentation of the self and to deny that this fragmentation constitutes *grotesqueness.* In this respect, Mead's social psychology of the self is akin to the Hegelian dialectic which, too, seeks to transcend the grotesque, and invest it with meaning.

For all his convergence with Romanticism, however, Mead was not - and we should not expect him to be - a nineteenth century German Romantic. He is, of course, a post-Darwinism American, who understood Romanticism in an optimistic mood and conceived it as a philosophy of evolution. As Anselm Strauss says, 'The Romantic treatment becomes in Mead's hands divested of its mysticism and is given biological and scientific traits.' Strauss is also substantially correct in interpreting mead as seeking to provide an 'empirical underpinning for the revolutionary but inadequate notions of evolution' that the Romanticists had inaugurated, on the one side, while, on the other, as using Romanticism as a lever to pry open the deterministic framework of modern science and to 'restate problems of autonomy, freedom and innovation'.

It was largely through Mead's influence, I believe, that systematic Romanticism permeated one wing of the Chicago School of Sociology, gave it its coherence and its unique character and marked it off as a school apart from - and, indeed, often in conflict with - the scientistic orientations more characteristic of Amercian sociology. The coherence and the vitality of this wind of the Chicago School of sociology derived as much from the unmistakable imprint of Romanticism, as from its own creative adaptation of Romanticism to distinctive American traditions and ideologies.

Methodology and Romanticism

In much that I have said so far, I have directed attention to the manner in which *conceptual* schemes and substantive *theories* in social science contain, on the level of their deep structures, certain distinguishably Romantic and Classical syndromes. In the remaining parts of this discussion, however, I want to change the focus somewhat. Here, in what follows, I want to concentrate, not upon conceptual schemas and substantive theories, but, rather, on what sociologists commonly call 'methodology'. In particular, I want to suggest that not only any substantive theories of social science differ when implicated in the different infrastructures of Romanticism or Classicism but so, too, may its 'methodologies'. Romanticism, for example, is not I believe manifested only by a rejection of all formal methods. Within almost all field of methodology there are some standpoints that are more Romantic and others more Classical. In saying this, however, I would not wish to deny that there is a Romantic standpoint that may take a radically *anti*-methodological standpoint. The most talented expression of this position is of course that of the philosopher Paul Feyerabend (especially in his *Against Method: Outline of an Anarchistic Theory of Knowledge*.)

Within sociology, the fullest expression of a Romantic methodology was Max Weber's with his concern for *verstehen,* for projected, imaginatively constructed ideal types as opposed to inductively established average types, and with his conception of the 'mental experiment' through which one might move toward causal inference. It is interesting to note that the specifically Romantic antecedents of the 'mental experiment' may be seen in Schlegel's remark, '. . . it is no idle speculation in history to inquire what, under different circumstances, might have occurred. . . What would have been the consequence, what form would Europe have assumed, if the Catholic powers had completely triumphed . . .'

The Nature of Data

While the effect of Romanticism on the methodology of the social sciences finds its culmination in the sociology of Max Weber, this is scarcely the earliest indication of Romanticism's importance for the methodology of the social sciences. One of the earliest of these was the encouragement that Romanticism gave to the direct and first-hand research - in short, to 'field work' methods - as a way of studying peasant and other pre-industrial cultures. As Anthony Oberschall remarks—

> The incentive for field work originated in the Romantics' discovery of the notion of the *Volk*, which brought with it a positive evaluation [*sic*] of the beliefs and customs of the German peasantry. Since the time of the Grimm brothers, a number of researchers were criss-crossing the land, noting down dialects and fairy tales as well as observing dress, customs, and inscriptions in the village houses and churches . . . Growing out of the romantic tradition but directed more to immediate social and political problems was the work of Wilhelm Heinrich von Riehl [and] his notion of *Volkskunde* as an empirical science. The purpose of the study of the *Volk* was to discover the laws of *Volklife*. . . The way to discover these laws was through direct observation of the people: 'Especially the research directed at contemporary *Volklife* is inadequate when performed on secondary sources. Whoever wants to represent the individuality [*sic*] of the *Volk* only through data that are in the libraries, archives or statistical bureaus will put together but a rattling skeleton and not a picture that breathes life. For that purpose first hand sources are necessary, and they can only be gotten by walking through the country on one's own feet'.

The most profound expression of the methodological influence of early Romanticism, however, was not its polemic against secondary sources nor its call for first-hand observation and field work. Rather, it was its conception of what was *Valuable* and worthy of study, on the one hand, and, correspondingly, of *who* provided legitimate and *valuable* sources of data, on the other hand.

Romanticists contributed to shaping modern social science's core conception of the very nature of data itself. Despite the common view of Romanticism as politically conservative (if not reactionary), Romantic pluralism actually contributed importantly to the 'democratisation' of the concept of data. Specifically, Romantic pluralism undermined the Classical metaphysics which had ordered reality hierarchically and which in consequence had, overtly or tacitly, conceived of some portions of reality as being 'high' and worthy of emulation and attention, and of others as 'low', indecorously deviant, and worthy only either of contempt or neglect. To the Romanticists, every object was a world in itself, every grain of sand a cosmos. Each object being uniquely individual was therefore worthy of attention in itself; it was valuable in itself not simply as a paradigm to be emulated or decried. It was seen as worth knowing quite apart from its *moral* implications, and not because it needed to be reformed and improved. Romanticism thus contributed to a concern with the lowly or deviant parts of the social world.

The nineteenth-century Romantic attitude toward objects was akin to that of the collector's aesthetic. Thus, Oberschall notes that 'a man like Mannhardt in the [eighteen] sixties was conscious of a race against time in collecting this material for genuine rural life was disappearing all around him'. Such a collector', orientation toward objects was quite distinct from the attitude of many nineteenth-century reformers who wanted to study and know under-privileged social worlds in order to uplift, reform, or protect them legislatively. The Romantic attitude toward social worlds - its collector's posture - was thus much more nearly akin to that of certain modern social science conceptions of 'pure' science 'objectivity' than it was to instrumental conceptions of a 'policy-oriented' or applied sociology. But even that is not entirely correct, for the Romantics' aesthetic relation to the objects seeks to possess or protect it, to 'appreciate' and understand it, and not to use it as grist even for generalisations or laws. The Romantic wants and appreciates the object in its concrete totality, in its uniqueness and individuality.

The Romantic conception of pluralistic worlds, each unique and each valuable, invited attention to hitherto lowly or neglected social worlds and people, thereby influencing conceptions of *what* was worth studying. It also encouraged direct contact and immersal in these worlds as ways of studying them, thus influencing notions of *how* to study them, and from whom one could derive 'data'. Romanticism thus transformed the ontology and epistemology of the social sciences. Most specifically, it moved beyond either aristocratic conceptions of 'taking evidence' or bureaucratic conceptions of writing to notables – to gentry, ministers, or schoolteachers - and asking them to describe the conditions of life of *others* in the 'lower orders'. Each order might now give testimony concerning its own condition. Romanticism created new conceptions of the 'sources' of data. Stressing the importance of the intuitive in the knowing process, and of the ineffable in the object to be known, Romanticism encouraged a research process that entailed a communion-generating direct contact between the inquiring subject and the object inquired about. In an extreme expression it might foster a radical relativism that held that 'you had to be one to know one' - e.g., that only Blacks could know Blacks, the epistemology of the 'Insider', as Robert Merton refers to it.

Romanticism also encouraged resistance to the quantitative study of what were taken to be unique and ineffable entities. By reason of the importance it attributed to the subjective and inward, of the significance it attributed to ideas, values, and world-views, it was a basic of concern with the subjective and phenomenological standpoints, and of resistance to the application of the mechanistic models of physical science and to 'external' conceptions of causation to the study of social worlds. In American sociology this crystallised, during the Classical period of the 'Chicago School', in the insistence of W. I. Thomas and Florian Znaniecki that whatever is *defined* as real is real, in its consequences. Thus, while the later growth of attitude surveys and public opinion polls represents an extension of an essentially positivistic methodology, it was paradoxically based upon a prior triumph of Romanticism and of a Romantic conception of what was sociologically important data.

Analytic Induction

Still another expression of a relatively Romantic methodology may be found in the concept of 'analytic induction' as developed by Florian Znaniecki and Alfred Lindesmith. In this technique, one arrives at general conclusions concerning a set of phenomena from the successive and intensive study of individual cases, treated one at a time, rather than from inferences drawn from a sample of cases that are simultaneously and statistically examined. Analytic induction is therefore a case-by-case technique and, in its emphasis upon the values of the individual event, is characteristically Romantic. In the light of my previous remarks about the distinctive importance of Romanticism for a wing of the Chicago School of Sociology, it is worth noting the special connection that the development of analytic induction had with the history of the University of Chicago, through Znaniecki who taught there and Alfred Lindesmith who was trained there.

To reiterate, my emphasis here is not that a Romantic social science rejects methodology but that it tends to have a distinctive orientation to methodology. Still, as my earlier remarks imply, if one were to compare two samples of modern social scientist, one of relatively pure Classicists and the other of relatively pure Romanticists, that we would find that Romanticists are, on the average, somewhat more hostile to highly codified and formalised metrologies. Perhaps the prototype of such a Romantic rejection of formalisation in the social sciences may be found in the work of C. Wright Mills.

C. Wright Mills as Romanticist

I am aware, of course, that in various works, Mills was at pains to exhibit his competence in handling a 'modern' research technology. This is especially notable in those works that he did when associated with the Bureau of Applied Social Research. I am also aware that, at one point, Mills even issued forth with the formulaic slogan that I.B. M. + humanism = sociology. But even in his statistically grounded researches, it is clear that Mills' major intellectual gratifications derived from *qualitative* analysis, for which his statistical materials primarily served as a springboard. Mills, however, was in many ways characteristically American in his enjoyment of various kinds of tools and machines. But perhaps it is neither unfair nor untrue to suggest that Mills loved especially those tools and machines that enhanced mens' sense of individual control and personal mastery. He loved machines or tools which would either strengthen individual independence or enable men to move freely and easily among different places. Perhaps this is in some part why Mills loved the motorcycle. But Romanticism need not entail a radical rejection of the machine, and perhaps Mills' love of the motorcycle was akin to Gabriel D' Annunzio's equally romantic love of the airplane. In short, twentieth-century Romantics need not be Luddites.

Far more revealing of Mills' central methodological position, however, are the main themes of his *sociological Imagination.* I believe these represent an essentially Romantic perspective, most particularly with regard to his rejection of any kind of autonomous and impersonal methodology. In his *sociological Imagination,* it will be remembered that Mills' critique was a twofold one: on the one hand, it was a rejection of mindless statistical empiricism and, on the other hand, it was a rejection of what he called abstracted grand theorising. Here Mills rejected formalisations that were used as substitutes for personalised thought and, in particular, insofar as they were emptied of data possessing concrete richness. He, too, wanted a picture of social worlds that 'breathed life.'

Mills' own conception of his methodology is revealed primarily in his metaphor of 'intellectual craftsmanship', and nothing could be more characteristically Romantic than Mills' remarks in his essay on 'Intellectual Craftmanship'. Here he held that the 'social science tradition of the last hundred years amounts to this: . . . in the *mind* that has hold of it, in the *mind* that has been formed by it, there sometimes comes about a kind of sociological *imagination.*

Mills'emphasis is clearly upon the value of the sociological *imagination,* and not on methodological *discipline*. As if the Romanticism of this perspective was not plain enough, Mills adds immediately thereafter that the sociological imagination resides 'in the capacity to shift from one perspective to another, and in the process to build up an adequate view of a total society . . .' It is, he insists, 'this *imagination* that sets off the social scientist from the mere technician'. A sociological imagination, adds Mills, contains 'an *unexpected quality* about it, perhaps because its essence is the combination of *ideas that no one expected were combinable'*. In short, the essence of the sociological imagination to Mills is a Romantic *pluralism of perspectives* blended with Kenneth Burke's version of the grotesque, namely, perspective by incongruity. For Mills, the collation of systematic data was above all 'one way to invite imagination'. In short, he suggested that it was not the formal machinery of research that produced results, but, rather, its stimulus to the imagination – a personal and inward quality. One may further stir the imagination, Mills adds in a bland aside, by a glass of Irish whisky.

It is in these remarks, I believe, that we have the essence of Mills' conception of a pluralistic, a personal, and an imaginative style of research that was plainly Romantic. Nor is it irrelevant to note, in passing, that an effort to trace the intellectual sources of Mills' outlook would surely lead to the seminal influence that was exerted upon him both by George Herbert Mead and Max Weber, two important viaducts of Romanticism in sociology.

It may seem that, while I have promised to discuss the influences of Romanticism on sociological methodology, the examples given thus far do not really represent the methodological concerns truly characteristic of the social sciences today. In other words, there may be some who agree that, once upon a time, there was such a thing as a Romantic methodology of the social sciences, but that this time is long since past, and that it is now useless to attempt to understand current developments in modern social science methodology in terms of the Romantic-classical distinction.

P.F. Lazarsfeld's Romantic Premises

With that in mind, let me briefly refer to the work of Paul Felix Larzarsfeld, who is surely the dean of social science methodologists in the United States today. The essence of Lazarsfed's methodological position is that the social scientist ought to be guided, first and above all, not so much by the formal canons of science, as these are articulated and codified by logicians, but rather, Lazarsfeld emphasises, by the *implicit* rules and procedures which successful social scientists *tacitly* employ and embody in their researches. In other words, Lazarsfeld's methodological position rejects a view of social science methodologies that sees them as a set of eternal and *externalised* rules of procedure or of proof. It is thus a distinctly anti-Classical conception of methodology, in its derivation if not in its application.

That Larzarsfed's methodological posture *ensues* in a Classical emphasis on the importance of codifying and formalising rules of research should not be allowed to conceal that it *derives* from quite different, Romantic premises. In other words, while Lazarsfeld is a Classicist as a methodological *moralist,* he is a Romantic who assumes that in the beginning was the creative deed.

What Lazarsfeld stresses is the search for the guiding proprieties, for the paradigms and the models that lie *implicitly in the* research of working social scientists. It is implied, by his view, that great social science proceeds on the basis of (at first) inarticulate operational rules and often ineffable information or experience. Here, then, in characteristically Romantic manner, Lazarsfeld's emphasis is on the inwardness of an effective social science methodology, on the inarticulateness of the creative, which needs, however, to be rendered articulate. In his unstated but evident premise, it is not the rulebook that is the measure, but, rather, the social scientist and his concrete work.

I might add here that this Romantic aspect of Lazarsfeld's methodological orientation seems to be of one piece with the style of the Bureau of Applied Research's statistics, at least insofar as it has treated tests of statistical significance in a relatively more 'flexible' way than some sociological statisticians elsewhere. Some, it has seemed to me, have objected to the neglect of tests of significance partly because this allowed too much variability in the interpretation of statistical tables, and placed undue reliance upon individaul choice and personal judgement. In short, they objected to the intrusion of the subjective. While sociological *theorists* at Chicago University were more Romantic than those at Columbia University, it may be that statistical *methodologists* at Columbia University were more Romantic than those elsewhere.

Computer-using Romanticism

This brief example may suffice to *suggest* that not all emphases upon methodology are intrinsically Classical in character, and that there are *Romantic* methodologists no less than Classical methodologists. This is true even with respect to the so-called 'hard' or computer-emphasising social sciences. For example, if one compares 'systems analysis' with, say, operations research, programme budgeting, or cost-benefit analysis it seems to me that systems analysis is by far the most Romantic. This conjecture appears to be borne out by the work of Aaron

Wildavsky. Thus, Wildavsky characterises the good systems analyst as a man whose 'forte is creativity'. And he also stresses that the good systems analyst strives to relate various elements 'imaginatively into new systems . . .'

Wildavsky also notes that E. S. Quade speaks of systems analysis as constituting a 'form of art' in which it is not possible to assert 'fast rules' that can be followed with exactness. 'In systems analysis,' says Quade, 'there is more judgement and intuition and less reliance on quantitative methods than in operations research'. Systems analysis is also very much concerned with the development of techniques - such as contingency analysis - for dealing with situations that contain a high degree of uncertainty.

Similar Romantic orientations to computer simulation may be inferred from the work of Robert Boguslaw. In an effort to develop computer programmes for playing chess, Boguslaw did with chess players essentially the same thing that Larzarsfeld had done with sociologists. That is, Boguslaw studied the work of good chess players, attempted to render explicit the 'heuristics' or working rules that they *tacitly* employed, and then proceeded to programme the computer in terms of these heuristics.

Résumé

In brief summary, the central assumptions I have made in the discussion above are:

(1) Serious historical studies of both sociology and anthropology - and these, I believe, are only now emerging - will find it illuminating to trace their connections with nineteenth century Romanticism. This constitutes *one* of the keys to the modern effort at the reconstruction of the history (and therefore of the consciousness) of the social science. It is this that will enable us to go beyond a concern for the narrowly political implications of various sociology's to their other and more complex social sources, particularly as they bear upon styles of sociological work as well as patterns of problem formulation.

(2) Romantic and Classical syndromes refer to enduring deep structures that underlie the theories of sociology even today. They are embedded in and help to differentiate various schools of thought and, also, various professional subcultures. In short, Romantic and Classical syndromes are in my view promising intellectual tools for the empirical study of the ongoing social sciences today - i.e., they are as valuable for a *sociology* of sociology as for a *history* of sociology.

(3) It is not only the substantive theories but the 'methodologies' of the social sciences themselves that bear the differentiating impress of Romantic and Classical deep structures.

(4) From both a developmental, historical standpoint and from a synchronic sociological standpoint, a core conflict within and among schools of thought centers on the tensions between Romantic and Classical (or other) deep structures.

We can, then, think of Romanticism and Classicism as syndromes or latent dimensions that underpin sociology and the other social sciences. We can think of them as different genotypes underlying certain phenotypes.

A 'Classical Sociology', then, would be one which - ideal typically - stresses the *universality* of the governing standards, norms, or values, or of the functional requisites of a society. A 'Romantic Sociology', however, stresses - again, ideal typically - the relativity, the uniqueness, or historical character of the standards or needs of any society or group. If Classicism tends toward *historicism*.

A Classical sociology is concerned with more careful statistical analysis of the 'average' case and with the fuller statistical distribution of cases, in its concern for 'the normal'. A Romantic sociology, by contrast, focuses on the reality of the deviant case and tolerates deviance from normative or role requirements; a Classical sociology places greater emphasis upon the indispensability of some measure of conformity to them. Classical sociology, then, focuses on the value of assimilating self and person to culture and role, while Romantic sociology, however, focuses on the values of distance from roles and values, and of those occasions when men have failed to be controlled by or assimilated to their roles and values.

The methodology of a Classical sociology stresses the importance of 'formal' reason, of codifications, and of self-conscious conformity to known rules. The methodology of a Romantic sociology places greater emphasis on the *Extra-technical* or social sources of theory and knowledge, such as the sociology of knowledge. A Classical sociology places greater stress on the situation-transcending potency of human reason. A Classical sociology therefore implies that there is one best model for work, and that it is the researcher's obligation to determine what this is and to attempt to conform to it at all times. A Romantic sociology, however, stresses that different intellectual problems and different research sites each have their own differing properties or paradigms. A Romantic sociology tends to attribute greater significance to informal procedures that are tailored to individual cases. That is, there is more than one best way, and appropriate techniques and methodologies are expected to change over time and with shifting values perspectives.

Classical sociology searches for the more enduring structures and seeks laws that are more universal in application. Romantic sociology seeks *historical* laws or may work only with ethnography, or with hermeneutic interpretations or descriptions of unique events, or concrete totalities. Classical sociology places its emphasis on order and order-inducing mechanisms in society; Romantic sociology, on the sources of change, process, of negotiations and becoming. To the Classical sociologist, 'objectivity' means conformity with the requirements of reason or the logic of science, and entails a kind of selflessness. To the Romanticist, however, objectivity means the consensus of scholars achieved through debate, and is grounded in a certain kind of subjectivity.

The Classical sociologist sees society's requirements for coherence and order; the Romantic sociologist stresses society's needs for conflicts and friction. A Romantic sociology believes that there are all manner of tensions and conflicts within society - among ideas, classes, institutions, types of men - and it expects that there is an inherent conflict between man and society. The Classicist sees the dependence of men upon some society for the realisation of their humanness. The Romanticist believes that men's humanness is limited by the established society. The Classical sociologist therefore sees the value of harmony, consensus, and decorum, while the Romantic sees the value of the grotesque, the dissonant, and the indecorous in society.

Clearly, then, I do not believe that Romanticism or Classicism is, by itself, a sufficient infrastructure for a valid social theory. Both, I believe, are necessary. But this needs qualification in at least two important ways.

First, if the theorist has access to both Romantic and Classical infrastructures, but if he *isolates* each from the other, then each will fail to provide a liberating perspective on the other. There may then develop a kind of theoretical schizophrenia, where one perspective is used for one purpose and the other for a different purpose. The most liberating relationship of the two exists, however, when neither is insulated from the other; when neither is repressed; when each can therefore provide a perspective on the other; and when each can be brought into a theory-energising tension with the other.

The above implication lean in a 'structuralism' direction. The following implications, however, lean in an 'historicist' direction: given the above implications (that is, invoking the same and not different assumptions), it follows that there can be specific historical conditions when one of the infrastructures is suppressed by the larger society, or by the professionally dominant technical tradition, and when, therefore, it may be intellectually valuable to place a compensatory *stress* on what has been culturally excluded. I believe that our own epoch, however shrill its 'counter-culture', is precisely such an historical period. The Classical infrastructure has been the dominant force in the development of the academic social sciences; developments of the late sixties have manifested what is only a counter-cyclical *trend of secondary* significance. In such an epoch, in which social theory has been exposed tc an establishment-sponsored

Classicism, it is especially necessary to protect theoretical creativity and the tensionful 'balance' of infrastructures by a compensatory emphasis on the special value of the *Romantic* infrastructure. In an epoch such as our own, where the Romantic largely remains underground, marginal to the dominant culture, there are also very grave dangers of its own equally one-sided development, particularly in irrational and anti-intellectual directions.

3

Emile Durkheim and the Critique of Socialism

Durkheim's study of socialism is a document of exceptional intellectual interest for several reasons. Not least of these is that it presents us with the now somewhat unusual case of a truly first-rate thinker who had the inclination to contribute to the history of sociological theory and to comment extensively on the work of a key figure in that history, Henri Saint-Simon. The core of this volume contains Durkheim's presentation of Saint-Simon's ideas, their sources and their development.

Indeed, Durkheim so subordinates himself in these pages that we might well with that he had developed his own critical reactions to Saint-Simon at greater length. This is somewhat unusual in the annals of current sociological scholarship in America, which has tended to leave 'mere' exegesis and historical commentary to text-book writers, and which sometimes unwittingly fosters the barbaric assumption that books and ideas more than twenty years old are beyond scientific salvation. In contrast to such current preoccupations with the modern, it is noteworthy that at the time Durkheim (1858–1917) wrote these lectures on socialism and Saint-Simon (1760–1825), the latter was dead some seventy years.

In some quarters a concern for the history of sociological theory is now regarded as misguided. Of course, it is easy to understand how the usual trite chronicle of thinkers and ideas could foster such a disillusioned appraisal. Yet this dim view of the history of sociological theory may be prematurely pessimistic about earlier theory and unduly optimistic about the state of current theory.

Though current theoretical accomplishments in sociology are frequently substantial and occasionally brilliant, nothing is to be gained by short-circuiting this discipline's sense of historical continuity. We may, of course, burnish our generation's attainments by neglecting the earlier sources from which they derive. But such a rupture of historical continuity may well undermine even our own generation's accomplishments. For it may set a precedent, disposing later scholars to turn their back on our work.

There is, it would seem, some inconsistency between the sociologist's growing recognition of the importance of deliberately cultivated theoretical continuity - as a methodological imperative - and a growing tendency to neglect the earlier contributors to sociological theory. An awareness of the historical development of sociology, of its past as well as its present state, is the only firm basis for evaluating whether we have 'progressed', and, if so, how much and in what ways. Alfred North Whitehead has said that 'a science which hesitates to forget its founders is lost'. But to forget something, one must have known it in the first place. A science *ignorant* of its founders does not know how far it has travelled nor in what direction; it, too, is lost.

There is one basis justification for a social scientist's neglect of the history of his discipline: he must demonstrate that current theory and research have substantially assimilated the problems and perspectives formulated by the earlier thinkers. Failing in this, he must demonstrate that these earlier problems and perspectives are no longer to be regarded as a proper concern of his discipline.

Since Durkheim's time, however, academic sociologists have increasingly neglected some of the central social problems of our time. For example, there are few sociological researches into the sources, growth, and diffusion of modern socialism, however numerous studies of the Soviet Union have become. While there have been careful studies of various marginal sects and cults, there are few detailed sociological analyses of a socialist or communist party.

Related to this lacuna is the common neglect of property institutions by sociologists, apparently on the assumption that this is the economist's job alone. If this is reasonable, however, one wonders why sociologists have not also left studies of industrial relations to economists, and studies of political parties and elections to political scientists. Furthermore, since the decline of the 'culture lag' school, which for a period flourished at the University of Chicago, there has been little systematic analysis of the role of modern science and technology, and these institutions now find only a peripheral place in the sociological theories current today. Finally, although there are numerous sociological studies of family discord and even some of industrial tensions, there are few sociological studies of international relations, of war and peace.

Durkheim's study of socialism and Saint-Simon assumes importance today precisely because, at various points, it considers all of these major questions and, in some measure, does so in their interrelationship to each other. Because it has something to say about these problems, it may be expected that educated laymen as well as professional sociologists will find much of interest in the pages.

One way in which this study is of special value to sociologists, and others interested in the development of sociological theory, is that it provides us with a basis for a fuller understanding of Durkheim's own contribution as a sociologist, producing greater clarity concerning some of the intellectual forces which shaped it, and, in particular, of its links to Saint-Simon, to the latter's disciple, Auguste Comte, and to Karl Marx. Some recent analyses of Durkheim's work have viewed it too much in terms of what it presumably became, and too little in terms of what it came from. There has also been a tendency to over-emphasise Durkheim's Comteian heritage and the influence which this had upon him, to the neglect of other influence.

Without doubt Durkheim's theory and research was much influenced by Comte's. But if Durkheim's work comes out of Comte's, it does not come *only* from this source; if there was continuity between Durkheim and Comte, there was also discontinuity. In Durkheim, we see a man who sometimes found himself constrained to oppose his own intellectual mentor. Durkheim, we may say, was an uneasy Comteian.

One striking demonstration that Durkheim was not simply the devoted disciple of Comte can be seen in this study of socialism. Here, Durkheim firmly denies to Comte, and bestows on Saint-Simon, the 'honour' of having founded both positivist philosophy and sociology. It should be clear from this alone that references to Comte as Durkheim's 'acknowledged master' are misleading simple; they do not portray their relationship in anything like its true complexity. Above all, the usual formula fails to indicate that, in certain pivotal ways, Durkheim's work constituted a deep-going polemic against Comte. Durkheim's study of *The Division of Labour* has been interpreted as an expression of his opposition to the utilitarian individualists, and particularly Herbert Spencer. In actually, this volume has another polemical target, namely, Comte himself, a fact which comes cut forcefully in its culminating chapter.

The Polemic Against Comte

In Comte's view, the increasing division of labour in modern society threatened its social cohesion. For it brought with it 'a fatal disposition towards a fundamental dispersion of ideas, sentiments, and interests. . .' The increasing division of labour was, in this analysis, subversive of social stability because it undermined the fundamental requisite of order, namely, the consensus of moral beliefs. It was one of the basic aims of Durkheim's *Division of Labour* to refute this Comteian view. Durkheim flatly rejected Comte's analysis, holding that it was not the division of labour as such which 'normally' induced social disorder.

Durkheim's argument, in effect, hinges on a Saint-Simonian assumption: namely, that with the emergence of the new industrial order, new social needs arose and new ways of satisfying old needs were required. Like Saint-Simon's, Durkheim's position was relativistic. The growing division of labour is 'natural' in modern society, Durkheim maintains; it normally produces social solidarity. Indeed, it produces what he seems to have regarded as a 'higher' type of solidarity, an 'organic' solidarity. This he contrasted with the 'mechanical' solidarity of earlier societies which had rested upon shared moral beliefs, or uniformity in their 'collective conscience'. Comte, he says, failed to see that the social solidarity produced by the division of labour with its web of interdependence, was gradually being substituted for the earlier solidarity which had rested mainly on shared moral beliefs.

Of course, says Durkheim, modern society requires consensus in moral beliefs. Shared moral beliefs as well as the division of labour both contribute to the maintenance of social solidarity. But modern society no longer requires the *same degree* of moral consensus, nor does this consensus entail the same items of belief, necessary for earlier periods. In Durkheim's view, the respective roles of mechanical and organic solidarity were changing. 'What is necessary is to give each, at each moment in history, the place that is fitting to it. . .' The division of labour 'more and more tends to become the essential condition of social solidarity'. Indeed, 'the ideal of human fraternity can be realised only in proportion to the progress of division of labour'. We cannot look to the past as a guide, says Durkheim. In a manner reminiscent of Saint-Simon, who has also held that the division of labour must become the basis of a new morality, Durkheim indicates, that contemporary society must develop a new moral code corresponding to changed modern conditions.

It is sometimes suggested that there was an important change in focus in Durkheim's later work, and that he gradually re-emphasised and saw new importance in the role of shared beliefs. Whatever the validity of this observation, here, in *The Division of Labour,* his first great work, Durkheim is unmistakeably conducting a polemic against Comte *for having overstressed the used for moral consensus in maintaining social stability.* It is certainly not the case that Durkheim neglects the role of shared beliefs in *The Division of Labour;* it is not that he is then unaware of their significance and only later works through to an understanding of them. From the beginning, he was fully aware of the significance which had long since been imputed to shared beliefs by Comte, but he deliberately chose to oppose Comte's estimate of their role in modern society.

Durkeim readily admits that the division of labour presently engenders social tensions. These arise, however, 'because all the conditions of organic solidarity [i.e., social solidarity deriving from increased occupational specialisation] have not been realised. His position is again fundamentally Saint-Simonian. Saint-Simon had held that social patterns engendering tension do so, either because they are the archaic survivals of earlier conditions which no longer obtain, or are the first growths of a new social system which has not yet matured. It is in both of these ways that Durkheim explains the tensions associated with the increasing division of labour.

He holds, for example, that the new moral rules appropriate to the new division of labour have not yet developed. Because of this, class war and crises of over-production result, for the relations between specialised functions are not yet properly integrated and regulated. Or, again, Durkheim states that the division of labour engenders tensions because people have been forced into occupations at variance with their natural talents. It is not the division of labour as such, but an archaic 'forced division of labour' that generates social tensions.

Occupational specialisation must be assigned, says Durkheim, in keeping with the natural distribution of talents and not on the basis of hereditary wealth or birth. He does not, however, develop this into a critique of private property, as had the Saint-Simonians, Bazard and Enfantin, in which it was indicated that private ownership of industrial property can inhibit its rational administration and productivity, since those owning factories may not be those who can best administer them.

In his *Division of Labour,* at any rate. Durkheim was not gropingly moving toward an appreciation of shared moral norms; he was, in fact, moving away from Comte's emphasis on their significance in modern society. Durkheim was, also, much more self-consciously aware than Comte of the ways in which *commitment* to certain types of norms might yield forms of social disorganisation. For example, in the *Division of Labour* he notes that it is because people in modern society *share* certain conceptions of 'justice' that they object to the 'forced' division of labour, and to the assignment of roles on the basis of inherited wealth or birth. In his later work on *Suicide,* Durkheim stresses that Protestant norms actually induce a higher rate of suicide. He stresses that normlessness (or anomie) is not the only source of social disorganisation or the only stimulant to a high suicide rate. A commitment to Protestant beliefs may also induce a disorganising 'egoism', Durkheim argues. And he regards anomie and egoism as having a close connection, a 'peculiar affinity' for each other.

Durkheim makes an interesting point in his discussion of 'acute anomie'. This, he says, arises during periods of sudden prosperity or depression which rapidly change people's class position. People exposed to such sudden class shifts are prone to suicide, he says, because they are normless. But here 'normless' is used in a peculiar sense. It does not mean that people lack norms, but rather that the norms which they *do have* no longer correspond to the new class position in which they suddenly find themselves. It is this disparity between their old norms and their new circumstances which induces tension. Thus, moral norms play a positive role in *generating* disorganisation; they can disrupt social order rather than strengthen it, unless they are in keeping with the changing circumstances of life. Social order does not rest on norms alone, Durkheim is saying here; it depends on the way in which norms are integrated with other conditions.

Similarly, Durkheim maintains that to the extent that people believe in 'progress' there will always be a strain toward anomie, involving a perpetually restless dissatisfaction with the *status quo.* A certain amount of anomie is therefore a normal condition in modern society. The 'enfeeblement' of the 'collective conscience' is an inevitable and normal development in a modern industrial society with an increasing division of labour.

Comte had stressed the need for social consensus, regarding its decline as the principal peril to modern society. Durkheim, however, maintained that *too high* a degree of social cohesion could also induce disorganisation. This is clearly expressed in his *Suicide* where he remarks—

> If, as we have seen, excessive individuation leads to suicide, insufficient individuation has the same results. When a man has

> become detached from society, he encounters less resistance to suicide in himself, and he does so likewise when social integration is too strong.

Thus, a collective conscience which was either too weak *or too strong* could induce social disorganisation.

In contrast again with Comte, Durkheim held that a certain amount of social conflict was normal and natural in modern society. In part, he sees it as the price of modern freedom. In the *Division of Labour,* for example, he makes the point that conflict and competition among individuals was natural. It was the prevention of such conflicts, by the imposition of outmoded arrangements based on inherited wealth and position, that was abnormal. Let natural talents rather than artificial institutions decide the issue, he says.

The contrast of Durkheim's position with Comte's also comes out forcefully in respect of their differing strategies for controlling the divisive effects of the increasing division of labour. Interestingly enough, Comte had held that the dispersing effects of occupational differentiation should be checked by government regulation. This is at variance with Comte's tendency to minimise the role of political intervention and his usual reliance on the 'spontaneous' sources of social solidarity. Durkheim takes issue with this proposal and is, in this respect, a more consistent Comteian than Comte himself. The central difficulty of modern society, Durkheim insists, is the lack of social structures mediating between the individual and the state. Comte's solution, he holds, would only compound the atomising heritage of the French Revolution.

Project for a Corporative Society

In the *Division of Labour,* he never proposes a clear-cut alternative solution to the problem, although the direction which his solution is to take is already manifest there. It is only in the *Suicide* that he proposes a specific remedy for the dispersing effects of the division of labour which he later expands upon in the preface to the second edition of the *Division of Labour.* In this he takes a step beyond and against Comte in maintaining that not only was the state incompetent to control this problem, but so too were the family and religious organisations. None of these could supply the necessary connective tissue in modern society.

What is needed, holds Durkheim, are new kinds of intermediary groups which can regulate the specialised occupational life of modern men. He advances a plan for the development of communal or corporative organisation among people working in the same occupations and industries. Men in the same segment of the economy will understand each other's problems well enough to respond to them flexibly. They can establish a viable group life which can exercise effective moral control over all the participants on the basis of intimate knowledge.

These occupational corporations were to be represented in a national assembly, with employers and employees each having separate representation. The number of representatives for each was to be determined by the importance that public opinion assigns to their group. The corporations are to be organised on a national basis, coextensive with the national development of the modern economy. They are to maintain carefully their independence of the state.

Ultimately, however, they will become the basis of political organisation and the fundamental political entity. This is notably convergent with Saint-Simon's conception of government in the new positivist-industrial order. In a formula later adopted by Marx, Saint-Simon had expected that government would cease being political in any special sense, and would not involve the coercion of men but the rational administration of things. Territorial and geographic bases of social and political organisation will not disappear, claims Durkheim, but will play a less important role in the corporatively organised society. This, too, converges with Saint-Simon's prediction that in modern industrial society loyalties will be less localistic and more cosmopolitan.

Durkheim's rationale for introducing this plan is noteworthy. In a manner at variance with Saint-Simon's, Comte's and Marx's evolutionism, Durkheim does not claim that the corporative organisation of society is already embedded in the evolutionary drift, or that it is inevitably predestined by evolutionary design.

Nor does he merely justify his proposal on the grounds that it conforms with certain values which he takes for granted. His position is that historical analysis shows that such corporative organisation has been functional in the past and that there are current social needs for which such groups could again be useful. In short, he does not simply describe what it is, nor does he hold that corporative organisation 'must be'; he maintains that it *can be* instituted, and that if it were it would prove useful in reducing current social disorganisation.

The plan is an interesting synthesis of diverse intellectual streams. It is a blend of the Comteian concern for small groups, with their complex and spontaneous bonds of social interaction, together with the Saint-Simonian emphasis on planned association. It is a 'utopian' plan in the sense that no plausible mechanisms are suggested for instituting it. Significantly enough, however, it is presented in a deliberately anti-utopian framework, in that it explicitly eschews any effort to specify particulars. Durkheim's formulations here bear the impress of the Marxian polemic against utopianism; indeed, the seems that Durkheim knew Marx well enough to quote the latter's metaphors freely.

What Durkheim seems to have been attempting was a synthesis of Marxist and Comteian veiws, a compromise which leads him back to Saint-Simonian formulations which had influenced both Marx and Comte. Above all, Durkheim was here seeking to combine the Comteian focus on regulating moral norms with the Marxian focus on economic institutions. The decisive need today, suggests Durkheim, is to provide a moral regulation not merely of society in general but of the economy in particular. What is needed is a regulation that will correspond to the characteristics of the new *industrialism* which, as Saint-Simon had also forcefully emphasised, Durkheim holds to be the distinctive feature of modern society.

> What brings about the exceptional gravity of this state [of anomie normlessness] is the heretofore unknown development that economic functions have experienced for about two centuries. Whereas formerly they played only a secondary role, they are now of the first importance. We are far from the time when they were

> disdainfully abandoned to the inferior classes. In the face of the economic, administrative, military and religious functions become steadily less important. Only the scientific functions seem to dispute their place, and even science has scarcely any prestige save to the extent that it can serve practical occupations, which are largely economic. That is why it can be said, with some justice, that society is or tends to be essentially industrial.

Durkheim also seems to have regarded his proposal for occupational corporations as consistent with socialist proposals. For even a socialist society, he insists, will require means of morally regulating interpersonal relations and adjusting the activities of different groups to each other. If socialist society is to be stable, it will have to do more than increase productivity and living standards; even elimination of the 'forced division of labour' will not suffice; socialism, too, requires a set of regulating moral norms, capable of daily implementation.

To reiterate the main line of Durkheim's argument in *The Division of Labour:* the increasing division of labour is a normal development in modern industrial society. It does not naturally produce social disorganisation, but does so only under certain conditions. The two most important of these are, first, where anomie prevails in the economy, that is, where there is a lack of moral norms governing industrial activities or relations. The second is where there is a 'forced division of labour', that is, where people are constrained to take up positions in the division of labour at variance with their natural talents.

At this point, Durkheim could have pursued two different directions: he could have focused either on the problem of anomie or on the study of the forced division of labour. If he had pursued the latter he could, for example, have examined the reasons why the hereditary transmission of wealth or position does not disappear and give way to new social arrangements more in keeping with the modern division of labour.

He does not take this direction at all. This cannot be explained by stating that Durkheim believed that the forced division of labour would naturally wither away in the course of time, and that it therefore required no planned remedy. For he clearly rejects this tack with respect to normlessness or anomie in the economic sphere. In the latter case, he does not count on the 'natural' or spontaneous development of new ethical beliefs to provide the required regulation of economic activities; he deliberately proposes a planned solution to the problem, the occupational corporation.

Attention is focused on the problem of anomie, rather than the forced division of labour, because Durkheim was still deeply committed to Comteian assumptions. He still believes that *some* degree of moral consensus is indispensable to social solidarity, either in a capitalist or a socialist society. It, however, he had further developed the problem of the forced division of labour this could only have obscured his differences with the socialists (as well as the utilitarian individualists) whose basic weakness, he maintained, was their neglect of the role of moral norms.

This tack would also, at some point, have constrained Durkheim into a concern with systems of stratification and power relations, in short into a greater convergence with Marxism. This would have made it difficult, if not impossible, for him to continue using the Comteian model of modern society which saw it as basically tending toward other and stability. Unlike Saint-Simon, who had stressed the role of social classes and of class conflict in providing an impetus or resistance to change. Comte had minimised the role of internal class conflicts.

To Durkheim, as to Comte, the basic features of the new society were already in existence - that is, modern industrialism with its rational methods and its increasing division of labour. Consequently, their problem was to develop a new moral order consistent with it, so that it might remain stable and develop in an orderly manner. Their central task was not defined as producing social change so much as facilitating a natural tendency toward social order. Their problem was, in short, that of 'fine tuning' the new industrial régime rather than basically reorganising it. They saw modern society as young and immature as an insufficiently developed industrialism. One merely needed to stimulate and gently guide the natural processes of its maturation. In contrast, of course, Marx - who had retained the Saint-Simonian emphasis on social classes and class conflict did not regard modern society as an adolescent *industrialism* but as a senile *capitalism* which, containing the ripe 'seeds of its own destruction', needed to be readied for burial. Expecting that the capitalist would resist his own dismissal, Marx believed that change would not be smooth and orderly, and that therefore modern society possessed deep-instabilities.

It is in part because he views modern society in the Comteian manner, as requiring moral rearmament rather than economic reconstruction, that Durkheim focuses on the problem of anomie and proposes the development of occupational corporations to control it. This is partly a supplement to and partly a polemic against the socialist's neglect of the role of moral norms. But even in this, Durkheim's attitude is no longer that of Comte's; he does not seem to view moral reform as necessarily prior to political or economic reform, as Comte had, but rather as corollary or coincident with it.

The question for Durkheim was *how* the needed moral reform was to be obtained. How could the new morality be developed? Saint-Simon and Comte had in part supposed that the new morality would not be developed but would be (indeed, had been) discovered by positive science and sociology. Durkheim, however, is not sanguine about this solution on several grounds. While he continues to believe that social science can ultimately provide a basis for values, and that a scientific ethics will some-by be possible, he nonetheless argues that, at this time, science is not sufficiently advanced to do so. Science could not yet discern the content or the particulars of the new morality '. . . it is vain to delay by seeking precisely what this law must be, for in the present state of knowledge, our approximation will be clumsy and always open to doubt.' The problem is too pressing to wait for the development of a positive or scientific ethic.

The Development of Moral Beliefs

How then could a new morality appropriate to modern circumstances be secured? It would have to be naturally or spontaneously developed, if it could not now be scientifically discovered. But this raises the question as to how, in general, systems of moral beliefs normally and spontaneously arise. For there is no reason to suppose that the spontaneous development of a new morality will differ from the spontaneous development of earlier moralities. The question of values then becomes a thoroughly empirical one. In short, Durkheim is led to a consistently positivistic position about moral beliefs, becoming concerned with the study of the ways in which they actually evolve and develop. This knowledge about the *spontaneous* development of values could then be used to further the *planned* development of a morality suitable for modern times.

It is in some part because he becomes growingly interested in the spontaneous development of social norms, the ways in which they emerge and become internalised in the individual, that he comes to focus on the role of educational institutions and of the family. This is also one of the reasons for his study of religion, which is essentially a study of the development of moral beliefs in their most dramatic expression. A central point in most of these studies is his concern with the factors that shape and sustain moral beliefs, and not merely in what *they* sustain. In this, again, Durkheim differs importantly from Comte who was basically concerned about the *consequences* of moral beliefs for social consensus and who had contributed little to an empirical understanding of the social forces fostering their development.

The problem was far from definitively resolved in Durkheim's work. Nonetheless, there is one theme which recurs in his studies. It is, above all, that moral norms grow up around sustained patterns of social interaction. It is clear, even in *The Division of Labour,* that he was beginning to focus on patterns of social interaction, as providing the focus around which moral beliefs emerge and develop.

The trouble was that Durkheim never clearly worked out an explicit analytic distinction between patterns of social interaction, or social structures, and patterns of moral beliefs or sentiments, the 'collective conscience'. This confusion is especially discernible in his *Suicide,* and particularly in his discussion of types of suicide. For example, the 'anomie suicide' is characterised as being both normless and socially detached, that is, he is described in terms of both his moral beliefs (or absence of them) and his social relations. The 'egoistic suicide is held to be burdened by norms calling upon him to take individual responsibility for his own decisions and, also, by being socially isolated from others. Despite this theoretical failure to clearly distinguish between patterns of moral belief and social interaction, Durkheim does break through to a clear solution in his *practical* proposals.

In the final chapter of *Suicide,* for example, he says that the problem of suicide 'bears witness. . .to an alarming poverty of morality'. We cannot simply 'will' the problem out of existence in a utopian way. A people's morality 'depends on the grouping and organisation of social elements', on the social arrangements which exist. Ways of thinking and acting cannot be changed without changing the collective existence itself and this cannot be done without modifying its anatomical constitution. By calling the evil of which the abnormal increase in suicide is symptomatic a moral evil, we are far from thinking to reduce it to some superficial ill which may be conjured away by soft words. On the contrary, the change in moral temperament thus betrayed bears witness to a profound change in out social structure. To cure one, therefore, the other must be reformed.

Since the older forms of social organisation, the family, the guild, the church, have been weakned or eliminated, new forms of social organisation must be erected in their place to stem the tide of anomie. What Durkheim seems to have been assuming is that patterns of social interaction form the basis upon which moral beliefs spontaneously develop. It is precisely for this reason that he advances as his remedy for moral anarchy in industry the establishment of new modes of social interaction, the occupational corporation. If science cannot yet invent or discover a new morality, then we must use what we know about the spontaneous development of moral beliefs to planfully foster their natural emergence.

Convergences with Marx

In many ways this is significant convergence with Marx, at least on the level of the working assumptions which they used in their roles as applied social scientists. For Durkeim was here saying something quite consistent with the Marxian formula that 'social being determines social consciousness'. What Durkheim did, however, was to generalise the Marxian formula. Instead of focusing mainly, as Marx usually did, on the manner in which class or economic relations shape patterns of belief, Durkheim holds that social (not merely economic) relations influence the development of beliefs.

Durkheim's analysis of religion and religious beliefs also has important convergences with Marx's, although it is much more acute and sophisticated than the latter's, particularly in its analysis of symbolism. For example Durkheim notes that in certain primitive societies the totem is the symbol of the god or godhead; but it is also a symbol or flag of the particular clan which worships it. The godhead and the clan are thus symbolically equal to each other. Consequently, concludes Durkheim, religious ideas emerge out of society.

In contrast with Marx, Durkheim does not deal solely with the relation between religion and class or work relations in a society. When Durkheim holds society to be the basis from which religion emerges, he conceives of society as containing a richer variety of relevant elements: power relations and economic conditions are included to be sure, but so, too, are kin and clan groupings as well as ecological factors. Here, too, he can be regarded as having relativised Marx's approach to the development of moral beliefs. Durkheim, then, was beginning to bridge the gap between Marxism the Comteianism.

What Durkheim began to see was that moral beliefs has to be treated in systematically scientific manner, that their emergence and development as well as their contribution to society needed empirical study. He began to see that the problem of values could not be handled in the manner of radical positivism, that is, by postulating that science could, or would ultimately, formulate and validate moral beliefs. Nor could values be coped with in a theological way, by regarding them as divinely given and thus without a developmental history. Both of these positions had placed values beyond scientific study.

But once existent moral beliefs are no longer taken as given, and once they come to be viewed as problems for empirical investigation, then they must inevitably be seen as inter-connected with many other elements of social life. Not only are many things contingent upon them, but they are reciprocally contingent upon many other things. Values then come to be regarded as one constituent of society, an important one to be sure, but still only one. Values and moral beliefs are no longer viewed as the sole or key constituent of society.

As Durkheim puts it, in the *Division of Labour,* society is the necessary condition of the moral world. This is almost a complete reversal of the Comteian position that moral consensus is *the* necessary condition of social order. Moreover, Durkheim adds, 'society cannot exist if its parts are not solidary, but solidarity is only *one* of the conditions of its existence. There are many others which are no less necessary and *which are not moral.*' (Our emphases).

The systematic exploitation of these early insights could have only been fatal to the Comteian position. For Comte had assumed that social solidarity was the prime condition for social survival, and he had further assumed that moral consensus was the basis of social solidarity. Durkheim's critique of Comte's stress on moral norms is inhibited, in part, by his simultaneous polemic against the socialists and individualist utilitarians for their neglect of moral norms. But though the critique of Comte is inhibited, it is, nonetheless, present and important to understand for a proper perspective on Durkheim.

To understand Durkheim's critical orientation to Comte, what needs to be remembered is that, unlike Comte, Durkheim was exposed to the full force of Marxism and to the growing challenge of European socialism. By 1870, the first French labour party had been formed. There was increasing class and industrial conflict in France, culminating in the great Décazeville strike of 1886, the year that Durkheim was drafting *The Division of Labour.* (One year later Durkheim gave the first French university course in sociology.) Durkheim's concern with 'solidarity' is probably related in part to the growing cleavages in French society which are reflected in the growth of socialism.

As a matter of fact, Durkheim began his sociological studies by focusing on the question of the relationship between individualism and *socialism.* These studies were interrupted and it was not until 1895, a decade later, that he returns to the study of socialism. Marcel Mauss, one of the intimate group of collaborators that Durkheim gathered around himself, relates in the introduction to this volume that some of Durkheim's students had been converted to socialism. There also seems to have been some mutual esteem between Durkheim and some of leading socialists of the time, particularly Guesde and Jaures. Mauss further indicates that, although Durkheim always remained uncommitted to socialism, 'he "sympathised" (as it is now called) with the socialists, with Jaures, with socialism'. The picture that emerges of Durkheim, supported in part by Mauss' introduction, is that Durkheim was under pressure to adjust Comteianism to Marxism. That there was somewhere a bridge between these two traditions was suggested by their possession of a common ancestor, Saint-Simon. Durkheim's sympathetic revisitation of Saint-Simon, the man most detested by Comte, may be understandable as an incompleted effort to find a passage and to mend the rift between two of the major theoretical systems of his time, Marxism and Comteianism.

This perspective on Durkheim's work finds further confirmation in his little known lectures on *Professional Ethics and Civic Morals.* In these, many of which consist of an examination of the evolution of certain Western values, Durkheim stresses the following points of relevance to our own analysis:

1. He holds that it is the existence of social classes, characterised by significant economic inequalities, that makes it in principle impossible for 'just' contracts to be negotiated. It is this system of stratification which, he argues here, offends the moral expectations of people in contemporary cultures, because it constrains to an unequal exchange of goods and services. The exploitation thus rendered possible by notable power disparities among the contracting parities conduces to a sense of injustice, which has socially unstabilising consequences. Thus, almost surprisingly, both Durkheim and Marx converge on a concept of 'exploitation' as a contributant to current social instabilities.
2. These power disparities derive largely, says Durkheim, from retention of the institution of inheritance.

Inheritance *ab intestato,* Durkheim firmly insists, 'is today an archaic survival and without justification'; it is in conflict with modern contractual ethics and practices. Testamentary dispositions, in his view, are also likely to be outmoded. Durkheim anticipates their ultimate elimination in modern society and looks forward to a time when property will no longer be transmitted through the family.

3. But if inheritance is eliminated, asks Durkheim, what institution would become the repository of private wealth, upon the death of its original owner? In his answer, we see a totally different and neglected aspect of Durkheim's project for the corporative reorganisation of modern society. The corporative organisation of people in the same industry or profession was not seen by Durkheim as having only a morality-building function. The occupational corporation was also expected to have important *economic* functions, inheriting and managing private property following the demise of its original owners. The occupational corporations were Durkheim's 'moral equivalent' for the Marxian nationalisation of industry by the state, and were expected to 'satisfy all the conditions for becoming . . . in the economic sphere, the heirs of the family'.

That Durkheim never succeeded in integrating the Marxian and Comteian traditions is evident; but he approached the foothills to an intellectual confrontation which challenges theorists to this very day.

4

Sociology and Marxism

Shaw's analysis falters here, I would suggest, for two reasons: first, because it *over*-ideologieses academic sociology and, secondly, because it *under*-ideologies Marxism. Let me clarify. Shaw totally rejects the possibility that academic sociology has any enduring rational and liberative kernel that deserves rescue. He adopts the manifestly unconvincing position that sociology's decades of labour have been in vain, totally. He argues that academic sociology is completely reactionary, indeed, hopelessly so, and that there is nothing at all in its more than fifty years of research and theory-making that retains any serious value for the human race. In my view, this judgement is in error on both logical and empirical grounds.

Shaw's standpoint on the hopelessness of sociology is strangely in contradiction with the Hegelianising, Lukàcsian Marxism, from whose standpoint he more generally views matters. As he makes quite clear, at the very start of his review, Shaw adopts an Hegelian view of ideology critique; from this standpoint, of course, ideologists are not merely apologists, as he tells us, and ideologies have some rational dimension. From the standpoint of an Hegelian 'ideology-critique' ideologies are not totally false and, therefore, not simply to be unmasked. Rather, their national dimension is to be separated out from their false consciousness and is to be transmitted into and sublated by the next, higher theoretical synthesis. Yet, after acknowledging essentially this conception of 'ideology-critique' in the beginning of his review, Shaw then proceeds to argue exactly the opposite way, so far as sociology is concerned, in the central part of his review. That is, he holds it to be wrong (illegitimate, in his words) to compare present-day sociology with Hegelianism (before Marx 'stood it on its feet'), maintaining that Hegelianism once had a revolutionary kernel that sociology never possessed. From the standpoint of an Hegelian ideology critique, however, it is not incumbent on sociology to have a 'revolutionary' component, it is rather incumbent on Shaw to clarify sociology's rational kernel (which need not be revolutionary to be rational). It would seem rather remarkable, from this standpoint, that every other major ideological standpoint should have some rational kernel that deserves rescuing, but not sociology. Perhaps, therefore, the failure is not in sociology but in Shaw. For his flat rejection of this as a possibility is, at the very least, a contradiction of his own premises.

Quite apart from the logic, Shaw's judgement on this matter - that is, the totally reactionary character of sociology - is also unsatisfactory on empirical and historical grounds. For even classical sociological positivism, at its crassest, was not a totally reactionary standpoint. In its opposition to the proliferation of metaphysical invisibles, positivism placed itself in abrasive opposition to conventional established religions and, in this, even positivism had its own rational kernel. We might also remember that, at least in their beginnings, positivists were commonly suspect, frequently despised, and occasionally prosecuted and jailed. The early-nineteenth-century positivists were, after all, the preachers of a humanitarian socialism - they were Saint-Simonians! And as such they were one of the main sources of Marx's own socialism. Here one would detail the roles of Ludwig Gall, the Baron von Westphalen, and possibly Eduard Gans. No Marxist can conceivably regard (at least) classical positivism as unambivalently reactionary and totally devoid of rational substance.

But the matter does not end with early positivism. There is a liberative tendency in positivism, even today, manifested by its attraction for many radicals and even Marxists. For example, it is evident that radicals such as Maurice Zeitlin or Richard Flacks have a manifest attraction toward positivism, Zeitlin having gone off to study the Cuban revolution, questionnaires in hand, and Flacks studying the student revolt with essentially the same methodological assumptions. French radicals, too, have long been attracted to positivism; one may regard Louis Althusser as simply the most current in a long line of this sort. Bear in mind, though it is hard to credit, that Althusser actually regards Auguste Comte as 'the only mind worthy of interest' produced by French philosophy 'in the 130 years following the Revolution of 1789. . .' If even a positivistic sociology had some rational, conceivably revolutionary but, in any event, emancipatory, dimension, it would seem that matters were even more hopeful for other, more reflective, sociologies.

In dealing with Talcott Parsons, of course, we are by no means faced with a positivist. Far from it. The 'young' Parsons rejects positivism, tends to prefer Weber rather than Durkheim as his model; and stresses the importance of a 'voluntaristic' sociology in which human striving, energy and values can make a difference. The young Parsons' theoretical position thus actually had much in common with the theoretical standpoint from which Georg Lukàcs mounted his critique of the Second International's mechanical evolutionism. Part of the reason for this convergence, of course, is that both Parsons and Lukàcs were alike influenced by the great classical German sociologists. It deserves to be stressed that, at precisely the time that the German social democrats were developing a 'scientific' and wooden Marxist determinism, German academic sociologists of that period, perhaps especially Max Weber, were developing a critique of *that* Marxism.

It is often said, and I have been one who has stressed it, that much of academic sociology's character was shaped by its polemic against Marxism. But it is rarely asked, Against *which* version of Marxism were these sociologists polemicising? I would suggest that much of their polemic was against the Engels-Kautsky-Plekhanov version of Marxism. That is precisely what brings them into some convergence with Hegelian Marxism's critique of Second International Marxism. Once again this suggests that sociology possesses some *liberative* dimension, rather than being hopelessly reactionary, as Shaw holds. It is because of this that Lukàcs was able to learn much, methodologically and substantively, from Max Weber, as seems clear from the former's analysis of class consciousness and of reification. Shaw, however, explores nothing of this in his broadside references to Max Weber. The fact, of course, is that Lukàcs was a pupil of Georg Simmel, an associate and student of Weber, to say nothing of his association with Karl Mannheim. Lukàcs' own development makes it evident that both academic sociology and Marxism had considerable potentiality for a mutually fruitful interaction.

The liberative potential of an academic sociology, its rational kernel, is perfectly plain in the importance that it has long given to a critique of bureaucracy. At a time when Kautsky was congratulating Social Democrats that they had avoided the danger of bureaucracy, Weber's far more profound critique warned that the era of bureaucracy was just coming into its own, and that 'socialism' - the kind of socialism, of course, that he saw around him in Germany - did not mean the dictatorship of the proletariat, but the dictatorship of the official. Certainly, the subsequent development of Stalinism would seem fully to justify Weber's critique. And if this is so, then how can sociology be regarded as an intellectually bankrupt and totally reactionary discipline?

One might say a great deal in criticism of academic sociology's failure to foresee the rise of Black militancy in the United States during the late sixties. But if one does, then one should also simultaneously ask: *Which* Marxists saw this any more deeply and clearly than the sociologists? All this aside, however, the fact remains that it was liberal sociologists whose research helped to sharpen the sense of the 'American Dilemma'; who continued to expose the life conditions of Blacks in some concrete detail; who continued to criticise 'prejudice' and 'segregation' in countless undergraduate courses during the 'passive' fifties, and who may well have contributed in a modest way to the eruption of the activistic sixties. Moreover, as is well known, these social scientists - 'liberals' to be sure - played some small but useful role in helping to bring about the United States Supreme Court's decisive desegregation decision of 1954.

Liberal reformism, of course; but it was also constructively emancipatory.

Again, not a little of what we know about the student rebellion, and about youth more generally, derives more from academic sociology, and even from Parsonian sociology which long since spotted the emerging importance of 'youth culture'; rather than from Marxism, which has generally had little of systematic value to say about the social role of youth. Much the same may be said about our knowledge of the emerging 'drug culture', which is of growing importance for anyone wishing to understand modern culture. For these and other reasons that might be cited, it seems that academic sociology retains a substantial liberative potential. Shaw would be better advised to maintain a consistently Lukàcsian position which sought to extricate sociology's rational kernel, rather than to condemn it wholesale.

The rational and liberative potential of sociology stems in part from its most fundamental *intellectual* commitments as a would-be social science, from the nature of its relationship to society and to the state, and, above all, from the contradictions involved in sociology's existence on these several levels. One of the central contradictions of academic sociology, as I discussed it in *The Coming Crisis,* derives from its role as market researcher for the Welfare – Warfare State. This induces two contradictory experiences: on one side, it limits the sociologist to the reformist solutions of the 'welfare state'; on the other, it also exposes the sociologist to the failures of this state and of the society with whose problems it seeks to cope. Their very work, then, makes sociologists intimately familiar with the human suffering engendered by such failures. While sociologists may be paid to help clean up the contemporary mess, they are often revolted by what their work necessitates them to see.

Secondly, the sociologist's conception of himself as a 'value-free' professional is, I have argued, a false consciousness. But it is a false consciousness which is real in its consequences. On the one hand, such a value-free self-conception allows one to take money from any source and to ignore societal values that are bolstered by one's professional work. On the other hand, however, the same value-free doctrine sometimes *inhibits* a reflexive loyalty for conventional values and, indeed, sometimes conduces to a certain anomie among sociologists. In short, if the value-free doctrine means that some sociologists are mercenaries and accomplices, they are, nonetheless, sometimes quite cynical about or detached from the very cultural values that are in effect supported by their work. Indeed, their entire professional code, especially that of objectivity, serves as a 'higher value' that may justify withholding the very reflexive loyalty that men in power commonly want, while at the same time providing a kind of protective covering for sociologists' own critical and often resentful impulses.

Again, the central concepts of sociology - 'society', the 'group', or 'culture' - point in two directions: on the one side, they point toward the importance of the group or of culture in shaping and hence in understanding the beliefs and actions of men, and this often underwrites a plea for submission to the conventional; on the other side, the emphasis on society served at one point to liberate men from earlier notions that they faced unchangeable destiny as the puppets of biological or supernatural forces. Now, if sociology held men to be the products of a reified 'society' or 'culture', then at least *these* could be changed, a better world *was* possible, and men need not resign themselves to what was.

In conceiving itself as an *empirical* science devoid of metaphysical presuppositions, in this most dubious expression of sociology's false consciousness, there is nonetheless an important way in which sociology contributed to human emancipation and continues to have a liberative potential. For now, with the emphasis on the empirical, the self-understanding of all societies (including their élites) was in principle made problematic; it could now be subject to systematic questioning, to examination, and to a demand for justification. There were now no social groups - neither priests, nor bourgeoisies, nor for that matter revolutionaries - whose pronouncements about themselves or their words needed to be regarded as sacrosanct, simply by reason of their self-confident affirmation or the authoritative position of those making the affirmation. Opposing the most ancient traditionalism or the newest dogmatics, sociology's empiricism insisted that a man's social position or his political allegiance did not suffice to establish the truth of his declarations. Sociology's sheer empiricism, then, necessarily creates tension for all authoritative definitions of social reality, for the claims of the conventional, the sacred, the socially privileged. These claims must now be confirmed 'empirically', confirmed, in short, by 'science', before they could be regarded as true, or, if demonstrated to be beyond such confirmation, they must run the risk – as some later positivists would hold – of being defined as totally devoid of meaning.

A positivistic sociology's contradictions are complex. On the one side, as emphasised above, it stands ready in principle to compare the claims of society (and the self-understanding of its élites) with its own studies of 'what is'. To that extent it discomfits the present: any 'present', whether the 'bourgeois' present that now exists or the 'socialist' present that might exist at some future time. At the same time, however, faced with a choice between the present and some conceivable future, positivism always in effect affirms the reality and rationality of 'what is', of the *status quo;* its impulse is to sidestep issues and problems by avoiding conflicts over values, goals, or ends, and it believes that it can somehow do this by confining itself to a presumably neutral *description* of the social world.

The built-in ambivalence of a positivistic sociology, then, is also commonly resolved in favour of the *status quo* (whatever *status quo,* socialist, or capitalist in which it finds itself) and all the more so by reason of the practical and material support that it derives from that *status quo.* The problem of transcending this ambivalence without surrendering its liberative potential boils down to the problem of how, on the one hand, sociology can be made to surrender its objectivistic false consciousness as value-free and openly to adopt a commitment to the values of emancipation and human fulfilment - without, at the same time, becoming another appendage instrumental to the practical politics of socialism.

That sociological positivism possessed a liberative potential is easy enough to see if one contrasts it with the alternative epistemologies that were and, in some cases, remain its historical alternatives. Essentially, these came down to the claimed right of legitimate authority, in the secular and the 'spiritual' sectors of society, to define the nature of social reality, and to do so with central concern for consistency with the prior commitments of faith. Social reality, in short, was that which was consistent with the faith of the Church and the claims of nobility, taken as unexaminable givens. To this positivism, in effect, replied that if the question is, What is the case?, the answer is not derivable *solely* from determining, logically or morally, what *should* be the case, nor from affirming beliefs required to maintain oneself in good standing as a member of the community. That this emancipatory, potential of positivism is not simply a matter of an archaic past but continues into the contemporary present is evident, as Jürgen Habermas reminds us, if we compare the objectivism of positivism with the party science of Stalinism or the racial doctrines of Nazism and their charismatic epistemologies that affirm the rightness of a single man's thought as a social standard.

On the deepest level, the rational core of academic sociology (in the tradition from Comte to Parsons) is in its concern with the self-maintenance of social systems. Much of this sociological tradition embodied a tacit generalisation of a 'free market' economy; sociology sought a set of social relationships that were as homeostatically self-maintaining as were market relations in the economy, at least in that traditions' self-understanding. In short, the sociological focus on the 'equilibrium' problem transmitted a latent ideological commitment to a free market. But if ideological compulsiveness led to a one-sided over-emphasis on consensus and equilibrium, it is precisely in this focus that sociological concern had its most abiding rationality. For after a very long experience of the dangers of bureaucratisation to the socialist movement and, especially, of a vast bureaucratised state apparatus that culminated in the overgrown and paranoid Stalinist state, socialists quite naturally concern themselves with the problem of how to avoid being crushed by a towering state apparatus.

This reduces itself to the question of how a socialist society may be maintained without or with only minimal - development of the state apparatus and how it can avoid a totalitarian state superintendence of life. There is, as many socialists already know, only one answer to this vital problem: there must be a 'self-governance' by those involved in the economy and society. The relations between people in a socialist society must be spontaneously self-maintaining, which also means they must be mutually satisfactory. This is precisely what Parsons' system theory is all about. When he formulates the equilibrium problem, he asks, How can a social system be self-governing, self-adjusting, self-correcting, self-maintaining? *The Coming Crisis* argues that there is no way in which a capitalist system can any longer be that. At the same time, however, this failure of the capitalist system does not at all guarantee that a socialist solution of 'Workers' Councils' will itself necessarily solve the problem of self-maintenance. Without a thorough-going theoretical analysis of the problem of spontaneously self-maintaining social systems, 'workers' control' could remain an inoperable ideology that serves only as a new window dressing for a familiar élitism.

Seen in the context of Western capitalism, Parsonian equilibrium analysis is conservative, when not merely irrelevant; but in the context of certain Eastern European countries which are massively controlled from a separate political centre, this same equilibrium analysis has liberative potentialities. It provides certain theoretical clues as to how a socialist society may be organised with a minimum of bureaucracy and of state control. In effect, then, the rational core of sociology is that it suggests theoretical guidelines for the creation and maintenance of a free community of men under socialism.

Before leaving this point, however, let me stress that it has *not* been my aim here to aruge that academic sociology as we know it is progressive or emancipatory, let alone revolutionary. In *The Coming Crisis* and elsewhere I repeatedly stressed that the ideological character of academic sociology is now *predominantly* conservative; but I have always added that I also believe that there is, underneath, an emancipatory potential that needs to be liberated from the domination of sociology's conservatism. My comments here have aimed to defend the latter judgement about this liberative potential; they are not to be understood, of course, as changing my overall judgement about the dominance of the conservative aspect of sociology.

There is a second basic reason why I believe Shaw's effort to protect 'Marxism' from subversion by radical sociology is misguided. This has to do with the contemporary condition of Marxism itself. If Shaw's treatment of academic sociology is mistaken because he sees it as all false consciousness and all ideology, then his view of Marxism is mistaken for the opposite reason, namely, that he sees it as in no way suffering from *any* false consciousness or ideologisation. Which is to say that Shaw seems inconsistent in two ways: first, when he refuses to consider that academic sociology might have some rational kernel and fails to clarify what this might be; and, secondly, when he fails totally to consider that *Marxism itself* might also have its own false consciousness and when he fails to explore what this might be. Having thus arranged that academic sociology shall be deemed totally mired in false consciousness and ideology, while Marxism presumably floats screnely above any contaminating contact with them, Shaw has contrived a melodrama of an unblemished good versus an unredeemable evil that would warm the heart of any fundamentalist preacher. In doing so, he *exhibits* the false consciousness of his own Marxism, even if he does not admit its existence or talk about it analytically.

This corporealisation of the false consciousness of Shaw's Marxism may indicate that the end is in sight not only for conventional academic sociologies but also for Marxism. Indeed, it would be surprising were that not the case. Both sociology and Marxism are essentially nineteenth-century theories which, however much engaged in mutual polemic, were also always joined together at the back like Siamese twins. The demise of one presages the demise of the other. They have a common destiny no *despite* the fact that they have developed in dialectical opposition but precisely *because* of it.

The most fundamental difficulty of Shaw's position, then, is that it premises a Marxism-in-being that can presumably be counterpoised to the non-being of academic sociology. This conception of the matter is essentially a positivistic one, implying as it does that Marxism now exists as a 'thing' to which we may flee, as a kind of *place* to go, as a *space* already carved cut and liberated and waiting for us as a haven. Those conceiving the situation in this reified manner manifest that they are simply going to substitute the crisis of Marxism for the crisis of academic sociology. If Marxism is already a constituted alternative to a radical sociology, *which* or *whose* Marxism is this to be? Do we rally around the Marxism of Lenin? Trotsky? Lukàcs? Korsch? Della Volpe? Althusser? Sartre? Do we rally around the Marxism of Engels or of Marx and, if Marx, the young or the older Marx? Certainly we cannot rally around them all, for they are often mutually contradictory and, are indeed in some cases, self-repudiated. So what, then, is the Marxism counter posed to the radical sociology that is to be repudiated?

5
The Red Guard

'Judging from this evening you seem to be in good condition,' I said. Mao Tse-tung smiled wryly and replied that there was perhaps some doubt about that. He said again that he was getting ready to see God very soon.

Interview with Mao Tse-tung, by Edgar Snow, *New Republic,* 27th February, 1965.

In isolating ourselves from China, we have placed the West in a situation where every turn in the Chinese Revolutions seems inexplicably mysterious and in which we are finally driven to explain mystery as due to madness. If the Russian Revolution seemed to be a 'mystery wrapped in an enigma', the Chinese Revolution seems increasingly – to certain Westerners – a mystery that enwraps and conceals a core of madness. When political fears are compounded by a confrontation with an alien culture the differences that become visible seem to be an expression of insanity. The explanation of political events as due to madness is a confession of intellectual impotence; it is another way of saying that we are incapable of offering rational explanations for events.

Nothing seems more insane, at first blush, than the recent reports of street skirmishing of the Red Guards with workers and detachments of the Red Army sent to curb them, attacks of Red Guards upon the home of Madame Sun Yat-sen, their damage to certain public properties, and above all their clashes with select local Communist Party cadres and headquarters.

Our job here is to seek and propose a sociological framework in which even the seeming madness of the Red Guard episode may be made intelligible.

First, we ought to be clear about what it is that needs explaining. What is it that seeks so mysterious to us in the West about the behaviour of the Red Guards?

Surely we would not find it strange if it were some kind of *coup d' état* that had been perpetrated by a section of the army against the Communist Party or against the régime. We have seen that before in Latin America and in Indonesia. But despite its military designation, the Red Guard is not a wing of the army but basically is comprised of militant students, rural and urban youth - in some reports numbering as many as six million - who have remained more loyal to the ideals of the Revolution than to the organisational forms of the conventional Communist Party establishment. The Red Guard has put itself forward not as an opponent of Mao Tse-tung but, to the contrary, as his most vocal protector and truest follower. The avowed aim of the Red Guard is to protect Mao and his teachings and, indeed, to protect the entire Central Committee of the Communist Party. The Red Guards are a generation-cohort whose revolutionary fervour has not been blunted by *Realpolitik*.

What is strange, then, is that successful and established revolutionaries should incite and accept protection from student militants even though the party hierarchy has created an enormous and far-ranging network of powerful institutions: the Communist Party, the Red Army, a newly emerging bureaucracy in almost all sectors of life, and upon whom – one might think – they might confidently rely for the perpetuation of the revolution and its régime.

The central question, then, is why has Mao turned to the students and allowed them – and quite probably, incited them – to speak on his behalf, on behalf of the Central Committee of the Chinese Communist Party? And why has he done so in this particular period in the history of the Chinese Revolution?

The question of its timing does not seem too difficult. Here, three considerations seem foremost. First, the succession problem grows increasingly critical with each passing year, and it must be seen as such by old leaders of the Chinese Communist Party, who are already venerable even by Chinese standards. Unlike Western leaders such as Joseph Stalin and Charles de

Gaulle whose public statements never intimated their mortality, Mao has for some time been publicly pondering his impending death. As his interviews with Edgar Snow and others indicate, he expects to die shortly. Whatever the publicity value of his recent swimming of the Yangtze river, it is clear that his private ratiocinations are sombre; he is thoroughly aware of his own mortality and of its political implications.

Second, this intensifying succession crisis has developed in an international context in which the old leaders of the Chinese Communist Party have become increasingly aware of the possibility that their own revolution, like any other, might be corrupted if not overthrown. The Chinese struggle against the Soviet Union (and in particular what they conceive to be its 'revisionism') has heightened their anxiety about the safety and future of the Chinese Revolution to which they have devoted their youth and their lives.

Third, the mobilisation of the Red Guard can be considered as part of a general intensification of fervour as the international crisis deepens from the Chinese perspective. The Chinese have suffered diplomatic as well as political losses in such far-flung places as Cuba, where the Chinese régime was denunced by Castro; in Indonesia, where Sukarno has been replaced by Suharto as the actual leader of the régime and where the Chinese no less than the Communist Party have suffered intensive persecutions; in Africa, where Boumédienne's régime in Algeria replaced Ben Bellas' thus causing the collapse of a major 'third world' conference; and also, in Ghana, where Nkrumah was displaced as leader precisely when he was on a state visit to China. All of these genuine setbacks have occasioned intensification of the internal conflicts. In some part the phenomenon of the Red Gujards is an answer to these recent defeats: they announce that the Revolution still lives. The Red Guards provide the form, if not always the substance, of the permanent revolution.

In this connection, it should be kept in mind that within the framework of Marxism there has always been a strong wing deeply troubled by national revolutions at the expense of the continuation of the revolution elsewhere. Whatever the basic differences between Maoism and Trotskyism on this point, there seems a common fear that stability can only bring about the conservating of the revolution. The Red Guards in such a context can symbolise the viability of the revolution, if not provide a guarantee against its natural aging and decadence.

But where do Mao and his associates see the danger coming from? Here, it would be misleading if we sought to understand the Chinese Revolution on the model of the Russian. There is a continual temptation to misread Chinese history by seeing it as repeating the problems and the stages of the Russian Revolution. But this is misleading because the Chinese Revolution took place after, and developed in the context of, a prior and successful Soviet Revolution; the two can no more be expected to be the same than the second child in a family can be expected to be like the first.

One difference between the two revolutions is this: unlike the Chinese, the leaders of the Russian Revolution conceived of the danger to their revolution as coming, primarily and most powerfully, from the world outside. And with good reason. Immediately following upon the October Revolution the Bolshevisks found themselves beset by the armies of more than a dozen nations. The political trails of the old Bolsheviks and of others commonly sought to link their 'betrayal' to the direct and deliberate intervention and scheming of foreign powers. Thus, even where the enemy was seen as being within, he was essentially defined as an 'agent of a foreign power' The Stalinist conception of the danger and of the enemy was thus very largely centered on the outside world.

But this does not seem to be the case for the Chinese Revolution. Certainly, the Chinese Communists believe that Chaing Kai-shek would like to invade their mainland and that, to do so successfully, he must and might receive the support of the United States. They were similarly aware of the possibilities of being militarily embroiled with the United States in any extension of the war in Vietnam. Yet these 'objective' dangers from without do not seem to be the dangers that weight most heavily upon the minds of the aging Chinese Communist Party leaders, but, rather, the dangers that abide within their own culture.

The most essential point being made is not so much with respect to the location of the perceived dangers to the Revolution but, rather, with respect to the location of the perceived resources of and possible help to the Revolution. The Russian Bolsheviks, prior to the October Revolution, never believed in their own ability to bring the Russian Revolution to a successful culmination without international support. They expected that their seizure of power in Russia would be the signal for a European-wide, and especially a German, revolution from which they could receive aid for the own industrialisation. They did not at first imagine they could overcome what they regarded as 'Russian backwardness' without outside assistance from industrially advanced nations. When the German and Hungarian revolutions failed, after the Bolshevik seizure of power in Russia, the Russian revolutionaries were despairing and disoriented.

The Russian Revolution was, from its earliest inception, a special sort of social movement: a movement for cultural revitalisation which saw the solution to its problems as deriving from the *importation* of Western technologies. Its attention was from the first fastened upon its relation to and its dependence upon the West. After the failure of the revolution in the West, the Soviet leaders remained sensitive to the manner in which their security and their prospects were contingent upon the new society's relationship to the outside world. Even when their anxiety and pessimism were overcome and bound by the slogan of 'Socialism in One Country', the Soviet leaders never doubted that developments elsewhere – such Fascism and Nazism – could (and were intended to) impair their new society. Russian intellectuals had long measured themselves by Western European standards and models and they continued to do so even when thrown back upon their own resources during the Stalinist 'anti-cosmopolitan' period.

The Chinese revolutionists have, to the contrary, long despised their subjection to outside influences of Western imperialism and to what they took to be its *alien* culture. Their basic impulse was not to import Western cultural models, not to emulate and overtake the West. Their basic impulse was to liberate themselves from such outside influences. In short, China was a colonially dominated nation in a way that Russia had not been.

The Chinese did not expect help from their former foreign colonial overlords. During the process of their gathering revolutionary efforts, from 1927 onward, they also found that the needs of their own revolution were being subordinated to those of the Russians. They began to view the Soviet Union not as a paragon of international revolutionary solidarity but rather as a more sophisticated expression of the nationalist selfishness of Western nations. They began to see the Soviet Union not as an example of revolutionary vitality but as a sad case of revolutionary corruption and softness demonstrated by the collapse of fervour among its own younger generation, the bureaucratisation of Communist Party workers, and the rise of party careerism. These sentiments finally expressed themselves in the Chinese attack on Khrushchev's 'revisionism', which was only one side of the coin. The other side entailed a demand that the revolution hew to its original purpose. They began to believe that the authenticity of the revolution depended more upon their internal spiritual purity than external material aid.

This internal preoccupation is evident in Mao's recurrent comments about the growing laxity of the Chinese youth, and of the possibility that they would not have the stomach to perpetuate the Chinese Revolution once he and his cohorts were gone. Again, it is just this sensitivity to the internal dangers that face the Chinese Revolution, and the willingness of the Chinese leaders to talk about them publicly - as they did, for example, on their recent visits to Eastern Europe - that makes their political diagnoses of their own situation *seem* to be surprisingly realistic, and quite different in character from those typically enunciated by the Russian leaders.

But there is not only a question of how they define and conceive the *location* of these dangers to the Chinese Revolution. There is also the further and equally important problem of how they conceive of the *Character* of these dangers. To understand this properly, to see what the Chinese regard as the source of their present danger, it is also necessary to see what they regard as the source of their previous *success* and victory. Here the matter must be set in its historical context and viewed as part of the long-range evolution of Communist strategy, from Marx onward.

A central shift in political strategy has occurred in the Communist world since the time of Marx. It has been a shift from a view which at first emphasised the importance of objective economic conditions for a successful revolution, to a view that increasingly emphasised the importance of political initiative, party organisation, and ideological commitment. This shift was first fully visible in Lenin's objections of Plekhanov's doctrine of 'spontaneity', which saw the revolution as a natural outgrowth of a mature working class. To this Lenin counterposed the need for a revolutionary élite that could seize and maintain the political initiative. The Chinese operated in an economy that was even less like that in which Marx had expected a socialist revolution than did the Russian Bolsheviks, and they developed an increasing emphasis upon the importance of ideology and the 'spiritual factor' as the mainspring and ultimate guarantor of the revolution. The Chinese emphasis on dialectics, on the power of self-criticism, can be interpreted as a further move away from the original focus on economics which Marx held in common with the classical economists. If Lenin added to the Marxist corpus the concept of party organisation as fundamental to revolution-making, Mao added to Leninism the concept of personal will and military fortitude as the essence of nation-building. In Maoism, Marxism has thus turned full-circle toward an unembarrassed 'utopianism'. It is the wilful struggle - not the organisational machinery - that the ageing leadership trust. Thus, the Chinese leadership is even ready to risk the possibility of internal strife, not because it is oblivious to the possibilities of ramifying civil conflict, but rather because it is more concerned with the purifying value of conflict.

The older generation of Chinese Communists had, certainly from an orthodox Marxist viewpoint, achieved something of a miracle ever since their long march north to the Shensi province in 1927. By classical Marxist standard they could very well feel that they had achieved the impossible. For they had come to power in a country which was even more industrially backward and economically depressed than revolutionary Russia, and in which modern science, modern industry and modern technology scarcely existed.

Indeed, it was only when the Chinese communists abandoned orthodox Bolshevik tactics that victories were registered. In the early 1920s, they tried to capture large cities, such as Canton, where it was hoped the factory workers would rally to the revolutionary cause; but such strata were either too small or too intimidated to forge a revolutionary phalanx. But when the Communists were driven from the cities to the countryside, they changed not only their tactical emphasis from factory workers to peasants, but more significantly, their leadership – from the Moscow – trained cadres who had secret headquarters in Shanghai to indigenous Chinese elements (Chu Teh was a war lord, and Mao himself was of peasant origins) operating in the open. Thus, the victories of the Chinese Communists coincided with a turn from town to countryside, from Bolshevik to native party cadres, and from clandestine to military actions.

The 'miracle' of the Chinese Revolution was thus even greater than that of the Russian Revolution, not simply because of the industrial backwardness of Chiang's China in comparison to Czarist Russia, but because the Chinese Revolution succeeded in totally reorienting the temperament of the rural masses no less than the urban classes, whereas the Russian Revolution only reoriented a strata of the working classes. The Chinese Red Army smashed the Kuomin-tang in civil war. This experience also re-emphasised the role of 'will' in the making of the Chinese Revolution in contrast to the role of organisation.

In short, their political and military experience leads the old Chinese leaders to conceive of themselves as having succeeded, not because of 'objective factors', but rather because of 'subjective factors' – because of correct theory, because of a steadfast commitment to ideology, because of a readiness for personal sacrifice. It is precisely this that leads them to emphasise the importance of the teachings of MaoTse-tung. This emphasis on Mao's writings is not, as is sometimes suggested, to be understood simply as a part of the process of the deification of

Mao. It is rather their conception of the meaning of Chinese experience: namely, that it was theory, indeed Mao's theory, that had made the primary difference for them and not objective conditions. In the hands of Mao, Marxism more than ever became a doctrine to live by rather than a dogma to abide by, and it is at this level that their exhortation to read and study Mao seems most intelligible.

In addition there has been a long-standing, if concealed, chasm between the struggling Communist movement of China and the established Bolshevik organization of the Soviet Union. From the 1920s onward it was clear that Stalin was less concerned with fostering the Chinese revolution than with maintaining a legal correctness in his dealings with foreign nations that could provide a protective international framework for the Soviet Union. The Chinese were not merely disappointed with the withdrawal of Soviet aid once their own revolution succeeded, but were newly convinced of the parochial national character and bureaucratisation of the Soviet revolution. The conversion of Chinese Marxism into a mass movement, such as that exhibited by the Red Guards, is an attempt to compensate for the loss of material foreign aid by strengthening their internal spiritual resources. For this reason the Chinese have ordered many slogans concerning the power of ideas to be put forward as a last gasp against the frustrations and inhibitions occasioned by the inexorable technological advance of Bloshevik Russia, no less than capitalist United States. Indeed, it might be said that Chinese Marxism-Maoism is the ultimate romanticisation of Socialist doctrine; it is the elevation to a supreme level of the role of heart over that of head, of will over economic conditions, and people over weaponry.

The old Chinese leadership understand their past success as the product of their will and ideological commitment. At the same time, this is how they understand their failure, or at least the threat of possible failure that they see hanging over them with the passing of the older generation. Because their political experience has led the Chinese to assign so much significance to the importance of theoretical, idological, and spiritual factors, they have come to define their present danger – no less than their former victory – as deriving from a decline in ideological commitment and from a loss of theoretical clarity. Correspondingly, if the danger is ideological and spiritual, then they must also see the solution and remedy as being ideological and spiritual. And that seems to be why the current turbulence in China has come to centre upon the problem of the completion of what is conceived to be a 'cultural' revolution, and thus on the need to complete the transformation of the values and believes of the Chinese people.

The aging Chinese political élite is a charismatic cohort: it not only stands above the institutions which it has created, but it also does not fully trust them – and indeed more than mildly distrusts them. It distrusts them, in some part, because it recognises that some sectors and echelons in these new institutions, many composed of men immediately beneath them, have been trained in Moscow. They are thus not simply politically suspect on nationalistic grounds but also may be seen as ideologically contaminated by Russian revisionism. And in one way this is quite realistic. Some Russian intellectuals have not entirely despaired of reconciliation with the Chinese because when the old leaders die they will be replaced by young men who have been students of the Russians. But the aging Chinese leaders not only distrust these younger leaders; they also and more generally distrust all the institutions that they man, for they believe that the life of the revolution is in the *spirit* and not in its institutions.

What then are the Central Committee and the Chinese leader-ship attempting to do in unleashing the Red Guards? Funda-mentally, they are seeking a revival of spirit and the purification of revolutionary ideology. The older generation is seeking to bypass part of the Moscow-tainted middle generation, and provide a check upon it, by allying itself with an ideologically reinvigorated younger generation. They are seeking to foster revolutionary fervour among a generation that has never known revolution, and thereby to commit this generation to a posture of ideological purity, thus providing a stable framework that will ensure the continuity of the revolution, as they conceive it.

In unleashing the Red Guards the Chinese Central Committee has also unlocked certain doors to social change. There were, indeed, middle-class styles and Western importations in Chinese urban regions. There were five per cent of men who lived off their previous commercial and land holdings. There were, indeed, bureaucrats unable or unwilling to perform everyday services in a competent manner. It would be a mistake to think that the enemy of the Red Guards is entirely a fiction. The enemy within was real, so much so that the Chinese leaders were willing to risk a paralysis of industrialisation to combat it. It could well be that the Red Guards form the fighting wing of a twentieth century Chinese puritanism, for their demand for purification has been made in the name of simplification of life styles, improving of work styles, and ordering of cultural styles. The fervour, the passion of such a movement may easily spill over into violence of an unbridled variety, but of a kind not unknown in the West and frequently found among those who are most fervently concerned with the purification of the spirit. The risks of the present course of action on the part of the Chinese leadership are indeed great. Undoubtedly they believe the possible consequences of its failure will be greater still.

One possible consequence of promoting the Red Guards may be to break the legitimisation system of orthodox Communists. Instead of a system that operates through the organisational channels of the Communist Party system, the Red Guards symbolise a return to spontaneity and to the importance of ideological purity rather than party loyalty. The wheels for such an approach were already set in motion by the emphasis on 'national liberation' movements outside the orthodox Communist Party apparatus in many parts of the 'third world'. Khrushchev, in his critique of Maoism made just prior to his retirement, exhibited considerable fears lest such emphasis on liberation movements turn into 'anty-party' vehicles. It might well be that the Chinese leadership has taken the next logical step, and declared that the protection of the Chinese Revolution is no longer to be the exclusive duty of the 'vanguard party', but rather of the people as a whole. In short, neither charismatic nor bureaucratic routinisation now obtains. Rather, China is witnessing a restructuring of both – made in a holy alliance between the militant antiquarians who have nothing to lose but their waning leadership and the militant youths who have nothing to lose but their reason for living.

If bypassing the middle generation - the transitional generation – can spare China the agonies of Stalinist totalitarianism, then the results of the 'cultural revolution' may well come to be judged as positive – even in the West. However, if this new generation coalition should tear Chinese culture apart in the name of ideological purity, it might well be that instead of sparing China the worst disruptions of the Soviet experience, it will make that seem a model of orderly evolution.

6

Comments on History and Class Consciousness

Georg Lukács' *History and Class Consciousness* is a truly extraordinary work, and its English translation, after almost fifty years of neglect by English and American publishers, is a major event. Indeed, its sheer eventfulness is so fraught with implication that exploring this might overshadow the intellectual content of the book itself. Certainly this long overdue translation tells us something about the ineffectual state of the translation industry and in particular about the American segment of it; for if the book is now available to Americans, it is primarily thanks to the initiative of its original translator, the British publisher.

That it took almost half a century to make this exceptional book available to English readers is due partly to the character of the publishing industry, but rather more, I would add, to the book's own intellectual character as a Marxist heresy; upon its original publication in 1923, it was assaulted at once by Social Democrats and Bolsheviks alike and, indeed, was officially condemned by Zinoviev at the 1924 Congress of the Third International. Europe, in short, has long known this book and taken it very seriously indeed. After its condemnation by the Third International, it remained an underground sensation even, and perhaps especially, among Communist intellectuals and other Marxists. That it appears now, along with a growing convoy of commentaries, is a symptom of emerging developments in Anglo-American culture as well as of the continuing crisis of Marxist 'orthodoxy'

The significant commentaries that will most deeply express and shape the American understanding of Lukàcs are only now being readied by young American scholars such as Paul Breines, Andrew Feenberg, Andrew Arato and Paul Piccone. Most Americans who know of Georg Lukàcs think of him primarily as a literary critic or as a sociologist of literature. But the narrowing concentration of his efforts to these fields signifies his political defeat in the Marxist world and embodies, in some part, a strategy of survival. For these were in a way the expression of his less controversial talents, even if of his first love. The full quality of Lukàcs' brilliance is most powerfully manifested in this 'youthful' work (done when merely 38!), where he reveals himself as by far and away the most talented philosopher among twentieth-century Marxists, and as their most penetrating critic of contemporary culture. While Susan Sontag's critique of Lukàcs as an uninspired sociologist of literature has something to justify it, Lukàcs work as a critic of general culture is an altogether different matter. In this general critique he anticipates and profoundly develops the whole current discussion of 'adversary' culture, and its recent emendation in Daniel Bell's thesis of a contradiction between contemporary culture and social structure.

In a recent book, *Georg Lukàcs: The Man, His Work and His Ideas,* edited by C. H. R. Parkinson (Random House and Vintage), Istvàn Mészàros gives a brilliant discussion of Lukàcs' dialectics and other contributors summarise Lukàcs' intellectual and political career. This portrays him as a rich young Hungarian Jew who assimilated the great traditions of German philosophical idealism and of classical academic sociology, as a student of Georg Simmel and associate of Max Weber and Karl Mannheim. Lukàcs was Commissar for Public Education in the ill-scarred Hungarian-Soviet Republic of 1919 and subsequently fled to Vienna there to edit *Kommunismus* in 1920 - 22, with an ultra-Left group that resisted all efforts to inhibit revolutionary militancy, whether these came from the newly prudent Bolsheviks or from the long revisionist Social Democrats. As Lukàcs later remarked candidly, he was then an advocate of 'revolutionary Messianism'; indeed, his *History and Class*

Consciousness was the high-water mark of Marxist political voluntarism in the Europe of that period. It was, on the one side, the legitimate heir of the voluntaristic turn marked by Lenin's *What Is To Be Done?* and, on the other, it was the great theoretical anticipation of the voluntaristic upsurge in Marxism that was later to culminate in Mao and Fidel.

After his work was condemned by the Third International, Lukàcs proceeded, as he says, to complete his 'apprenticeship's in Marxism, in the course of which he supported Stalin on the question of 'socialism in one country': indeed, after 1924 Lukàcs was a Stalinist. In 1929, and in order to survive politically, he issued a self-criticism of his political line on the Hungarian Revolution. In 1933 and, strangely enough, for the first time, he issued a public repudiation of *History and Class Consciousness,* a recantation that he later indicated was primarily a matter of political prudence, although subsequently affirming that there were indeed many things in *History and Class Consciousness* that he no longer accepted, and which we must, I think, believe him to have meant.

After his 1929 defeat, Lukàcs says that he concluded that he was not very effective as a political figure, and so devoted himself increasingly to intellectual and literary work. Nonetheless, he was imprisoned briefly in 1941 and released after world protests. In 1944 he returned to Hungary after a long sojourn in Moscow, and in 1951 he once more came under political attack, once more recanted, and once more retired from political life, only to re-emerge as the aging phoenix of the Hungarian Revolution of 1956. After this was crushed, he was deported to Rumania but was later allowed to return to Hungary, where, in his last years, he was immensely fruitful and fortunate in his work with many talented and devoted students. He died on 4th June, 1971.

The crux of Lukàcs' Marxism is that it does not one-sidedly stress the distictiveness of the Marxian contribution but *also* emphasises its continuity with its mother traditions in German philosophy and, most particularly, Hegelianism. It is in part because of his emphasis on this continuity that Lukàcs, whose work has a most contemporary ring, repeatedly stressed the value of the works of the 'young' Marx. The decisive difference between Marxism and bourgeois thought was not the primacy of economics and of economic motives but, rather, the fact that Marxism takes the standpoint of the 'totality', refuses to study social objects in isolation, and refuses to submit to the existing division of intellectual labour and separation of the different disciplines. Thus, Lukàcs' Marxism does not acknowledge the validity of the autonomous sciences of economics, history or law.

In clarifying his notion of the social totality, Lukàcs spells out a conception of its *systemness* which, while superficially akin to Nikolai Bukharin's, is less deterministic and more dialectical. The social 'totality' is composed of an interaction of social elements that, unlike interacting billiard balls, do not remain the same; they change not only their positions but also their character. The social system must be seen as a historical product, as a thing made and fashioned by men as active 'subjects', as continually remade and daily enacted by the ongoing doings of men, and hence as capable of being undone or redone by their future actions.

The system, in short, depends upon men. The social system is not something given in history, but is a social object that is selectively interpreted and is actively conceptualised by men in the here and now; it is seen as the product of the interaction of 'subject' and 'object'. Lukàcs understood that men establish their social worlds by constituting them conceptually, as well as by their practical enactments. In Lukàcs' Hegelian Marxism, then, thought and existence are regarded as different sides of one and the same reality.

For Lukàcs, the liberation from capitalism means a liberation from the domination of the economy. It will be the elimination of a society in which economic life was not a *means* to social life, but had become its dominating *end.* It is this autonomy and domination by the economic that is one of the major sources of the corruption of contemporary culture. Lukàcs had no doubt that capitalist culture can and does, from the very first, mount a critique of capitalist society; thus capitalist culture is *limited* by the interests of capitalist society, but also gives voice to the contradictions of capitalism. In short, while a cultural expression can be an authentic outcome of capitalist society it may still be in opposition to its interests.

At this point, let me stress that my focus here is on the young Lukàcs who wrote *History and Class Consciousness* from the stand point of a Marxism that was heavily Hegelian. Lukàcs himself subsequently repudiated many of the 'excesses' of his early Hegelianism, and this auto-criticism is incorporated in the introduction to the volume. But the book has been published, and the book will be read not for this repudiation, but for what it repudiates. I am thus in the strange position of having to centre my critique on a text that Lukàcs himself criticised. But it is right, I believe, that *History and Class Consciousness* should be read primarily for its text and not its repudiating introduction. For it is this text that epitomises one historical potentiality of Marxism. And it is this text which has had a liberating historical role, precisely because it was both politically militant, and, at the same time, philosophically creative, never echoing the increasingly empty Bolshevik rhetoric.

For Lukàcs, a socialist economy will be one which, unlike the capitalist, will no longer be characterised by the blind autonomy of its own economic laws but will, rather, be subject to control by human reason operating through the planning process and the State administration. Here we have a paradoxical 'opening on the Right' to the development of bureaucratisation, even though Lukàcs own view of the revolutionary process was often critical of such tendencies. One cannot but wonder: How is it that a romantic, revolutionary messianist such as the young Lukàcs could hold such a pre-bureaucratic vision of socialism? In some part, this may have been because, for the young Lukàcs, the focus was on the revolution and not on socialism as such; his concern was to make the revolutionary 'leap', rather than with the nature of the ground onto which the leap would be made.

The bureaucratic vulnerability of Lukàcs' tradition of socialism also links up with the importance attributed to the role of consciousness in revolution-making and, in particular, with the cognitive, rational and shaping character of consciousness that derives ultimately from German idealism. If rational deliberative consciousness is prized, then we must not be surprised to find that those prizing it will have created a social system in which rational planning is stressed and which, in turn, creates its organisational conditions in the form of a bureaucracy. For all his revolutionary Messianism, then, Lukàcs began with a rationalistic pre-bureaucratic conception of socialism, and it is this, and not only his political defeat, that created in him an inner vulnerability to Stalinism. There was a part of Lukács that was in tune with Stalinism, that welcomed it rather than simply capitulating to it. For 'Stalinism', the skeleton in the Marxist closet, is not to be understood only as Asiatic backwardness, nor merely as a corruption extrinsic to Western rationality, but as a vulnerability inherent in its overweening ambitions, activated when it encounters recalcitrance, opposition or backwardness.

Like Marx, Lukàcs understood the proletariat as the prime historical actor, as the agency through which the programme and ambitions of classical German philosophy would be fulfilled. A vital difference between the two, however, is that Marx was a 'materialist', while Lukàcs, certainly the Hegelianising Lukàcs of 1923, was somewhat embarrassed by this and primarily defined himself as a *dialectician.* Insofar as this is true, Lukàcs' Marxism exalted consciousness and held, in George Lichtheim's terms, that the, '. . .role of consciousness (and of conscience) is decisive. . . .'

While it was precisely this dominating position of consciousness that Marx originally sought to control with the bridle of materialism, nonetheless consciousness was at least half the conceptual universe for Marx, even if the subordinated half. And he, too, prized consciousness in the form of a stress upon deliberately established social relationships and planned organisation. Marxism contains, and Lukàcs made it perfectly plain that it contains, a cryptic polarity between the 'natural' and the 'social'. Thus, to 'socialise the means of production', the very definition of socialism, meant on the one hand to *denaturalise* them and, on the other, to *rationalise* them. 'Our task,' says Lenin in *What Is To Be Done?* 'is to fight the natural run of things, to divert the labour movement from its natural drift towards trade unionism.' To socialize the means of production meant to remove them from the 'blind' governance of nature and to bring them under conscious planning and deliberate control.

A decisive question here, of course, is who is actually in control of socialism. The claim that socialism means that the workers themselves will indeed control the means of production was once a humane hope; today it is only a vestigial archaism; but it was always, and it remains, the core ideological mystification of Marxism.

My point, then, is that there was always an élitist potentiality in Marxist socialism, and that this is not an accidental corruption arising from Russian 'backwardness'. The Bolshevik organisational plan, after all, was in part inspired by the German Social Democrats. The élitist potentiality is part of the indigenous character of Marxist theory. It is grounded in the importance attributed to consciousness, an emphasis controlled, repressed, yet active even in orthodox Marxism, but salient and unbridled in its Hegelian formulation. It is this exaltation of consciousness that tends to transform the proletariat into the political raw material of history, to be assembled and reprocessed by the Party organisation, which justifies its leadership precisely in the name of its possession of theory and consciousness. Under the banner of consciouness, the most 'conscious' elements proclaim themselves an *avant-garde* and endow themselves with the right to rule.

Behind the Hegelianisers' stress on the importance of consciousness, on the subjection of the world to consciousness, that is to say, on the 'identity of the subject-object', there is an abiding suspicion of nature, distrust of alienness and of otherness, partly because it is an autonomous thing, *vis-à-vis* man. There is a desire to define even 'nature' as a product of man, an impulse to reduce it to a socially shaped concept, to see it only as part of 'social reality'. Anything autonomous, anything 'other', anything not a part of ourselves, anything not controllable by ourselves is, from this perspective, to be rejected. The impulse is to eliminate anything in the world that is not us, or not totally dependent on us. What the Hegelianisers want is a world in which men will control and indeed dominate the universe. They are, in short, the proponents of a humanistic imperialism; they must therefore be the foe of the natural even in man. For the 'natural' is intrinsically that which has its own laws, spontaneities, and autonomies; it is not us, but another.

A Hegelianised Marxism may emphasise different sides of 'consciousness' and is vulnerable to breakdown in different directions. On the one side, it may become politically deactivated academic Marxism; on the other, it may slide into a revolutionary Messianism. For a Hegelian Marxism may stress either the importance of the *knowing* consciousness, of awareness, or it may stress the wilful consciousness, both commonly rooted in an assumption concerning the ultimately unlimited potency of men. If a Hegelian Marxism stresses the importance of knowing or awareness, however, this may be experienced as an unbearable constraint upon the revolutionary will.

Hegelian Marxism thus has a paradoxical vulnerability to an anti-intellectualism in which theory is seen as a subversion of revolutionary militancy, thereby transforming itself into revolutionary Messianism. Presenting itself as a philosophy of consciousness, it attempts to conceal its anti-intellectualism by calling ritualistically for the 'unity of theory and praxis'; Messianism really seeks to *subordinate* theory to praxis, to use it really to disguise the mindlessness of its political practice. This, at any rate, seems one important pathology that is a potential of a Hegelianising Marxism, although not a necessary consequence of it.

The other outcome of this contradiction between the willing and knowing consciousness is the atrophy of the will, and its total subordination to the knowing consciousness. In short, another outcome of this contradiction may be to *academicise* Marxism, a critique which has been directed against the 'Critical School' at Frankfurt.

A Hegelian revolutionary Messianism such as Lukács' is a philosophy of the 'leap' which transports men and societies away from the jurisdiction of routine processes and the natural regularities of laws. It seeks the defiance of routine and an escape from the everyday world. It substitutes consciousness-raising and courage for knowledge and discipline. The paradox of Hegelian Marxism is this: in the beginning it is most attractive to those Marxists who have a respect for mind and freedom. In the end, however, it may be they who have the fewest inhibitions about revolutionary adventurism and adopting élitist measures to destroy the corrupt old order, precisely because it is they who most feel themselves in legitimating contact with the Absolute Consciousness.

The élitist potentialities of the Hegelianisers in Marxism are not to be underestimated, precisely because of the extent to which they exalt consciousness. For under what conditions is the need for consciousness invoked? Primarily, when there is a hiatus between the immediate and the long-term gratifications available to men; between their experiences and their expectations; between gratifications known and gratifications promised. Workers are said to need 'consciousness' precisely because consciousness is required to act against or to depart from their short-run, therefore visible, interests. One needs no 'theory', however, when one is acting only in accordance with one's own immediate and hence visible interests. One needs theory, that is to say, one needs a rationale, for diverging from the immediately apprehensible, from the 'natural', from the most obvious course of behaviour.

Consciousness always embodies a measure of 'idealism', because consciousness always entails the overcoming of one's natural, materially and situationally-rooted impulses. Men 'need' theory in order to defy the evidence of their senses and their experience and to live, instead, by their ideas and their imaginations. Theory and consciousness, then, have an uprooting function. It is precisely because the socialist consciousness does *not* stem from the material conditions of the proletariat's existence but must rather, as Lenin clearly saw, be brought to the proletariat from the *outside,* that it becomes the mission of the Party to cultivate theory and to protect it from corrupting contact with the world. Which is to say, the Party appoints itself the guardian of the working class's long-range interests. As Lukàcs put it—

> The form taken by the class consciousness of the proletariat is the Party. . .The Party is assigned the sublime role of bearer of the class consciousness of the proletariat. . .The Party is the historical embodiment and the active incarnation of class consciousness. . .

In his *History and Class Consciousness,* Lukàcs spoke on behalf of the 'methodology' and not of the substantive theories of Marxism. The essence of Marxism is not to be found in any of its doctrines about capitalism, in any of its predictions or analyses concerning the capitalist economy, but, rather, in its dialectical apprehension of the totality. Marxism is thus above all a method. We can therefore still commit ourselves to Marxism today, argues Lukàcs, even if all of Marx's predictions about capitalism were proved wrong. This then loosens the specific connection between Marxism and capitalism. It transforms Marxism into a dialectic of the generalised revolution, into a consciousness of the imminent revolution, of the revolution anywhere and at any time. And this is precisely why the Lukàcs of 1923 is the most modern of Marxists.

To reduce Marxism to a method is, in effect, to deprecate, if not to eliminate, questions of observation, statistics, data, fact; it is a surrender of the empirical, a willing surrender, because the empirical is after all the manifestation of concern for the 'other', for alienness, for nature in its own autonomy. The young Lukàcs' methodological Marxism tables empirical interests precisely because he was a consciousness-enthralled Hegelian and partly, also, because he wished to outflank revisionist views about the reformed character and possibly peaceful evolution of contemporary capitalism. Lukàcs' methodological Marxism, therefore, sees the question of the day not as one of the objective readiness of capitalism for revolution. What counts is the will to revolution, not the established, structured, socio-economic conditions. For such callers to the Revolutionary Leap, what matters is will and consciousness. For them, revolution is always on the order of the day.

Yet it is precisely as a methodologist that Lukàcs firmly distinguished between Marxism and Bolshevism, refusing to reduce the former to the latter. It is in this sense that the Lukàcs of 1923 was very much an occidental or Westernising Marxist. The Russian Revolution was made by socialists in a relatively underdeveloped industrial society and was fundamentally at variance with the deepest expectations of Marx and Engels. It thereby established the historical foundation for a thorough-going transformation of Marxism, the gist of which was to loosen its connection with a specific social system, capitalism. Lenin already saw many of the world implications of this, but he saw these from the standpoint of someone immersed in the experience of the Russian revolutions. Lukàcs, however, saw these from the standpoint of Western Europe. He could thus begin to develop a Marxism in which the Russian Revolution, vital paradigm that it was, was still only a dominating but never the *culminating* event.

Lukàcs thus contributed to a new epic in Marxism, an epic in which it achieves a deeper level of self-awareness; it is a new level of Marxist self-reflection which is not confined intellectually by the Russian Revolution, even though it was subjugated politically by its subsequent diversion. The new level of Marxist self-awareness crystallised by Lukàcs then becomes the bridge between orthodox Marxism and the subsequent development in Frankfurt of 'the Critical School', as G. E. Rusconio makes plain in his *La Teoria Critica della società*. In short, Lukàcs' importance is also to be found in the fact that he is a major stimulus in the development of what is certainly the most creative school of social theorists in the twentieth century, and of whom Herbert Marcuse is only the best known member. For all this, then, we owe homage to Georg Lukàcs.

7

The Two Marxisms

This is the project: to begin a Marxist critique of Marxism itself. But on what would such a Marxist critique of Marxism focus? What would its central assumptions be? I submit that, at the minimum, a Marxist critique of Marxism would do two things. One of these is to situate its analysis of Marxism itself in an *historical* way. It would see, and insist on seeing, Marxism as an historical and social product. There is absolutely no doubt that Marxism itself requires and constrains us to understand all social theoreis in their own historical context. Despite this, however, it is also true that all too little has been done to understand Marxism as an historical product. There has been a great reluctance by Marxists, no less than non-Marxists, to view Marxism historically, perhaps because they feel that to view it in such a manner serves to devalue or 'unmask' it. Yet a Marxist standpoint requires us, it insists, that we see Marxism historically; that we do *not* see it only as a source or cause of historical development but, also, as an historical product. From our own standpoint, and from a Marxist standpoint, no social theory can be properly understood by viewing it only within its technical tradition, and by seeing it simply as the outcome of a previous set of theories, philosophies, or even ideologies. (But there is certainly a problem here, for if we wish to understand Marxism in its historical setting we will also have to clarify what we understand by history, and what kinds of things will be included or excluded under that heading).

The second minimal requirement of a Marxist critique of Marxism itself is that it absolutely must see Marxism itself as possessing its own internal *contradictions.* A Marxist critique is concerned with the understanding of the internal contradictions of *any* object it studies; thus a Marxist critique of Marxism must identify and concern itself with the contradictions of Marxism itself. This objective will of course be threatening to a certain kind of Marxist – specifically, to a vulgar Marxist. But a concern with the contradictions of Marxism will not only seem indispensable but commonplace, from the standpoint of the most realistic Marxism of our own time, the Marxism of Mao. This is clear from Mao's 1937 lecture *On Contradiction.* An auto-critique of Marxism, then, must insist that Marxism, too, has its own contradictions; it must insist that these contradictions be its own, not simply the vestigial remnants of Marxism's past - its bourgeois heritage or Victorian prejudices – and that these contradictions remain an ongoing and living part of Marxism today, and that they are an essential key to an understanding of its present condition and its future prospect.

This stress on the unrestricted universality of contradictions is clearly one of the central thrusts of Mao's paper *On Contradiction.* Here, this question of the contradictions of Marxism can be opened only very provisionally and partially. I shall begin with the problem of the contradictions of Marxism as a theoretical-cultural system.

Among the most ingrained *theoretical* contradictions of Marxism is its ambivalence with respect to science. As an intellectual system, Marxism vacillates concerning its most fundamental 'paradigm' – to use Thomas Kuhn's term. At times Marxism looks to science, indeed to positive science, as its paradigm. Thus, Marx's introduction to the second edition of *Das Kapital* could applaud the Russian reviewer of the first edition, who had interpreted it as an effort to apply the method of *science* to political economy. Indeed, Marx quotes approvingly from that laudatory review at some length:

> The one thing which is of moment to Marx is to find the laws of the phenomena with whose investigation he is concerned. . . This law once discovered, he investigates in detail the effects in which it manifests itself in social life. . .Marx only troubles himself about one thing: to show, by rigid scientific investigation, the necessity of

> successive determinate orders of social conditions. . .Marx treated the social movement as a process of natural history, governed by laws not only independent of human will, consciousness and intelligence, but, rather, on the contrary determining that will, consciousness and intelligence.

In the same introduction, Marx also affirms that there are 'naturalistic laws of capitalist production. . .working with iron necessity towards inevitable results'.

If at times Marx thinks himself a scientist among scientists, and of his work-paradigm as 'science', there are, however, *other* times when he clearly thinks himself something different; when he regards himself as a *critic* and his work as '*critique*'. Thus, *Das Kapital's* sub-title is, of course, not 'A Scientific Analysis of the Laws of Capitalism', but, rather, *A Critique of Political Economy.*

It is no easier to clarify the meaning of 'critique' than of science. Certainly, the object of a critique is *not* simply to produce a new and more correct set of scientific laws. A critique takes a given belief system, a theory, ideology, or indeed science itself - or any cultural 'objectification' – as problematic. It seeks to de-reify it, to de-mystify, to remove its objectivistic false consciousness, to offer an interpretation of it in terms of the everyday life of men living in and constrained by a specific society.

The aim of a critique is not simply to show a theory to be in error, formally or empirically, for the problem is not only the reliability of the theory's assertions. The 'truth' of a theory does not boil down to its reliability but also involves the nature of its selective perspective on the world. A critique is concerned with the meaning of this selective understanding, examining it in terms of the social forces that led to the *focalisation* of certain perspectives and to the *repression* or rejection of others. As the structuralists might say, a critique is as much concerned with the '*silences*' of a theory as with what it dramatically accentuates. A critique, then, is an hermeneutic. It seeks an interpretation of the meaning of a theory or belief-system by linking it to the society or culture in which it lives - to show that the theory was not born of mind alone - and thus to undermine its false consciousness. It seeks to establish the manner in which the thoery relates to and serves the larger society, especially its leading élites, and to show how this relation has shaped the theory itself.

To clarify Marx's notion of critique one should remember that the very model of a critique at the root of his concrete experience was the critique of *religion* developed by the Left Hegelians. The fundamental question of this critique of religion was to account for what appeared to be, from one standpoint, a certain fantastic quality in religious beliefs and in their theological systematisations. In the critique of religion, the primary object was not to reject, deny, or even test the truth of religion, but, rather, to account for its attraction. This, in turn, was interpreted, as implying that, however fantastic, religion had a certain rational dimension and human serviceability, and it is this that lent it persuasiveness. This critique of religion was the historically specific paradigm from which the more generalised Marxist notion of an ideology-critique developed into a critique of politics and political economy.

Marxism created itself as a distinctive socialism precisely by developing its own critique of other socialisms. The *Communist Manifesto* begins with a critique of bourgeois society, but it culminates in a critique of *socialism;* of so-called reactionary socialism, feudal socialism, petit-bourgeois socialism, German or 'true' socialism, and conservative socialism. Marxism begins, then, as a critique of both capitalism *and* socialism.

Of special relevance here is the *Manifesto's* critique of 'Utopian' socialism. This socialism was doomed to failure, says the *Manifesto,* 'owing to the then undeveloped state of the proletariat, as well as to the absence of the economic conditions for its emancipation'. Lacking 'the material conditions for the emancipation of the proletariat, they therefore search after a new social science, after new social laws, that are to create these conditions. . .' Utopian socialists endeavour to win converts by creating small Utopian communities and they develop a 'fanatical and superstitious belief in the miraculous effects of their social science'.

Here Marxism as a critique of socialism specifically rejects Utopian socialism's reliance upon *social science* and social '*laws*' as the vehicle of socialism. At the same time, however, the *Manifesto* tacitly supposes that certain socio-economic conditions are indeed necessary for proletarian revolution. It suggest that the relation between these conditions and the revolution has a certain kind of knowable *regularity* if not lawfulness, being productive of their consequences seemingly apart from the will of men. The *Manifesto's* critique of 'Utopian' socialism thus actually premises a lawful social science not altogether different from the very positivistic socialism that it expressly criticised. Ironically, then, in the very act of exhibiting its 'critique', the *Communist Manifesto* manifests its *ambivalence* between *critique* and *science.*

For the purposes at hand, I think I need only indicate the existence of two different paradigms in Marxism which constitute models of intellectual analysis that are partly interdependent or complementary and partly divergent. They are divergent paradigms because, as the Russian reviewer of *Das Kapital* made plain, the object of science was to discover laws independent of human will and determinative of it, while a 'critique' aims at establishing the manner in which human history is an outcome of the hidden potency of men. The basic conclusion of the Left Hegelian critique of *religion* was to show that God's being was entirely a postulation of *Man* and an expression of *Man's* own alienated being. A critique, then, aims at making men's potency more fully manifest so that men might then make their own history consciously rather than blindly. A natural science, in contrast, will, by providing laws that presumably determine the human will, allow those having technical knowledge of these laws to apply their knowledge in a technological way and to formulate the problem of social change as a *technical* problem.

In a 'scientific' socialism, the technical conferences of bureaucratised 'vanguards' tend to be substituted for the political discussion and education of masses. A critique, however, aims to transform the political process by deepening the mass consciousness and liberating it from its false consciousness. Here the political process and outcome are seen as profoundly affected by the nature of men's consciousness. The politics and praxis of a socialism conceived as a critique will thus differ substantially from that conceived as science. There are, then, two tendencies in Marxism: one toward critique, which I shall call 'Critical Marxism', and another toward science, which has called itself 'Scientific Marxism'. The way forward for Marxism, as theory or practice, requires that it surmount this contradiction. Whether this way forward can be found remains to be seen. In the meanwhile, it continues to provide one of the main bases of structural differentiation among Marxists today.

It is well known that theorists of the Marxists world have for some time now been divided between those conceiving of Marxism as some kind of critical theory and others conceiving it to be science. Among the former, there are the early Karl Korsch and Georg Lukàcs, Antonio Gramsci, J.P. Sartre, Lucien Goldmann, the *Telos* circle, the 'News and Letters' group and such members, or one-time members, of the 'Frankfurt School' as Max Horkheimer, T.W. Adorno, Franz Neumann, Leo Lowenthal, Erich Fromm, Walter Benjamin, Herbert Marcuse, or its 'younger' men such as Albrecht Wellmer, Alfred Schmidt, and its eminence in self-exile, Jürgen Habermas. Opposed to this remarkably distinguished group, there are other Marxists who eschew critical theory as mere ideology, and who conceive Marxism as a true science. They include such men as Galvano della Volpe, José Artur Gianotti, and the Marxist mandarin of l'École Normale Supérieure, Louis Althusser, and those influenced by him, such as Nicos Poulantzas, Maurice Godelier, Andre Glucksmann, Charles Bettelheim, the intellectual leader of their Swedish outpost in Lund, Göran Therborn, and an editor of the British *New Left Review,* Robin Blackburn. The divergent membership of these two networks is the sociological counterpart of an intellectual skirmish that has manifested itself among Marxists for some fifty years now. That it still continues vigorously is evident from the November-December 1971 issue of *New Left Review,* where Gareth Stedman Jones develops a sharp Althusserian critique of Lukàcs as the 'first irruption of Romanticism within Marxism'.

Much of this theoretical conflict among marxist theory is most visibly organised as a conflict between those supporting and those rejecting Hegelianism, the importance of Hegel for

Marx and a more Hegelian conception of ideology critique. It is in one part, then, a theoretical conflict between those stressing Marx as the culmination of the tradition of German idealism, and those others emphasising Marx's differences from and superiority to that tradition. It is therefore also a difference between those who accept the young, and consequently more Hegelian, Marx as authentically Marxist, and those others who regard the young Marx as still mired in ideology.

On each side of this division there is then a syndrome of correlated commitments that is the mirror image of the syndrome of correlated commitments on the other side. Thus, the Critical Marxist or Hegelianisers conceive of Marxism as critique rather than science; they stress the continuity of Marx with Hegel, the importance of the young Marx, the significance of the young Marx's emphasis on 'alienation', and adopt a more historicism ontology. The Scientific Marxists or anti-Hegelianisers stress a radical break (*a coupure epistémologique*) with Hegel after 1845; Marxism is then science, not critique, entailing a 'structuralist' methodology whose key is the 'mature' political economics of *Capital* rather than the ideologised anthropology of the 1844 Manuscripts. In one part, the controversy about the young *versus* the old Marx is to be understood as a discussion on the *concrete* and metaphoric level of the contradictions between critical and scientific Marxisms, a more serious and analytic distinction.

Despite their historicist sensitivities it is the Critical Marxists who stress the *continuity* between the young and old Marx, for they wish to establish the abiding influence of the Hegelian concern with alienation even in the technical political economy of the mature Marx. Correspondingly, while one might suppose that the Scientific Marxists' structuralist proclivities would dispose them to stress the structural continuities in the work of the young and old Marx, it is they who tend to stress the quantum leap that Marx presumably made from ideology to science, as well as emphasising qualitative differences between ideology and science.

The Critical Marxists have at least won the battle against Althusser on the textual and biographical levels, but it is not all that clear what they have actually won on the analytical level. That is, does their victory on the textual level mean that Marx's continued concern with (or use of the concept of) alienation *meant* the same thing to the young as to the older Marx? When embedded in his early philosophical anthropology as in his later technical, political economy? And when in his early, more 'Promethean' optimism for a total human emancipation as in his later more limited stress on liberating men from the specific constraints of capitalism? (In my view, there is no more valuable discussion of these issues than that of the independent Swedish Marxist-sociologist – in self-imposed exile in Copenhagen – Joachim Israel, who is fully sensitive to both the continuities and the important changes in Marx's concept of alienation. Even if inconclusive, Israel's analysis is unblemished by any sectarian impulse, and he accomplishes something not done since Lukàcs, namely, the re-establishment of a productive liaison between modern academic sociology and Marxism.)

While there is little doubt that the older Marx remained committed to the concept of alienation, there is much doubt that his understanding this underwent no serious change. Marx's *understanding* of alienation changed, substantially and inevitably, as his theories deepened and developed, for these theories were the concept's defining context, and especially as they shifted in focus from Man as a species to a concern with men as members of capitalist societies. As Marx situates his concept of alienation within an historical analysis of capitalism as a constraining social system, the prospects of human liberation implicit in the notion of alienation are shifted. Human liberation is now increasingly guaranteed by the contradictions of capitalism itself, rather than by any qualities of man that may transcend that society. Increasingly, it is the contradictions of this society that not only produce alienation itself but, also, guarantee that men will *revolt* against that alienation.

In the mature Marx there is a growing movement toward a 'sociologism' or 'economism' in which it is the *structures* of *society* and their contradictions that determine social outcomes. To stress that it is the contradiction between the 'forces' and the 'relations' of production that ensures the uprooting of capitalism, say Albrecht Wellmer quite correctly, is substantially different from the *Manifesto's* stress on the liberating potential of class *struggle*. Both Althusser and Wellmer agree on the presence of this objectivistic focus on structures in Marx. Althusser, however, values it and sees it as an ontology appropriate to a true social science, while Wellmer subjects this aspect of Marx to profound critique.

It is precisely in this vein that Althusser and Ètienne Balibar suggest, in *Reading Capital* (a truncated version of the French edition), that Marx's view that 'men' make their own history is an unexamined and deceptive idea. Their view is that this is the standpoint of the immature Marx, the philosophical anthropologist who is still an ideologist rather than a true scientist. (Marx's aphorism – men make their own history, even if in circumstances imposed on them – dates from 1853, and is thus after his supposed break from ideology, the *coupure épistémologique* which according to Althusser occurred in 1845.) In effect, Althusser and Balibar claim that it is not men and men's actions, but the social structures, formations and systems that invisibly move them, that really shape history, and that these, therefore, comprise the proper object of a scientific Marxism. The Althusserians apparently conceive an emphasis on 'man' as a manifestation of 'subjectivity', and on (the plural) 'man' as a mere 'intersubjectivity'. Quite apart from the intrinsic merits of this for a conception of a sociology, this correctly suggests the difference between the young Marx, where 'men' in all their 'vulgar', visible embodiment are manifestly the acting subjects who make history, and his *Capital,* where 'social formations' such as the mode and relations of production become the subjects of history, and where men's conformity to or revolt against that social system is essentially determined by its social structures and their contradictions.

The unsparing condemnation of Althusser by some Hegelian Marxists, or by Kolakowski ('commonsense banalities. . .Vague and ambiguous. . .striking historical inexactitudes. . .self-contradictory. . .ideological') gives no impression of the power and complexity of Althusser's mind. For all the venom directed at it, Althusser's reading of Marx is one of the most methodologically instructive that we have, telling us not only much about Marx but also a great deal about how to read *any* theorist. Althusser's stress on the importance of a 'symptomatic reading' of Marx, as attentive to his omissions as to his emphases, is an intellectual milestone in the development of Marx interpretations. In my view, the most fundamental limitations on Althusser's reading of Marxism are not Althusser's personal shortcomings, nor even the limits imposed by his Communist affiliation. Rather, they are those inherent in the Marxism he reads, in Marx-Engels 'themselves', in *their* contradictions, and in the inability of anyone to resolve these contradictions and still remain a 'Marxist' in more than a sentimental sense. One might say that just as he argued that Marx was pregnant with a new methodology that he was not yet able to articulate so, too, Althusser has undertaken a task of which he could not allow himself to become fully aware. For what Althusser has attempted is not so much a new interpretation but a thoroughgoing reconstitution of Marxism. His failure, and I believe it is a failure, derives most basically from his inability to accept the fact that Marxism itself has its own internal contradictions, from an avoidance of their analysis, and hence from an inability to transcend them.

Most especially, Althusser seeks to resolve Marxism's ambivalence about itself as science, on the one side, and as critique, on the other, essentially by a process of denial and splitting. He denies that the young Marx is importantly continuous and consequential for the older one; he denies that the young Marx is Marxist. He denies that Marxism contains ideology and insists that 'true'Marxism is science and science alone, free from its Hegelian origins. But this is not the Marx that was. It is a purified, logically possible, but not historically evident Marx. Like Lukàcs' early work, it is one of the objective possibilities of development in Marxism, but it is not Marxism itself. The objective possibilities of Marxism are not the same as the historical Marxism that existed or exists. The trouble is that Althusser is working within a concrete intellectual and political tradition that has transformed the works of Marx into untouchable texts so that the inevitable need to leave them behind cannot be openly and matter-of-factly acknowledged, but must instead be concealed and obscured. This commitment to the *concrete* Marx is a basic source of the false consciousness of Marxists. Althusserianism is a social theory that is in the process of becoming something more nearly like a 'socialist sociology' or, more ecumenically, a 'radical social theory'. To put the matter in another way: Althusser is about as much of a Marxist as August Comte was a Saint-Simonian.

That Althusser may have set himself a kind of Comteian mission is suggested by his remarkable praise for Comte as the only mind worthy of interest produced by French philosophy in 130 years after the French Revolution! Just as Comte sought to remove the contradictions of his mentor, Henri Saint-Simon, to systematise the latter's sprawling genius and, above all, to scientise it, so Althusser attempts much the same for Marx. And as Comte sought to divorce his sociology from metaphysics, Althusser seeks to foster the 'end of ideology', declaring that authentic Marxism is not ideology but science. If, however, Conte's false consciousness manifested itself by denying any indebtedness to his mentor (the 'depraved juggler' Saint-Simon) and by stressing his own originality, Althusser's false consciousness manifests itself by piously affirming that he is simply exhibiting the authentic Marx rather than inventing a new one.

The most basic strucural polarity in Althusser's conceptual system is its dualism between 'science' and 'ideology'. Yet, fundamental as these are for him, they both remain profoundly unclarified. In the end, we come away with no clearer a picture of the 'science' that Althusser prizes than of the 'ideology' he despises. His conception of science is that of an intellectual discipline essentially definable in terms of its theoretic constitution and problematic, rather than its empirical component. What one must do to justify any claim to knowledge, in Althusser's vision of Marxism as science, remains badly blurred. All the more so because Althusser renounces any pragmatic standard or even praxis as the criterion of truth, and holds that Marxism succeeds because it is true rather than being true because it succeeds. At most, Althusser's science requires the making of a reasonable argument within the framework of an articulated theory. But much the same might be said about scholasticism or astrology. Are the claims of science, then, to be justified in no manner different from those of theology? From the standpoint of the methodological 'anarchism' of a Paul Feyerabend one might accept such an ecumenical conclusion with equanimity. But this is quite impossible for an Althusser who started with the central aim of differentiating sharply between science and ideology and establishing Marxism's credentials as a science.

Quite apart from the method of science, Althusser is also vague concerning the character of the scientific product. For example: Is Althusser's Marxism scientific because it produces warranted laws? If so, what are they? Or is it scientific because it produces careful ethnographies and discursive historical analyses of concrete events? In some part, Althusser is inhibited from clarifying his conception of science because he needs one broad enough to encompass the diversity of scholarly works actually produced by Marx and Engels in their 'mature' lifetimes. In short, it must include both the *Capital* and the *Eighteenth Brumaire,* which exemplify (but do not exhaust) the tension between science and critique in originary Marxism. Althusser's awkward commentaries on these crucial questions conceal the fact of his essentail silence about them which, in turn, betrays the presence of contradictions fundamental to Marxism itself.

There is, I believe, still another reason for Althusser's failure here. It is apparent that Althusser does not always view Marxism as a science such as physics. This is implicit in his own theoretical borrowings, which are from psychoanalysis and structural linguistics. Althusser thus sometimes operates with a working (if inarticulate) distinction between the physical and the social sciences. 'Inarticulate', because to confront the issue fully would run the risk of pushing Althusser back to the distinction between the *Naturwissenschaften* and *Geisteswissenschaften,* and this is exactly where his old enemy, Georg Lukàcs, began more than fifty years ago. Such a distinction implies a profound difference between the nature of the object studied by the natural and social sciences. If that is so, then what reason is there to believe that the methods adequate to the established natural sciences will suffice for the new social sciences? Althusser never tells us.

While vague about it, one nonetheless gets the impression that sometimes he tacitly assumes that the object studied by Marxism as social science has essentially the *same* character as the objects of the natural or physical sciences, being objects whose unique *subjectivity* does not fundamentally alter them so that they may be treated and studied as 'things'. Thus, for all his recognition of the role of theory in science, Althusser converges with sociological positivism. In general, however, Althusser never tells us much about his method of studying society. All he really exhibits is his method of studying social *theory.* This is fundamentally a form of qualitative analysis, a kind of hermeneutic in which I, for my part, think he is greatly talented and profoundly informative, but scarcely 'scientific'.

Anti-Hegelian Marxism sank some of its deepest roots in the Bolshevik rejection – as early as 1924 – of Karl Korsch's and Georg Lukàcs' Hegelian Marxism. This rejection was originally prompted by the Bolshevik effort to avert a challenge to the hegemony of Leninism, then crystallising as the official ideology of the Third International. (Lenin's close study of Hegel had come rather late in his political and intellecutal development.) This rejection of Hegelianism was further crystallised in the Soviet Union during the hegemony of Stalinism, while the Soviet attitude toward Hegel appeared to have softened after the Twentieth Congress of the C. P. S. U.

Robin Blackburn and Gareth Jones warn us, and quite properly, that it is wrong to over-emphasise the Stalinist character of Althusser's politics. They remind us that Gauchists, Maoists and Trotskyists have found Althusser interesting. Blackburn and Jones tend to view Althusser's involvement with the Communist Party as a kind of sentimentality, a wish to retain solidarity with the French proletariat, as the expression of a kind of emotional need for a Marxist ecumenism. Yet it may not be wrong to suggest that one difference between the Scientific and Critical Marxists is that the former make heavier organisational commitments, and that they value the organisation as such; this in contrast to the Critical Marxists, whose deepest commitment is to a set of values, to a conception, a consciousness, the 'spirit' or ends of the revolution. The first grouping of Scientific Marxists risks surrendering the ends sought by the revolution in order to protect the *means* – the organisational vanguard. The pathological potentiality of this tendency is thus toward a kind of political 'ritualism' in which what were initially regarded as means have come to be viewed as ends in themselves. In the language of Marxist diagnosis, this is 'revisionism'.

The Critical Marxists' outlook, however, is not, of course, immune to political pathologies, but merely has different susceptibilities. Their lunge toward the revolutionary end is so dominating that they have less commitment to any specific organisational instrument such as the vanguard party, or even to any specific 'historical agent' such as the working class. They are in general less insistent on the prior presence of certain 'objective' historical conditions as the requisite for the revolutionary leap. If the political pathology of the Scientific Marxists is ritualism and revisionism, that of the 'Critical Marxists is adventurism or (as Georg Lukàcs once termed his early position) 'revolutionary messianism'. In one part, then, the tension between the Critical and the Scientific Marxists is the theoretical counterpart of an underlying sociological dilemma - the classical pitfalls of revolutionary politics: sectarianism and opportunism. Perhaps another difference between the two outlooks is a difference in their mental 'horizons'. The Scientific Marxists are seemingly more circumscribed in their attachments, being 'locals'of a sort; the Critical Marxists, for their part, seem more likely to be 'cosmopolitans' continually striving to link Marxism with a larger tradition and world.

If each side has pathological political potentials, each also has its own characteristic political strength. For the Critical Marxists, this is in their refusal to submit to 'what is', their refusal to wait interminably, their belief that the time is always right to change the world, that there is always some way to exert pressure against the *status quo* – in short, that one can always find some path forward to the revolution. In effect, they are constantly on guard against the dangers of political exhaustion, apathy, and of undue reliance upon forces external to men's own commitments or outside of their own control. Theirs is a political position that insists that people count more than technology and weapons; that men can and should do something without waiting interminably for other 'forces' to mature. They see the importance of courage and commitment in politics; of consciousness; of the here-and-now transformation of human relationships. In its *strengths,* no less than its weaknesses, Critical Marxism is, of course, the more Romantic.

The Scientific Marxists, however, have different political talents: they stress the cultivation of political endurance and patience; the husbanding and developing of their cadres until the time is right; the careful appraisal of historical conditions for what they are, and not confusing them with what they would like them to be. Above all, the Scientific Marxists seek to protect their ability to act when objective conditions promise to maximise their chance of success. They place their greatest reliance on the development of the forces of production, and on the opportunities and contradictions this will create.

Critical and Scientific Marxists may each be committed to the revolution, but each views the revolution's future as protected in diferent ways. The Critical Marxists see the future of the revolution as depending on the clarity of awareness and vigour of conscious commitment, on a consciousness that can be imprinted on history like a kind of germ matter. The Scientific Marxists, however, see the future of the revolution as essentially vouchsafed not by the heroism of the revolutionary, but by history itself; by the inexorable contradictions of each society; by the scientific appraisal of these contradictions; and by seizing the political opportunities created by the crises brought about by these unfolding contradictions. The mission of a Hegelian Critical Marxiam is to safeguard revolutionary purpose and élan; the mission of an anti-Hegelian Scientific Marxism is to protect the organisational instrument and its future options. It is thus easier for revolutionaries out of power to be Hegelians, while those in power will find more congenial the prudence of an anti-Hegelian Marxism.

The stress on consciousness typical of Hegelian or Critical Marxists crystallised in the work of Karl Korsch and Georg

Lukàcs in the early 1920s, after the defeat of the revolutions in Hungary and Germany and, also, in the wake of the successful revolution in Russia. The defeat of the revolution in nations that were industrially *advanced,* and its success in one that was *backward,* was then the most important historical conjuncture undermining the authority of a 'scientific' and materialistic Marxism and supporting a critical and idealistic Marxism.

An Hegelian or Critical Marxism is one that compensates for the deficiency of economic and technological conditions (once deemed) requisite for socialism, and it is, therefore, a Marxism appropriate to revolutionary efforts in 'underdeveloped' or Third World nations. Such a Marxism is, in effect, an effort to counterbalance deficient material socio-economic conditions by stressing the significance and potency of the 'human' agency and of his awareness, consciousness, sacrifice and discipline. Underlying the 'consciousness' of the Hegelian revolutionary, then, is his inability to rely on material conditions to lend support to his efforts, and his sense that the 'natural' drift of things is inimical to the revolution. The call to consciousness, then, is the ideology of those who do not believe that time is on their side, or that 'history is on our side'.

To develop this point further: Scientific Marxism relies on history and on the unfolding of certain natural tendencies in history to fulfil its socialist expectations. It sees itself as allied with history and nature. Correspondingly, however, a Scientific Marxism also sees such objectified history and objectified social structures as that which it would rely upon *rather than* 'men', and their will and consciousness. In short, a scientific socialism is sedimented with a tacit judgement of *human* nature as having a kind of unworthiness, as somehow falling short of the requirements of history, so that it cannot be relied upon to solve the historical problem. This contrasts with the tendencies of a Critical Marxism that does not rely upon an objectified history, on social structures or on nature but, rather, on men and on their will and consciousness to overcome the deficiencies of nature, history and economic structures. The adventurism of a Critical Marxism derives in part from its embattled and desperate sense that it must overcome (and perhaps combat) nature and history themselves. The bureaucratism of Scientific Marxism derives from its distrust of man himself and the feeling that it may use men as things on behalf of the higher purposes of history with which it sees itself allied.

The subsequent *embourgeoisement* of the working class in the most industrially advanced nations and its accommodation to capitalist society, as material standards of living improved, further and profoundly undermined the claims of scientifc socialism. For the latter had supposed that it would be the economic contradictions of advanced capitalism that would be most acute and that it would be these that would make their societies vulnerable to socialism. When it was the proletariat's militancy rather than the capitalist class's hegemony that succumbed, scientific socialism came into continuous contradiction with the experience of everyday life. All the more so as some of the most manifestly militant of socail strata, such as college students, were not economically impoverished or exploited.

The experience of everyday life, then, lent new support to the importance that Hegelian Marxists attributed to consciousness and to the flawed quality of everyday life in modern society. In moving from a scientific to a critical socialism, the socialist critique of modern society correspondingly moved from a condemnation of capitalism's economic exploitation to a denunciation of its sociological dehumanisation: alienation and reification. The new Marxist emphasis on alienation and reification is most fundamentally rooted in capitalism's increasing gross national product, in the Keynesian control of the business cycle, and in the improving standard of living among the working class. The movement toward a Hegelian Marxism, then, has in part resulted from an effort to reformulate Marxism so that it would be consistent with the experience of everyday life under advanced capitalism.

A major transition occurred in the history of world communism when the Bolsheviks rejected the standpoint of the Second International. The Bolshevik position, however, did not entail the embracing of a fully Hegelian Critical Marxism so much as a partial and limited rejection of the wooden evolutionism of the Second International. Plekhanov and Lenin had learned much from Kautsky and they still accepted certain aspects of his politics as well as of his economics. This reflected itself, on the one side, in Lenin's emphasis on the importance of the 'professional revolutionary' and the party vanguard that would bring a socialist consciousness to the proletariat from the outside and which would take revolutionary initiatives.

On the other side, moreover, practically all of the Old Bolsheviks were committed to the economic premises of a scientific socialism; they thus at first believed implicitly that Russia lacked the economic conditions requisite to establish socialism, and that it was these economic conditions that were decisive. The Old Bolsheviks therefore looked forward to the coming of the revolution in Central Europe as the guarantor of their own socialism. When they found that the revolutionary lunge there had failed, leaving behind their own revolution as an isolated beachhead, they then fell back on the tactic of 'socialism in one country'. But this was an improvisation aimed at accommodating to what was, from the standpoint of their 'scientific socialism', a totally unexpected and highly threatening situation.

The Leninists had effected the Soviet Revolution by shifting (but not completing the movement) toward a political voluntarism consistent with a consciousness-stressing Hegelian Marxism. In short, the first 'successful' revolution made by Marxism predicated Lenin's movement toward a critical Marxism and a kind of Romanticism of the organisation. But the Bolsheviks had not made a corresponding change in their *economics* or in the primacy attributed to it. Indeed, the theoretical change they had made did not fully register in their self-understanding. They did not, for example, conceive of themselves as having *changed* Marxism but, rather, as having merely adapted it to new historical circumstances. Their self-understanding was that they had changed only the political superstructure or 'starting mechanisms' of Marxism, but not its fundamental political economy. With the development of 'socialism in one country' and, most especially of Stalinism, Soviet socialism was essentially guided by a kind of Second

International 'scientific' socialism in which primary emphasis was placed on the building of the right industrial, technological and scientific requisites. If socialism had once been conceived by Lenin as a fussion of 'electrification' × Soviets, Stalinisation meant a conception of socialism that totally destroyed the latter and dwelt exclusively on the former.

Soviet Marxists could never face the fact that the success of their revolution was based on assumptions deeply deviant from the very version of Marxism they employed in building 'socialism' in one country. From the standpoint of the consciousness subsequently fostered by the Soviet State, the Soviet Revolution itself was an anomaly. It was something that should not have happened. The different consciousness that had guided the revolutionary Bolsheviks – 'Leninism' itself – inevitably became an embarrassment and a threat to those who later succeeded to the Soviet power. Stalinism, we might say, was an effort to deny and to extirpate the revolutionary voluntarism that was the heretical heritage of Leninism, because it threatened Soviet power internationally and domestically; it was an effort to conceal the fact that the Soviet State diverged from the requirements of 'scientific' socialism, while attempting to enact these requisites by a forceful imposition from above. Whatever else it was, Stalinism was the product of a consciousness that assumed that it did not matter how men behaved toward one another, but that what mattered were the social structures they created, and the 'objective', technological, scientific, industrial and economic conditions they left behind. These, it was believed, would 'absolve' them.

The Soviet State and its leaders thus defined themselves increasingly as the product and the defender of a scientific socialism, and they developed a corresponding false consciousness concerning their historical relation to Hegelian Marxism. The Stalinist development, then, meant regression from Lenin's halting movement toward a Hegelian Marxism back to the scientific socialism of the Second International. It was this model of Marxism with which the Soviet State then associated itself. After the Leninist seizure of power in Russia, the maintenance and protection of the new Soviet State (the 'bastion') and its conception of Marxism became the fulcrum of Communist politics wherever Soviet influence held sway. The break away from Soviet influence on world socialism, as in Cuba and China, to a policy that was at once more autonomous and more militant, could thus only take the direction of a return to the Hegelian model of Marxism, but this time it was an uninhibited embrace, involving the resurgence or reinvention of a full-scale Hegelian Marxism, even if not of a concrete commitment to Hegel himself or to his specific works.

Maoism and the Contradictions of Marxism

Cuban and Chinese Marxism both converge with a Hegelian Critical Marxism far more than with a 'scientific' socialism. In both cases the importance attributed to revolutionary will and voluntarism, so characteristic of Critical Marxism, is indicated by the crucial place each assigns to military initiative, to the guerrilla column, to its *foco* and tactics, and by their common conviction that power comes out of the barrel of a gun. Both believed that the revolution need not require the prior maturation of the objective conditions of an advanced industrial economy. If the limited Leninist tendency toward voluntarism was indicated by the emphasis Lenin placed on the initiative of the political instrument, the party vanguard, then the fullblown voluntarism of Cuban and Chinese Marxism is indicated by the imporance each attributes to the military instrument, the army, and to its influence on (if not priority over) the vanguard party itself.

Maoism, say Robert Jay Lifton, assumes two things: first, it views—

> . . . the human mind as infinitely malleable, capable of being reformed, transformed and rectified without limit. The second is a related vision of the will as-powerful, even to the extent that (in his own worlds) 'The Subjective creates the Objective.

Much the same may be and has been said of Castroism.

In a converging analysis, Richard R. Fagen stresses that the style of Cuban revolutionary politics was crystallised by the guerrilla experience in the Sierra Maestra during 1958-59, whose enduring legacy was voluntarism, egalitarianism and ruralism. Voluntarism, Fagen indicates, refers to—

> The expansive sense of efficacy, competence and personal power generated during the guerrilla period. . .[and denotes] a philosophy which conceives human will to be the dominant factor in experience and thus history.

Whether Cuba's voluntarism *derives* from (was 'generated by') the guerrilla period or, as seems far more likely, whether it preceded it and was the underlying consciousness that allowed Castro to launch guerrilla warfare, is a secondary point. The essential consideration here is that this voluntarism is clearly a salient feature of Castroism and a central symptom of its convergence with an Hegelian model of Marxism.

For my part, and unlike Fagen, I regard this as a salient but *not* as a *distinctive* feature of Castroism. I would also say the same about the two other components Fagen deems distinctive of the cuban style of revolutionary politics, ruralism and egalitarianism. They are distinctive only in that they set it apart from political models consistent with a 'scientific socialism', but they are certainly *not* peculiar to *Cuba*. Exactly this same triad or voluntarism, ruralism and egalitarianism also characterises Mao's Marxism.

Fagen's analysis may be taken to suggest that the egalitarianism of Cuban socialism was accentuated by the experience of shared danger and shared struggle characteristic of a military brotherhood and that this brotherhood became the guerrillas' tacit paradigm of a good social order, which they subsequently sought to reproduce in society at large. It may be that it is precisely this use of the military brotherhood as societal paradigm that helps explain how egalitarianism can be associated with concentrated decision-making at the top and with strict control over dissent. ('In Cuba, a radical economic, social, and cultural egalitarianism is married to an authoritarian and hierarchical decisional structure.) For the stress of men in combat frequently generates informalities, mutual reliance, and a sense of shared fate without, however, actually changing the formal hierarchical social structure of the military unit and the differential authority of officers and men. As battle and danger recede with victory, the informal egalitarianism gives way to the abiding formal hierarchy. This was precisely the experience of the Yugoslavian Partisan fighters and it may be a central source of the disillusionment of those, such as Djilas, who somehow retained a vivid image of the older military brotherhood and therefore keenly resented the emergence of new socio-economic distinctions – the 'New Class.'

Cuban (and, as we will indicate, Chinese) voluntarism was also associated, in the manner characteristic of Critical Marxism, with a stress on the importance of consciousness and awareness. In Castro's view, socialism or communism is not simply a socialisation of the means of production but the *transformation of men,* the creation of a new revolutionary man, 'a man devoid of *egoismo,* guided by *conciencia,* who puts service to society above service to self'. 'A communist society,' in Castro's own words, 'is one in which man will have reached the highest degree of social awareness ever achieved. . . To live in a Communist society is to live without selfishness. . .' Certainly this is far more reminiscent of the young Marx's philosophical manuscripts than of his *Capital.*

Castro's model of development, like Mao's, does not give first place to the classical verities of scientific Marxism: resources, capital, technology, efficiency or growth. Instead, it stresses 'mass participation, determination, selflessness, enthusiasm, and faith. . .' Again: '. . .a profound general faith in achieving economic progress through the *formation* and utilisation of revolutionary man certainly pervades the highest decisional circles.' The leadership's commitment to development rests less on technological factors than on the transformation of human relations and consciousness. It rests, in Castro's own Hegelian formulation, on 'factors of a moral order, factors having to do with awareness.'

Essentially the same portrait of Maoist development policies has been drawn by E. L. Wheelwright and B. MacFarlane. In their analysis they note that—

> a fundamental axiom of Maoist thought is that public ownership is only a technical condition for solving the problems of Chinese society. . .the goal of Chinese socialism involves vast changes in

> human nature, in the way people relate to each other . . .Once the basic essentials of food, clothing and shelter for all have been achived, it is not necessary to wait for higher productivity levels to be reached before attempting socialist ways of life.

In an unusually probing discussion of their analysis, Michael Kosok expressly counterpoises the 'Moscow' view of development with the Chinese, adumbrating the economistic side of 'scientific' socialism with penetrating clarity. Kosok holds that the economist of Scientific Marxism (what I have elsewhere called its 'utilitarianism') implies that 'the structure of society is essentially the development of *productivity* and the "level of production". . .' and regards man as an 'efficiency machine serving the dictates of technology. . .Communism and socialism are seen [by Scientific Marxism] as contingent upon the availability of a sufficient number of things. . .,' quantification and reification being characteristic of it. Again, Scientific Marxism stresses the importance of rational planning rather than will or motivation, and in holding that expertise is more important than 'redness', ultimately surrenders the economy to the control of specialists.

Kosok's insight into the development policy of Scientific Marxism is, I believe, essentially correct, and it was a policy basically accepted by Stalin also. Stalin defined the basic law of socialism' (i.e. of the Soviet economy under his régime) as

> the securing of the maximum satisfaction of the constantly rising material and cultural requirements of the whole of society through the continuous expansion and perfection of socialist production on the basis of higher techniques.

Some subsequent Soviet planners, it has been argued, have reduced the priority Stalin assigned to production and given greater emphasis to consumer satisfaction. Actually, however, Stalin's development policy is not best characterised, as certain formulations seem to imply, in terms of its focus on efficiency or rationalisation. Indeed, Stalin expressly rejected the view 'that it is only necessary to organise the productive forces rationally and the transition to communism will take place. . .' Rather, Stalin tended to counterpoise growth to efficiency and to assign priority to the former.

Rationality of economic organisation and economic growth are somewhat independent considerations. There can be great economic growth with relatively little increase in rationality, and increased rationality without economic growth. Stalin opted for the primacy of growth: 'It is necessary to ensure not a mythical "rational organisation" of the productive forces, but a continuous expansion of production of the means of production. To the extent, the economic imperatives of capitalism and Scientific Marxism converge. The issue, then, is whether it is the growth imperative or the efficiency imperative that controls the economy of a scientific socialism. In my view Stalin is quite correct, if he is thought of as having described the imperative controlling the Soviet economy and thus the forces that shape the character of much of everyday life in the Soviet Union. Soviet leaders, in contrast to some of their planners, opted for growth over efficiency; in some part because they were concerned with the aggregate power of the Soviet Union in comparison with that of the United States; in some part because labour has been relatively cheaper there; in some part because the criterion of 'catching up' is more readily visible on the 'growth' than on the 'efficiency' level; and in some part, finally, because the decline of traditional living standards means that consumers are always seeking *more* than they formerly had.

The question is a practical one of much significance; Kosok's focus on rationality leads him to define scientific socialism as rooted in and corrupted by the division of labour. The alternate view suggested here would, rather, view the trouble as rooted in the cold war or the hot competition between Soviet and American societies, and in their common insistence - now ecologically critical - on a policy of indefinite growth. This, in trun, is rooted in their common failure to develop a stable conception of a proper standard of living which, not being ever expanded, could therefore be capable of being satisfied. Once the importance of some morally validated conception of a standard of living is recognised, we are then thrust back to the decisive problem Èmile Durkheim saw some sixty years ago - the need for a socialist *morality* as a requisite for a fulfilling and stable socialism. In any event, there is little question that scientific socialism, sedimented with the nineteenth-century mythos of an all-conquering science, rests solidly on the assumption of indefinite and unlimited economic growth, which is in flat and fundamental contradiction of all we are now learning from modern ecologists.

I have previously suggested that any social theory, including Marxism, changes when it is no longer vindicated by or consistent with the experiences of everyday life. It changes when everyday life changes and gives rise to sentiments, to a personal vision of what is real, or fosters a new set of assumptions that are at variance with those premised by and built into the social theory. A social theory may change, however, not because the old everyday life is changing into a new one, but simply when the theory is *transported* to a different culture in which everyday life generates and rests upon a quite different set of assumptions, sentiments and conceptions of what is real. Here the theory is under pressure not because a once-congenial everyday life has ceased to be compatible with it, but simply because this theory is now brought into a new contact with an everyday life that was never compatible with it.

Transformations in the everyday life of Western capitalism seem to underlie the decline of Scientific Marxism and the rise of Critical Marxism: successful revolutions in industrially backward countries; the accommodation of the proletariat in industrially advanced countries; the militancy of non-impoverished groups, etc. The emergence of Maoism, however, as a special case of a Critical Marxism distinct, in part, from that of Cuban socialism, illustrates the way in which a theory is changed by diffusion to a society which has an everyday life that is (and always was) different from the everyday life of the society in which it first originated.

As suggested earlier in the first part of this analysis Maoism seems distinguished by the emphasis it places upon the universality of contradiction. To that extent Maoism represents a new and distinct stage in the world development of Marxism because it has achieved a reflexivity superior to that of Western Marxisms; it can and has faced the 'bad news' about its own internal contradictions. (This clearly was one aspect in the struggle between Mao and Liu Shao-chi whom Mao saw as ignoring the contradictions of socialism itself.)

Western Marxism, unlike Maoism, was developed in a Christian culture whose everyday life has long been sedimented with millenarian religious fantasies that were often sublimated into the political vision of some final, climactic coming. Western Marxism's conception of socialism and Communism have rested tacitly upon such profoundly ingrained (but not always manifest) millenarian expectations. Maoism, however, is the first Marxism that matured in a non-Christian civilisation. Nourished in a deteriorating Confucian culture that has no concepts of salvation or of an afterlife, and which is oriented to an immanent order rather than one that is transcendental, Maoism is the most secular of Marxisms. It regards those Marxists who think socialism devoid of contradictions as naïve if not as faintly uncivilised.

There are, of course, various other conditions under which a theory may undergo change. Another of these is when the social strata that had created and had fostered the theory itself changes or passes away. And so it is with Marxism. It is not only the change in the everyday life of industrially advanced societies, and not only its move from the everyday life of a Christian to that of a Confucian society, but, also, a change in the social strata with which Marxism has been associated, that promises a radical change in Marxism. Here I refer *not* to the passivity and accommodation of the *proletariat* and its failure thus far as the promised historical agency of socialism, but, also, to the changes and crisis of the academic *intelligentsia*, the social strata by which Marxism was created, that brings us to the deepest level in the crisis of Marxism.

The most profound indication of this development is to be found in the societal re-mapping sought by Maoism which is laying the groundwork for the elimination of the academic intelligentsia. As Robert Guillain remarks in *Le Monde,* 'It is no over-simplification of the massive series of reforms [of the 'Cultural Revolution'] . . . to say that their key objective - defined by Chairman Mao himself – is the elimination of the "academic intellectual". As the intensity of the Red Guard movement subsided, it became increasingly evident that the elimination of the academic intelligentsia was one of the most important items on the agenda of the Cultural Revolution. This effort is resonated in the West by the anti-intellectualism of the bureaucratised *lumpen* intelligentsia and in the self-hatred of certain *gauchiste* intellectuals.

Jean-Paul Sartre expresses an essentially Maoist view of the intellectual's future when he remarks: 'his privileged status is over. . .it is sheer bad faith, hence counter-revolutionary, for the intellectual to dwell on his own problems. . .he owes his knowledge to [the masses] and must be with them and in them: he must be dedicated to work for their problems. . .Asked whether the recent publication of his massive book on Flubert was not in contradiction to this very position, Sartre humbly replies, 'My book on Flaubert may, indeed, be a form of petty-bourgeois escapism. . .'

Maoism is a Marxism that, according to its self-understanding, strives to live in the purer morality of ordinary people, rather than through the theoretical acumen of a privileged élite. In this view, Mao's closing of the Chinese universities was a kind of sociological surgery that sought to create a new social order devoid of an academic intelligentsia. From June 1966 until about September 1970, universities throughout China were closed down and many (some ten out of forty in Peking) still remain shut. And not only the universities but Chinese culture more broadly appears, even in Guillain's sympathetic account,

> to be in a state of suspended animation. Literature has virtually disappeared. . .Painters and sculptors produce endless versions of the Great Architect. The cinema has almost ground to a halt and the theater has a repertory of half a dozen plays which are presented time and again. . .

According to B. Michael Frolic of York University, the latest foreign book on the shelves of Peking University's library dates from 1966; and many municipal libraries, museums, research institutes and bookstore still remain closed.

Marxism, however, was in the beginning the creation of a library-haunting, bookstore-browsing, museum-loving – and hence leisure-possessing - academic intelligentsia of the very sort that Maoism now seeks to excise. It does not matter, of course, that Engels himself had no university training; and it does not matter that Marx never achieved the professorship that, when young, he had coveted; for both were mandarins at heart. They had both assimilated and embodied the culture of the Western University. Marx was the product and possessor of a high European culture who knew his Goethe by heart; who read his Aeschylus in the original; who had a boundless respect for Shakespeare, whom he had his daughters memorise; who took pleasure in reading two or three novels at one time, ranking Balzac and Cervantes before other novelists; who, when disturbed, might take refuge in algebra; and who actually wrote an infinitesimal calculus. In a letter to his daughter Laura in 1868 he describes himself as '. . .a machine condemned to devour books. . .When Marx died, on 14th March, 1883, he was where one might expect him – at his desk.

Whatever its ultimate destiny and destination, Marxism was originally a creation of the West. Born of European culture, Marxism is simply unthinkable without the complex of institutions that centre on the university, which trains and provides livings for a secular intelligentsia. Marx and Engels, and all the epigones of every nationality that follow after them, are unthinkable without the countless books, journals, newspapers, libraries, bookstores, publishing houses, and even Party schools, whose cadres and culture constitute a dense infrastructure at whose centre there is the Western university. No university, no intelligentsia, no Marxism.

The gulf between Maoism and Soviet Marxism derives largely from the fact that Soviet Marxism understands and respects this, while Maoism understands but rejects it. Soviet Marxism and Stalinism sought to control the university and to guarantee the loyalty of intellectuals and scientists to Party precepts and leadership; it never sought to stop the university and to eliminate the self-reproduction of the academic intelligentsia, as Maoism has.

Intellectuals are an historically recent social stratum, essentially emerging with the bourgeois revolution during the onset of modernisation in the West. They have, however, been largely recruited from the secular professions of relatively older and more humanistic vintage. They have more likely been scholars, journalists, academicians, artists, writers or lawyers, rather than engineers or scientists. Characteristically, then, the intelligentsia have been associated with long-established (but no longer well-protected) occupations, and were linked to educational and socialising systems that possess and insist on some measure of autonomy.

Unlike the new engineers and scientists, who almost immediately had greater career opportunities and public prestige with the advent of the bourgeois economy, the occupations with which intellectuals were associated had an ambivalent relation to the modern bourgeois order. On the one hand, some were given increased support by the state, in order to win the allegiance of secular ideologists who might help it in controlling the Church, and, in general, they were increasingly released from the personalised controls of partisans or from personalised service as tutors. On the other hand, however, their livelihoods were now often subject to the insecurities of the impersonal marketplace and, except for a few 'stars', the new world of emerging industrialism did not hold this language-manipulating élite in great esteem.

Intellectuals, then, were a social stratum that were freed of corporate and patron controls, but were also limited in the enjoyment of their new freedom by poverty and neglect: bohemia with its deprivations was not only a preferred style of life but for many it was also a necessity. Intellectuals were an élite possessed of a privileged education, but usually lacking in any commensurate *power* - to which they felt their superior education, entitled them - as well as lacking a commensurate *income*. They were, in short, characterised by the tensions typically generated by such status disparities. The very society that had created intellectuals allowed them only a marginal place, so that they were at once both beholden and hostile to the new society. They were the structurally alienated.

Despite the differences between Enlightenment and Romantic intellectuals, Western intellectuals, Marxist or bourgeois – nonetheless shared certain important values. They were committed to the importance of intellectual productivity and performance; whether courtly *philosophes* or bohemian Romantics, they were commonly hard workers. They usually believed in the value of advanced education and of universities, even if they did not always agree on what constituted a good education. They were rationalists even when promulgating an anti-intellectualism. Even the Romantics, despite their special interest in Oriental civilization and languages, undoubtedly viewed European and Western societies as their paradigms – willy-nilly, all were Westernisers. Intellectuals were, too, commonly 'universalistic' in their value commitments, believing that a man's rewards should be proportionate to his performances and achievements. Thus, even Marx says that under socialism the slogan should be: from each according to his ability, to each according to his work! In this universalism, intellectuals were essentially sanctioning the requirements of the *educated sector* of the middle class while embarrassing the *propertied* sector of the middle class, which believed that its property entitled it to unearned incomes. They were also commonly critical of established, respectable religions; if intellectuals were by no means uniformly atheists, they were often modernisers who felt that religion needed to adapt to the requirements of modernity. They commonly resented and challenged authority based on lineage and ascription, affirming the rights of the talented, whether talent was seen as due to educated practice or to inborn genius. While Romantic intellectuals might nostalgically idealise rusticity, even they were not slow to seek their fortunes in salons, courts, marketplaces and other urbane environments, and they had the cosmopolitans' urge to keep in touch with the urban centres. If intellectuals did not always say (with Socrates) that the city was their teacher, they had no doubt that the people of the city were important audiences and markets.

In contrast, Maoist socialism does not regard either urbanisation or 'Westernisation' as the last word. It is *not* obvious, moreover, that Maoism even conceives itself as engaged in 'modernisation'. It is not modernisation but 'cultural revitalization' to which the Chinese Revolution seems committed; it seeks an historically unique kind of revitalisation, since it does not look to the glories of the past, and in that sense is not 'nativistic', and does not to change itself by Westernisation. It is this unique 'development' policy that undergirds the educational policies of the Cultural Revolution and its effort to alter the intelligentsia. In the self-understanding of Maoism, the aim is to de-bourgeoisify the intellectual; to eliminate the rift between intellectuals and masses; to change the class character of intellectuals by changing their class origins, so that in future they derive predominantly from workers or peasants, and themselves have an extensive personal experience of labouring as peasants or workers. This, to repeat, is Maoism's self-understanding of its policy toward the intelligentsia.

Yet if Maoism is a critique of the bourgeois intellectual in terms of egalitarian values, if it rejects the old intellectuals because they were an élite set above the masses, it remains difficult to understand why Maoism has allowed a great gap to persist in the income levels of workers and intellectuals. Top academicians may earn as much as seven to eight times more than the average worker, and the ratio of the top and bottom levels in the university itself is about 12 to 1, and has over the years been growing. This inconsistency, however, would be reconciled if we did not accept the self-understanding of Maoism and, instead of conceiving it as an effort to overthrow *all* élitism, we would think of it, rather, as an effort to make a *new* élite, an élite which has broken radically with the traditions of the past, an élite which rejects Western models of development.

Maoism's policy toward the intelligentsia is, in part, grounded in the very special conditions of the Chinese economy and social structure. Michael Frolic quotes a Chinese official who makes the major point: 'The new Chinese educational system is designed to maximise the even development of a peasant society.' The crucial statistic is that China has 150,000,000 city dwellers but some 690,000,000 peasants. (Contrast this with the United States where the college population now exceeds the farm population, even when the latter includes women and children.) Maoist policies, Frolic also indicates, limit the priorities assigned to urban development and aims to curb urbanisation as well as to decentralise industry.

Kosok formulates this development from the standpoint of a critical Marxism:

> . . .the Chinese are attempting to destroy at its root the classical Western antagonism between city and country, industry and agriculture, culture and the hinter-lands, 'production-control-direction' centers and 'consumption-living' centers. . .To decentralise and ruralise the land instead of regimenting the countryside to the city and turning the whole land into a gigantic production unit.
>
> (The proletariat is therefore not just the *industrial* worker, but the entire working population which is alienated from its praxis and the control of its living process.)

This is an historically unique policy of economic development that must be understood as the domestic counterpart to the *foreign* policy of a country whose technologically superior enemies threaten it with nuclear blackmail. In one part, Mao's slowdown of urbanisation is an effort to arrange. China's internal social order so that, if it must, it will be able to survive even nuclear warfare. China will therefore for a long while remain a predominantly peasant and rural society, and, given Maoism's unique conception of development, it has far less need of academic intellectuals. Indeed, Guillain claims that 'China's need for university-educated personnel is still relatively limited . . .[and] the country even had a glut of graduates before the Cultural Revolution.'

Maoism's policies toward intellectuals have in part to be understood, then, in the light of China's limited need for them at this stage of its development. Mao's unique policy of economic development is the infrastructure of his policy concerning the intellectuals. Nonetheless, the central fact remains that Mao's policies were *militantly* anti-intellectual. They were inspired less by market considerations of supply and demand than by *political* considerations: they were inspired, specifically, by the intellectuals' tendecy to suspect and to resist precisely Mao's fundamental policy of limiting urbanisation and decentralising industry. It is, I believe, the intellectuals' resistance to *this* unique conception of development that Mao regards as proof of their abiding bourgeois and antisocialist character. It is, above all, intellectuals' resistance to a new and non-Western form of development – including a commitment to an anti-élitist egalitarianism – that led Mao to seek the radical transformation of intellectuals.

> In the Chairman's view the intellectuals are suspect because. . .they have been a source of resistance or reaction to Communist ideas. . . A characteristic Mao statement given wide publicity during the Cultural Revolution ran: 'I shall always believe that the vast majority of intellectuals, both within and outside the party, are basically bourgeois'.

Mao's attack upon intellectuals is grounded in an impulse to make a great repture with the past, to make a vast leap forward away from it. It is thus not simply that intellectuals had a different, more Westernizing conception of economic development but also that their link with the past is so profound, that led Mao to come down against them. Inevitably, intellectuals do embody the heritage of the past. However, radical they are, intellectuals are, in the history-rootendness of their learning, inevitably if unwittingly engaged in the *preservation* of the past. Their very 'bookishness' marks them as the agents of cultural continuity. Mao, however, wanted to make a break with the history of China; more than that, he also wanted to make a break with the history of *socialism* itself and with the history of revolutions past. Mao's anti-intellectualism, then, is a way of destroying the links with the past and the limits of the past itself; it is not an expression of a contempt for mind.

Mao has proceeded from the profound understanding that the most fundamental limits on the revolution were not located outside, in the enemy. The diagnosis that the main danger to the revolution is to be found in the resistance and power of the enemy society *outside* was certainly compatible with the experience of the Soviet State. But a voluntaristic Marxism such as Mao's, which believes in the potency of consciousness and commitment, is especially sensitive to the dangers that derive from ambivalence and faintheartedness. From a voluntaristic standpoint, intellectuals have a very speacial importance and, for that reason, it becomes especially important that they be viewed as politically trustworthy.

Those whose ideological view has been sharpened by a kind of Hegelian consciousness look out on the world from a very special perspective. They have a firm insight into the way in which the 'Object' is the creation of the 'Subject'- even if the Object be the enemy and the Subject the revolutionary Self – and they therefore always know that the trouble is not only in the stars but also in themselves. They are not, in short, given to vulgar externalising; their talent and weakness is instead for the subtle searching out of the enemy within, and for internecine vigilance and struggle against him.

Maoism has the deepest and most troubling understanding that a Marxist can have: it understands that Marxism, too, has a false consciousness; it knows that the weakness of Marxism is not only a weakness of its *enemies* but also of Marxism's *friends*. Maoism understand *this:* that Marxism is the child of the very society that it seeks to overthrow and that, as such, there is a way in which Marxism not only has a critical knowledge of the Old Régimes but also a measure of affinity with them. Maoism understands that if the capitalist order gives birth to the 'seeds of its own destruction', then the new order is indeed the affinal product of the old order's seed, not only its enemy, and that there is a certain continuity between Marxism and the old order, not only a revolutionary rupture. Maoism's fear is this: that the old order *lives on* in the new one; that the old order conquers in the midst of its defeat; that the old order passes part of its seed-heritage on and lives *through* the very triumph of the new order. Maoism understands that this is how it is with Marxism, too, in its relation to the old order that it seeks to destroy.

The wistful wisdom of the Chairman, then, is this: there is no permanent revolution, no way forward for a revolution that seeks to live, except by eating its own children; for it is they who constitute the last bridge to the past, and it is they who set the sturdiest limits on the revolution's future. Sartre's Maoist consciousness understands all this very well:

> . . .in the past, the winners have always thought about stopping. Historians claim revolutionaries never know where or when to stop. But it is the contrary. They always do stop, so that the next generation of revolutionaries has felt obliged to go after the previous generation. It happened four times during the French Revolution of 1789–94. Perhaps it would be better if for once a revolutionary movement was ready and willing to go all the way. . .of all the groups within the left today, the undogmatic Maoists. . .are most prepared to do that. . .

Maoism is the Marxism that recognises - or better still, senses without recognising – that there is no way forward for the revolution except through the death of Marxism; that the final limits on the revolution are those imposed and built into Marxism itself; that these limits lay sedimented in the revolutionary intelligentsia, and in the university system that socially reproduces the intelligentsia. Maoism is the Marxism that was brought to the brink of understanding that one has to choose: either Marxism or the permanent revolution – but not both!

One pole from which the crisis of Marxism spreads is the wandering and floundering of the working class; of the proletariat that surrendered its initiative to self-anointed vanguard parties; which accommodated itself both to the great economic crises of capitalism as well as to the seductions of capitalist affluence. At the other pole from which the crisis of Marxism spreads is the decline of the academic intelligentsia.

The relationship between the intelligentsia and proletariat is a relationship between an author and his protagonist, between the cameraman and the actor; between latent structure and manifest structure. Or, as Marx once spoke of them, it is a relation between the head and the heart of the revolution. Together, the proletariat and intelligentsia once constituted the basic infrastructure of enacted Marxism. As both are in the process of being historically transformed, the sociological foundations of Marxism itself are crumbling.

The ultimate false consciousness of Marxism is that the historical role attributed by it to the proletariat was assigned by an invisible intelligentsia, by an intelligentsia that never made an appearance in its own theory, and whose existence and nature are therefore never systematically known even to itself. It is precisely because Maoism has seen through to this ultimately concealed level in Marxism itself that Maoism marks the highest and final stage in the historical development of Marxism. It is precisely because of this that Maoism cannot allow itself to recognise what it gives every evidence of so clearly understanding, namely, that the way forward for the revolution requires an end to the contradictions of Marxism - which is to say, and end to 'Marxism.'

8

Deviance and Social Control

What is Deviance?

A contemporary text on deviance and social control begins, "The subject of this book is knavery, skulduggery, cheating, unfairness, crime, sneakiness, malingering, cutting corners, immorality, dishonesty, betrayal, graft, corruption, wickedness, and sin. . ." (Cohen, 1966, p.1). This description is only partly true, for, as we have seen, even a saint may be considered deviant. *Deviance* is a blanket term that covers everything from genius and saintliness to crime and insanity, rebellion and eccentricity. Indeed, any behaviour that violates social expectations, breaks social norms, strays from the "straight and narrow" path of respectability may be labelled *deviant*.

The sociology of deviance may have begun with Emile Durkheim's observation that behaviours that qualify one person for sainthood may condemn another to prison, a mental asylum, or the stake, (Indeed, the same person may be considered a saint and a sinner, a hero and a heretic in his or her lifetime by different social groups, as Saint Joan was.) Sociologists, Durkheim wrote, "should completely abandon the still too widespread habit of judging an institution, a practice or moral standard as if it were good or bad in and by itself, for all social types indiscriminately" (1964, p. 56). His point, quite simply, was that no act is *inherently* deviant. Deviance is defined by social norms. Even killing another person is considered normal and right if the attacker is wearing a soldier's uniform and fighting for his country. (We never say that a soldier murdered one of the enemy.) Thus, one person may be honoured and another sent to prison for committing the same act.

The changing nature of the social definition of deviance is illustrated by the rise in marijuana smoking. Although possession of the drug is still illegal and subject to severe penalties, as many as 15 million Americans had at least tried marijuana by 1972 (Gallup, April 1972, no. 72). According to Gallup Polls, only 5 per cent of college students surveyed in 1967 had tried marijuana, but 55 per cent of students surveyed in 1974 had smoked it. Although arrests for possession of marijuana rose 43 per cent in 1972 along (*Uniform Crime Reports,* 1973), public attitudes towards the drug are changing. It will be interesting to see if the penalties against marijuana-smokers are softened, in line with greater public acceptance of the drug.

Deviance varies not only with time and from group to group in one society, but it varies cross-culturally as well. In parts of the Near and Far East, for example, opiates are sold on a cash-and-carry basis in open markets, and people smoke marijuana and hashish publicly. Even in this country attitudes toward drugs in general are highly inconsistent. There is little or no stigma attached to taking tranquilisers, sleeping pills, or pain killers obtained with a doctor's prescription, drinking large quantities of alcohol (at socially appropriate times), or smoking tobacco, all of which pose clear health hazards.

Just as ideas about what is and what is not deviant vary, so do explanations of nonconforming behaviour. Once, almost all Americans considered homosexuality an expression of depravity, a sin, a "crime against nature" that showed a person morally unfit for life among decent people. Then homosexuality "became" a mental illness, an unfortunate compulsion that might be cured through psychotherapy. But in 1974 the American Psychiatric Association voted to remove homosexuality from its catalogue of mental illnesses, declaring it to be a "sexual orientation disturbance," not an illness. Similarly, behaviour that was once considered a sign of possession by the devil and evil spirits, punishable by exorcism or burning, became symptoms of mental illness in the twentieth century, treatable by various kinds of therapies and drugs. Indeed, some contemporary psychologist and psychiatrists even argue that the concept of mental illness is a myth (Szasz, 1970).

Whether an act is stigmatised and the person who commits it labelled evil or sick depends, in part, on his or her social status. Many white-collar criminals who violate tax laws, antitrust laws, and the like are fined relatively small proportions of their incomes, but rarely imprisoned (Gibbons, 1968, p. 319). Former vice-president Spiro Agnew walked away from admitted extortion charges a free man. (His penalty was resigning from office, not going to jail.) And Richard Nixon, after his resignation from the presidency, was fully pardoned for any crimes that he might have committed during his years in the White House. In contrast most car thiefs (71 per cent in one study) are sentenced to prison for three years (Mitford, 1973, p. 76). In the final analysis, then the definition of deviance is at least partly a matter of social powers the people who have the power to enforce their definitions decide what is proper and what is deviant.

Explanations of Deviance

During 1972 police learned of more than 18,000 murders and over 40,000 rapes committed in that year. Close to 375,000 people were robbed and an equal number assaulted. Some 880,000 Americans stole cars. There were 1.8 million cases of larceny (thefts of $ 50 and over) and 2.3 million burglaries (*Uniform Crime Reports*, 1973). Undoubtedly, the true figures are much higher: many crimes are never reported. Data on crimes without victims (gambling, prostitution, drug addiction, and so on) are even less reliable. We know only about those people who come to the attention of authorities. Why do people break the law? As we will show in the pages that follow, the answer to the question of why people deviate isn't obvious at all. Numerous theories have been advanced.

Biological Explanations

In the nineteenth-century world view, people were considered rational. They were supposed tö act only in ways advantageous to themselves. "Crime does not pay," so how could someone be rational and yet be a criminal? Cesare Lombroso, an Italian criminologist, suggested an explanation—people could be *born* criminals (Lombroso, 1911). Misinterpreting Darwin's evolutionary theory, he suggested that criminals were throwbacks, more nearly representing our primitive and savage ancestors than modern men and women. This flash hit Lombroso as he examined Villella, an Italian master criminal. He reported excitedly that :

> At the sight of that skull, I seemed to see all of a sudden, lighted up as a vast plain under a flaming sky, the problem of the nature of the criminal—an atavistic being who reproduces in his person the ferocious instincts of primitive humanity and the inferior animals. Thus were explained the enormous jaws, high cheekbones, prominent supercillary arches. . .found in criminals, savages, and apes, insensibility to pain, extremely acute sight, tattooing, excessive idleness, love of orgies, and the irresistible craving for evil for its own sake, the desire not only to extinguish life in the victim, but to mutilate the corpse, tear its flesh, and drink its blood. (Lombroso, in Cohen, 1966, p. 50)

Lombroso and his students made dozens of measurements on the heads and bodies of scores of prisoners, and every criminal fit the "animalistic" pattern. But Lombroso made one serious error—he measured only criminals. When a British physician, Charles Goring, measured ordinary citizens, he found that they were no different, at least physically, from criminals (Goring, 1913).

Although Lombroso's theory was abandoned, the search for a biological explanation for deviance lived on. William Sheldon, an American psychologist and doctor, developed another theory linked to physical characteristics (Sheldon, 1949). He grouped people into three body types: soft and round (endomorphs); hard and rectangular (mesomorphs); and lean and fragile (ectomorphs) Endomorphs, Sheldon claimed, are easygoing friendly, self-indulgent types—the fat jolly person everyone likes. Mesomorphs, he argued, are energetic, hyperactive, impulsive people who rarely stop to think about what they are doing. Ectomorphs are nervous, sensitive and withdrawn. To test his classifications, Sheldon examined two hundred boys at a Boston rehabilitation center, studying their biographies and analysing their physical types. He found that most of the delinquent youngsters were mesomorphs and concluded that their physiology predisposed them to deviance. Mesomorphs, Sheldon argued, are quick to translate impulses into action and lack the sensitivity to consider what they are doing.

Using Sheldon's typology, Sheldon and Eleanor Glueck (1956) compared five hundred delinquent boys to five hundred nondelinquents and found that significantly more of the delinquents were mesomorphs. They concluded that under the right conditions, the "excessive instinctual energy and weak or erratic inhibitory apparatus" of mesomorphs would be expressed in deviant behaviour. The Gluecks added that the relatively small numbers of endomorphs and ectomorphs who became delinquent did so to compensate for their less than ideal build. In this way the researchers covered all possibilities. If an ectomorph conformed to the rules, he was doing what they would predict from his body type. If, on the other hand, he became delinquent, he was also doing what they would predict, namely compensating for his body type.

Although biological explanations of deviance have lost popularity, the possibility of physiological *predispositions* for deviance has not been forgotten. The discovery that Richard Speck, who murdered seven nurses in Chicago in 1966, was genetically abnormal stimulated new research in this field. (A nomal man has an XY chromosome pattern, a normal woman an XX chromosome pattern; Speck has an XXY pattern.) Although the 'XXY' theory of born criminals has been disproved, research in this area continues. Researchers have discovered chemical differences between schizophrenics and other people, and between hyperactive and normally active children. But to date there is no firm proof that genetic or chemical abnormalities produce deviant behaviour.

Psychological Explanations

Freudian psychologists maintain that all people have deviant impulses, but that in the process of growing up most of us learn to inhibit them most of the time. Freud argued that through identification with their parents, children acquire a superego, or conscience, that forbids certain kinds of behaviour, and an ego that enables them to deal realistically with internal drives and social demands.

Psychoanalytic theory suggests that children who are neglected or mistreated may not relate to their parents or other adults in this important way. As a result they do not learn to take the position of the other—to, for example, see burglary or mugging from the victim's point of view. They develop only weak inner controls, and it is these people who violate social expectations. The technical term for a person who does not feel remorse or guilt for harmful actions and has little sense of right and wrong is *sociopath*. This model is often invoked to explain wanton cruelty and crimes committed without apparent motives.

Other deviants, according to the psychodynamic view, have a weak or erratic superego. Although they know that they are about to do something wrong or cruel, they cannot help themselves and succumb to their impulses. For example, a woman may lead an exemplary life, fulfil her responsibilities toward her family and job, but find the desire to shoplift irresistible. Or a person may conform to social norms among his or her "own kind," but not apply these norms to outsiders. A member of a teen-age gang, for example, may treat fellow gang members as brothers, but may feel no qualms about cheating members of rival gangs. Finally, an *overdeveloped* superego may also lead to deviance. People who are repulsed by their own urges may commit deviant acts to receive the punishment they feel they deserve, for hating their parents or for having sexual fantasies, for example (Cohen, 1966, pp. 56-57).

Other psychologists do not agree that we all have aggressive impulses which must be controlled, but simply argue that we learn from those around us. Alberty Bandura and Richard H. Walters, for example, compared groups of delinquent and nondelinquent white adolescent males from financially stable homes (1959). They found that continuously harsh, physical discipline or over indulgence could lead to delinquency. Boys whose fathers frequently beat them tended to rely on external controls, that is, they based decisions on the chances of being caught, not on inner feelings of right and wrong. Furhtermore, they emulated their fathers' violent, retaliatory approach to life. On the other hand, boys who had their parents' uncritical approval grew up believing that anything they wanted to do was good—an assumption the outside world did not always share. Most successful were loving but firm parents.

Sociological Explanations

Although psychological theories of deviance provide insights into individual cases, they do not explain why *rates* of deviance (the number of deviant acts per unit of population) vary from group to group, from neighbourhood to neighbourhood. Sociological theories address this question. Sociologists have found that social environment influences many kinds of deviance—even something so psychological as psychosis and so personal as suicide.

Deviance and Anomie

One sociologist who tried to account for varying rates of crime in different social classes was Robert K. Merton (1957). Merton linked high rates of deviance to anomie. As defined by Durkheim, *anomie* is a state of normlessness or confusion that occurs when cultural formulas for living do not match social realities. For example, the culture may decree that every man must have a job, but the social structure may not provide enough jobs for every man. Merton reasoned that all people internalise, to some degree, the goals that are considered worth striving for in their culture. Everyone, too, internalises the norms governing proper and legitimate ways of striving for these goals. When opportunities for achieving highly valued goals (as the culture defines them) do not exist, people seek alternatives. Thus, "some social structures exert a definite pressure upon certain persons in the society to engage in non-conforming rather than in conforming behaviour (Merton, 1957, p. 132).

Merton defined *conformity* as seeking culturally approved goals by culturally approved means. He outlined four types of deviant behaviour that may occur when social realities do not match cultural expectations (see Table 8.1). The first type is *innovation*—pursuing culturally validated goals by deviant means. A thief, for example, is pursuing the same objectives as a working person—namely money, the things it can buy, and the prestige it confers. They are playing the same game, but with different rules. Merton stresses that poverty alone does not boost crime rates. In a rigidly stratified society the poor do not expect to move up the social ladder. "It is only when a system of cultural values extols, virally above all else, certain *common* goals for the *population at large* while the social structure rigorously restricts or completely closes access to approved modes of reaching these goals for a *considerable part of the same population,* that deviant behaviour ensues on a large scale". Innovations may also occur because culturally prescribed goals are unreachable. The fact that success is defined as more in American culture helps to explain the high incidence of white-collar crime.

Table 8.1
Merton's Model of Adaptation to Cultural Goals

Modes of Adaptation	*Culture Goals*	*Institutionalised Means*
1. Conformity	+	+
2. Innovation	+	–
3. Ritualism	–	+
4. Retreatism	–	–
5. Rebellion	±	±

Source: Robert K. Merton, *Social Theory and Social Structure* (New York: The Free Press, 1956), p. 140.

A second way to resolve conflicts between goals and means is *ritualism,* adhering rigidly to norms at the expense of goals. A bureaucrat who follows regulations to the letter regardless of whether he or she gets the job done is the prototype for this type of deviance. Following the rules becomes a virtue, a goal in itself. Police and firemen, who are prohibited by law from striking, often use ritualism to bring City Hall to the bargaining table. A teacher who maintains order in the classroom and delivers lessons in the prescribed way regardless of whether students learn anything is a ritualist.

Merton notes that ritualists are often not labelled deviant. People may consider bureaucratic rule-sticklers stupid or aggravating, but generally do not put them in the same category as criminals. However, Nazi officials who obeyed inhumane orders were treated as criminals; so was Lieutenant Calley, who was held responsible for the murder of civilians at My Lai.

Merton uses the term retreatism to describe giving up. Retreatists are people who have lost the desire to pursue certain cultural goals as well as the belief that following certain norms is intrinsically worthwhile. Drug addicts, alcoholics, many psychotics, drifters, and bums are examples. These people have withdrawn; they are "*in* the society but not of it." In Merton's view retreatism is an escape mechanism, a way in which people protect themselves from confusion and failure.

Cloward and Ohlin (1960) agreed with Merton's description of retreatism. After comparing different types of delinquency, they concluded that youngsters who become involved in the drug subculture are usually "double losers" who lack the opportunity and ability to succeed both in the legitimate world, as conformists, and in the illegitimate world, as innovators.

Retreatism may also explain the high rates of mental illness among poor people in America, where the strain between goals and opportunities is greatest. Hollingshead and Redlich (1958) and Myers and Bean (1968) have found that rates of commitment to mental hospitals vary inversely with social class—that is, the lower the social class, the higher the rate of hospitalisation. Data also indicate that outpatient psychiatric care is inversely related to income as well (see Figure 8.1).

Finally, people who are alienated from both the goals and standards of their culture may create new ideals and new rules for pursuing them. Merton calls this *rebellion*. The Weathermen, the Panthers, and the Minutemen (right-wing radicals) are examples. Rebellion need not be political, however. Seeking economic self-sufficiency on a rural commune, rejecting conventional marriage and family for freer relationships are also examples of rebellion.

Figure 8.1 : Family income and psychiatric outpatient care, 1969

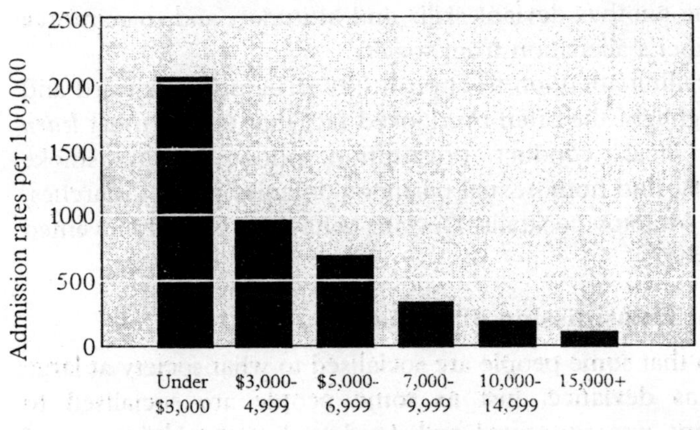

Source: Statistical Note = 47, National Institute of Mental Health, Survey and Report Section, Biometry Branch.

Whether these data reflect the incidence of psychological problems or merely rates of treatment in outpatient clinics is debatable. In all likelihood, more middle and upper class people have problems than the statistics show, but because they are treated privately their problems are not a matter of public record.

The question still remains as to why rebellious subcultures develop in some corners of society an criminal subcultures in others. Cloward and Chlin addressed this problem in their study of delinquency (1960). They concluded that the kind of adaptation people who are denied access to legitimate avenues to legitimate goals make depends on the *opportunity structures* in their environment. Just as some communities offer young people opportunities for education, role-models of people who have achieved success by conventional means, and contacts with people who can advance their careers, so other communities offer opportunities for learning how to hustle and evade authorities, role-models of people who have achieved success as gamblers or pimps, and contacts with the underworld. Ironically, illegitimate opportunity structures thrive in reform schools, prisons, and other institutions whose putative goals are to rehabilitate deviants. Here, people caught breaking rules are segregated from conforming people and have unlimited time to teach one another deviant skills and attitudes, and to reinforce one another's alienation from society.

By calling attention to opportunity structures, Cloward and Ohlin highlight the often overlooked fact that people must *learn* how to steal, conduct prostitution, shoot heroin, smoke marijuana, find homosexual partners, organise protest marches, or make Molotov cocktails. Deviant behaviour is rarely invented on the spot.

Cultural Transmission of Deviance

The idea that some people are socialised to what society at large regards as deviance, just as some people are socialised to conformity, was conceived and developed at the University of Chicago in the 1920s and 1930s (Cohen, 1966, p. 94). Clifford Shaw and Henry McKay (1929) found that high crime rates persisted in the same Chicago neighbourhoods for over twenty years, even though different ethnic groups and come and gone. Obviously, ethnic traditions could not explain the crime rate. Shaw and McKay concluded that newcomers learned deviant ways from established residents, primarily in play groups and teenage gangs. Eventually they passed these norms and values on to new waves of immigrants. Thus, deviance may be learned through the natural process of cultural transmission. In a similar way, people might be socialised to the drug subculture, the homosexual subculture, the radical subculture, and so on.

The effects of norms and values on young people growing up in high-crime neighbourhoods was the subject of a study conducted by Walter B. Miller (1958). During a three-year participant-observation study Miller identified the "focal concerns" of lower-class, urban, adolescent males: trouble (with the law and with women); toughness (physical prowess and playing it cool); smartness (being able to outsmart and con others and avoid being conned oneself, as well as a respect for verbal quickness and ingenuity), fate (a sense that many forces are beyond one's control, that success is a matter of luck); and autonomy (a resentment of outside controls—"No one's gonna push me around"). Miller argues that such delinquent acts as drinking or stealing cars are expressions of these important subcultural concerns. Like all adolescents, ghetto youth are eager to demonstrate their adulthood and to gain and maintain status among their peers. Miller argues that delinquency is "a directed attempt. . .to adhere to forms of behaviour, and to achieve standards as they are defined in that community" (p. 5).

Of course, ghetto youngsters also encounter many role-models who conform to and advocate conventional goals and means. Why do some youths choose deviant over conforming styles. In *Principles of Criminology*, Edwin H. Sutherland (1960) pointed out that *everyone* is exposed to different, often conflicting definitions of right and wrong—to people who value obeying the law and to people who consider the law merely a hindrance and the police as enemies. The standards people adopt as their own depend on the frequency, duration, priority, and intensity of their association with procriminal or anticriminal, radical or conservative, heterosexual or homosexual ideas. Thus, if those who matter most to a person devalue conformity, he or she will try to learn techniques for committing deviant acts and will accept rationalisations for committing them.

Labelling and Deviant Careers

In the late 1950s some sociologists began wondering if they hadn't been asking the wrong questions about deviance. Virtually everyone breaks rules at one time or another. A survey of nearly seventeen hundred New Yorkers, for example, revealed that 99 per cent had violated the penal code at least once. And a random sample revealed that as many as one in five residents of midtown Manhattan is severely disturbed, though none of these are hospitalised (Srole et al., 1962). And Kinsey found that 37 per cent of American men reported one or more homosexual experiences. Most of these people do not think of themselves as deviants—nor do other people. Their nonconformity is one, perhaps secret, aspect of an otherwise respectable life. However, others who have performed the very same acts (or been falsely accused of doing so) are branded criminal, psychotic, or queer for the rest of their lives. A key question, then, is why some people get labelled as deviant while others, who commit the same acts, do not.

Labelling

Suppose a man meets a girl in a park; they talk and later go to bed together. The affair lasts a month or two, and then they part. But, suppose the girl is only fourteen, although she looks and pretends to be older. She has become pregnant, and to save face tells her parents she was raped. The man is taken to court and convicted. He loses his job and cannot find another. His future, in that town at least, is ruined. Even if he is acquitted, the accusation and trial would tarnish his respectability. Wherever he goes, people stare and whisper: RAPIST. For the girl, refusal to tell anyone who the father of her child is would burden her with the full stigma of unwed motherhood. If she reveals the father, her fate partly depends on how her parents react—on whether they agree to help her support the child, arrange an abortion, or declare her incorrigible and send her to a reform school. In this way she, too, might be labelled deviant.

As Howard S. Becker suggests in *Outsiders* (1963), people perform deviant acts for various reasons. They even may not know they are doing anything wrong, like the man in the story above. Or people may know they are breaking a rule, but calculate that the ends justify the means. Or they may simply have no reputation to maintain, no stake in appearing to be a normal and conventional person. Whatever their reasons for deviating, their fate depends, *not* on the reason, but on whether they are caught and publicly *labelled* deviant.

Deviant labels—queer, lunatic, thief, junkie—have an almost magical quality. They tend to wipe out whatever favourable impressions a person may create. One day he is the man next door, a good friend and neighbour. The next day people discover he is not what he was supposed to be, he *is* a homosexual. "The question is raised: 'What kind of person would break such an important rule?' And the answer is given: 'One who is different from the rest of us, who cannot or will not act as a moral human being and therefore might break other important rules' (Becker, 1963, pp. 33-34). The deviant label becomes a master status, colouring all other aspects of the person's identity.

Who Gets Labelled

As the statistics at the beginning of this section indicate, only a fraction of the people who break rules are caught and publicly discredited. Sociologists are interested in discovering the kinds of people who *do* get labelled. In the 1960s William J. Chambliss (1973) spent two years as a participant-observer at "Hannibal High School". During this period he became acquainted with the members of two gangs, the Saints and the Roughnecks. The eight members of the Saints came from upper-middle-class families; they were good students and active in school affairs. On weekends and on days when they sneaked out of school (most days, Chambliss found), the Saints amused themselves with various forms of delinquency: heavy drinking, reckless driving, games of "chicken," petty theft, and vandalism. A favourite pastime was removing the wooden barricades and lanterns from street repair sites and watching unsuspecting drivers cruise into the hole. Although their activities were hazardous, townspeople considered them good boys who were sowing a few wild oats. Stealing small items and breaking into empty houses were considered pranks. Not one Saint was arrested in the two years Chambliss spent at "Hannibal High".

In contrast, the six Roughnecks were in constant trouble with the police, and townspeople considered them good-for-nothings. The Roughnecks came from lower-class families and were not particularly good students. Most weekends they could be found hanging around the local drugstore, drinking from concealed bottles. Almost every month they got into a fight—usually among themselves. Like the Saints, they stole, more for profit than for thrills. Even so, Chambliss estimates that property damage by the Saints cost townspeople *more* than the Roughnecks thefts. And although the Saints rarely fought, they endangered their own and other people's lives nearly every time they got behind the wheel of a car.

Why did townspeople wink at the Saints but condemn the Roughnecks as delinquents? One reason was that the Saints had cars and left the immediate community for their drinking bouts. The Roughnecks, too poor to own cars, were more visible. In addition, the police knew from experience that the Saints' upper-middle-class parents would cause trouble if their children were arrested insisting their sons were just having fun and putting police on the defensive. The Roughnecks' parents did not have the power and influence to protect them. Finally, the Saints dressed nicely, drove good cars, and spoke politely to teachers, police, and other authorities. Anyone could see they were "good boys," tomorrow's leaders. The Roughnecks were different: "everyone agreed that the not-so-well-dressed, not-so-well-mannered, not-so-rich boys were heading for trouble" (p. 27). In short, the community's social structure protected the Saints but not the Roughnecks. Additional studies of social power and labelling are discussed in the Box 8.1.

Table 8.2
Effect of Four Types of Legal Folders On
Job Opportunities (by per cent)

	No Record	*Acquitted with letter*	*Acquitted without letter*	*Convicted*	*Total*
Positive response	36	24	12	4	19
Negative response	64	76	88	96	81
Total	100	100	100	100	100

Source: The Other Side (New York: The Free Press, 1963), p. 110.

The Consequences of Labelling: Stigma and the Deviant Career: Typically, people who are labelled criminals, declared mentally ill, or branded queer are excluded from conventional social life. They may or may not be isolated physically, that is, in a prison or a mental hospital, but nearly always they are isolated socially. A man convicted of a crime describes the experience :

> And I always have this feeling with straight people—that whenever they're being nice to me, pleasant to me, all the time really, underneath they're only assessing me as a criminal and nothing else. It's too late for me to be any different now to [sic] what I am, but I still feel this keenly, that that's their only approach, and they're quite incapable of accepting me as anything else. (in Goffman, 1963, p. 14)

Box 8.1

Social Power and Deviant Labels

A study conducted by Richard Schwartz and Jerome Skolnick offers proof that middle - and upper-class people are often able to "get away" with the kinds of behaviour that earn deviant labels for the poor and the powerless. Schwartz and Skolnick sent four different applications to a total of one hundred employers. All four described a thirty-two-year-old, single, male high-school graduate who had held a series of jobs including kitchen helper and handyman. One of the applications stated that the man had been convicted for assault; the second noted that he had been tried for assault and acquitted; the third included a letter from the judge certifying that he had been found not guilty, and the fourth said nothing about a criminal record. The responses (Table 8.2) show clearly that employers made little distinction between conviction and acquittal, even when a judge certified the applicant's innocence.

In a second, parellel study, Schwartz and Skolnick interviewed fifty-seven medical doctors who had been accused of malpractice (which is roughly equivalent to being arrested for assault). Thirty-eight had won their cases, fifteen had settled out of court, and four had lost in court. Fifty-two of the doctors reported that the malpractice suit had no effect on their careers, and five indicated that their practices had actually *improved* after the suit. In fact, the doctor who suffered the heaviest loss in court reported the most improvement after the case. He reasoned that other doctors felt sorry for him and were sending him more referrals. Thus, a doctor who was found guilty escaped labelling, but a high-school graduate who was found innocent was nevertheless stigmatised.

Source : Richard D. Schwartz Jerome H. Skolnick, "Tow Studies of Legal Stigma," in Howard S. Becker, ed., *The Other Side* (New York Free Press, 1964), pp. 103–117.

The stigma of deviance may even extend to a person's family, as when a poor family is denied public housing because one child has been arrested or convicted for juvenile delinquency. In the Box 8.2, a respected member of the medical profession explains that for years he hid his homosexuality to avoid the severe consequences that revelation would have brought for both himself and his family.

Box 8.2

In The News

The Agony of Secrecy

In December 1973, Dr. Howard J. Brown, professor of the public administration of health at New York University, publicly acknowledged his homosexuality in a statement to a symposium of six hundred physicians.

Dr. Brown revealed how the fear of being discovered had shaped every aspect of his life. Should he be seen in restaurants or theaters with male friends? Could he live with another male? Admit that he liked to cook? As a young man, Brown had hoped to become a small town doctor, but moved to New York City's liberal Greenwich Village when he realised the problems for homosexuals in small towns were insurmountable. In 1967 he resigned as New York City's health services commissioner after hearing rumors that a journalist was planning to write a column about homosexuals in city government.

Why did Dr. Brown issue his statement? He told reporters:

> You get to a point in your own life where you want to leave a legacy—in a sense this can help free the generation that comes after us from the dreadful agony of secrecy, the constant need to hide.

He added that he knew of many highly respected clergymen, politicians, and doctors who were homosexual, but doubted they would follow him in public disclosure.

> They feel such a disclosure would ruin their professional career, destroy their reputation and wreck many friendships. And indeed in my own case, until recently I would have assumed that following my public appearance as a homosexual, that the only proper next step would be suicide.

Interestingly, the Skolnick and Schwartz study we discussed earlier suggests that public disclosure of medical malpractice may carry a lighter stigma than homosexuality. But times are changing. Brown's disclosure led not to ostracism, but to his appointment as chairman of committee to combat discrimination against homosexuals for the Public Health Association of New York.

Source : Marcia Chambers, *The New York Times* (Oct. 3, 1973): 1, 42.

Deviant labels tend to become self-fulfilling prophecies. Chambliss found that with few exceptions, the Saints and

Roughnecks lived up (and down) to community expectations. As Goffman has written, "one response to this fate [being labelled deviant] is to embrace it" 1963B, p. 30). This is the final step toward a deviant career. Cut off, the addict begins to associate almost exclusively with other addicts, the prostitute with other prostitutes (Often these associations are made in prisons and in other institutions aimed at *correcting* deviant inclinations.) Gradually the person develops new understandings and routines. He or she learns techniques for deviating from more experienced offenders. Equally important, career-deviants learn rationalisations for deviant behaviour. For example, prostitutes grow to regard their work as a social service and consider those who condemn sex for money as hypocrites. The deviant subculture begins to play an increasingly central role in the person's identity and life-style. As one addicted told a researcher, she realised she was addicted when she noticed that all of her friends were junkies (Becker 1963, p. 38). Thus, in labelling certain people deviant and shutting them out of conventional life, society virtually *assures* the behaviour it is trying to control, an outcome few people consider.

A Critique of Labelling Theory

While this description of the drift into deviant careers is compelling, in several ways it verges on "liberal overkill" Labelling theorists imply that the people who fill the wards of mental hospitals, for example, are there because someone more or less arbitrarily decided to label them sick and subject them to the consequences. They tend to ignore the fact that most of the people in mental hospitals were unable to cope with their lives and their problems outside. Many, too, are dangerous or highly disruptive to themselves and to others. At least one researcher found that both families and authorities consider commitment to a mental hospital a very last resort, and exhaust all other alternatives before launching commitment proceedings (Gove, 1970).

This is not to say that labelling theory is "wrong," but that it only partly explains deviant careers. It does not say why people violate rules in the first place or why some people are able to resist or overcome the stigma of deviance. But labelling theory does help us to focus on the social structure of power behind the rules. What really matters is who makes the rules and who has the power to make the labels stick. This is the underlying theme of social control.

Social Control

In any community, the purpose of social control is to encourage conformity. The chapter on socialization partly answered the question: Why do most people conform? In different ways each of the theorists discussed in that chapter explained how and why cultural standards become part of the growing child's personality structure. Sociologists use the term *internalisation* to describe this process. Internalisation means that people have so thoroughly accepted certain norms and values that deviating from them is largely unthinkable. They abide by these rules not because they fear being labelled and perished for nonconforming behaviour, but to avoid *self*-condemnation. Deviating from these norms makes most people feel guilty and disoriented. In effect, each person learns to distinguish between "me" and "not me," between behaviour that seems consistent with his or her self-image or identity and behaviour that does not.

It is easy to forget that internalised norms and values are the basis of social order: people police themselves. But socialisation is never "perfect" : people may not internalise all of the rules society considers "right." A variety of informal and formal social controls fill this gap.

Informal Social Controls

Fear of ostracism pressures people to conform to norms and values they have not fully internalised. A silent stare, the "cold shoulder." Gossip, laughter, ridicule, verbal and physical threats, a parent's or spouse's tears and exhortations—as well as smiles and other rewards for conformity—are everyday mechanisms of *informal social control.* Often the mere anticipation of disapproval from family, friends, co-workers, even strangers in a public place stops people from engaging in deviant activities. Indeed, disregard for public opinion—as when people talk to themselves or masturbate in public—is considered a primary symptom of mental illness (Goffman, 1963A).

However, informal controls can work in the opposite direction, pressuring conforming individuals into deviant acts. For example, an adolescent may steal or take drugs to gain prestige among his or her peers, or adults may embezzle to maintain the standard of living people expect of them. In addition, the norms of family and friendship require people to protect deviants who are close to them. The words *tattletale, fink* and *informer* are not terms of praise. As a result, modern societies depend heavily on institutionalised formal controls.

Formal Social Controls

Formal social controls are all those organisations and roles specifically designed to enforce conformity in a society, including police departments, courts, prisons, juvenile facilities, mental hospitals, drug rehabilitation centers, and settlement houses and other social-work agencies. Police, judges, and prison and hospital guards are the most obvious agents of social control, but psychiatrists, social workers, ministers, teachers, and lawyers are also in positions to enforce conformity. In the pages that follow we will focus on society's efforts to determine how much crime there really is and on efforts to control it.

Measuring Crimes and Corrections

Each year the FBI issues the *Uniform Crime Report,* a compilation of national statistics on seven serious crimes: murder, rape, robbery, aggravated assault, burglary, larceny of $50 or more, and auto theft. In 1972 a total of 5,891,900 crimes were committed, including 828,150 crimes of violence and 5,063,800 crimes against property. The FBI also converts the number of crimes into crime rates (crimes per 100,000 population) and measures trends. Crime rates ensure that crimes are related to the appropriate population base. Between 1967 and 1972 the violent-crime rate rose 67 per cent; and the rate of crimes against property rose 53 per cent (see Figures 8.2 and 8.3).

Is the *Uniform Crime Report* an accurate measure of criminal activity in this country? Yes and no. The FBI tabulates only those crimes that come to the attention of police. By all estimates the number of unreported crimes is much higher. For example, in 1965-1966, the National Opinion Research Center (NORC) polled a national sample of ten thousand households, asking whether anyone in the family had been the victim of crime during the preceding year. According to this survey crime rates are about twice as high as FBI statistics indicate. A similar survey conducted in Washington, D.C., revealed an even wider gap (see Figure 8.4). When asked why they hadn't reported crimes, most people told NORC interviewers they knew the police couldn't do

Figure 8.2 : Crimes of violence 1967–1972

+70
+60
+50
+40
+30
+20
+10
0

Violent crime up 67%
rate up 50%

1967 1968 1969 1970 1971 1972

Limited to murder, forcible rape, robbery and aggravated assault.

Source: Uniform Crime Reports (Washington, D.C.: Government Printing Office, 1972), p. 4.

Figure 8.3 : Crimes against property 1967–1972

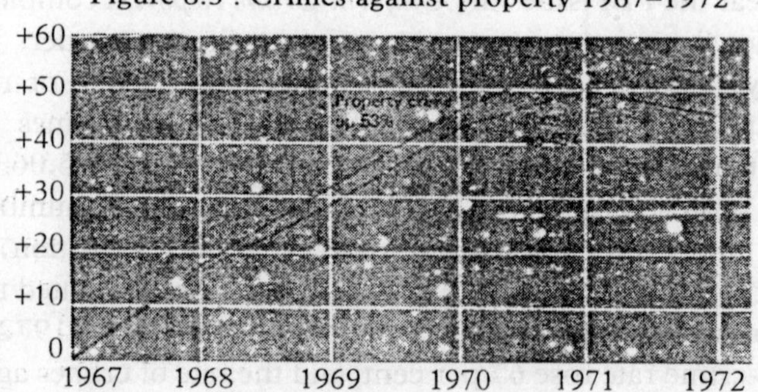

Limited to burglary, larceny $50 and over, and auto theft

Source: Uniform Crime Reports (Washington, D.C.: Government Printing Office, 1972) p. 3.

Figure 8.4 : Estimated rates of offence[1] : comparison of police[2] and bureau of social science research survey data, 1967

Three Washington, D.C. precincts
rates per 1,000 residents 18 years or over

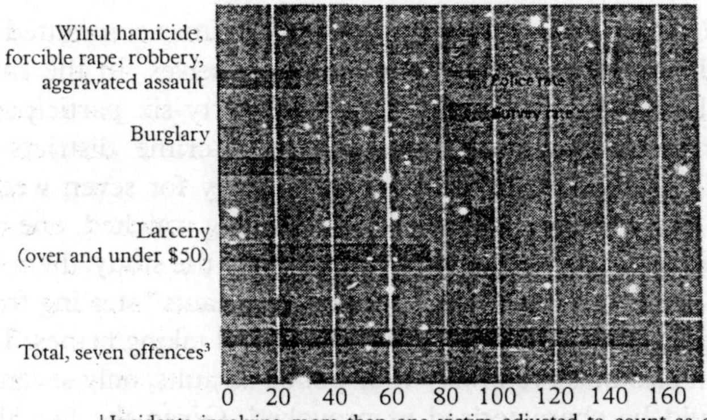

Wilful hamicide, forcible rape, robbery, aggravated assault

Police rate

Survey rate

Burglary

Larceny (over and under $50)

Total, seven offences[3]

0 20 40 60 80 100 120 140 160

[1] Incidents involving more than one victim adjusted to count as only one offense. A victimisation rate would count the incidence for each individual.
[2]Police statistics adjusted to eliminate nonresident and commercial victims and victims under 18 years of age.
[3]Wilful homicide, forcible rape, robbery, aggravated assault, burglary, larceny (over and under $50), and motor vehicle their.

Source: Albert Biderman, *The Annals,* November, 1967, page 20.

The extent of unreported crime during one year in Washington, D.C., can be seen in the above graphs. The survey rates for various offences are from three to ten times greater than the reported rates.

anything, so why bother? A smaller number said they didn't want to get the offender in trouble. (Eighty-eight per cent of murders, 66 per cent of rapes, and 75 per cent of assaults are committed by family members or acquaintances, [Mitford, 1973, p. 61]. Others said they feared reprisal. Presumably many white-collar crimes go unreported because businesses would rather avoid an investigation of their books, and find it easier to charge consumers an extra 1 or 2 per cent than to prosecute embezzlers, shoplifters, and so on.

Nor does the FBI collect statistics on murder, assault, and theft committed by mine owners, slum landlords, construction companies, car manufactures, and other corporations that violate health and safety codes (resulting in death an injury) and rob consumers through deceptive advertising and packaging (Mitford, 1973, p. 64). In most cases such violations are not even considered crimes, and charges against companies are settled in civil suits or out of court. (No one goes to jail when workers are killed in a mine that has been repeatedly cited for fire and safety violations.)

The *Uniform Crime Report* also ignores crimes committed by police, who, of course, do not report themselves. In the mid-sixties Albert J. Reiss, Jr. and a team of thirty-six participant-observers accompanied patrolmen in high-crime districts of Boston, Chicago, and Washington, D.C., daily for seven weeks. Although the policemen knew they were being watched, one out of five committed crimes during the course of the study, the most common being stealing from drinks and "deviants" stealing from establishments that had been burglarised, and taking bribes. The Reiss team also observed forty-four police assaults, only seven of which could be characterised as provoked. Given the fact that these officers knew they were being watched and presumably modified their behaviour, Reiss concluded that police routinely break more laws than his observations indicated (1971).

The FBI's calculation of rising crime rates is also deceptive. The increase in larceny, for example, reflects higher prices as well as more crimes. The fact that bicycles cost $50 or more today may account for much of the increase in larceny rates. The "crime explosion" also reflects improved, computerised methods of recording crimes. After all, it is to the FBI's advantage to find dramatic increases in the crime rates; the more crimes reported, the more money Congress allocates to the bureau for law enforcement procedures (Mitford, 1973, p. 64).

How do the police and courts handle the 5 million or more crimes that are reported? In 1972 police arrested 22 per cent of the close to 5.5 million reported law-breakers—which means that 78 per cent went unapprehended. Eighty-three per cent of the adults arrested were prosecuted in the courts. Of those, 59 per cent were found guilty as charged, and 12 per cent were guilty of a lesser charge. About 30 per cent of the cases were either acquitted or dismissed.

In 1972, 36 per cent of all murder defendants were either acquitted or their cases dismissed at some stage in the prosecution process. Forty-nine per cent of those charged with forcible rape were acquitted or had their cases dismissed, and 41 per cent of the persons charged with aggravated assault won their freedom through acquittal or dismissal *(Uniform Crime Reports,* 1972, pp. 35, 107). In 1965 less than 3 per cent of known, serious crimes actually resulted in prison terms. What these figures show is that the correctional system is highly selective: very few of the people who commit crimes are prosecuted to the full extent of the law. And the majority of these are young, male, poor, and in four cases out of ten, nonwhite (Mitford, 1973, p. 133). In other words prisoners are selected.

The Social Dynamics of Crime Control

In theory a policeman's job is to enforce the law. In practice though, police decide *when* and *how* to enforce the law, because arresting all law-breakers would be impossible. In the course of a day police make numerous decisions about what constitutes a crime and what persons should or should not be arrested. In making such decisions, usually in the heat of the moment, police must consider their responsibility to the public and to their superiors for maintaining order. They must also think about maintaining their own authority on the street, if they are to do their job at all (Reiss, 1971). In the end they rely on their own judgment (on "instincts" and experience) in deciding who is a danger to the community and who threatens police authority. In plain language, they arrest people whom they "know" to be potential or actual trouble-makers.

This discretionary application of formal controls was clear in police harassment of the rough-mannered, back-talking Roughnecks and toleration of the smooth, middle-class Saints, mentioned earlier. Jessica Mitford (1973) discovered an even more startling example of police "discretion". Several years ago seniors from a wealthy California high school went on a rampage of vandalism, arson, breaking and entering car theft, assault, and rape. After a conference with local leaders, police returned the young people to their parents, who promised to discipline them. No formal action was taken. In a nearby ghetto that same week, a nine-year-old boy was arrested for stealing a nickel from a schoolmate and placed in a detention center for six weeks to await a hearing (pp. 55-56). The ghetto child fit the police image of a criminal type; the wealthy vandals did not. In one experiment at the University of California, twelve sociology students who had clean driving records put Black Panther stickers on their car bumpers. Within seventeen days they had collected thirty citations and used up the $1,000 allotted for the experiment (Mitford, 1973, pp. 53-54).

This screening process continues in the courts. Studies of bail hearings held shortly after a person is arrested indicate that judges tend to trust white middle-class offenders to appear for trial, but demand bail from the poor (white and black), who are least able to afford it (Bell, 1973). Why? The President's Crime Commission (Katzenbach 1967) reasoned:

> Most city prosecutors and judges have middle-class backgrounds and a high degree of education. When they are confronted with a poor, uneducated defendant, they may have difficulty judging how he fits into his own society or culture. They can easily mistake a certain manner of dress or speech, alien or repugnant to them but ordinary enough in the defendant's world, as index of moral worthlessness. They can mistake ignorance or fear of the law as indifference to it. They can mistake the defendant's resentment against the social evils with which he lives as evidence of criminality.

Despite the presumption of innocence in our legal code, a defendant who cannot raise bail is held in jail and in large cities many wait a full year to come to trial.

Ninety per cent of people who are arrested and charged agree to plead guilty to a lesser charge. By doing this, they avoid the risk of receiving a verdict of guilty and a more severe penalty. This procedure is known as plea-bargaining or "copping a plea". The Supreme Court declared it legal in 1969, acknowledging that it saves the state the expense of lengthy trials and lessens the already staggering burden on the courts. The Supreme Court only required that the defendants be thoroughly informed of their right to trial and that the "bargains" be officially recorded.

The most notorious example of plea-bargaining in recent years was Spiro T. Agnew's plea of "no contest," whereby he avoided prosecution for extortion and other serious crimes that could have sent him to jail. More often however, it is the poor who, lacking the money for a good defense, plea-bargain. Statistics indicate that defendants who insist on a trial, if found guilty, receive sentences twice as long as those who plead guilty (Mitford, 1973, p. 76).

Unless a state imposes mandatory penalties for specified crimes, sentencing is left to the judge's discretion. And, as with labelling and arrests, social status and power play a role. Nonwhites typically serve longer terms than whites found guilty of the same crime, but blacks who commit crimes against blacks serve shorter terms than blacks who commit crimes against whites (Bell, 1973). As a rule white businessmen receive very light penalties. "Most judges justify the minimal sentences they give to businessman-criminals—fines, probation, or exceedingly short jail terms—on the grounds that when such a man is convicted, he generally loses his job, his standing in the community, and his family's respect" (Lesley Oelsner, in Mitford, 1973, p. 75). Spiro Agnew, for example, was fined $10,000 and given a suspended sentence, but the average car thief goes to jail for three years.

Prisons

Prisons are a relatively modern invention. One-hundred and fifty or two hundred years ago, convicted criminals were killed, maimed, branded (for example, with a scarlet A for adultery), or deported (as often as not, to the New World). The idea of locking people up, which began to take hold in the mid-nineteenth century, was based on the equation of crime with vice and the assumption that isolation and hard work would make the sinner reconsider his or her errant ways and repent. But once prisons were established, they became institutionalised.

What functions do prisons perform? Most obviously, they *punish* criminals for their wrongdoings. Clearly, prisoners do suffer, and most people consider this just. (The desire for retribution may be fading, however. See Table 8.3). Second, prisons are supposed to *protect the public* by taking known deviants off the streets. In addition, they are thought to act as a *deterrent,* discouraging those on the outside from breaking laws and those on the inside from ommitting crimes after they are released. Finally, there is much talk of prisons *rehabilitating* offenders through training programmes and counselling, so that when they are released they approach life with a new, law-abiding frame of mind. These different goals present each prison warden with a difficult and conflicting mandate.

Table 8.3
Present and Ideal View or Purpose of Prison (by per cent)

Response	*Prisons Are*	*Prisons should be*
Mainly corrective	57	77
Mainly punitive	19	11
Not sure	24	12
Total	100	100

Source: Harris Poll, *Los Angeles Times,* August 14, 1967.

> Somehow he [the prison warden] must resolve the claims that the prison should exact vengeance, erect a specter to terrify the actual or potential deviant, isolate the known offender from the free community, and effect a change in the personality of his captives so that they gladly follow the dictates of law - and in addition maintain order within his society of prisoners and see that they are employed at useful labour. (Sykes, 1958, pp. 44-45).

Prison Life In *The House of the Dead,* Dostoevsky wrote :

> Besides the loss of freedom, besides the forced labour, there is another torture in prison life, almost more terrible than any other—that is compulsory life in common.
>
> I could never have imagined, for instance, how terrible and agonising it would be never once for a single minute to be alone for the ten years of my imprisonment.

Loss of privacy is one of the characteristics of total institutions. Under constant surveillance, crowded together with other inmates at all times, required to use open showers and toilets, a person is deprived of the ability to manage the impression he or she makes on others; there is no time off-stage. Public physical examinations (anal and, for women, pelvic) made upon arrival to detect contraband seem designed to strip prisoners of all dignity. Often, new inmates are paraded naked in front of cat-calling residents. As Goffman (1963A) suggests, humiliation and violation of a person's physical integrity are part of the breaking in (or more accurately breaking down) process.

Censorship also represents a violation of privacy. Today many states forbid prison authorities from opening letters to and from a prisoner's lawyers and public officials, but letters to family are read. Prisoners who hope to win parole must say the "right" things, limiting themselves to safe banalities in a way that further weakens family bonds (Schwartz, 1972).

One prisoner told a researcher that the worst part of prison is having nowhere to go when tensions begin to mount. On the outside people can avoid confrontations and consequent "trouble" by leaving the scene; in prison, there is no escaping challenges or insults.

The second biggest problem in this prisoner's view is the absence of heterosexual activity. Homosexuality is more widespread in prisons than most officials would like to admit. Alan J. Davis (1971) estimates there are about a thousand homosexual rapes each year in the Philadelphia prisons alone. Only a handful are reported—because victims fear retribution or being locked in solitary for their own protection. Rape victims also fear that guards will expose them to outsiders. Reasoning that masturbation is a more likely way of coping with heterosexual deprivation, Davis concludes that these attacks are more aggressive than sexual. The aggressor gets his "kicks" from degrading the victim. David A. Ward and Gene G. Kassebaum (1971) found that 50 per cent or more of female inmates engage in homosexual activity while in prison. For almost all it is a temporary habit.

The prisoners' third main complaint is the deprivation of meaningful work and of the right to make decisions about how to spend their time. Prisoners do work, but usually at boring, unskilled jobs (such as making license plates) in antiquated, overstaffed shops that bear little resemblance to work on the outside. At one New Jersey prison that houses mostly black offenders who will return to cities, prisoners work in the fields and barns (WNBC, 1974). What use will learning how to milk a cow be to them on the outside?

Do Prisons "Work"?

The cost of locking a person up for a year is between $6,000 and $10,000 (as prison critics note, this is enough to send a person to Harvard with a handsome allowance and a summer vacation in Europe). This amounts to nearly $12 billion annually (WNBC, 1974). What does this money buy?

Clearly, prisons do not protect the public. Only 3 per cent of the people known to have committed crimes ever go to jail; 1.5 per cent if we include unreported crimes. Moreover, most prison officials estimate that, at most, 15 to 25 per cent of inmates are actually dangerous (Mitford, 1973, p. 285).

Nor do most prisons accomplish anything that might be called rehabilitation. Between 67 and 80 per cent of inmates return to prison again and again. Indeed, prisons may socialise people *to* deviance, as suggested earlier. Many observers consider them "schools for crime," where one-time offenders learn the tricks and rationalisations of deviant careers. In the seventies it might be more accurate to call prisons "schools for radicalism," where the young, alienated prisoners learn to see themselves as victims of oppression. For example, the Symbionese Liberation Army, which kidnapped Patricia Hearst in 1974, apparently originated in California's Vacaville Prison (Sykes. 1974).

And there is little evidence that prisons act a deterrent to potential law-breakers. In 1961 the penalty for assault with a deadly weapon in California was one to ten years. In 1966 in California legislature raised the sentence for assaulting a police officer with a deadly weapon to five years to life. That year the rate of attacks on police was 15.8 per hundred officers, compared to 8.4 per hundred officers in 1961. In 1961 California raised the sentence for possession of marijuana from an optional one to twelve month to a mandatory one to ten years. Between 1961 and 1966 the number of arrests for possession of marijuana *rose* 500 per cent, from 3,500 to 18,000 (Mitford, 1973, pp. 280-81).

Prison Reform

Are there any alternatives to prisons as we know them? Efforts to reform prisons—whether motivated by humanitarian principles or the desire to reduce crime - have focused on three general areas: work programmes, conjugal visits, and group therapy (Bloch and Geis, 1970, pp. 469–74). In this country North Carolina led the way with "work furlough" programmes, wherein inmates are permitted to leave prison for up to sixty hours a week to work on the outside. Although 16 per cent of the inmates have been taken out of the programme (most for drinking or visiting friends and family), none of the 1,046 prisoners committed violent crimes. As a result more than thirty states launched similar programmes in the 1960s, but usually on a small scale. In the Swedish penal system, widely regarded as the most enlightened in the world, providing prisoners with steady, useful jobs and requiring them to support themselves and their families, while paying restitution to their victims, are central to the rehabilitation effort (Durham, 1973).

Only one prison in this country allows conjugal visits (Parchman State Prison in Mississippi), but many other nations permit spouses to visit prisoners, and some allow prisoner to visit their families for short periods. After six months of good behaviour, a Mexican prison (located on a 34,000-acre island) permits prisoners to bring their families to live with them. Sweden sends some convicted criminals on vacations with their families, when the only requirement is that the prisoners attend morning classes. The idea behind conjugal visits is that the people who are most likely to discourage convicts from entering criminal careers are spouses and children. In fact, Sweden gives priority to "hard-core" prisoners in assigning a limited number of family apartments. Only about 2 per cent of prisoners use family visits as an escape route.

Group therapy programmes are difficult to assess. Nearly all forms of psychotherapy depend on uninhibited self-revelation and open expression of feelings. But the psychologists who run such programmes in prisons are, after all, prison officials. The inmate is thus put in a double-bind: total openness might well delay his parole, but self-concealment renders the programme useless.

Undoubtedly, the most radical approach to penal reform is to eliminate prisons altogether. Surprising to most people is the fact that this has been tried in Massachusetts. Dr. Jerome Miller became Commissioner of the Department of Youth Services in that state in October 1969. By the fall of 1972 he had reduced the population of juvenile prisons from about 1,350 to 90. Instead of being imprisoned, young law-breakers were returned to their families or placed in foster homes, small unlocked residences, or a few prep schools that ordinary cater to middle and upper-class youngsters. Officials helped older boys and girls to find their own homes and jobs. Only forty or fifty who were considered "dangerous," and an equal number who were "seriously disturbed," were housed in locked facilities. The staff, which included professionals as well as college students acting as "big brothers," had wide discretion in handling youngsters.

The goal of this programme was first, to stop the process of labelling youngsters "delinquent," and second, to help them to cope with life on the outside, rather than socialising them to the authoritarianism and brutality of prisons. As of January 1973 there was no evidence of an increase in juvenile delinquency in Massachusetts (and some hint of a drop), and Miller was able to return $2 million of his $10 million 1972 budget to the state treasury (Mitford, 1973, pp. 282–85).

It is doubtful that the American public is ready to tear down its prisons; one experiment with juveniles is hardly conclusive evidence that prisons are useless. In a report on prison reform, sponsored by the Roscoe Pound American Trial Lawyers Foundation, Herman Schwartz (1972) concluded:

> The prison problem is beginning to be seen as part of the overall problem of social justice, as a crucial element in the movement to eliminate the racial and other oppression that has stained our history for so many years. . .On balance, I think we have come a very long way in expanding prisoners' rights in the last few years. But again, the satisfaction must be tempered. Our prison system is so diseased and bankrupt that these achievements represent only the smallest and earliest steps of a very long journey. Whether we can successfully negotiate that journey is indeed problematic.

9

Population and Health

Studying Population

The study of population centers on just three variables: birth rate, death rate, and net migration (inflow minus outflow). Together, these silent, powerful forces not only produce increases or decreases in population but determine the very shape of society—the size of the labour force, the demands for food and shelter, the proportion of young and old people, the ethnic composition.

Demographers are concerned, then, with the changes in the demographic variables, with the causes of such changes, and with the consequences. They ask: Is the birth rate increasing? Did the baby boom occur because parents wanted larger families or were there simply more families with parents of child-bearing age? As the crop of boom babies grows old, will their predominance turn us into a national of conservatives? To find answers, demographers need sources of raw information. Two sources they rely upon are government and community records, and the census.

Counting Population

In our highly organised society, key events in one's life—being born, graduating, marrying—quickly become statistics. The recording of such facts by a government or other agency is known as *registration.* Registration has been compared to a motion-picture record of a continuous stream of data on a specific subject.

The periodic head count called the *census*, on the other hand, resembles a still photo, taken with a wide-angle lens and capturing a single moment. The census collects a mass of data about each citizen: sex, age, occupation, and much more.

Census taking dates back about five thousand years. The ancient Sumerians counted heads for the sake of more efficient tax collecting. Other ancient peoples—Chiness, Hebrews, Egyptians—used the census for taxation or to identify men who could serve in the army or as forced labourers. In America, the Comanche Indians counted their people by dividing reeds into five bundles. Each represented a group; warriors, young men, wowen, children, and dwellings. The colonists also conducted censuses: Virginia in 1624; Connecticut in 1759; and Massachusetts in 1764 (Thomlinson, 1965, p. 41).

According to our Constitution, the government must take the census every ten years to determine congressional representation and taxes. In 1790 the first national census reported upon 3,929,000 individuals in a fifty-six-page pamphlet. The 1970 census counted 204,879,000 people and presented its findings in numerous reports, in varied forms from microfiche to computer tape. The modern census is more than just a head count; it collects many kinds of information about the American people to aid in social prediction and planning.

Even a computer, however, cannot assure total accuracy of a census. For one thing, the Census Bureau admits to underestimating the population. In 1970 about 1.9 million blacks and 3.4 million whites were not counted, for a net undercount rate of 25 per cent (U. S. Bureau of the Census, *User's Guide*, 1970, p. 5). More recent research estimates the black undercount to be 8 per cent (Coale and Rives, 1973, table 5). As a result, these "missing citizens" are under represented in government. Because many black people live in cities, the undercount means that federal allotments to cities may be less than they should be, depriving many people of needed services.

If such inaccuracies can be found in the census of a nation with advanced communications technology and a long tradition of census taking, it is mind-boggling to imagine the problems of counting population world-wide. In 1962, for example, Nigeria took its first census since becoming an independent nation. To prepare the citizenry, radio programmes made daily announcements in song, and posters were displayed in every town and village. Nevertheless, census takers were beaten and even kidnapped by people who feared they were tax collectors. Some diligent census takers discovered whole new communities, such as a group of fishing villages whose twenty thousand inhabitants has been totally unknown. Too often, however, officials sabotaged the census takers' results. To get more money from the central government for welfare and economic development. They exaggerated the number of people in their districts (Peterson, 1969).

Some countries produce censuses even less accurate than Nigeria's. Consequently, we should allow for significant marigns of error in world population statistics. Estimates do indicate that world population statistics. Estimates do indicate that world population was about 3,706,000,000 in 1971. It appears to be increasing at an average annual rate of 2 per cent, the highest rate in history (United Nations, 1971).

Whatever its faults, modern societies could not do without the census. As societies become more complex census data become more varied. So do the uses to which they are put: to plan where and when new schools will be needed, to anticipate tax revenues, to figure out the potential market for a new soft drink. And demographers must rely upon the census for data about population growth or decline.

Population Growth

To determine population growth, demographers study the interaction of birth rates, death rates, and net migration. *Crude birth rate* represents the number of births per thousand people during a given time span. In 1947, during the postwar baby boom, our crude birth rate soared to twenty seven per thousand. At its low points—during the depression and in the early 1970s—it plummeted to eithteen per thousand. Meanwhile, our *crude death rate* (deaths per thousand people) has fallen and remains well below the birth rate. In 1900 the death rate was about seventeen per thousand, in contrast to nine per thousand in 1970. Population growth reflects the excess of births over deaths (*Statistical Abstract,* 1973, p. 51).

But population growth also depends upon migration. The United States has traditionally attracted more people than it has lost. In demographic terms, our immigration (or in-migration) has exceeded our emigration (out-migration), resulting in population growth. *Internal migration,* or movement within a country, is also important to measure. The frequency with which a group moves may affect its way of life, for example. And population clusters, such as the concentration of the elderly in Florida, may create distinctive cultures. The rate of population growth or increase is the amount by which the crude birth rate and immigration together exceed the crude death rate and out-migration (see Figure 9.1).

Birth Rate

From menarche (first menstruation) to menopause (the cessation of fertility) the average woman's fertile period lasts about thirty years. But biological potential for reproduction or *fecundity,* is only one aspect of a society's birth rate at a given time. No society has ever reached, or even come near its theoretical biological potential. The *fertility rate* shows the number of children actually produced per thousand women between the ages of fifteen and forty-four.

Clearly, the number of fertile women in the population at any one time will influence the birth rate. However, our postwar baby boom took place at a time when the proportion of potential mothers was not at a peak. Demong raphers must take into account the number of potential fathers, as well. World war II temporarily lowered the *sex ratio,* or the number of men per hundred women, because so many men were away in the armed services. When the war ended, the sex ratio suddenly increased. Twice during this century, however, war decimated the population of mariageable males in Germany and Russia. In these countries, birth rates continue to reflect the low sex ratio.

Because most children are born to married parents, the proportion of people getting married can affect the birth rate. For example, many American couples postponed their

Figure 9.1: The key demographic variables

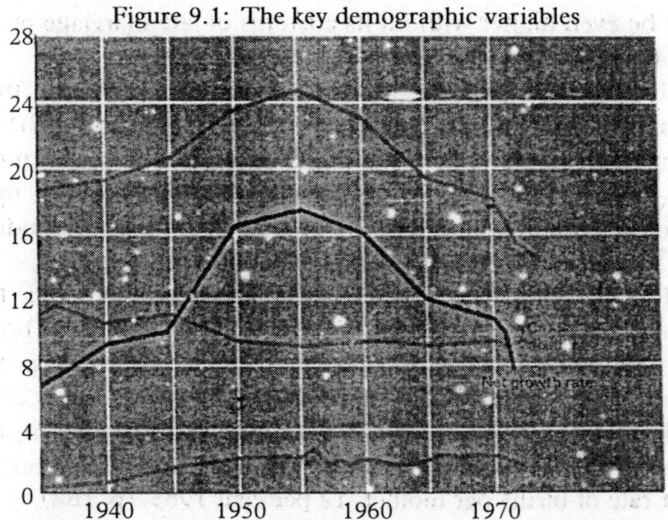

Source: Statistical Abstract of the United States, 1973. (Washington, D.C.: Government Printing Office. 1973): table 9, p.11.

The rate of population growth is the total of the crude death rate minus the crude death rate plus the net migration rate. In the United States the variations in growth mirror changes in the birth rate rather than the other variables. The death rate is relatively low and stable because many of the forces that carried off large numbers of people - such as influenza or widespread crop failures - have been tamed. Net migration is only a small (though positive) component of growth, since emigration is relatively insignificant and immigration is limited by legal quotas. Earlier in this century immigration played a much larger role in American population growth.

marriages during World War II. Then, from 1946 to the early 1950s, the proportion of married persons in the population rose significantly, and so did the birth rate. But in Ireland, where about a quarter of the men and women are not married by age forty-five (compared to 6 per cent in the United States), the birth rate is far higher than ours Why? Because the fertility rate is much higher. The couples who do marry have lots of children (Knnedy, 1973, tables 49, 50, 58). The age of marriage can affect the birth rate, too. But again Ireland, which has the highest age of marriage of any other country, does not have the low birth rate to go with this. Of course, the Irish birth rate might be even higher without its customs of late marriage or no marriage at all.

Birth control allows couples to control family size, thus helping to lower the birth rate. Some societies control births by placing a taboo on intercourse—sometimes as long as three years—while a mother is still nursing a child. Other societies may permit, abortion, sterilisation, or infanticide to limit fecundity. Most birth control consists of abstinence or contraception.

How did these four factors—fecundity, the sex ratio, the proportion of married couples, and birth control—help to bring about the postwar baby boom? Thomlinson divides. the responsibility as follows: the larger number of women 24 per cent; the higher proportion of women who married, 30 per cent; the higher percentage of wives who bore children, 34 per cent; and the higher rate of births per mother, 12 per cent 1965, (p. 168).

These figures represent an intelligent quess, not a certainty. Birth rate—its causes and consequences—remains elosive, especially when someone attempts to manipulate it. In 1966, for example, the Romanian government was worried. A few years earlier fertility had dropped below the replacement level. Romanian women were relying upon inexpensive, legal abortions for birth control. To raise the birth rate, therefore, officials suddenly outlawed abortion in November 1966. Unable to get abortions and lured by government incentives to have larger families, Romanian women tripled the birth rate only eleven months after the law went into effect ! Two years later, however, previous cultural patterns began to reassert themselves. Women found other means of limiting births, and the birth rate declined once more (Clark, 1973). Clearly, the availability of abortion alone was not responsible for the low birth rate. If our baby boom produced radical changes, imagine the effects of that sudden, brief bulge in Romania's population. For one thing, in 1974 the first three elementary grades were mobbed. Just a few years later, enrolments in those grades will drop suddenly by up to two-thirds!

A more revealing statistic than either crude birth rate or the fertility rate is the *age-specific fertility rate,* or the number of births per thousand women of a given age range. Since women bear children during a limited number of years, it is clearly more significant to know how many children are born, for example, to women twenty to twenty-nine years of age than to all women. The *net reproduction rate* (NRR) is an average of the number of female children born per woman of child-bearing age; that is, the rate at which a woman replaces herself by producing a female child to bear children in the next generation. An NRR of 1.0 would indicate that, on the average, one woman produces one daughter.

Zero population growth (ZPG) occurs when the crude birth rate is equal to the crude death rate. An NRR of 1.0 may eventually bring about ZPG. However, to achieve constant population in the United States once an NRR of 1.0 was reached would take several decades, because of the large number of women of child-bearing age and because of the age composition of the population as a whole.

Table 9.1
Life Expectancy and Age-Specific Mortality Rates, 1969

Age	*Life expectancy*[1]	*mortality rate*
Under 1	70.4	21.08
5	67.2	0.63
10	62.3	0.26
15	57.8	0.85
20	52.8	1.41
25	48.1	1.45
30	43.5	1.56
35	38.8	2.15
40	34.3	2.24
45	29.9	4.88
50	25.7	7.44
55	21.8	11.42
60	18.1	17.26
65	14.8	25.60
69	12.4	35.53

1. 'Note that the longer a person survives, the greater the total number of years he or she can expect to live. Thus, if a person lives to sixty, he or she can look forward to living to seventy-eight, whereas an infant can expect to live only seventy years.

Source : Statistical Abstract of the United States, 1973 (Washington, D. C.: Government Printing Office. 1973), table 80, p. 58.

Death Rate and Life Expectancy

Life span, the maximum number of years that a human being can possibly live, has not changed substantially over the centuries. But *life expectancy,* the average number of years of life remaining for an individual of a given age has increased dramatically in the last seventy-five years or so. An infant born in 1920 had a life expectancy of 54.1 years; by 1970 the life expectancy at birth was 70.8 years. This gain looks impressive, but life expectancy at age 60 is only a few years longer now than it was in the past. Only now more people are reaching age 60.

The crude death rate does not fully explain the reasons for the change; age-specific mortality rates are more revealing. The *infant mortality rate,* or deaths per thousand children under one years of age, shows clearly that most of the gain in life expectancy has come because of fewer infant deaths. The 1972 crude death rate of 9.4 per thousand was not much lower than the 1935 figure, 10.9 per thousand. But in 1935 infant deaths stood at 55.7 per thousand, significantly higher than the 18.5 deaths per thousand infants in 1972 (*Statistical Abstract,* 1973, table 65, p. 51).

The chances of dying in the first year of life are still quite high. Age-specific tables show that after the first year the mortality rate drops quite sharply until the later years of life. An infant under one year is now about as likely to die as a person in his early sixties.

A Close Look at Immigration

Since the discovery of the New World, one of Europe's big exports has been people; 45 million of them to North America, 20 million to Latin America, 10 million to Australia and South Africa combined. This movement of people from one country to another is called *international migration.*

Why do people migrate? Demographers use the term *push* to describe their reasons for leaving or being forced out, and the term *pull* for the attractions of the new place. In Israel, peopled primarily by immigrants from other nations, both forces were at work in its settlement. World War II forced many Jews to leave their European homelands. And Israel exerted pull—the emotional appeal of a traditional homeland; its attraction as an existing independent nation for Jews; and its open immigration policy. Immigration patterns have had an immense impact on Israel, in a number of ways.

From 1948 to 1951, immediately after the establishment of Israel, the new country grew by 24 per cent a year. Ninety per cent of this growth was due to immigration. For some years after 1952, the growth rate slowed to 3 per cent, of which half was still due to immigration. By 1970 fewer than half the Jews in Israel were natives, or Sabras (named for a native desert plant); 28 per cent were of European and 26 per cent of Afro-Asian origin (Friendlander and Sabatello, 1972).

Box 9.1

In The News

Long Life—A Regional Specialty?

Franklin, Neb.— Hanna Sanger should have died 7.05 years ago, according to the statistics.

She has always been stubborn and indpendent-minded, though, so she didn't. And in living a long time here (she's working on her 80th year now) Mrs. Sanger is carrying on a local longevity tradition.

For Nebraskans, according to the Federal Government, can expect to live longer than the residents of any other state, an average of 71.95 years.

Franklin citizens seem not just longer-lived, but unusually active—bowling, chopping wood, and gardening long after most Amercans have retired to their rocking chairs. What makes Nebraskans so hardly?

Some say "hard work". Others think it's the extreme climate, or the water, or the air. Dr. Harmon Denham, president of the American Aging Association, believes it's a combination of things.

"Historically, rural residents live longer than urban ones," he said, "and Mid-westerners live longer than coastal residents. They have a lower food intake. The pace of life is slower.

"Most importantly, people seem to keep busier in retirement. They don't sit around [and] worry about their health. . .And there's probably a selective factors the hardiest residents stay on while the others move out".

Box 9.1 *Contd.*

Beaufort, S.C—Aging, leather-tough Aldridge Glazer has been retired for some years now and he gets a monthly pension check, but it doesn't always stretch over his expenses. . .Mr. Glazer is an agile, quick 75 years old—a happy state that cannot truly be called rare in this part of the country but that is worth noting.

Why does South Carolina have the lowest life expectancy rate in the United States (66.41) while Nebraska has the highest? There is no one simple explanation, but a network of related causes. For one thing, many Sourth Carolinians are black, and blacks die sooner than whites on the average. Poverty, the coastal climate, poor sanitation, high infant mortality, and few doctors make the picture bleak. So does the high incidence of diseases related to hypertension. Among black males 55 to 64 years of age, 649 in every 1,000 die of such diseases in South Carolina. In Nebraska 42 of every 1,000 white males of the same age die of such diseases.

A reporter asked Thomas C. Barnwell, Director of the Beaufort-Jasper Comprehensive Health Care Service, Inc., why the difference between South Carolinians and Nebraskans is so great.

"We really don't know", Mr. Barnwell concedes, "but we'd like to".

"I grew up in Beaufort County", he says holding up a small box of pills.

"I take one of these every morning. They're for hypertension. I have it, too".

Source : Wayne King, "Life in Beaufort, S.C." and Andrew H. Malcolm "Hearty Longevity at Franklin, Neb.", *The New York Times* (March 17, 1974): 45.

Israel's *population pyramid* shows graphically how immigration patterns have affected the distribution of the population according to age and sex. The pyramid representing native-born Israelis shows that in 1972 some 60.5 per cent were under fifteen years and nearly 70 per cent under age twenty, while only about 20 per cent were between twenty and sixty-five. This profile indicates a country with few productive workers and an extraordinary number of dependent children. But a pyramid representing Israelis born in Europe and America clearly shows where

Figure 9.2 : Population pyramids for Israel, 1970

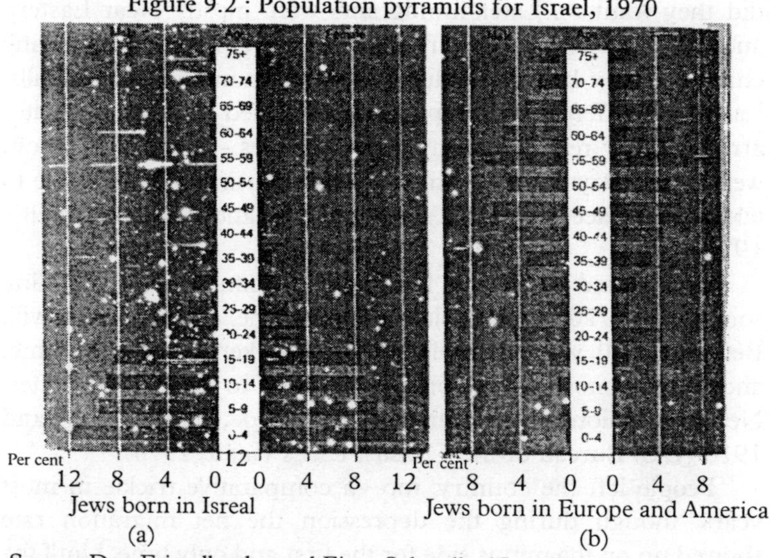

Source : Dov Friendlander and Eitan Sabatello, "Isreal", in *Country Profiles* (The Population Council, February 1972) pp. 4, 5.

A population pyramid shows the composition of a group by age and sex. The Sabras of Isreal are a young group, the children of immigrants by and large, as population pyramid (a) shows. Most Israelis born in Europe and America, (b) belong to the older generations.

the missing adults were to be found. This group included few children (only about 3 per cent were fifteen or under) but many adults (more than 80 per cent) between fifteen and sixty-five.

Consider how such immigration patterns affect the daily lives of Israelis. For one thing, status depends in large part upon immigration. Those who have been in the country the longest—Sabras and pre-Independence immigrants—find themselves at the top of the status ladder. Prestige may be granted to those with more education, but it also depends upon country of origin. Sabras and European immigrants enjoy higher status than other immigrants.

Not surprisingly, the immigrants brought with them a host of problems. The first wave of immigrants, before 1951, came largely from Europe. Many were elderly, and those of working age had skills appropriate to urban life. They had not farmed, nor did they want to. Later immigrants were mostly Near Eastern and North African. Their families were large, with many children. They had little education, little money, and few skills. Language differences and prejudice weighed against these later arrivals. They required many social services - health, education, welfare, employment and training, and housing—if they were to take their place in Israeli society (Friedlander and Sabatello, 1972).

The United States, too, is a nation of immigrants—including some 10 to 20 million slaves who came against their will. Between 1820, when official statistics were kept for the first time, and 1972, almost 46 million people came to the United States. Nearly 9 million of them came in one decade, between 1901 and 1910 (U.S. Bureau of the Census, *User's Guide, 1970*).

People left the country, too—a comparative trickle in most years, though during the depression the net migration rate showed up on the minus side for the first and only time. Until the 1920s immigration was almost unrestricted; the United States welcomed newcomers to help settle and industrialise the nation. During the 1920s, however, immigration policy began limiting the number of immigrants, easpecially those from non-European countries. Objections to the discriminatory aspects of this policy led to its modification in the Immigration Act of 1965. Each year nearly 400,000 people enter the United States legally. (Illegal immigration also adds its share; in 1971 officials tracked down 420,000 deportable aliens, most of them Mexican.) We continue to feel the impact of immigration; from 1960 to 1970, immigration accounted for 16 per cent of population growth (*Population and the American Future*, 1972, p. 114).

The Population Explosion

Terms like *population explosion* have become familiar, if frightening, in recent years. One of the first to sound a warning about population growth was a gentleman-scholar the Reverend Thomas Robert Malthus (1766 - 1834). First published in 1798, his theories went into a sixth edition in 1826, entitled "An Essay on the Principle of Population, or A View of his Past and Present Effects on Human Happiness, with An Inquiry into Our

Prospects Respecting the Future Revomal or Mitigation of the Evils Which it Occassions." Malthus's theory, briefly, was this: People require food, and people will continue to have children. Population, he said, increases in a geometric progression (2, 4, 8, 16) while food supplies increase only arithmetically (2, 3, 4, 5). No population can continue to grow indefinitely, because people will simply run out of food. Increase the standard of living and reduce the number of deaths, and the population will simply increase, thereby wiping out the gains. The standard of living will fall and mortality rise again.

To Malthus, the only answer was to marry late and have fewer children (he did not approve of birth control or abortion. Otherwise, population would inevitably be checked by drastic means: starvation, pestilence, or war.

As Malthus predicted, when the death rate declines and fertility remains high, the population grows very fast. From 1650 to 1850, world population doubted from 500 million people to 1 billion. But it took only eighty years—from 1850 to 1930—for the population to double again. In the 1970s world population is increasing at about 2 per cent a year and doubling every thirty-five years (Ehrlich and Ehrlich, 1972, p. 450). Just like interest in a savings account, population increases by compounding.

Is human population reaching the limits of growth predicted by Malthus? Some demographers are haunted by the Malthusian specter of starvation, plague, and war. Others believe that humanity may be able to avert such a disaster. Some evidence suggests that we can achieve a population with low mortality and fertility, or even zero population growth. In fact, industrialised countries have gone through the demographic transition which has brought their repid rate of population growth down.

The Demographic Transition

The demographic transition summarises in four stages the population dynamics in Europe and America during the last two centuries. Initially, there was a high, steady birth rate and a high death rate, which varied with famines and epidemics. Then gradually in the second phase, the death rate declined. This decline was due less to medicine than to sanitary water and

Figure 9.3 : The demographic transition

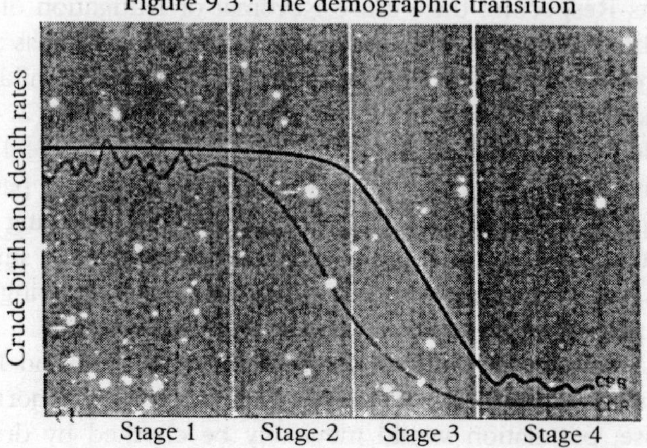

This schematic graph shows the differences in behaviour of birth rates and death rates during the demographic transition in the industrialised nations. The gap between births and dealths in stages 2 and 3 produced rapid population growth. Today the gap has narrowed, although jumps in the birth rate may produce spurts of population growth as in our postwar baby boom. Even though its population is not growing as fast as that of the developing nations. The industrialised world still must be concerned with population growth because of the heavier demands its people place upon the environment. The United States, for example, has one-sixteenth of the world's population but consumes over one-third or the world's resources.

sewage systems, soaps and disinfectants, better transportation for shipping foods, and more productive farming techniques. Because the birth rates remained high, the rapid population growth Malthus observed began. Slowly in the third phase, the birth rate declined, as people realised they needed to bear fewer children in order for the same number to survive into adulthood. Nevertheless, the widening gap between the two rates meant that population continued to grow faster than at any time in human history. Toward the end of this phase, the death rate levelled out. Today the industrialised nations are in the final phase, with a low, steady death rate and a low but fluctuating birth rate. Population growth in these countries is no longer so explosive.

In the past few decades, the rest of the world has also experienced something like the demographic transition.

However, the change has been so rapid and the circumstances so different that there is serious question whether the developing nations will experience the full transition.

Death rates in developing nations have been dropping more rapidly than they did during the demographic transition in the West. In just five years, from 1945 to 1950, their death rates dropped an average of 24 per cent. A more impressionistic view from a Calcutta man reveals the radical change:

> "When I was a boy, they took away forty or fifty bodies after a cholera epidemics. It happened every five or ten years. Now they come and vaccinate our children. I have lived here almost seventy years. The biggest change in my time has been health. We've learned how to keep from dying." (Thomlinson, 1965, p. 25)

Philip Hauser tells why :

> The same ship that anchors in the harbour of Colombo, Ceylon, can carry in her hold virtually all of the means by which morality declines were effected in the Western world during the three centuries of the modern era. The ship can carry, in one delivery, fertiliser and tractors for increased productivity; chlorine, insecticides and tooth brushes for improved environmental sanitation and personal hygiene; and the methods of modern medicine, including chemotherapy. (1969, p. 16)

United Nations and government agencies contribute to falling death rates by providing sanitation, public health, and preventive medicine.

With death rates—especially infant mortality—lower, population grows at an astounding rate. Ehrlich provides a graphic description of one teeming city, Delhi:

> My wife and daughter and I were returning to our hotel in an ancient taxi. The seats were hoping with fleas. The only functional gear was third. As we crawled through the city, we entered a crowded slum area. The temperature was well over 100, and the air was a haze of dust and smoke. The streets seemed alive with people. People eating, people washing, people sleeping. People visiting, arguing, and screaming. People thrusting their hands through the taxi window, begging. People defecating and urinating. People clinging to buses. People herding animals. People, people, people, people. As we moved slowly through the mob, hand horn squawking, the soot, noise, heat, and choking fires gave the scene a hellish aspect. Would we ever get to our hotel? (1971, p. 15).

This pattern is duplicated on every continent. Rural overpopulation in developing nations is an equally pressing problem as well.

Why Birth Rates are High

Three main variables seem to control fertility in the developing nations: social values governing marriage, number of children, and contraception: the resulting age structure of the population; and the lack of economic development that might make lower birth rates both possible and more advantageous. These combine to produce the Malthusian nightmare of runaway population.

Marriage in developing nations is universal—and early. Take Africa and Asia, for example. Here, the average woman marries before she is twenty. By their late thirties, less than 5 per cent are single (Coale, 1973, p. 56). Most women are able, even encouraged to bear children all through their fertile years.

And most of these women want children. One study of rural Moroccan women found out that nearly half wanted more children than they already had. On the average, they wanted 4-6 children. To have four or five children survive, a woman might have to bear eight or nine. Moroccan values clearly favour fertility not contraception ('Morocco,' 1970).

To what degree does ignorance of contraception enter in? Researchers are not sure. Rural Moroccans seemed unfamiliar with birth-control methods. Only a third of the women and about half their husbands admitted knowing anything about how to prevent births. Only 14 per cent of married women under fifty could name any contraceptive methods. But 60 per cent could identify at least one method when researchers read them a list. Thus, "ignorance" is hard to distinguish from feeling.

The high birth rates that result from such social values produce a large population of young people. On the island of Mauritius in the Indian Ocean, 44 per cent of the people are under fifteen. Older people, born and raised when mortality was higher, are relatively few. Only 3 per cent have lived to age sixty-five. The effect of this age distribution is a large *dependency ratio,* or proportion of people of nonproductive age (under fifteen or over sixty-five) in the total population. In Mauritius, 47 per cent of the people are in the dependent age group; therefore, the dependency ratio is forty-seven. Developed countries have very different ratios. Japan's, for example, is only thirty-nine.

This large young population means a continuing cycle of high fertility, as these young people have their own babies. We have seen the effects of our postwar baby boom—but imagine what would happen if the boom were continuous!

Lack of economic development also contributes to the high birth rate. Some optimists point out that economic development helped the Western nations to bring down their birth rates by making it advantageous to have fewer children and could do the same for developing nations. No longer would parents need a huge brood to ensure enough surviving offspring to support them in their old age, for example. Ironically, however, one of the greatest obstacles to economic development is overpopulation itself.

Overpopulation and Economic Development

Increased population is quite likely to eat up any economic gains a nation makes. If total national income goes up by 2 per cent, for example and the population grows by the same amount, *per capita income* (or the income available to each citizen if the total of the country were divided evenly) remains the same and people are no better off than before. In some countries where population is growing faster than the economy, per capita income is actually declining!

There are other aspects to the problem. When population grows, the number of jobs must grow, too, or there will be greater unemployment or underemployment. In most developing nations too many people are already farming for efficient use of the land. What happens to the leftover people when they seek employment?

This depends on how much industrial capacity there is and how fast it is growing. Economists estimate that investment in machinery, factories, and so forth must increase annually at a rate two or three times greater than the increase in the labour force, if per capita income is not to fall. A working population increasing at a rate of 3 per cent annually would thus require an increase in capital investment of from 6 per cent (Freedman,

1964, p. 161) to 9 per cent (DeFleur et al., 1973, p. 251) just to maintain productivity. To increase productivity and thereby raise per capita income, capital investment would have to be substantial—a 12 per cent increase in investment per year is considered the rate necessary for a developing country (Keyfitz, in Freedman, 1964, p. 161). Furthermore, a labour force needs training and education, and providing this requires another large investment. Where can this much capital come from in those countries just emerging from a subsistence economy? The land base and income levels are so low that taxing the citizens would accomplish little. Thus, over-population and slow economic growth form a vicious cycle, with each worsening the other.

Figure 9.4 : The geography of hunger

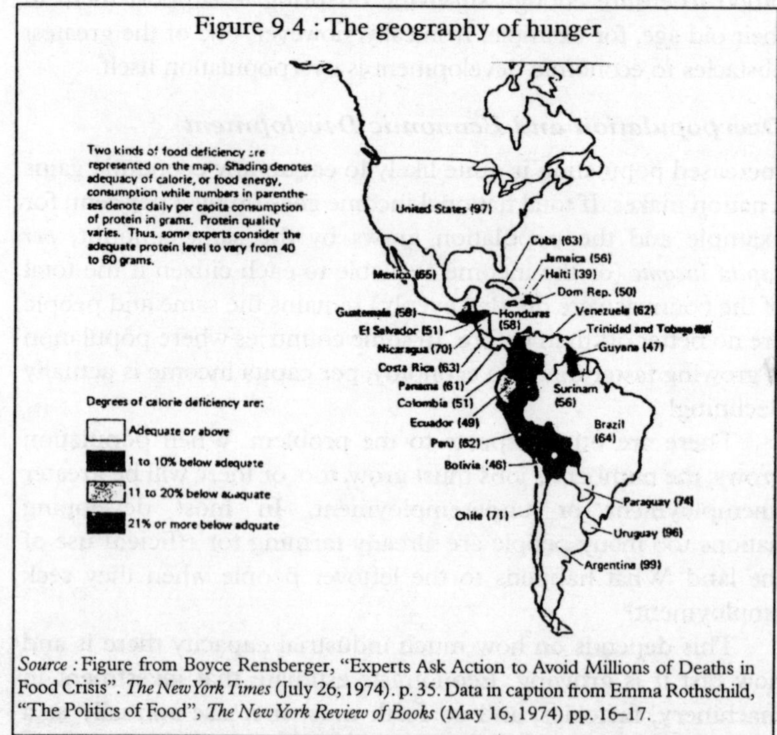

Source : Figure from Boyce Rensberger, "Experts Ask Action to Avoid Millions of Deaths in Food Crisis". *The New York Times* (July 26, 1974). p. 35. Data in caption from Emma Rothschild, "The Politics of Food", *The New York Review of Books* (May 16, 1974) pp. 16–17.

Undernourishment and malnutrition are chronic in three areas of the world: southern Asia, Africa and western South America. Countries in these areas must import food. Developing nations as a whole imported 38 per cent of all wheat, 55 per cent of soybeans, 50 per cent of cottonseed oil and 74 per cent

Overpopulation and Hunger

These abstract figures on economic development can be translated into something more elemental: the lack of enough food to provide sufficient calories (undernourishment) or sufficient nutrients (nalnutrition). In 1967 the president's Science Advisory Committee Panel on the World Food Supply estimated that 20 per cent of the people in developing nations were undernourished and 60 per cent were malnourished. At the least this means a total of one and a half billion people. Another half billion are either chronically hungry or starving. And this estimate did not include the large number of hungry and malnourished people in developed countries. In the United

Figure 9.4 : contd.

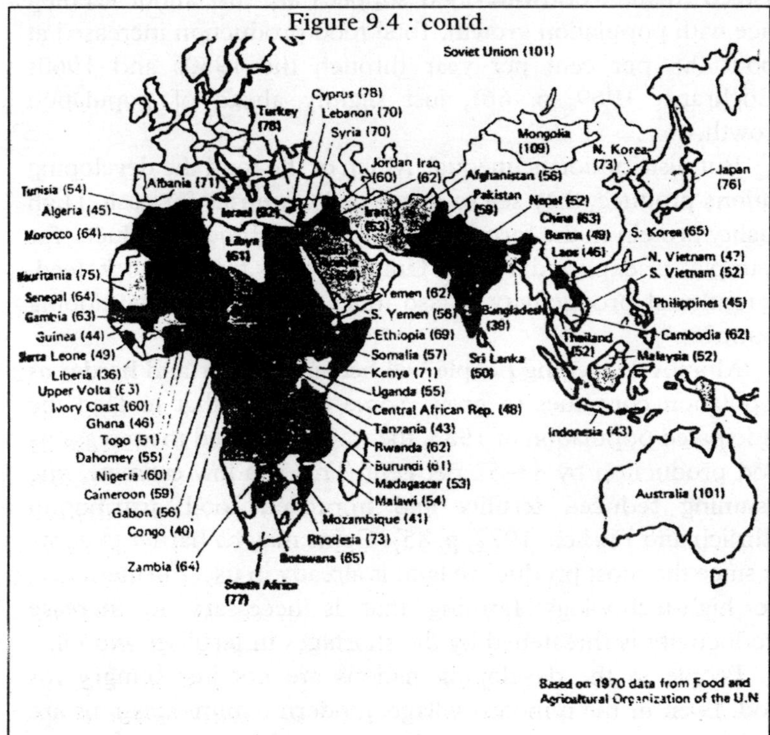

of the rice in the international market. The prices of these products have been rising rapidly. In 1978, for example, the prices of food exports from the United States rose by 55 per cent. The result was that American export earnings on foot to developing nations alone increased by $3.4 billion.

States, a Public Health survey uncovered 10 to 15 million chronically hungry Americans, a large proportion of them children. Another 10 to 15 million had such low incomes that malnutrition was inevitable (Ehrlich and Ehrlich, 1972, p. 94). In other words, from 20 to 30 million Americans are suffering from natritional problems like those of people living in developing countries.

Why should malnutrition and undernourishment be so widespread? Famines have always existed; they are disastrous of course, but temporary and limited in extent. Famine, however, is not a primary cause of the word's food problems. If food could be distributed to all who need it, enough is now being produced to feed them. Worldwide food supplies are just about keeping pace with population growth. Total food production increased at about 2.8 per cent per year through the 1950s and 1960s (Cochrane, 1969, p. 66), just slightly ahead of population growth.

But distribution is unequal. Much of the food the developing nations produce, they sell to developed countries for cash. High quality protein in the form of soybean and fishmeal products, for example, is exported to the United States for livestock feed. Agricultural productivity is also much lower in the developing countries.

Moreover, feeding people will become harder and harder as population continues to grow. Some estimate that to feed the anticipated population of 1985, the world will need to increase its food production by 43–52 per cent. This is a low estimate, one assuming reduced fertility and improved food distribution (Ehrlich and Ehrlich, 1972, p. 85). Gains may be harder to come by since the most productive land is already in use. Furthermore, the high-technology farming that is necessary to increase productivity is threatened by the shortages in fertiliser and oil.

People in the developing nations are not just hungry for food. Even in the remotest village, modern communications are awakening poor people everywhere to one important fact: other people live better. Other people have cars, hospitals, bicycles, plenty of food. Aware of such things, the poor have learned to want and even to expect them. Cochrane sees 1948 as the turning point in a "revolution of expectation" (1969, p. 3). Armed with new wants, the have-nots may create social unrest as they struggle to catch up with their more affluent neighbours. The question remains: What is to be done?

Bringing the Birth Rate Down

To attack the problem directly many countries attempt to use family planning programmes as a means of persuading citizens to limit their families. The experiences of Costa Rica and Japan reveal just how complicated it can be to stem the tide of births.

Costa Rica and Birth Control

This Central American nation was a classic example of population gone wild. Before 1950 the birth rate was forty-five per thousand and the death rate slightly over fifteen per thousand. This meant a net increase in population of 3 per cent annually, or a doubling every twenty-three years. The 1950s brought economic and social development, including better health standards. These helped reduce the death rate to ten but also to increase the birth rate to fifty, a net rate of growth of 4 per cent, or a doubling of population every seventeen years! (To determine the time it takes for populations—or your bank account—to double, divide the per cent into sixty-nine.)

Then cultural values and family practices started to change and the birth rate began to decline. In 1967 Costa Rica started a family planning programme. The programme worked, but in large part because it began *after* values favouring small families had taken hold. The birth rate declined 28 per cent in the 1960s.

Nevertheless, Costa Rica's problems continue. The economy faces the task of absorbing young adults born during the period of high fertility. As these young people have families of their own—even if they limit births—the recent decline in birth rates will be less rapid in the next decade. A work force of 534,000 in 1970 will expand to nearly twice that by 1985. It will be a long time before zero population growth comes to Costa Rica (Sanders, 1973).

The Remarkable Transition of Japan

In Japan, on the other hand, both fertility and mortality began to decline as early as the 1920s. Except for a post-World War II baby boom, these declines accelerated until the rate of natural increase (crude birth rate minus crude death rate reached 1 per cent a year in 1956.

Improvement in the standard of living and in sanitation helped to bring about the early reduction in mortality. Traditionally, literacy and knowledge of personal hygiene have been high in Japan. These conditions laid the groundwork for public health improvements (especially the introduction of DDT and antibiotics) that kept mortality on its downward path after the war. From 1920 to the mid-1960s, mortality dropped from 25.4 to about 7 per thousand (Muramatsu, 1971, pp. 11-13). Note that this death rate is 30 per cent lower than ours, though our per capita GNP is four times that of Japan.

In fertility Japan presents a contrast with other developing nations. In the twenty years before the war the birth rate dropped from 36.2 to 29.4. After a rise to 34.3 in 1947, the rate again declined very dramatically, reaching a low of 16.9 in 1961 and moving slightly upward to 18.5 in 1965 (Muramatsu, 1971, pp. 16–19). The slight prewar fertility decline credited to postponement of marriage and the modest beginnings of family planning, prepared the Japanese for more intensive fertility control after the war. Abortion became legal in 1948 and 1949: a few years later, national family planning began to furnish all Japanese with contraceptive information and services. Designed to promote maternal health and allow the individual greater choice, these policies encouraged lower birth rates as well. Their effect is clear: population growth declined much more rapidly after they went into effect.

A population growth rate of only 1.0 since 1956 helped Japan achieve its postwar economic "miracle". A stable population allowed substantial capital to be reinvested in industry, while living standards remained high. Now some Japanese worry about a labour shortage!

Government policy helped the lower birth rates along, but we should not lose sight of the ways in which Japanese society itself fostered population limits. Literate and free from taboos on frank discussions of sexual matters, Japanese could read about family planning in their equaivalents of the *Ladies Home Journal* and the *Reader's Digest* (Freedman 1964, p. 171). The media spread the word quickly: small families are desirable. As living standards rose, the benefits of having fewer mouths to feed became even clearer, and the low-birth-rate cycle continued.

Modernisation or Birth Control?

As we have seen from these exmples, the key to lowered fertility is motivation, shaped by social values. A striking example of the link between values and fertility was recently uncovered in a study of Spain (Coale, 1973, p. 63). A demographer drew a map showing the birth rates in Spain's forty-nine provinces and showed it to a language specialist. The areas of similar birth rates almost exactly matched the areas of different Spanish dialects. In other words, fertility patterns corresponded with cultural and linguistic variations. Only regional differences in culture could account for the differences in fertility.

If fertility is to decline, three conditions must be found together. First, the community must accept smaller families. So must the individual. And once men and women have decided that fewer children mean economic and social advantages, they must be able to find effective means of birth control. Birth control, then, must be *acceptable, advantageous* and *available* (Coale, 1973, p. 65).

As we have seen, some nations enjoy all three conditions. There, fertility starts declining even before industrial modernisation begins. In some countries birth rates stay high because all the preconditions are absent. Most nations fall somewhere in between. High mortality may not be a hindrance to modernisation, but high fertility certainly is. Lower fertility is still essential to modernisation, but modernisation need not take place for the three basic fertility-lowering conditions to exist.

Population Growth in America

The developing nations may outstrip us in population growth, but we will still have about 300 million Americans by the year

Table 9.2
Unwanted Fertility in the United States, 1970

Race and Education	*Most Likely Number of births per woman*	*Per cent of Births 1966 - 1970 Unwanted*	*Per cent of Births 1966 - 1970 Unplanned*[1]	*Theoretical Births Per Woman without Unwanted births*
All Women	3.0	15	44	2.7
College 4+	2.5	7	32	2.4
College 1-3	2.8	11	39	2.6
High School 4	2.8	14	44	2.6
High School 1-3	3.4	20	48	2.9
Less	3.9	31	56	3.0
White Women	2.9	13	42	2.6
College 4 +	2.5	7	32	2.4
College 1-3	2.8	10	39	2.6
High School 4	2.8	13	42	2.6
High School 1-3	3.2	18	44	2.8
Less	3.5	25	53	2.9
Black Women	3.7	27	61	2.9
College 4+	2.3	3	21	2.2
College 1-3	2.6	21	46	2.3
High School 4	3.3	19	62	2.8
High School 1-3	4.2	31	66	3.2
Less	5.2	55	68	3.1

[1]Unplanned births include unwanted births.
Source: Population and the American Future. The Report of the Commission on Population Growth and the American Future (Washington, D. C.: Government Printing Office, 1972), table 11.1, p. 97.

2,000, about 100 million more than in 1970 (*Statistical Abstract*, 1973, table 3, p. 6). More people demand more food, more energy, more resources—and create more pollution. If we want to keep up our comfortable way of life, then some feel we had best halt population growth.

If contraception that allowed women to have the number of children they wanted at the time they wanted them were available to all, would this be the answer? Many demographers say no, pointing to the fact that people want more than the replacement level of 2.25 children per family. In 1965, for example, married women aged thirty-five to forty-four were asked how many children they would like to have. Their answer—an average of 3.4

children per family—would lead to an awesome rate of growth. Other investigators approached this question differently, in subtle way they determined how many unwanted babies a representative group of women had had, then subtracted this number from the total number of children these women had borne. By this measure, the average ideal family turned out to have 2.5 children, far closer to the replacement rate (Bumpass and Westoff, 1970). A 1970 National Fertility Study concluded that of all births to married women from 1966 to 1970, 15 per cent were unwanted. Another 44 per cent were wanted but would have taken place later. A total of about 2.65 million babies were unplanned. Clearly, if contraception had been acceptable, advantageous, and available to all Americans, the problem of population growth would have been greatly alleviated.

Contraception

Americans now use more effective contraceptive devices than ever before. About four-fifths of couples using contraception in 1970 favoured the most effective methods—the pill, the IUD, and sterilisation (Westoff, 1972). Use of these methods increased from 37.2 per cent in 1965 to 57.9 per cent in 1970. Young couples, especially, chose the pill or the IUD more often than ever before. Older couples, on the other hand, were using sterilisation more than before. By 1970 about a third of the couples using contraception chose the pill. Charles Westoff sees the rapidity with which American women have accepted the pill since it first came on the market in 1960, despite its potential side effects, as "an indication of the wide market for effective contraception" (1972, p. 11).

Catholic Americans and Birth Limitation

Despite religious prohibitions, Catholics are using birth control much the way their compatriots are. In 1968 Pope Paul VI issued an encyclical, *Humanae Vitae,* reaffirming the traditional Roman Catholic prohibition of any birth-control method except rhythm (abstinence during fertile periods). All the same, American Catholics increased their use of other methods. A series of studies in 1955, 1960, 1965 and 1970 bear out this generalisation. In 1955 only 30 per cent of Catholic women used methods other than rhythm. By 1970 the proportion had gone up dramatically—to 68 per cent (Westoff and Ryder, 1970).

This trend has been even more marked among younger Catholic women: 78 per cent of those aged twenty to twenty-four used methods other than rhythm in 1970 (Westoff and Bumpass, 1973, p. 41). Even in 1965, when the rhythm method was still the most popular form of birth control for Catholic women (used by 36 per cent of all who practiced contraception), the pill took second place (18 per cent). The trend toward less dependence on the rhythm method and greater use of the pill held true for Protestant women as well (Westoff and Ryder, 1967, pp. 4-5).

One survey questioned Catholic women on their reactions to the papal encyclical. Typical of those who acted in opposition to church doctrine was this woman: "I don't think the Church has any right to dictate how many children you should have. I don't think any Church has a right to pry into anyone's private life. The Church doesn't help raise the children nor provide for them. It's just not the business of the Church" (Westoff and Ryder, 1970). Many priests now support women in their decision to use artificial birth-control methods. To sum up, Catholic women seem to be following the American trend toward use of more effective contraception.

Abortion

Until recently abortion was illegal in the United States. Therefore, it was hard to tell just how important it was as a means of birth control in America. In 1973 a Supreme Court ruling (*Roe v. Wade*) reflected a changing climate of opinion about abortion. *Roe v. Wade* held that abortion during the first twenty-four weeks of pregnancy was a private matter between a woman and her physician; state statutes could not interfere with it.

The following commets from citizens hint at the bitter struggle over abortion in recent years. One population expert expressed support for legalized abortion, calling its illegality "ludicrous". Why? Because, she pointed out, "from what I see of present population problems in the United States, in ten to twenty years women will be prohibited from doing what they are now forced to do and forced to do what they are prohibited from doing now" (Schulder and Kennedy, 1971, p. 127). But a Black Panther spoke out against abortion: "Abortion hides behind the guise of helping women, when in reality it will attempt to destroy our people" (Schulder and Kennedy, 1971, p. 156). And a New York doctor, a Catholic, refused even to provide contraception, on the grounds that women have no right to decide whether or not to bear a child (Schulder and Kennedy 1971, p. 172).

More generally, approval of abortion has increased markedly from 1935 to the present. A substantial majority of women now approve of abortion if a mother's health is in danger, if she has been raped, or if her child is likely to be born deformed. A small but significant minority (16.5 per cent) approve of abortion for any reason. In general, education goes hand in hand with approval of abortion. College graduates are most likely to approve of abortion under various circumstances (34.6 per cent). Working women and non-Catholics approve more often than housewives and Catholics. But surprisingly, young women are *less likely* to approve of abortion than are somewhat older women of child-bearing age (Jones and Westoff, 1972).

Legally available abortion immediately reduces the birth rate. In the two years after New York State passed its liberalised abortion law, New York City experienced dramatic declines in the number of live births. However, legal abortion accounted for only half the decline. The rest was due to new attitudes, which reduced births not only in New York but nationwide. Furthermore, many women who had legal abortions during this period would undoubtedly have had illegal ones otherwise. But making them legal has improved maternal health, especially for the poor, by replacing hasty, often dangerous back room procedures with sanitary, medically superivised ones. Legal abortions are cheaper, and thus available to nearly everyone. When fertility counselling accompanies abortion, the practice often reinforces and expands regular contraceptive practice (Tietze, 1973).

Table 9.3
The Baby Boom and the Birth Dearth

	1945	*1950*	*1955*	*1960*	*1965*	*1970*	*1973*
Live births (millions)	2,858	3,623	4,104	4,258	3,760	3,718	1,141
Crude birth rate (per 1,000 population)	20.4	24.1	25.0	23.7	19.4	17.8	15.0
Fertility rate (births per 1,000 women 15–44 years)	85.9	106.2	118.5	118.0	96.6	87.6	69.3
Children per family	2.5	3.2	3.6	3.6	3.6	2.4	1.9
NRR (female children per female adult)	1.42	1.55	1.73	1.62	1.38	1.24	1.00

Source: Statistical Abstract of the United States, 1973 (Washington, D. C.: Government Printing Office, 1973), tables 66 and 68, p. 52, figures for 1973 are from Harold M. Schmeck. Jr,. "Birth, Fertility Rates at a New Low in U.S." *The New York Times* (March 16, 1974): 14, based on data from the National Center for Health Statistics, U. S. Census Bureau. NRR rates by five-year averages with 1973 estimated from *Population Index, Vol. 39 (April 1973), p. 286.*

Although by 1965 the crude birth rate had droppe below the 1945 rate, the *number* of births remained higher in 1965 until 1970 because of the increasingly larger number of women of child-bearing age. Moreover, women were having more babies, than in 1945, as shown by the higher fertility rate (96.6 and 87.6 *versus* 85.9). In this case the fertility rate is a much more accurate reflection of trends than the crude birth rate. Notice the dramatic fall in the Net Reproduction Rate from 1.73 in 1955 to about 1.00 today, foreshadowing eventual zero population growth if this rate continues for a number of years.

The Birth Dearth: Will it Last?

After running its course, the postwar baby boom was followed by a baby bust. After the boom peaked in 1957, the crude birth rate fell steadily through the 1960s and into the 1970s (see Table 9.3). Our birth rate reached a low of fifteen per thousand in 1973. If the decline continues, we can achieve zero poulation growth much faster that people even five years ago had hoped.

But population growth may not be over yet. As the boom generation moves into its own child-bearing years, an echo boom is expected to take place. To some extent the recent decline occurred because the women bearing children were part of the

Box 9.2

Teenage Mothers

Imagine a television ad for baby food. The mother is in her twenties or thirties. In soft focus she cuddles her smiling, cooing baby. Her home is sunlit and middle class, and you can be sure she is wearing a wedding ring. The hard facts don't quite resemble this dreamy picture.

One-sixth of all babies are born to mothers in their teens. And of these, two-fifths are born out of wedlock. Teenange motherhood is shared by over a quarter of the girls born in 1950. One out of four of these teenage mothers had at least two children before age twenty. Believe it or not these figures represent a decline in teenage mothers from 33.9 per cent in 1939.

Unwed motherhood is largely teenage motherhood. The younger the mother, the less likely she is to be married when her child is born. Half the illegitimate births each year are to teenage mothers. Of births to mothers aged fifteen to seventeen, 40 per cent are illegitimate; slightly older mothers (eighteen or nineteen) are twice as likely to be married. We must not overlook the babies made legitimate only by hasty marriage. Nearly six out of ten first babies of girls aged fifteen to nineteen were conceived before marriage (Menken, 1972, p. 46).

While illegitimacy rates have declined for other age groups, they have been increasing for teens. In 1968 single girls fifteen to nineteen years old gave birth at a rate of 19.8 per thousand, up from 16.0 in 1961.

Having a baby out of wedlock has drastic consequences for a teenage girl. As Arthur Campbell put it, "The girl who has an illegi mate child at the age of sixteen suddenly has 90 per cent of her life's script written for her. She will probably drop out of school, even if someone else in her family helps to take care of the baby; she will probably not be able to find a steady job that pays enough to provide for herself and her child; she may feel impelled to marry someone she might not otherwise have chosen. Her life choices are few, and most of them are bad" (Campbell, in Menken, 1972, pp. 45-46).

Health complications plague the teenage mothers as well. More babies born to teenage mothers die before age one, especially when the mother has borne other children. Fetal mortality, too, is higher than for the babies of mothers in their twenties. Girls in their teens tend to have babies closer together than other mothers do. Shorter intervals between babies go hand in hand with stillbirth, prematurity, and infant

Box 9.2 Contd.

moratality (Menken, 1972, p. 49). Teenage mothers have more complicated pregnancies and they bear more premature infants. Prematurity has been associated with increased mortality and the development of a variety of congenital illnesses and birth defects, such as cerebral palsy, epilapsy, mental retardation, and blindness (Menken, 1972, p. 50).

Why do so many teenagers bear children? Probably because so many fail to use contraceptives. A national survey of never- married fifteen-to-nineteen-year-olds showed that nearly half of those with sexual experience had not used any method of contraception at last intercourse. Fewer than a fifth had always used contraception. Those who took no precaution rationalised that they could not get pregnant because they were too young, it was the wrong time of the month, or they had sex too seldom. About one-fourth believed oral contraceptives to be unsafe. Clearly, some misinformation contributes to the high birth rate among these girls.

Perfect contraception is "a model in which couples can avoid having more children than they want and do not have children before they want them" (Bumpass and Westoff, 1970, p. 1177). If teenagers precticed perfect contraception, the results would be startling. Here are some sample projections: if no females under eighteen had babies, the total birth rate among teenagers fifteen to nineteen years old would be reduced by 30 per cent. At this rate, in fifty years the population would be 5 per cent smaller than it would if the 1968 teenage birth rate continued unchanged. If 75 per cent of births to teenagers were postponed till the girls were twenty to twenty-four, and the rest to ages twenty-five to twenty-nine, the population in fifty years would be 6.6 per cent smaller. And if there were no teenage births at all, the population would be 15.1 per cent smaller. This drop alone would reduce the NRR to just over 1.0—almost a stationary population.

Sources: Larry Bumpass and Chaties F. West off, "The 'Perfect Contraceptive' Population," *Science,* vol. 169 (September 18, 1970): 1177–1182; Jane Menken "The Health and Social Consequences of Teenage Child-bearing." *Family Planning Perspectives,* vol. 4. No. 3, July 1972: 45–53.

unusually small group of depression babies. In 1965 there were just a few more women of prime child-bearing years than there were in 1935 (11.1 million as compared to 11 million), although the total population had grown by over 50 million people during those years. But this age group has been growing steadily, to 16 million in 1972. In 1980 there will be about 20.1 million, nearly twice as many as in 1960 (*Population Bulletin*, 1966, p. 65).

Thus, the current low *rate* of births may still result in large crops of babies because there are so many more mothers. Will twice as many mothers mean twice as many children? Probably not, according to most indicators. Young women today are having their children later. Furthermore, they are planning to have smaller families. Women now in their late thirties have, on the average, three children; but in 1971 married women aged eighteen to twenty-four expected to have an average of 2.4 children per family (Ehrlich and Ehrlich, 1972, p. 36). However, experience shows that families usually end up larger than people expect them to be.

Figure 9.5 : United States growth with two-or three-child families.

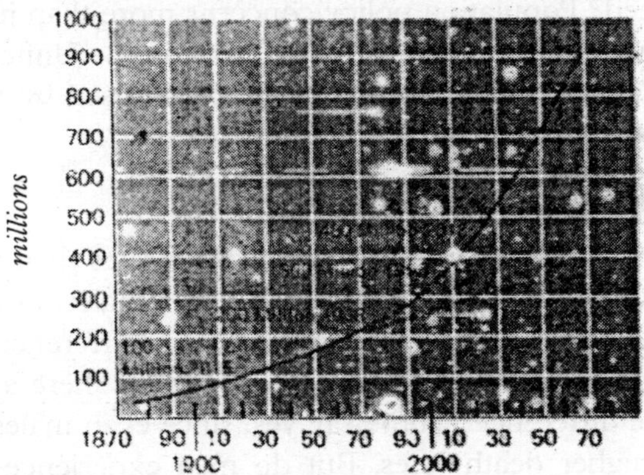

Source : Population and the American Future. The Report of the Commission on Population Growth and the American Future (Washington, D.C.: Government Printing Office, 1972) figure 2.3, p. 23.

The difference between having two children and three seems small enough until examined for a whole population. Had American families continued to have three children apiece the population would double by 2013 (from 200 million in 1968 to 400 million 55 years later). Recent trends however make the two-child family more typical. Even so there will be another 100 million Americans by the year 2015.

In late 1972 births fell below replacement level for the first time. Optimists hailded this as zero poulation growth. One called the day of the announcement “a milestone . . . a day as historic as the fourth of July, the birth date of any President, or the termination date of any war” (Kahn, 1974). But had we really achieved a constant population? On the contrary. Even if we hold to replacement-level fertility—a big “if”—it will still take from sixty-five to seventy-five years for population growth to end, because of the age structure of the population. From replacement level in 1974 to ZPG in about 2040, our population would increase by 81million (Ehrlich and Ehrlich 1972 pp. 38-39)!

Health in America

While many Americans worry about the population crush, others wonder about the fate of those who are born. Will they lead long, Realthy lives? Will they be able to pay for the health care they need? Population policy concerns more than just birth rates and death rates. Though the death rate in the United States is relatively low, it could be even lower. It is raised by the high death rates of certain groups in the population.

Excess Death

From birth to death males have higher death rates than females. At birth there are 106 males for every 100 females, but by age sixty-five the sex ratio has dropped to 72. A difference of this magnitude raises some provocative questions. Is there a genetic cause for the difference? Some say yes, since even males one to eight have higher death rates. But do men experience greater stress and greater pressure to achieve than women? Is the higher male death rate partly a penalty for success as the world sees it? As liberated women put themselves under similar pressures, their death rate may rise to match that of the men. Some optimists look for a different outcome. Suppose men took a hint from the Women's Liberation Movement and began to get off the treadmill. Would their death rate start to decline?

Beside an excess of male over female deaths, avoidable deaths result from smoking (Brody, 1974, p. 8). In the ten years since 1964, when the surgeon general of the Public Health Service officially reported on the hazards of cigarette smoking, about 29 million people stopped smoking. Still, there were 52 million smokers, including a large number of young people (3,000 teenagers begin smoking every day). Americans are smoking new types of cigarettes, with less tar and nicotine—the substances considered harmful. Neverheless, the Public Health Service estimates that 300,000 people die annually as a direct result of complications from smoking such as lung cancer and heart disease. Smokers miss 40 per cent more working days than non-smokers do, visit doctors more often, spend more time in hospitals, and require surgery more often (Brody, 1974).

The American people have the highest incomes in the world, and they second more than anyone else on health care, nearly 7 per cent of the GNP. Nevertheless, the United States has a higher crude death rate and a higher infant mortality rate than a number of other nations. More than fifteen other nations have rates of infant mortality, for example. Many underdeveloped countries, such as Mexico and Iran, have far lower crude death rates than the United States. However, the discrepancy is only apparent. Because these countries have high birth rates, and correspondingly high proportions of young people in their overall population, they have fewer people in the years of high mortality. It is more informative and accurate to compare the crude death rates for the United States with those for other developed nations. Even here, however, several countries such as Sweden have lower mortality rates, an indication that they deliver health care more effectively than we do. Likewise, the United Nations found that the life expectancy for males born in 1972 in the United States was lower than life expectancies for males in at least sixteen other nations (United Nations, 1973, tables 13, 15, 18). Once again evidence indicates we could improve our health care.

Socioeconomic factors help to determine mortality rates. As one demographer puts it, "the relatively high mortality of the United States compared with other advanced nations is undoubtedly in large measure a reflection of the high mortality of the disadvantaged in the nation—the lower socioeconomic

Table 9.4
Excess Mortality in the United States, 1960 (by per cent)

Sex Colour, Age and Years of School completed	*25 and over*	*25–64 years*	*65 and Over*
Total population	19	26	15
Males	11	25	1
Females	30	29	30
Whites	17	21	15
Nonwhites	36	52	18
White males	10	21	2
0–4 years of school	9	30	3
5–7 years of school	12	29	2
8 years of school	10	25	1
High school, 1–3 years		24	
High school, 4 years	11	16	0.1
College, 1 year or more	0	0	0
Non white males	25	45	0.5
0–4 years of school	25	51	5
5–8 years of school	23	43	-8
high school or college	28	39	-3
White females	27	21	30
0–4 years of school	42	53	40
5–7 years of school	33	36	32
8 years of school	31	30	31
High school, 1–3 years		12	
High school, 4 years	18	4	26
College, 1 year or more	0	0	0
Nonwhite females	49	60	39
0–4 years of school	51	70	41
5–8 years of school	50	63	34
High school or college	44	42	41

Source: Evelyn M. Kitagawa and Phillip M. Hauser, *Differential Mortality in the United States: A Study in Socioeconomic Epidemiology* Cambridge, Mass.: Harvard University Press, 1973, table 8.1.

groups of whites and the even more disadvantaged minority groups" (Kitagawa, 1972, p. 106). Kitagawa's studies show, for example, that those with the lowest incomes have higher overall mortality rates, higher infant mortality, and a higher incidence of infectious and chronic diseases. Education, as well as income, corresponds with lower mortality. Racial differences are particularly marked. From 1959 to 1961, for example, all nonwhite females had a death rate 34 per cent higher than that of white females. The rate for all nonwhite males was 20 per cent higher than that for white males at all ages. The difference was even greater with the young, especially infants (Kitagawa, 1972).

These statistics led Kitagawa to ask: How many people die unnecessarily in the United States today? To find out, she devised an Index of Excess Mortality, which in simple terms measures the deaths that would not have occurred if every subgroup had the same, relatively low, death rate as whites aged twenty-five years and over with at least one year of college. In 1960 this figure was 292,000, or 19 per cent of all deaths, (17 per cent of deaths among whites, and 36 per cent of deaths among nonwhites (Kitagawa, 1972) . These deaths must be considered preventable.

Health Care and the Poor

Could we imporve mortality rates by improving education for all, thus preparing people for better jobs, more income, and thus better health care? Or can we approach the problem differently, making helath care equally available to all? At present the system of health care in the United States falls short in several respects. In proportion to population, there are simply fewer medical facilities in poor areas, both rural and urban. In 1970 the fifteen counties with highest per capita incomes had seven times as many hospital beds per person than did the fifteen counties with the lowest per capita income (Schultze, 1972, p. 222).

Poor people visit doctors less frequently; especially for preventive care. This pattern is particularly striking for children. On the average, poor children under sixteen visited the doctor only 17 times a year, while wealthy children the same age averaged 5.7 visits. Only 10 per cent of low-income children have ever visited a pediatrician, compared with 30 per cent of upper-income children. School examinations turned up some children with defective vision. Of those from the lowest income group, 31.1 per cent received no treatment for the condition; only 13.5

per cent of children in the upper-income bracket went without treatment (Hurley, 1970, pp. 91-93). Of children from families with incomes of $ 3,000 or less, 20.9 per cent have not received vaccinations against smallpox and 18.9 per cent have not received diphtheria-tatanus vaccinations. For children from families with incomes of $9,000 or more, the figures are 3.9 per cent and 1.7 per cent, respectively (Hurley 1970).

The inequities show up in many other areas. The poor of all ages have less private health insurance, easpecially for children. In 1968, 90 per cent of families with incomes over $10,000 had some private medical insurance, while only a third of those earning less than $ 3,000 did. Of children covered by insurance plans, less than a quarter of those at the lowest economic level were covered for hospitalisation expenses. Nine-tenths of those at the upper level had such protection. Medicaid and Medicare have attempted to improve health coverage for the poor and the elderly, respectively. But these programmes do not provide for preventive care, and what they offer varies widely from state to state. The states also administer and regulate their own programmes. Thus, one state, for example, limits payments to only fifteen days of hospital care. Only a few states include payments for drugs, the services of dentists and optometrists, and private nursing.

Until we solve some of these problems in delivery of health care, some Americans will continue at a disadvantage. In a civilised society population control means maintaining the citizens's good health, not just regulating their numbers.

10

Power and Politics

The Basic Dimensions of Power and Politics

The foundations for the sociology of power and politics were laid by Max Weber; his essays on the subject are reprinted in *From Max Weber: Essays in Sociology* (1946). There he defines *political power* as the ability of a person or a group of people "to realise their own will in a communal action even against the resistance of others who are participating in the action" (p. 180). How is such power acquired?

Political Power: Its Sources and Uses

The most obvious source of political power is the right to use or to threaten *physical force*. President Kennedy did not have to detonate nuclear weapons to stop the Soviet Union from establishing missile bases in Cuba, for example. Premier Khrushchev believed that as president of the United States, Kennedy had the capacity to inflict serious damage and that he was willing to do so. The risks of "calling his bluff" seemed too high. Often threats and bluffs of force succeed because they are incorrectly estimated or go unchallenged (Bierstedt, in Olsen, 1970).

Other sources of political power include numbers, organisation, and such resources as *money, land, prestige* and *knowledge*. Consider the issue of equal pay for equal work. If only five women in a large company refuse to do their jobs unless they are paid as much as men earn in equivalent positions, their employer may fire them and hire replacements. However, if all or most of the women in the company demand equal pay with men, management will probably be forced to bargain. The principle of majority rule is based on the fact that majorities have the potential to enforce their will. "The power which resides in numbers is clearly seen in elections of all kinds, where the majority is conceded the right to institutionalize its power as authority—a right which is conceded because it can be taken" (Bierstedt, in Olsen, 1970, pp. 17-18).

But numbers alone do not constitute political power. Throughout history small elites have dominated hugh majorities because "the masses" lacked organisation and resources. Individually, the women in the example above will not be able to change the policy of underpaying female employees. A hundred or even a thousand angry but isolated women will have little effect. Unless they mobilise, establish communications net works, and coordinate their activities, they will accomplish little. They may use their financial resources to buy out the current owners or, more likely, to support themselves while they strike. They might persuade influential public figures to back them or use the media to stimulate public pressure. If they know something about the company that would be damaging to its public image, or if they possess skills the company cannot find elsewhere, they may use these as powerful levers.

Powerful individuals and groups can enforce their will in political decisions in one of several ways. Power can be used to compensate others for complying with one's wishes. The classic example of compensation is political patronage—awarding political appointments to loyal supporters, ambassadorships to campaign contributors, and the like. Paying generous government officials "under the table" to vote a certain way, or awarding a contract to a particular company, or bribing a witness to testify in one's favour are other forms of political compensation. In effects the briber is paying the other person for the risk he or she takes in lying under oath. Power can also be used to punish people who do not comply with one's wishes, and to withhold expected rewards. This is known as *coercive power* because compliance is involuntary. The National Guard opening fire on protesting students at Kent State or a mayor refusing to issue permits to demonstrators are examples. On a different level, expelling students who are caught cheating, and withholding diplomas from students who have not fulfilled all requirements for graduation are also forms of coercive power. Finally, people can use power to persuade others to comply by manipulating information, emotions, norms, and values. As Marvin E. Olsen observed (1970, p. 6), applying punish-ments or withholding rewards obtains only reluctant compliance, and is therefore less reliable than compensation, from which both parties expect to benefit. To the extent that persuasion succeeds in changing people's minds about an issue or a candidate so that they do not feel they are being coerced or even compromised, it may be the most effective and long-lasting use of power.

Box 10.1

Political Persuasion

When attempting to persuade the public that the war in Vietnam was an expression of our noblest traditions, the late President Johnson was a master at manipulation information, emotions, norms and values. His November 1966 speech to an audience of Gl's stationed in the Demilitarised Zone was an effective use of the power of persuasion.

The avergae fellow in the world doesn't ask for much. . .He wants. . .a roof over his head, a chance for his kids to go to school. . . a little recreation for his family, a movie now and then, or to be able to load them all in the old jalopy and take them to see Grandma on Sunday. But except for you, people couldn't do that. . . You weren't born into this world. . .to liquidate the freedom and liberty that your grandfathers fought for with bows and arrows or old muskets. You have a heritage, a tradition to carry on.

Johnson added, "My great-great-grandfather died at the Alamo."It reminded newsmen of the times he showed them the little shack where he had been born. According to Johnson's mother, he had definitely not been born in a shack; nor had any of his ancestors been anywhere near the Alamo. But Johnson knew the powerful *symbolic* value of humble origins and frontier heroics.

Lyadon Johnson also used his persuasive talents to convince Congress to pass the Civil Rights legisiation of the 1960s and to "sell" the War on Poverty to the American people.

Source: David Wise, *The Politics of Lying* (New York, Vintage, 1973), chap. 2.

Influence

Influence is related, but not identical to authority. We say people have *influence* when they are so highly respected, so well liked that they can change people's minds without resorting to compensation, threats, or manipulation. Although enhanced by official position, influence is ultimately a personal quality. Eleanor Roosevelt, for example, never held public office but she did hold much of the public's attention, respect and admiration. And while she lived in the White House, Jacqueline Kennedy influenced women's fashions, although she never made a single speech on dress design.

Authority and Legitimacy

For Weber naked coercive power was only one source of political influence. In all of his writings, Weber stressed the difference between coercive power and authority. *Coercive power* rests on the threat or use of violenc; it is the ability to *force* people to comply with one's designs. *Authority* rests on the consent of the governed; it is power exercised in a way that people consider necessary and legitimate. Every year the Internal Revenue Service takes money from all working Americans. Although people grumble about taxes, few question the government's legitimate authority to collect them, and fewer still refuse to pay them. As Weber suggests, all organisations and particularly governments depend on "a certain minimum of voluntary submission; [on] an interest (based on ulterior motives or genuine acceptance) in obedience" (Weber, 1947). Power to which people willingly submit is authority.

Weber identified three types of authority: legal/rational, charismatic and traditional. *Legal/rational authority* derives from a system of explicit rules or laws that define legitimate uses of power. Authority is vested in offices or positions, not in the people who temporarily occupy those posts. It is limited to "official business". For. example, a boss has considerable authority over the way employees spend their working days, but he does not have the authority to tell workers how to spend their weekends. In systems based on legal rational authority, loyalty tc the system largely replaces loyalty to a paricular person. Public officials, professionals (doctors, lowyers, teachers, etc.), and to some extent businessmen and women are expected to put their professions first and to disobey superiors who ask them to break the law or organisational rules. One of the main revelations of the Senate Watergate hearings was how aides in the Nixon administration overlooked this principle. Numerous officials confessed to placing their loyalty to the man above their duty to obey laws and expose criminal acts.

Charismatic authority is the opposite of rational/legal authority. It derives from exceptional personal qualities that people perceive as a "gift of grace". People follow a charismatic leader because they are personally devoted to him or her. But as Weber observed, "The charismatic leader gains and maintains authority solely by proving his strength in life. If he wants to be a prophet, he must perform miracles; if he wants to be a war lord, he must perform heroic deeds" (1946, p. 249). Routine is the antithesis of the spontaneous force of charisma. This is why succession can be problematic. The unique, irreplaceable qualities of a charismatic leader are not likely to appear twice in a row. There are no second Gandhis, Malcolm Xs, or Martin Luther Kings. For this reason charismatic authority is inherently unstable. Nevertheless, such leaders have overcome overwhelming odds. Examples of charismatic leadership in recent history include Gandhi. Martin Luther King, Jr., Malcolm X and Cesar Chavez.

Traditional authority lies between rational legal authority and charismatic authority. In traditional societies people tend to regard the way things have always been done as sacred; kings, chiefs, priests, councils of elders, and the like are part of this sacred order. Although traditions may limit a king's or chief's authority, they do have some personal latitude in making decisions. Positions are hereditary and people feel a sense of personal loyalty to the occupants. Thus, traditional authority is vested in both the office and the holder. A familiar example is parents' authority over children.

In practice the three types of authority Weber identified may overlap. John Kennedy, for example, had rational/legal authority by virtue of his election to the presidency, the traditional authority that surrounds the office of the presidency, and charismatic appeal as well.

Whatever system of authority prevail leaders or people in positions of power invariably try to *legitimise* their acts in terms of existing values, thereby attempting to establish authority. The legitimacy of an administration or system of government depends on its capacity "to engender and maintain the belief that existing political institutions are the most appropriate one for the society" (Lipset, 1970, p. 40).

Box 10.2

In The News

King of Kings

Every year on the morning of the spring equinox, His Imperial Majesty, Mohammed Reza Pahlevi, King of Kings, Light of the Aryans, holds court amid the glittering splendor of Teheran's Gulistan Palace to receive the homage of Iran and the world. . .[I]t is a ceremony of power. . .At one end of the room, under a massive arch of mosaic mirrorwork that throws back the light of the chandeliers in a million rays of silver, stands the giant divan of jewel-encrusted marble known as the Peacock Throne. At the other end are the tall, white doors through which, every half hour, the monarch and his Empress enter to send a shiver of excitement and apprehension around the room.

He is not very tall, this Shahanshah . . .[but] he carries the authentic, unmistakable scent of power; and as he leaves the room again his subjects smile and release their breath in mingled pride and relief, euphoric in the afterglow of his presence.

Seventy per cent of Iranians are illiterate, 60 per cent live at a subsistence level, and hundreds of villages in this rich country do not have a doctor. But it seems unlikely that the Shah will be deposed. He not only maintains the legal and political power to dissolve Iran's parliament, he is also a religious leader, the guardian of the Iranian way of life according to the tradition of Shilsm (Iran's dominant Moslem sect). He thus combines charismatic, legal/rational, and traditional forms of authority.

Source: David Holden, "Shah of Shahs, Shah of Dreams," *The New York Times Magazine* (May 26, 1974): 9.37; and *The New York Times* (June 3, 1974*)*: 1, 12.

Power and the State

The concept or legitimacy is central to Weber's definition of the state. The *State* differs from other organisations in a society, Weber wrote, in that it successfully "claims *the monopoly of the legitimate use of physical force* within a given territory" (1946, p. 78). Organised crime may use physical force to coerce people, but ordinarily not with social consent and approval. Only the state is conceded the legitimate right to forcibly arrest, jail and in some cases kill people.

The way in which political power is organised in a country depends on its history and culture, as Gabriel Almond's classification indicate (1956). Almond identifies four types of political systems, focusing on their different cultural orientations toward politics. He compares *Anglo-American political systems* to political marketplaces, where different groups bargain for decisions that are favourable to them. Decisions are made through a system of exchange. In simple terms, Group A wants to build a highway, Group B wants to preserve a park, Group C wants additional funds for school recreation. Group A may promise to vote for school funds if Group C supports the highway, or Group B may offer Group C use of a park if it votes against the highway. Ideology is less important in Anglo-American systems than in the other three types identified by Almond. People see politics as a way of solving problems and pursuing self-interest, not as a "holy cause." Power and responsibility are diffused into a number of autonomous but interdependent government agencies and departments and private organisations. Because the division of political labour is so complex, Anglo-American systems depend on some degree of consensus about the basic values of freedom, mass welfare and security.

Preindustrial Political systems develop when "large groups have fundamentally different 'cognitive maps' of politics and apply different norms to political action." Such systems embrace at least two cultures—the traditional culture, and the Western colonial culture. The two exist in what often appears to outsiders as an incompatible relationship. For example, political parties may center around powerful families, as tribal governments do.

The people may elect a mayor (following Western custom), but see nothing wrong in his awarding all appointed positions and contracts to members of his family. Different ideas of correct and incorrect political behaviour make preindustrial systems extremely volatile: the one thing on which people generally agree in such systems is nationalism.

Totalitarian political systems rest on modern methods of communication, organisation, and violence, over which the state has absolute control. It alone supervises the media, the schools, the police and the military. Power is highly centralised in such governments; any and all opposition is suppressed. Much of the state's power comes from the fact that any behaviour may arbitrarily be defined as treasonous and punished. The arbitrary use of power applies to public officials as well as to private citizens, and prevents and opposition from gathering support. But totalitarian systems do not rest on force alone; as we suggested earlier, this would be impossible. No government can, as yet, oversee every moment of every citizen's life (except in novels such as George Orwell's, 1984). Totalitarian systems depend on relatively high degrees of conformity and apathy among citizens.

Continental-European political systems (those in France, Germany and Italy) include a number of parties that have conflicting and mutually exclusive designs for politics. Workers demand one kind of government, traditional parties (such as Catholic parties) another, secular, middle-class parties demand still another. Each seeks to convert the opposition, to transform the political system. Whereas political affiliation in Anglo American systems is based on practical considerations in Continental-European systems it is an act of faith. Political activities take on religious overtones; ideologies become causes. As a result, the centers of power and authority tend to be in parties and in political subcultures rather than in the formal government.

Power, Politics and Law

Whatever form politics takes, one of the primary functions of the state is organising and controlling the use of power. Most modern societies rely on legal systems to confer the authority to use force for social control. Legal systems also limit the authority that people in powerful positions can exercise.

Law and Social Control

"The essential talent of the law," wrote Harvard law professor Roger Fisher, "lies not in producing perfect order but in *coping with disorder in an orderly way.* Contract law, negligence law and criminal law 'work' not in the sense of producing a community with no broken contracts, no negligence and no crimes, but by telling us how to respond when things go wrong" (Fisher, 1974, italics added).

The official purposes of law include (a) defining and suppressing deviance (through criminal law); (2) protecting individual and group rights (through civil transactions); (3) preventing powerful organisations from abusing these rights (through financial and corporate law); (4) preventing government from abusing these rights; and (5) settling disputes.

In performing these functions the law gives certain groups the power to say what is acceptable or not as well as the power to enforce their view. For example, in defining marijuana, gambling, prostitution, homosexuality, and other "victimless crimes" as deviant, the law in effect criminalises these activities. Deviant labels often become self-fulfilling prophecies: stigmatised individuals may be forced into the underworld the law is designed to suppress. Even people who have not broken the law may be stigmatised if police keep arrest as well as conviction records and release them to employers, banks, and others who hold social power. And sometimes vague laws against loitering, vagrancy, creating a public nuisance, or obscenity may give police an excuse to arrest almost anyone they consider a troublemaker.

Similarly, the practice of law may deprive members of certain groups of their guaranteed rights. In this country, every person is presumed innocent until found guilty and every person is entitled to counsel. In reality, the poor often serve time in jail before they are tried because they are unable to raise bail. Court-appointed lawyers often represent so many clients that they cannot investigate and prepare a case as throughly as private lawyears, and often work *with* the district attorney's office.

Finally, the law can be used as an instrument for political repression, even in democracies. For instance, in the late sixties and early seventies, the United States government used conspiracy laws to punish dissenters. For example, the Chicago 7 were tried for conspiring to cross a state line to incite a riot. The decision against the Chicago 7 was overturned by a higher court, which found that the presiding judge had not conducted a fair trial. Thus, even though it lost the case, the government effectively prevented these dissenters from carrying on their normal lives for many months. In summary, the law is not a neutral instrument. It can be manipulated by the powerful to harass groups they consider threatening to the existing power structure, as well as to preserve the common good.

Constraints on Government Power

The legal system in this country is an adversary system. The prosecution presents evidence in a way calculated to incriminate the defendant; through an attorney, the defendant presents evidence in a light that demonstrates his or her innocence; the jury or judge decides which argument is true. Similarly, our political system is based on a structure of checks and balances among the three branches of government. Both systems assume that, given the chance, people will use the power they have to further their own interests, and that the best way to prevent the abuse of power is to pit self-interest against self-interest. Competing branches of government, the minority party, elections, the press, and public opinion all act as checks on government power. As a last resort, the Constitution provides for the impeachment of "civil officers," up to and including the president.

The authors of the Constitution met to consider presidential accountability on july 20, 1787. Should the Chief Executive be subject to impeachment and removal from office? George Mason of Virginia thought he should. "Shall any man be above the law?" he asked. "Above all, shall that man be above it, who can commit the most extensive injustice?" North Carolina's

Charles Pinckney had reservations: "Mightn't Congress use impeachment as a rod over the President's head, destroying his independence? Elbridge Gerry of Massachusetts returned, "A good magistrate will not fear impeachments, a bad one ought to be kept in fear of them." When a vote was taken, the "ayes" had it: *The president, vice-president and all civil officers of the United States, shall be removed from office on impeachment for, and conviction of, treason, bribery, or other high crimes and misdemeanors* (Article II, sect. IV of the Constitution).

Only twice since 1787 has Congress considered removing a president from office. The first impeachment move began in 1867, after Andrew Johnson refused to implement Reconstruction programmes Congress had passed over his vet. Johnson was eventually impeached for breaking a law the Supreme Court later declared unconstitutional, but he was cleared in a Senate trail. In July 1974, the House judiciary Committee approved three articles of impeachment against Richard Nixon. On August 5 of that year, the White House released tapes that indicated the President had indeed been guilty of "obstruction of justice." When it became clear that Mr. Nixon would be impeached and found guilty in the Senate, he resigned, turning the presidency over to Gerald Ford on August 9.

The rise and fall of Richard Nixon, and of Lyndon Johnson before him, show the extent to which political leaders depend on public trust in democracies. In politics, trust is like a blank check. It means that authorities can make decisions and claim the loyalty of individuals and groups without specifying in advance what their cooperation will entail. People are more likely to tolerate delays and sacrifice if they trust the leaders who demand them. When politicians lose public trust they must "waste" some of their resources trying to restore their credibility (by visiting foreign leaders, for example) and perhaps enforcing decisions that might be accepted willingly if they were trusted (Gamson, 1968, pp. 42 - 51).

In 1964, President Johnson was reelected by a landslide; by 1968, however, he had begun to lose legitimacy with the American public, and decided not to seek a second terms. Similarly, in 1972, President Nixon was reelected by an overwhelming margin, but as the Watergate cover-up began to unravel, his popularity declined. By the summer of 1974, when Nixon resigned, a majority of Americans had indicated they disapproved of his conduct in office. An equal number gave Congress a poor rating (Gallup Polls, April 28; May 19, 1974). But despite widespread disillusionment with politicians, most Americans apparently had not lost faith in the political system of the nation. Seven out of ten respondents in one poll expressed confidence in America's future (Gallup Poll, May 19, 1974). Two sociologists have found that many adult Americans retain a blanket admiration for and loyalty to the political system (if not to specific administrations, while a smaller percentage commit themselves to specific policies and candidates (Easton and Dennis, 1969). French adults, in contrast, tend to be highly cynical about politics or to ignore politics whenever possible (Dowse and Hughes, 1972, p. 188). How are these attitudes acquired? Like attitudes toward sex, money, and other things, it is during the process of socialisation.

Box 10.3

Youth in the Seventies: Political Skeptics

If the nationwide survey conducted by the Daniel Yankelovich research organization in 1973 is accurate, attitudes toward power and politics are changing. According to this survey, a majority of young Americans—in and out of college—are satisfied with their lives, optimistic about their futures, and feel our society is basically healthy. At the same time, however, six out of ten believe that "special interests" (big business and self-interested politicians) run the government, and that American society is democratic in name only. A majority (54 per cent) believe corporations are the real centers of power in this country, and nine out of ten think big business puts profits too far ahead of social responsibility. Only one in five young people thinks the war in Vietnam ended with honour. Critical of American foreign policy, four out of five believe "new Vietnams" are inevitable. The percentage of college youth who feel our political parties need fundamental reforms grew from 57 per cent in 1969 to 61 per cent in 1973; the percentage of noncollege youth who agreed grew even more dramatically, from 44 per cent to 64 per cent.

Almost half of those surveyed identified themselves as Democrats (45 per cent youth, 49 per cent of noncollege youth) . Noncollege respondents were more conservative than college respondents' (53 per cent of whom said they were radical or liberal). More favour the death penalty for some crimes (52 to 44 per cent), life sentences for drug pushers (45 to 30 per cent), and a crackdown on pornography (44 to 26 per cent). Fewer (14 to 35 per cent) describe themselves as active in politics. Both groups, however, seem to be developing a "broad new agenda of social rights." Many young people feel *entitled* to things their parents only hoped for, including the best medical care, whether or not they can afford it (54 per cent), the right to participate in decisions affecting one's job (53 per cent), a college education for one's children (48 per cent), and secure retirement (37 per cent).

Yankelovich concludes that one of the most important political questions today is whether our system will prove responsive to the new values and expectations of the noncollege majority. While not as politicised as young workers in Europe and South America, this group is beginning to evidence resentment. "If four institutions prove rigid and unresponsive and our political leadership shows insensitivity to the changing needs and values of our youth, then the underlying potential for discontent will become all too real and we will face a period of instability and demagoguery."

Source: Daniel Yankelovich, *Changing Youth Values in the 70,s:A Study of American Youth,* New York: JDR 3rd Fund, 1974.

Political Socialisation

Studies of children's attitudes toward government indicate that political socialisation "begins early, if unsystematically," in the family, where youngsters develop assumptions about "human nature," attitudes toward authority, concepts of legitimacy, group loyalties, and so on. Many of these lessons are implied, not explicit. By the time children reach school, most have definite feelings about such political symbols as the president, even though they know little about the political system (Dowse and Hughes, 1972, chap. 6). Attitudes toward politics, then, seem to predate understanding.

In the early sixties, David Easton, Jack Dennis, Colleagues questioned a national sample of schoolchildren on their ideas about and attitudes toward government. They found that most young children identified government with the father of the country, George Washington, and with President John Kennedy. When asked who made the laws in America, 76 per cent of second graders said the president. This personalised image of government begins to change in the fourth and fifth graders, with more and more young people defining government in terms of Congress and voting (see Table 10.1). Fifty-seven per cent of fifth graders and 85 per cent of eighth graders knew that Congress makes the laws in America. The authors attribute this change to a growing awareness that government is a collective enterprise (not the actions of single person) and a deepening understanding of the representative nature of democracy. Young children viewed government in terms of personalised, charismatic authority: older children grasped the concept of legal/rational authority. Virtually all of the children pictured the government in glowing terms, as "something" that protects people, helps them, and cares for them in times of need. The government is not only helpful, in childrens' view, it exercises leadership ("makes important decisions"), knows more than most people, has power over almost everyone ("can punish"), and practically never makes mistakes. French children, in contrast,

Table 10.1
Children's Developing Awareness of Who Makes the Laws

Grade	*Congress*	*President*	*Supreme Court*	*I Don't Know*	*Total*	*N. Resp-onding*	*N Not Respon-ding*
Grade 2	5%	76%	11%	8%	100%	1627	28
Grade 3	11	66	17	6	100	1648	30
Grade 4	28	44	21	7	100	1723	26
Grade 5	57	19	20	3	99	1793	10
Grade 6	65	13	18	3	99	1743	6
Grade 7	72	9	16	3	100	1712	11
Grade 8	85	5	8	1	99	1690	5

Source: David Easton and Jack Dennis, *Children in the Political System*, New York: McGraw-Hill, 1969.

see their president as someone who commands others and sees that his orders are obeyed; rarely do these children mention that he is "good" or "helpful" (Greenstein, 1973).

Anthony Orum and Roberta Cohen's recent comparison of black and white schoolchildren indicates that not all American children idealise our government (1973). Black children, like black adults, are more cynical about politics than their white counterparts, and they are less likely to regard to government as benevolent or to idealise the president. Black young people generally know more about the political system than do whites from similar socioeconomic backgrounds, participate in more political discussions and activities, perceive greater differences between parties, and are more likely to take sides. These differences appear as early as fourth grade and remain relatively constant through high school. The authors conclude that political attitudes do indeed develop very early, and that children adopt the political norms and values of their community.

Studies such as these suggest that income, education, religion, and other factors that correlate with party choice and voting have only an *indirect* effect on the formation of political attitudes. Parents, peers, teachers and neighbours orient children to politics, and insofar as these people's political opinions reflect their incomes and so on, income can be said to influence the development of political attitudes.

Theories of Political Power

Throughout history philosophers and statesmen have debated the questions—who exercises social power, why, and what are the consequences? Contemporary theories of political power are largely an elaboration of and reaction against Karl Marx.

Marx: An Economic Theory of Power

Before Marx, political philosophers more or less assumed that social power resided in the state and related organisations, such as the military. Any discussion of politics centered on government. Breaking with tradition, Marx argued that power is rooted in economics. The people who own the "means of production" (the factories, raw materials, and so on) control society; the state is little more than their servant (Olsen, 1970, p. 70).

Marx went on to elaborate a philosophy of history. With the rise of capitalism, society had begun to split into two hostile camps, two diametrically opposed classes—the bourgeoisie (the owners) and the proletariat (the workers or masses.) The owners' very existence depends on their ability to exploit the workers. They create "a class of labourers, who live only so long as they find work, and who find work only so long as their labour increases capital. These labourers, who must sell themselves piecemeal, are a commodity, like every other article of commerce, and are consequently exposed to all the vicissitudes of competition, to all the fluctuations of the market" [Marx and Engels, (1847), 1967]. And herein lie the seeds of the bourgeoisie's destruction. Workers, Marx argued, will become increasingly insecure and alienated. The traditional and emotional ties that bound lord and serf do not exist between owner and worker in capitalist economies. Work ceases to be a moral duty and source of satisfaction. (There is little craft in performing an assembly line job—workers become appendages to machines—and the products of that work do not belong to them.) "At this stage, "Marx and Engels wrote, "the labourers still form an incoherent mass scattered over the whole country, and broken up by their mutual competition. "But it is only a matter of time before they realise they are being exploited (develop class consciousness) and rise up against the industrialists, pitting the power of numbers against the power of wealth. In Marx's view, class revolution is inevitable. Beyond revolution he envisioned a temporary "dictatorship of the proletariat" that would restore ownership of the means of production to the workers, laying the groundwork for a classless and just society. Eventually the state would "wither away"

Pareto and Mosca: The Elitist View

Many of Marx's contemporaties disagreed sharply with his reasoning and his predictions, among them Vilfredo Pareto and Gaetano Mosca. Neither of these sociologists thought a classless society was possible, much less desirable. Pareto began with the simple observation that some lawyers are sharper, some royal mistresses more influential, some thieves more successful than others, so that in all human activities there are elites. "I am not interested here in what is desirable," Pareto noted. "I am making a simple study of what is. In a broad sense I mean by the *elite* in a society people who possess in marked degree qualities of intelligence, character, skill, capacity, of whatever kind": (Pareto, in Olsen, 1970, p. 115). And politics is not exempt from this general rule. Throughout history small governing elites, distinguished by their talents and organisation, have ruled the masses by virtue of their superiority. As Mosca put this:

> In all societies—from societies that are very meagerly developed and have barely attained the dawnings of civilisation, down to the most advanced and powerful societies—two classes of people always appear—a class that rules and a class that is ruled. The first class, always the less numerous, performs all political functions, monopolises power and enjoys the advantages that power brings, whereas the second, the more numerous class, is directed and controlled by the first in a manner that is now more or less legal, now more or less arbitrary and violent, and supplies the first, in appearance at least, with material means of subsistence and with the instrumentalities that are essential to the vitality of the political organism. (Mosca, in Olsen, 1970, p. 123).

By elite or ruling class, neither Pareto nor Mosca, meant a strictly hereditary class. To the contrary. Both believed that hereditary ruling classes, like strings of horses that have been inbred for too long, degenerate. Once this occurs the capacity of the elite to govern is lost. As Pareto wrote. "History is a graveyard of aristocracies. . . They decay not in numbers only. They decay also in quality, in the sense that they lose their vigour," But rarely does a closed aristocracy stay in power to the point of incapacity. "The governing class is restored. . .by families rising from the lower classes and bringing with them the vigour and the proportions of residues necessary for keeping themselves in power. . .In virtue of class circulation, the governing elite is always in a state of slow and continuous transformation" (Pareto, in Olsen, 1970, pp. 117-18). This new blood is drawn from sub- or nongoverning elites who are situated between the rulers and the ruled and have the talent and ambition to govern.

Thus, Pareto and Mosca agreed with Michels' "iron rule of oligarchy" (see the Box 10.4), but added the qualifier that the make-up of governing elites is constantly changing. (This is what Pareto meant by "circulating elites.") Naively perhaps, both believed that ruling classes are more or less open to people

Box 10.4

Michels' "Iron Rule of Oligarchy"

Writing in 1915, German political scientist Robert Michels attempted to explain why power tends to fall into the hands of a small group of leaders in *all* organisations, whatever their goals and ideology. After studying the labour and socialist movements of his time, Michels concluded that as organisations grow in size and complexity, the need for leadership becomes more and more pressing. Informal decision-making in which all members participate becomes impractical: there are too many issues to resolve; the organisation must present a united front to the outside. Leaders, chosen for their special talents in administration, and public relations, gradually take command. In time these leaders develop a vested interest in maintaining their position. A combination of admiration and apathy in the rank-and-file accelarates this concentration of power in the hands of a few. Within the ruling clique, maintaining the organisation becomes an end in itself. Leaders tend to become conservative, to seek compromises with enemies, to avoid risks, and to modify extreme and unpopular goals—to protect their positions. Nowhere is this process more obvious than in successful, radical political movements; revolutions, Micheles argues, are little more than the replacement of one elite by another. In Michels's view, "Who says organisations says oligarchy."

Sources : Robert Michels, *Political Parties* (Glencoe, III.: Free Press, 1949).

with "intelligence and charatcter," and that in the long run, governing elites "represent" the interests of the ruled. Underlying this, of course, is the assumption that the masses are neither desirous nor capable of governing themselves.

Since the turn of the century political theorists have been divided into two camps: Marx's heirs, who argue that power is held by economic elites and stress the coercive and exploitative uses of power, and Pareto and Mosca's heirs, who believe there are many diverse and competing elites.

C. Wright Mills: The Power Elite

> I should contend that "men are free to make history," but that some men are indeed much freer than others. (Mills, in Olsen, 1970, p. 254).

Among American sociologists, C. Wright Mills took the lead in documenting the existence of an American power elite, above and beyond the official political system. (Marx assumed the existence of an elite, but never actually said who they were.) Mills began with the fact that many people who occupy high positions in government have also held high positions in corporations or the military and seem to move back and forth among these centers of power. America's governing elite, wrote Mills, is "a coalition of generals in the roles of corporation executives, of politicians masquerading as admirals, of corporation executives acting like politicians" (1959, p. 278). Tracing their personal histories, Mills found that, by and large, these people come from similar white, Anglo-Saxon, Protestant, old American back-grouds, attend the same Ivy League schools, belong to the same exclusive clubs, visit the same resorts, and so on. Thus, if the president of an oil company doesn't know the federal "energy czar" personally, he surely knows someone who knows him (and can place a confidential call, if necessary). Through their psychological and social affinity, the power elite's coinciding interests are reinforced.

Mills argued that the different branches of the elite are interlocking. Congress approves billions of dollars in military appropriations every year, dollars that go more or less directly into corporate pockets. Why? In part for national defense; in part because military contracts create jobs for their constituents, and because business leaders are important campaign contributors. Thus, politicians tend to support big business, and business leaders often support politicians tend to support big business, (Ceilings on campaign contributions may lessen the influence business has with government.) All three sectors—economic, political and military—have a vested interest in what Mills calls "military capitalism".

Mills argued that democratic procedures have become empty rituals. Neither elections nor congressional debate restrain the power elite. Over a decade before Americans learned about the concentration of power among a small group of aides in the Nixon White House, Mills wrote, "the executive bureaucracy becomes. . .the arena within which major conflicts of power are resolved or denied resolution. 'Administration' replaces electoral politics; the maneuvering of cliques. . .replaces the open clash of parties" (in Olsen, 1970, p. 259). Important decisions are made behind closed doors. The middle-level society, which works for the elite, and the lower level have little or no effect on these decisions.

Mills believed the trend toward centralisation of power would continue unabated. "The top of modern American society is increasingly unified, and often seems will fully coordinated: at the top there has emerged an elite whose power probably exceeds that of any small group of men in world history" (in Olsen, 1970, p. 261).

The Pluralist View

But where is the evidence that America's political, military and corporate chieftains are all of one mind or that they cooperate with one another? Isn't the reverse more likely, that is, that they see one another as rivals? This is the question pluralists ask. They agree with Mills that some people are freer to make history than others and that unorganised individuals (the masses) are powerless. But they do not see a ruling clique, a power elite at the top of the power structure in this country. Rather, pluralists argue that social power is *dispersed* among a variety of competing interest groups—the oil industry and the coal industry, car manufacturers and ecologists, unions and business associations, hunters' lobbies and wildlife funds, and so on. All of these groups influence the political process at different times and with varying degrees of success, but no one group commands. In most cases, they can do little more than veto programmes that threaten their interests. In David Riesman's words, "Today we have substituted for [centralised, mercantile-aristocratic leadership a series of groups, each of which has struggled for and finally attained a power to stop things conceivably inimical to its interests and, within far narrower limits, to start things" (1951, p. 242). See also Dahl, 1961; Kornhauser, 1961; Keller, 1968).

Mills, as indicated, believes that coinciding interests, reinforced by social similarity, bind America's executives together in a single, cohesive power elite. Riesman maintains that diverse, often conflicting interests preclude united policy or action. Mills argues that the power elite settle important questions among themselves, behind closed doors; "fundamental issues never come to any point or decision before Congress, much less before the electorate" (1958). Riesman disagrees, arguing that fundamental issues are decided through bargaining among interested parties, and the parties who exercise power vary with the issue. (The American Rifle Association, for example, is not interested in farm subsidies or the National Endowment for the Arts.) Mills laments the erosion of democracy, the loss of responsible and accountable centers of power, the alienation of the powerless many. Riesman laments the erosion of leadership and the lack of direction in American politics.

In *The Power Structure* (1967), Arnold Rose concludes that both sides of this argument are true of America. Rose concedes that foreign affairs seem to be dominated by a small group of people who resemble Mills's power elite, but he suggests that the growth of the federal government and the emergence of new pressure groups (such as Civil Rights organisations) have undercut big business and no such elite dominates domestic affairs. In his view there are many power structures in America, not one, and nationwide decisions are made through a process of bargaining among them (the pluralist view). However, the power structures themselves (political parties, government agencies, legislatures, businesses, and so on) tend to be dominated by oligarchies (the elitist view). Rose also notes that senators, approximately one in five of whom are millionaries (what Mills calls social similarity), tend to vote according to their own, presumably upper-class convictions. In short, Rose sees the American power structure as a complex plurality of elites.

The Organisation of Power in America

The one point on which theorists of all persuasions agree is that single, isolated individuals have little impact on the political process. This section will examine the different types of political organisations that fill the considerable gap between the high levels of government and "the people".

Political Parties

Drawing on Weber, Robert Michels defined a political party as a "society or propaganda and of agitation seeking to acquire power (1949, p. 134). Although these are not the words contemporary Americans might choose, this definition is essentially correct. *Political Parties* are organisations designed for the explicit purpose of gaining and holding legitimate control of government policies and personnel. Parties perform several crucial functions in large, complex political systems. Ideally, they link the people and the government, transmitting public opinion up the ladder to where decisions are actually made, thereby converting public opinion into legislation. In the other direction, parties mobilise grass roots support for policy decisions. Parties also serve as a link between different branches and levels of government (executive and legislative, federal and state) and between official (governmental) power structures and unofficial (non-governmental) power structures. On the practical level parties play a dominant role in recruiting personnel for elective office (Dowse and Hughes, 1972, pp. 339–41).

The Two-party System

Although we are accustomed to thinking in terms of two parties, in some countries there are five or more parties, in others only one (and the struggle for power takes place within the party rather than between or among parties). The two-party system in this country dates back to the early days of the nation, when Republicans (an agrarian, States' Rights party led by Jefferson) vied with Federalists (a mercantile party led by Hamilton that sought to increase the powers of the federal government). Although the Federalist party did not last, a two-party split developed again when Andrew Jackson led the new Democratic party to victory over neo-Republicans Clay and Hamilton (who now called themselves Whigs) and again, in the Civil War, when Lincoln's Republicans enforced federal domination on the South and Southerners fled to the Democratic party. Greadually, the agrarian-based Democrats aligned themselves with labour, the Republicans with big business, preserving the two-party alignment.

True, there have been third and fourth party entries into the politcal arena—Theodore Roosevelt aligned himself with the Bull Moose party in 1912; Progressive Henry A. Wallace and States' Rights candidate Strom Thurmond opposed Harry Truman in 1948; George Wallace ran for president on the American Independent party ticket in 1968. In most cases a third party is little more than a distraction, splitting the vote for one of the majority-party candidates. Why is this? Why does the United States consistently generate two parties, while Italy consistently generates several? The answer lies in the structure of the elecoral system.

French sociologist Maurice Duverger (1954) argues that two-party systems emerge when there can be only one candidate from each party and the winner of the election takes all. This simple-plurality system discourages third parties because a vote for a minor party is, in effect, a wasted vote. There is almost no chance that the third-party candidate will win. In contrast, in proportional-representative systems, such as Italy has, a party receives the same percentage of seats in the legislature as it receives in the election. In this kind of electoral system a vote for a minority-party candidate is not wasted, for even if the party receives only 10 per cent of the votes, the party receives a tenth of the seats in the legislature.

The simple-plurality system not only determines the number of parties in the United States, but also their character. To win state-wide and national elections. American parties must embrace diverse kinds of people and a wide range of interests. Differences of opinion must be settled *before* elections. Critics like Duverger argue that the American system forces parties into bland positions and prevents many groups from being represented. Both the Democratic and Republican parties must lean to the center and create policies that sound attractive to everyone and offend no one. Duverger's analysis suggests that politicians cannot be blamed for political double-talk; the social structure of American parties *forces* them to be that way. However, Duverger points out that the simple-plurality system is more stable than proportional representation, where coalitions must be formed issue by issue in the legislature.

Interest Groups

In a sense, interest groups make up for the amorphous and tentative character of political parties in this country. An *interest group* is an organisation created to influence political decisions that directly concern members. They range from business associations (such as the National Association of Manufacturers), to labour unions (most notably the powerful AFL-CIO), agricultural groups (including the National Milk Producers Association), professional associations (the American Medical and Bar Associations), Civil Rights groups (the National Association for the Advancement of Coloured People, the American Civil Liberties Union), political groups (Americans for Democratic Action, the John Birch Society), and special interest associations (such as the National Rifle Association). Corporations may form their own lobbies—the most notorious example in recent years being the International Telephone and Telegraph Company's attempt to gain favourable settlement of an antitrust suit by offereing to underwrite the 1972 Republican National Convention. In addition, agencies and departments within the government may lobby, using their resources and spokesmen to influece Congress. For example, members of the Defence Department regularly testify in favour of increased military spending. Foreign governments also place lobbies in Washington to look out for their interest (see Milbrath, 1963).

The activities of the National Rifle Association (NRA) illustrate the way interest groups work. The NRA has an annual budget of over $5 million, most of which is used to publish *The American Rifleman*, circulation 900,000. In 1963, the year President Kennedy was shot, the House Judiciary Subcommittee on Juvenile Deliquency began to consider legislation that would forbid the mail-order sale of firearms to minors. *The Amercian Rifleman* responded with articles characterising the bill as irrational and emotional, and urged readers to write congressmen (supplying their names). The committee decided to defer action. In March 1965, President Johnson called for strict gun control in his message on crime to Congress. The NRA sent an urgent letter to members, distorting the administration's bill and warning, "If the battle is lost, it will be your loss, and that of all who follow." This plea was successful, and in December the NRA thanked readers for letters that effectively prevented the passage of gun-control laws. No legislation reached the floor of the House or Senate in 1967, but the NRA continued its attacks, now focusing on individual legislators whom it called "do-gooders" and "fanatics". "All of these people would like to bury your guns. Some of them would like to bury us, also"an editorial read. Not until June 1968, when Robert Kennedy was assassinated, did letters to Congress supporting gun controls outnumber letters opposing it. In October of that year, Congress passed a law limiting interstate shipment of long gun (*Congressional Quarterly,* April-October, 1968).

Interest groups may also negotiate directly with the executive branch (as ITT did), or work through the courts (as the NAACP and ACLU have done). Some support sympathetic candidates with endorsements, campaign funds, and campaign workers. In addition to pressuring law-makers, lobbyists may direct public relations and propaganda campaigns to improve their constituents' image and win popular support for their views.

In most cases lobbyists work for the elite of an organisation; they are hired by the leaders of a union, for example, not by the rank-and-file, and are accountable to those leaders. Still the diversity of interest groups creates numerous cross-currents. Many people are active in (or at least responsive to) different groups at once. For example, a conservative southern Democrat may find herself aligned with outspoken liberals on women's rights; political leaders in the ghetto, fighting for community control, find George Wallace seeking the same goal (but with different motives). Seymour M. Lipset suggests that diverse and conflicting interests, which prevent the formation of solid political blocs, are essential to modern democracies. "Multiple and politically inconsistent affiliations, loyalties and stimuli reduce the emotion and aggressiveness involved in political choice. . .The available evidence suggests that the chances for stable democracy enhanced to the extent that groups and individuals have a number of crosscutting, politically relevant affiliations" (1963, p. 77). If interests and affiliations did not overlap, the country might split in half, as America did in the nineteenth century.

Community Power Structures

The organisation of political power at the local level has attracted a great many researchers in recent years, if only because it is possible to test theories of power empirically in the microcosms of towns and cities. Sociologists and political scientists have identified several different types of local power structures in this country, but there are no firm explanations as to why these variations occur (Rossi, 1960).

In "Power and Community Structure", Peter H. Rossi (1960) suggests that important variables in the way power is organised at the local level include the degree of professionalisation of public officials (whether officials work full time at community work), the number of elected officials (as opposed to appointed officials), the level of partisanship (whether there are clearly defined, competing parties), the political heterogeneity of the electorate, and the extent to which parties represent different ethnic and economic groups. With these factors in mind, Rossi defines four types of community power structures.

In *pyramidal communities* one person or a small clique decides all-important issues, and lower-level officials serve mainly to implement their policies. The ruling clique may operate within the official political system, or it may exert pressure from without. An example of the former is Mayor Daley's Chicago machine, a machine so powerful in its day that no Democratic presidential hopeful dared cross the Mayor.

Rossi's second type is *caucus rule,* where a larger group of prominent individuals make decisions by "manufacturing consensus" among themselves. An example would be Atlanta, Georgia, of the 1950s, which Floyd Hunter (1953) renamed Regional City in a classic study of community power. Hunter interviewed residents to find out who they thought influential, then tried to learn who had pulled strings on certain decisions. He concluded that a group of forty "influentials". Most of whom were businesspeople who operated behind the scenes (and a few of whom had connections in Washington and abroad) dominated local affairs. The mayor, treasurer, and other public officials never made decisions without consulting this group. Caucus rule seems most likely to develop in homogeneous, middle-class suburban communities where "the class basis for countervailing power does not exist," and in cities where the lower classes constitute a majority, prompting businesspeople and professionals to undermine democratic procedures to protect their own interests.

Polylithic communities include a diversity of influential cliques and groups, each with its own sphere of authority. The government is usually run by professional politicians who have relatively solid support; businesspeople and professionals dominate civic organisations. This is what political scientist Rober A. Dahl (1961) found in New Haven, Connecticut. The upper class had largely withdrawn from politics, rather than mingle with "new elements" in the population. In many cases members of the upper class had actually withdrawn from the city itself, moving to the suburbs and enrolling their children in private schools. At the opposite end of the spectrum, the working and lower classes were excluded from decision-making groups. This left the governing of New Haven to a number of different middle-class groups who used their power and influence in different issue-area (that is, in issues that directly affected their interests). The power structure was "a coalition of public officials and private individuals who reflect the interests and concerns of different segments of the community." As Rossi indicates, power struggles in palylithic communities tend to center around individual and group efforts to expand their spheres of authority.

Rossi's fourth type, *amorphous structures,* would include any community that did not evidence stable patterns of power and influence. (It is a hypothetical type; Rossi could think of no examples.)

In a paper read at an American Sociological Association meeting (1973). John Walton concluded that center cities (particularly in the North and Midwest) are becoming increasingly decentralized or polylithic, while younger cities and suburbs tend to have pyramidal or caucus rule. Among the reasons he cited for the decentralisation of power in the cities are the concentration of the poor and nonwhite in cities and the white middle-class exodus to the suburbs; the loss of jobs and declining tax base in inner cities escalating demands for services (such as mass transit, police protection, and day care); and competition for federal funds. Today's élites depend heavily on state and federal programmes to provide services for their residents. As a result local leaders control only part of the resources the city needs. The heads of urban renewal, mass transit, and job-training programmes may, for example, report to state and federal officials, not to the mayor, creating numerous centers of power in a city. Looking ahead, Walton suggests that the urban politics of the future will center around group rights (including minority rights and community rights, which often conflict) and the quality of life (environmental problems, crime, and the like).

The Politics of the Powerless

> Victory comes to mean achieving a position of power that will enable members of a movement to work out their own destiny. (Killian, 1968, p. 128).

On May 17, 1954, the day the Supreme Court declared the separate-but-equal doctrine unconstitutional, it looked as if the battle against Jim Crow had been won. But within weeks it became clear that white southerners were willing and able to use civil disobedience to maintain their privileges. The NAACP, which had led the Court fight, was an elitist organisation, founded at the turn of the century by radical black intellectuals such as W.E.B. DuBois who rejected Booker T. Washington's philosophy of accommodation. NAACP leaders had done many things *for* black people, but they had not done things *with* black people (Killian, 1968, p. 55).

At this early stage, the black population lacked both a strategy and a prophet. Martin Luther King, Jr., supplied both, at least for a time. He was, as Louis Lomax observed, "the first

Negro minister I have ever heard who can reduce the Negro problem to a spiritual matter and yet inspire the people to see a solution on this side of the Jordan, not in the life beyond death" (Lomax, in Killian, 1856, pp. 55-56). King preached that integration was right and segregation evil. He encouraged thousands with the belief that "right makes might". Inspired by the religious/political father of modern India Mahatma Gandhi, King taught the non-violent tactics of civil disobedience and non-voilent protest.

What many white liberals overlooked at the time, however was that Gandhi and his followers did not stop at reforming the British—they forced them out of India (and precipitated the collapse of the British empire). Like Gandhi in India, King appealed to America's conscience; and like Gandhi, he forced America to listen. King and other black leaders at that time had no rewards to offer white Southerners in exchange for admitting blacks to white schools, restaurants and so on; they could not promise to build new factories, raise farm subsided, or win elections. They had no resources, no positive inducements. But they could create a state of emergency with sit-ins and adverse publicity, and *then* offer racial peace—a restoration of order—if the other side gave in. Thus, King spoke of peace, brotherhood, and reconciliation while engaging in a display of naked power. In fact, he condemned violence not only because it was "wrong" but also because it would be ineffective (the other side had more guns). "There is more power in socially organised masses on the march than there is in guns in the hands of a few desperate men. . .Our powerful weapons are the voices, the feet, and the bodies of dedicated, united people moving without rest toward a just goal" (King, in Killian, 1968, p. 75).

The latent power King mobilised in the black community in the late fifties and early sixties has since become a staple in American politics, a weapon for the powerless. César Chavez's National Farm Workers Association, for example, had $ 85 in its treasury when members voted to join the Filipinos' strike against the multi-million-dollar California grape industry in September 1965. A few years earlier, a massive strike would not have been possible. A federal law had allowed growers to import millions of

Mexicans who were not citizens, had no legal rights, and could be deported instantly if suspected of "starting trouble." In 1965, however, Congress had repeated this law—in large part because Chicanos had begun to exercise the power of the ballot in the Southwest (giving massive support to President Kennedy in 1960).

As the grape strike gathered momentum, Chavez emerged as the spiritual leader of his people, much as King had. Under Chavez's leadership an economic issue (wages and benefits) became a moral crusade, under the rallying cries of *La Huelga* (the strike) and *Venceremos* (we will win). Chavez used Gandhi's and King's tactics: mass demonstrations, marches and fasts. He drew on the sentiment for minority rights which blacks had generated, appealing to Civil Rights leaders, student political organisations, the Catholic church, the AFL-CIO (which gave strikers $5,000 a month), and such national figures as California's Governor Pat Brown and Robert Kennedy. Although the army continued to buy California grapes, the national boycott succeeded in bringing growers to the negotiating table (see McWilliams, 1968; Steiner, 1970; Meier and Rivera, 1972).

Inadvertently, perhaps, the government itself inspired another "revolution of the powerless" when it hired thousands of social workers, lawyers, and VISTA volunteers to bring about the "Great Society" in the mid-sixties. In a short time, poverty workers—often Office of Economic Opportunity staff members—were organising clients in local welfare centers around the country. The National Welfare Rights Organisation (NWRO) was founded in 1966 by George A. Wiley, a veteran of the Civil Rights struggle, to coordinate these different groups. Since its inception, the NWRO has concentrated on informing welfare recipients of their rights and, when necessary, staging mass demonstrations to force agencies to give them what they are entitled to under the law. This is more revolutionary than it sounds. If all the people in Los Angeles or Chicago who were legally entitled to welfare received their full benefits, the amount of funding required would probably break the city's budget.

In *Regulating the Poor* (1971), Frances Fox Piven and Richard A. Cloward argue that one of the primary functions of public relief is to "mute civil disorder." When the poor are threatening to disrupt the social structure, as they did in the 1930s and again in the 1960s, the government responds by handing out more and more money—until calm is restored. When the poor are acquiescent, benefits are withdrawn. In the absence of true economic reform, full employment, or a guaranteed income, Piven and Cloward see rising demands as the only source of reform. In their words, "a placid poor get nothing, but a turbulent poor sometimes get something" (1971, p. 338).

The groups we have been discussing are but a few examples of people who, though lacking money, position, and other conventional resources, are making themselves heard. The Civil Rights Movement inspired the powerless in this country. As a consequence, both Humphrey and Nixon advocated ending the war in Vietnam in the 1968 election, the Democratic party reformed rules for selecting delegates to its national conventions, many men are supporting women's rights, many "straights" are backing Gay Liberation. And although the political scene is quieter today than it was in the late sixties the attitudes of American youth have changed (see the Box 10.3).

11

The Family

"Happy families are all alike; every unhappy family is unhappy in its own way." This is the sentence with which Leo Tolstoy began his novel *Anna Karenina*. But Tolstoy was wrong Happy families are not all alike not if we look at them from the sociological perspective. Throughout the world both happy and unhappy families assume many different forms and shapes and fulfil many different functions. In Samoa, for example, a newly married couple does not move into its own home, but become part of an already existing family. In *Coming of Age in Samoa* (1959). Margaret Mead wrote that "the young couple live in the main household simply receiving a bamboo pillow, a mosquito net and a pile of mats for their bed. . . The wife works with all the women of the household and waits on all the men. The husband shares the enterprises of the other men and boys. Among the Trobriand Islanders of New Guinea children are the complete responsibility of their mother's brother. In fact, among the Trobrianders children are not even considered to be the biological offspring of their own natural fathers (Malinowski, 1929).

And even within one society happy families are not all alike. In America, for example, the ideal happy family celebrated in movies and television consists of a devoted house-bound mother, a work bound father and two or more delightful children. (The "ideal" number of children per family varies with the times. Right now it is two: in the past it has been three, four or more). Although many American families (happy and unhappy) may in fact fit this ideal many and perhaps a majority do not. In millions of American families one or more of the ideal elements is missing: there are childless families and families with a dozen children; there are extended families (where grandparents or other kin live under the same roof) and families that are disrupted through death, divorce, separation or desertion; there are families with working mothers and families with unemployed father; and, with increasing frequency, there are new family forms altogether (like communes, group marriages and unmarried parents).

Because the forms of family life vary enormously throughout the world, it helps to forget the familiar mother-father-child unit and to think of the "family" sociologically. Free of our narrow experience and stereotypes we can think of the family as whatever arrangements people make for creating and raising children. It may not be the biological parents' children, as in societies where uncles or grandparents do the raising, or it may be a commune which serves as a public family (Kanter, 1974). The growing importance of day care centers, schools and other institutions forces us to think about them as socially part of the family. Whether we like it or not, they care for and socialise children.

In the first part of this chapter, we discuss the ways social scientists have defined the family, focusing on its three main functions. Next, we consider the family cross-culturally, paying particular attention to the Nayar, the Dani and the Israeli kibbutzim. In that section, we discuss explanations for the variety of family forms found throughout the world. The next part of the chapter focuses on the American family—the meaning and reasons for the nuclear family and the way social class affects both family form and child-rearing. We also discuss both romantic love and divorce in America. Finally, we examine the changing American family and consider contemporary alternatives to traditional marriage.

Defining the Family

If it is true that different human groups devise different means for nurturing and training their young, how are we to come up with a single, all-encompassing definition of *family?* The most famous attempt at such a definition was made by anthropologist

George Peter Murdock after he had surveyed the family forms of 250 different societies. Murdock suggested that: "The family is a social group characterised by common residence, economic cooperation, and reproduction; it includes adults of both sexes, at least two of whom maintain a socially approved sexual relationship, and one or more children, own or adopted of the sexually cohabiting pair" (Murdock, 1949, pp. 2-3). But Murdock's definition does not include the Nayar of southern India, for instance, whose families contain neither sexually cohabiting adults nor adults who reside or work together. (For details on the Nayar, see our discussion later in this chapter.) Kathleen Gough (1974) an anthropologist who studied this group, suggested that Murdock's definition must be revised. For Gough a family is a group characterised by the union of a man and a woman in which the children born to the women are recognised as legitimate offspring of both parents. While Gough's definition would allow the Nayar families to be called families, her definition would exclude such tribes as the Nuer of East Africa. There, an older, wealthy, childless woman may marry a younger woman and claim her children as her legitimate heirs (Levi-Strauss, 1956.)

However, the family is defined (and the issue has never been happily resolved) there seem to be three crucial *social functions* that are carried out by families throughout the world :

1. Reproduction of new members of the society.
2. Child care.
3. Socialization of children to the values, traditions and norms of the society.

Thus, in all societies there is one constant feature: a reliable arrangement for producing, sustaining and socialising succeeding generations. We call this institution the family.

The Family as a Biological and Social Unit

While it is clear that family arrangements involve important biological elements like heterosexual intercourse, conception and gestation; birth, and infant care, it would be a mistake to think of the family as merely a biological unit. The social contexts, the traditions and sentiments that surround and shape these biological givens, determine the form a particular family system will take. While the biological givens are unchanging, the social forces that channel and direct them are extremely variable. *Social forces,* not personal desires, dictate the types of people who will have intercourse leading to pregnancy. For example, American culture has strong norms against pairs of lovers consisting of old women and young men, old men and teenage girls, or partners who are already married to others; and in nearly every society, incest is forbidden. The biological acts of intercourse don't vary in any of these cases but their social meanings vary dramatically.

The distinction between biological and social determinants of family life becomes even clearer if you consider the meaning of "illegitimacy". A so-called illegitimate child surely has two biological parents and is therefore perfectly legitimate from a biological point of view. But a child (at least in America) who is conceived out of wedlock and whom no male acknowledges as his child and whom no male assumes responsibility for, is illegitimate from a social point of view. A child will be socially legitimate only if *some* male, even if he is not the actual, biological father (or *genitor* as social scientists call him), assumes public paternity and responsibility. Thus, at least with paternity, the biological and social bases of family life may be separate.

In the case of maternity the separation is a little more complicated since the biological connection between mother and child is so unmistakable: no woman could ever wonder whether or not she had carried and delivered a particular child. Nonetheless, even with this strong biological connection there are cases where physical and social maternity do not coincide. Consider, for example, the cases of children offered up for adoption by their natural mothers, who later want them back. The adoptive mothers, who have cared for the children from an early age and have formed great bonds of mutual attachment with the children, are surely these children's psychological mothers. In such cases the biological and social bases of motherhood are clearly separable. And, in fact, in recent years the courts have begun to recognise the legitimacy of social motherhood, sometimes allowing adopted children to remain with their adoptive parents.

Once we recognize the distinction between social and biological parenthood we can also begin to appreciate how closely the two are intertwined. In no society in the world is biological parenthood uncontrolled. As the British anthropologist Malinowski once observed. "The relation of mother to child, clearly dictated by natural inclinations, is yet not entirely left to them." Thus, everywhere, "biological facts are transformed into social forces" (Malinowski, 1964, pp. 6, 8). By this Malinowski means that all phases of procreation—conception, gestation, and infant maintenance—are everywhere governed by some social rules. The biological sex drive is always harnessed in some way. Thus, in our own society, for instance, we have many rules that limit the random expression of sexual desires, particularly if that expression is likely to lead to conception. We have rules about incest, rules about marriage between kin, rules about child marriages, rules about bigamous marriages, and even in some places still, rules about interracial marriages.

It is clear, then, that while family units are based on biological processes, these biological features are universally channelled by social rules and traditions. Having a baby may be a biological fact, but creating family is clearly a social one.

Cross-cultural Perspectives

Once we have acknowledged the social nature of family life, it is intriguing to compare the different social forms of the family that have emerged at different times in different places. By comparing family patterns we not only broaden our cultural perspectives, but we also become aware, through contrast, of the precise nature of our own family patterns. Numerous forms of the family have been recorded by anthropologists and sociologists, and although many of them are very different from our own, none are more or less valid or correct than ours.

The Nayar, the Dani and the Israeli Kibbutzim

One of the more fascinating forms of family life was found among the Nayar of Kerala India (Gough, 1974). During adolescence a Nayar girl was encouraged to have several lovers. If she became pregnant, one or more of these lovers was obliged to acknowledge paternity and to pay the delivery expenses, but beyond this none of the lovers had any further obligations to the girl or to her child. The mother's kin were completely responsible for both the child's care and for the mother's support. The Nayar did have a form of marriage, but it was a ritual marriage that marked a girl's passage to adulthood; it was not a ceremony that heralded the beginnings of a family as we know it. During the ritual marriage, the women's tribe chose a man to be her husband for three days. After these three days, husband and wife might never see each other again. Their only further obligations arose when the husband died and the wife had to observe his funeral rites.

Once a Nayar woman was ritually married, her sexual relations with other men came under no social control whatsoever. If she gave birth to a child, some man of her own rank was assigned the status of biological father (whether or not he actually was the father). But this assigned father had no rights or obligations concerning the child. Thus, among the Nayar, social fatherhood (that is, acknowledge paternity) was totally unrelated to biological fatherhood. And yet, the business of re-creating the Nayar culture went on just as smoothly as it did elsewhere; children were conceived; born, and socialised in an orderly, socially determined way, and the expectations and rules concerning family life were regular and predictable.

The Dani, of West Irian, Indonesia, have a family system that is equally unfamiliar to us. For the Dani the family is not a very meaningful unit and, in fact, the Dani language does not even have a word for "family" (Heider, 1972, p. 13). Social life is organised not around private, family households, but around compounds which continually shift (sometimes as frequently as every three days). While the Dani do have a ritual marriage (and one man may ritually marry several women), husbands and wives do not necessarily live in the same compounds, and they rarely get together as a unit. There is some cooperation between spouses in regard to house-building and cooking, but family life is at best short-lived. Children, especially boys, spend much of their time away from their parents, and by the time they are ten years old, they generally move in with distant relatives.

The most striking feature of Dani life, for those of us raised in Western cultures, is the seeming indifference to sex. Men and women in Dani compounds generally sleep in separate quarters: the men sleep in the men's houses and women in the women's houses. Dani also practice long periods of ritual sexual abstinence, particularly after the birth of a child. Husbands and wives may abstain from sexual relations for as long as four to five years after a baby is born, and there is no feeling among the Dani that this abstinence creates special hardship. "Thus. . .both men and women remain celibate for long periods of time without discomfort. . .and this is accomplished without rigorous, overt mechanisms of social control" (Heider, 1972, p. 15). Despite its strangeness to us, however, the Dani family system produces healthy, socialised children, just as families do everywhere.

The collective communes in Israel, called *kibbutzim,* provide yet another example of an unfamiliar family life-style. On the kibbutz many of the activities we have come to associate with family life are transferred to the community as a whole. Men are not responsible for the economic support of their wives, but instead both men and women work for the community and are supported by it. Women are not exclusively responsible for the care of their children; instead, child care is the responsibility of the community as a whole (Talmon-Garber, 1962). While the biological mother is responsible for nursing her own children during the first six weeks of life, after this time children are cared for by communal nurses in separate children's houses. Since the children's houses are organised into homogeneous age groups, each child spends his or her childhood with the same group of peers. This group plays an enormously important role in each child's life.

On the kibbutz such household activities as food preparation, laundry and recreation are all communally organised. The experience of the kibbutz has exploded a number of cherished myths about the indispensability of the small, intimate family and about the tight connection between biological and social parenthood. Psychological and sociological studies of kibbutz, life have revealed that communal child-rearing has many virtues and does, in fact, provide a viable alternative to the traditional, isolated nuclear family as we know it (Rabin, 1965; Bettleheim, 1971). An *isolated nuclear family* is defined by social scientists as a husband and wife and their dependent children living apart from other relatives. It is the family form idealised in our own society.

Origins of Different Family Forms

Once we recognise that different societies throughout the world promote different family forms, we must face the complicated question of why. Why do particular societies come to practice their specific forms of family life? Why do the Dani men have several wives simultaneously? Why do some Israelis raise their children communally? Why do the Trobriand Islanders base family heritage on the female's line? While it is true that attributing causes after the fact is always risky, because we cannot study the beginnings of a process that is already completed, nonetheless social scientists have suggested some convincing explanation for the origins of different family forms.

Some Theories of Family Formation

In the nineteenth century Frederic LePlay, a French scientist, suggested that different family arrangements resulted from different combinations of geographic environment and types of human work. Thus, for example, among the ancient Hebrews work was organised around shepherding activities and, because of the harsh terrain tribes were forced to move continuously to find more fertile fields. This nomadic existence and the precariousness of the environment led to the development of a rigidly organised social life centered around the leadership, knowledge, and experience of the elders (typically the oldest males). Without printed agricultural manuals, knowledge about the location of fertile lands and methods for food production were stored in the memories of the elders. LePlay argued that these men were granted power and authority because they held the clues to survival (1877 - 1879). The Hebrews' patriarchial family and community structure was therefore an adaptive response to the environment and to the forms of work the Hebrews performed to survive.

By contrast, the fishermen of northern Europe developed a more democratic and egalitarian form of family life. Because the men were so frequently away at sea, the women became extremely self-reliant and enterprising, assuming a great deal of responsibility for family life in and outside of the home.

A third type of family form developed among hunting tribes, where family members were encouraged to be independent and individualistic. As many social scientists now agree, family forms emerge from the subsistence needs of the society. In agricultural and herding societies, where compliance and cooperation are crucial, the family structure is tightly organised and hierarchical. Individual members of such societies might endanger the limited food supply if they did not adhere to established customs and rules for raising food. By contrast, among hunting tribes innovative techniques might produce *more* food rather than less. Therefore, family life is more flexible, more egalitarian and less tightly organised (Barry, Bacon and Child, 1957).

In a study of family life in 549 different societies, two researchers discovered a close connection between family organization and patterns of subsistence (Nimkoff and Middleton, 1960). In societies based on agriculture and fishing, family networks are large and cooperative, thereby assuring the survival of all through the cooperative labour of all. In hunting and gathering societies, where subsistence is based on individual enterprise and extensive mobility, family networks are small and cohesive in order to facilitate the groups' continual movement and to ensure the constant availability of a limited food supply.

Modern industrial societies, where families are highly mobile, are more like hunting tribes than like agricultural settlements, and the small nuclear family, stressing independence and individualism, tends to predominate. In a careful analysis of the connection between the modern nuclear family and modern forms of industrialisation, sociologist William Goods (1963) suggested several reasons for the fit between the two.

Goode points out that the geographic mobility demanded by modern industrial societies (that is, the demand that people move to areas where work is available) requires a small family unit that can, in fact, be moved readily. When a member of a family must move to increase economic or social opportunities, it is far simpler to take along a small nuclear family than to consult and accommodate large number of kin. In addition small nuclear families cannot build up the power and independence that large family dynasties can, and therefore small families are subject to the whims of the marketplace rather than being able to control or oppose industry. For these and other reasons (for example, the lack of space in urban areas to house large family homesteads) the small nuclear family is the one that is idealised in contemporary American society.

The American Family

If we recognise that family forms more or less conform to social requirements (and particularly economic and survival requirements), we can begin to explore the *consequences* of different family forms for the members of particular societies. What, for instance, are the consequences for Americans of the small, isolated nuclear family? (It is isolated in the sense that each new couple set up a household that is independent of either of their parents' homes.) In the first place, married couples become extremely dependent upon each other both emotionally and physically. In the absence of large members of kin living under the same roof, the couple must be all things to each other. They must protect and comfort each other; they must provide for each other in times of stress; they must be self-supporting; and they must accomplish all household chores (including child care) on their own. This kind of mutual dependence leads to society's institutionalising love as the social glue which replaces the structural supports that traditionally bind the family to society. The nuclear family floats relatively free of social bonds. As a result, feelings of love receive much more emphasis in modern society as a basis for marriage. Paradoxically, the prevalence of love as a bond in marriage correlates with high divorce rates.

Another important consequence of the isolated nuclear family is that the division of labour between a married couple must allow one member to always be at home during the child-rearing years. In societies where grandparents, cousins, aunts and uncles all live together, there is always some adult around to care for children. But when the family structure consists of an isolated nuclear family, the child-rearing tasks as well as the bread-winning tasks must be divided between only two adults. Until recently the American ideal has been for the husband to earn the money and the wife to keep the home fires burning (again, we must remember that between this ideal type and the actual reality there has always been much disparity). Of late the traditional model is beginning to change, but however the chores are divided up, whoever earns the money or tends the house, the labour must be divided between two people rather than being spread about among a group of competent adults.

The great dependence of couples on each other also makes the American family extremely fragile. When one member of an isolated nuclear family is absent (through death, separation, or divorce), the family disruption can be enormous, whereas in large extended families, the death or departure of one member can be absorbed and relieved by the several remaining members.

Table 11.1
How Family Members Help Each Other

Major forms of help and Service	*Direction of Service Network*				
	Between Respondent's family and related Kin	*From Respondents to Parents*	*From Respondents to Siblings*	*From Parents to Respondents*[1]	*From Siblings to Respondents*
Any from of help	93.3	56.3	47.6	79.6	44.8
Help during illness	76.0	47.0	42.0	46.4	39.0
Financial aid	53.0	14.6	10.3	46.8	6.4
Care of children	46.8	4.0	29.5	20.5	10.8
Advice (personal and business)	31.0	2.0	3.0	26.5	4.5
Valuable gifts	22.0	3.4	2.3	17.6	3.4

[1] Totals do not add up to 100 per cent because many families received more than one form of help or service.

Source : Marvin B. Sussman, "The Isolated Nuclear Family Fact or Fiction," *Social Problems* 6 (Spring 1959), p. 338

The forms of the isolated nuclear family also severely limits the life span of any particular family. Since children are encouraged to strike out on their own as soon as they reach maturity, married couples are often left with empty households after their children become adults. This pattern colloquially labelled "the empty nest syndrome," often causes much loneliness and anxiety for parents who are used to feeling useful, needed, and protective. In addition, when the parents grow old and less capable of attending to their own needs, the ideal of the isolated nuclear family inhibits them from moving in with their grown children. They must either manage on their own or be turned over to institutions specifically designed to care for the aged. Thus, while the isolated nuclear family may, in fact, snugly fit the economic system, it also causes many problems for individuals in societies where it prevails.

Variations of American Family

One of the great American myths is that most families consist of a loving husband and wife and their well-adjusted, happy children. Generations of schoolchildren learned to read from books describing such a family and their dog. Spot, living in their own name behind a white picket fence. Minority groups with somewhat different life-styles and family structures simply did not exist.

Sociologists, too, have perpetuated the myth of the singular family type in America. The people who study and write about family life most frequently describe young, white, native-born, middle-class families with children (Heiskanen, 1971). And since these types of families most closely approximate the American ideal, it is not surprising that the myth marches on. If we look closely, however, we can find considerable variation in American family life.

Social Class Differences

Of all the factors that tend to influence the nature of family life, social class is one of the most important. No matter how social class is defined (by income, education, occupation, or family background), it invariably affects the organisation of family life.

Of course, on the superficial level, this statement is self-evident. A family's resources clearly influence the quality of the food it consumes, the amount and kind of leisure activities it has, the amount of space it has to live in, and the schools its children will attend. But beyond these obvious options that money will buy, there are other class differences in family life.

Some of the most important differences among classes are demographic. That is, the number of children born to each family, as well as death rates, tends to vary with social class. Families lower in the social hierarchy are more likely to have (and desire) more children than families in the higher strata. More children mean more expenses, more crowded living quarters, more emotional and physical strain for the parents. Mortality, like fertility, is also related to social class. The death rate is substantially higher among lower-class families, which means that people in the lower social strata are likely to die younger than people in higher strata. The death rate is, of course, related to other class variables as well, such as health care, nutritional variety, living conditions, and occupational hazards. In addition, lower-class families are more likely to be disrupted by illness, early death, desertion and divorce.

Families from different classes also appear to raise their children in somewhat different ways. Since people who live at different levels in the social hierarchy will have different life experiences, they will also tend to see the world from different perspectives. Thus, a college professor might value educational achievement, intellectual agility, and innovative approaches to problems (all of which are necessary for academic success), whereas a construction worker might value trade expertise, physical prowess, and the ability to carry out orders (all of which are necessary to the competent performance of construction work). With different sets of values about what is good and important in the world, it is only reasonable to expect that men and women from different classes will approach child-rearing in distinctly different ways, particularly since an important part of child-rearing is, precisely, the transmission of parental values.

Sociologist Melvin Kohn (1959), who has studied the relationship between social class and child-rearing, argues that in order to understand why different classes raise their children differently, we must know what the parents value and want for their children. Kohn suggests that one of the most significant value differences between middle and working-class parents concerns obedience to authority versus inner controls. "Working class parents want the child to conform to externally imposed standards, while middle-class parents are far more attentive to. . . internal dynamics" (Kohn, 1974, p. 283). Kohn found that working-class parents :

> value obedience, neatness and cleanliness more highly than do middle-class parents and that middle-class parents in turn value curiosity, happiness consideration and—most importantly—self-control more highly than do working-class parents. . .To working-class parents it is the overt act that matters; the child should not transgress externally imposed rules; to middle-class parents, it is the child's motives and feelings that matter: the child should govern himself . (1974, p. 283).

Kohn suggests that these differences in values stem, in large part, from differences in occupational conditions. Working-class parents anticipate that as adults their children will have to follow the orders of a foreman. Conformity and obedience, then, become highly valued traits. Middle-class parents tend to envision their children in professional careers, where initiative and self-discipline bring success. But values also stem from education and from experiences in the economic marketplace. If we think about it for a moment it seems quite logical that individuals whose economic and occupational situations are reasonably secure will be more willing to take social and political risks, more willing to be nonconforming than will people whose positions are insecure, because the price of nonconformity will not be nearly so great among those who are economically safe.

What differences do these values make in terms of actual family behaviour and child-rearing practices? Apparently, a considerable amount. One of the pioneering studies of child-rearing techniques concludes that, "In matters of discipline, working class parents are consistently more likely to employ physical punishment, while middle-class families rely more on reasoning, isolation, appeals to guilt and other methods involving the threat of loss of love" (Bronfenbrenner, 1958). This finding is certainly consistent with class value differences. Working-class parents, who are more concerned about overt acts of disobedience, will attempt to stop it directly and immediately. The difference between the two classes in punishment behaviour seems to hinge on different conceptions of what constitutes punishable behaviour. For working-class parents acts with negative *consequences* are punishable (for instance, marking up the furniture with crayons), whereas for middle-class parents acts with negative *intentions* are punishable (for instance, deliberately knocking down a sibling's pile of blocks). Often, of course, the two negatives coincide in a universally punishable activity (for example, stealing candy from the neighbourhood drugstore), but when there *are* class differences in punishable activities, they often stem from different conceptions of what is wrong or naughty.

Discipline, of course, is not the only arena in which class differences in values are reflected in class differences in behaviour. Since lower-strata families are more concerned with apparent behaviour than with some vague notion of inner development, it makes sense that among lower-strata families in general the emphasis would be on maintaining order and exacting obedience rather than on promoting individuality and developing equality within the family. These differences show up not only in behaviour toward children but also in the kinds of relationships that parents have with their children. Middle-class fathers are expected to be supportive and considerate of their children. Since this is also expected of middle-class mothers, the differences in the roles that middle-class mothers and fathers play is not so vast (see the Box 11.1). Both concentrate their energies and efforts on the inner development of the child.

In working-class families, however, where constraint and obedience are the keynote of upbringing, the mother is more likely to be the supportive parent and the father, if he is meaningfully involved with child-rearing at all, will be the constrainer. When the lower-class father is not involved extensively with the children's upbringing (as is the case in many lower-strata families), then the mother will play both the roles of supporter and constrainer, and the father will bring home the bacon. This sharp division of labour is likely to become blurred as the forces of social change (for example, Women's Liberation and increased occupational opportunities for women) begin to influence young working-class people. But for the time being, the values and practices of each class will continue to perpetuate themselves, if only because people tend to raise their children much as they themselves were raised.

Box 11.1

In the News

The Future of Fatherhood

Whatever happened to Father—to the father who ruled *his* household with unquestioned authority? Teachers, policemen, social workers, therapists and mothers have usurped his role in the family, according to psychiatrist and family therapist C. Christian Beels:

> The children, no longer dependent for education, protection, patronage or the right to marry, have staged a fairly successful revolt. Most recently, Mother, no longer dependent for income and protection, has declared her independence.... [T]he father as we once knew him has become irrelevant.

After analyzing the middle-class father's three traditional roles—as authority figure, disciplinarian and model for male children—Beels finds that all three have been weakened. Consider authority: fathers do not have time to meet with teachers and other authorities, and important decisions about child-rearing go to mothers by default. When crises arise, families consult professionals who are experts in family problems. Does working and supporting the family give a father authority in the home?

> No—the job is something that makes him tired, that takes up his time, that alienates him from his family. He works hard, and [feels he is] entitled to things that will compensate him and make him feel better, rather than positively entitled to dictate policy because of his authority as the breadwinner.

His role as disciplinarian has also faded. Child-rearing has become a psychological science in America (in a sense, we are all Dr. Spock's children), and psychologists generally do not approve of fathers being called in to administer punishment.

Box 11.1 Contd.

Often the father is the nice man who is home in the evening and on weekends, whose time with the children is so precious that he should spend it developing his relationship with them and not hounding them to [clean] up their rooms. . .The ultimate father in our society is an agency: family court or the policeman.

Fathers ceased to be full-time role models when they first began to work away from the home, and then moved their families miles from work to suburbia. Until recently, American men maintained a private world of sports, cars, home repair, and hobbies, into which they could initiate their sons when they came of age.

They were the separate arenas where father and sons could find both the language and the subject-matter with which to communicate about the values, problems and solutions inherent in being a man.

But, with sex roles becoming more flexible, mothers and daughters have entered these areas. Beels concludes: "[Today's] father is overworked at work, played out and unable to give himself to full-time fathering when he gets home. His wife is also fed up with full-time mothering. Both seems to want part-time work and part-time parenting. Perhaps we should redefine fatherhood altogether. It should not be the full-time job of one parent but the part-time function of both parents in accord with their ability and knowledge."

Source: C. Christian Beels, "Whatever Happened to Father?" *The New York Times Magazine* (August 25, 1974): p. 10ff.

Love and Marriage

In any society, when two people marry their union binds many other people together as will. Nowhere in the world is marriage a simple, unguided act of commitment involving only two people in love. Just think of the numbers of people immediately involved in any one marriage ceremony. The groom's family, for instance, includes :

1. Groom's mother
   (a) her mother (and her mother's family)
   (b) her father (and her father's family)
   (c) her siblings (and their spouses, their children and their spouses' families).
2. Groom's father

(a) his mother (and his mother's family)
(b) his father (and his father's family)
(c) his siblings (and their spouses, their children and their spouses' families).

3. Siblings
(a) siblings' spouses (and their families)
(b) siblings' children.

When this limited list is duplicated for the bride's side, we find literally dozens of individuals *immediately* linked to each other as a results of two simple "I do's".

Given the numbers of people who are potentially affected (for better or worse) by two lovers' decisions to "tie the knot," it is no wonder that every society has patterned means for guiding its young people toward "appropriate" marriages. With so many people involved in the outcome, it is risky to leave such an important decision to the discretion of the impractical young.

In some societies, like our own, the guidance is subtly concealed. In others it is codified into systems of arranged marriages. But whatever the strategy there are always some forces at work in every society that channel and influence the romantic impulses of the unpredictable young.

Although systems of arranged marriages seem cruel and unusual to those of us raised with values of individualism and free choice, it is easy to understand why such systems develop and flourish. Think for instance of societies in which newlyweds move into the husband's family's household (patrilocal residence). The husband's family will, in this case, have an important stake in the type of woman the son brings home. They will be concerned, at least, about the following characteristics of the woman :

1. Tribal (or class) background. Does she come from a similar background so that :
(a) she will share the family's value system about what is good and worthwhile;
(b) she will already know the behavioural codes and expectations;
(c) she will have been brought up to expect and understand her role as a junior member of the household.

2. Personality characteristics. Is she submissive and flexible so that:
   (a) she will readily adjust to the family's unique patterns of behaviour;
   (b) she will submit to the authority of the husband's parents;
   (c) she will work hard in order to pull her weight in the household.
3. Physical characteristics. Is she physically sound so that :
   (a) she can be a hard-working member of the family;
   (b) she will bear healthy children for the family.

If a new wife is to live in her husband's household forever, it is reasonable for the members of that household to have some say about their new addition.

But over and above these positive reasons for arranging marriages, there are also cogent reasons for actively discouraging romantic love as a basis for marriage between young people in societies where the newly weds live with either the bride's or the groom's family. Romantic love, in such situations, would have an enormous potential for disruption. A young person might fall in love with an "inappropriate" mate who would be unacceptable to the existing household. But even if the mate were acceptable, the bond of love between the lovers might create jealousy and competition for attention among other household members. In addition, if the husband were strongly devoted to his wife, he might join her in a coalition against other household members and thereby threaten their authority over her. For these reasons, at least, traditional societies don't leave affairs of the heart to the discretion of the young, but rather attempt to control them through arranged marriages.

Our own society has a different set of requirements that affects the nature of our love-channelling activities. Since newlyweds in the United States typically set up their own households (neolocal residence), the acceptability requirements of new spouses are not so stringent. But neither are they totally absent. While the new couple may not be *geographically* integrated into a preexisting household, they are, to be sure, *socially* integrated into preexisting families and therefore are subject to certain familial requirements. Since an "inappropriate" marriage may "scandalize the family," whereas an "appropriate" one might bring glory and pride, parents and the rest of society subtly shape children's marriage aspirations from a very early age.

Such parental decisions as those concerning residential neighbourhoods and school districts influence the kinds of peers that children will find first as playmates and later as spouses. Such intangibles of family life as the development of a sense of "we" and "they," of "our kind" and "their kind," influence young people's values concerning "attractive" others. Such family patterns as the choice of recreational activities, the selection of vacation spots, and the style of celebrating holidays and special occasions all influence the kinds of potential mates that young people will meet or eventually seek on their own.

These kinds of subsurface controls effectively direct a young person's love interests toward an appropriate pool of eligible mates. And, in fact, the effectiveness of these subtle processes shows up in the marriage statistics. Intermarriages in the United States between different races, religions and nationalities are relatively rare, particularly among the higher strata of the society (Udry, 1971. Homogamous marriages (that is, those between social equals) are still the order of the day in America. Despite our doctrines of equality and classlessness, we continue to promote marriages between socially equal partners. Once the general screening process has taken place, however, and young people have learned what other sorts of people swim in their pool of eligibles, then the impulses and emotions of romantic love are encouraged to take over.

Romantic love is idealised and exalted in American society. We need only think of our clucking responses to someone who marries for money (or power or prestige) to realise how firmly we uphold the virtues of love. From an extremely early age we are taught about the glories of romance. In fairy tales, the prince and princess fall madly in love and, after some travail, live happily ever after. In comics and magazines, in movies and songs, on radio and television, men and women are forever falling in love. From the very beginnings of our lives we learn that all "normal" people eventually fall in love and marry. Our parents did it and so did their parents. Our teachers, leaders, heroes and friends all do it, and so, eventually, will we.

Much of our youthful energies and emotions is devoted to the quest for love, and many a psychiatrist's couch groans under the burden of those who have failed in this culturally exalted quest. There are good reasons why romantic love has become an important basis for marriage in our society (just as there are good reasons why arranged marriages have developed in more traditional societies). When a couple in the United States marry and sets up a new household (as approximately 2 million American couples did in 1972), the new family unit is relatively independent (at least geographically) of other kin. As a result the partners are free to love one another without creating tensions, jealousies, and competition among other household members. Also, since the new couple will depend on each other for a wide range of emotional and physical supports, they will be batter able to meet each other's needs if they are guided by love rather than by strictly defined rights and obligations. Romantic love also helps young people to lessen the strong emotional ties that bind them to their own families and allows them to move more comfortably out of the familial nest into their own, independent worlds.

But romance as the basis of marriage has its limitations. In some ways, romance is completely antithetical to the daily demands of married life. As it is promoted in songs, fables, and movies, romance thrives on mystery, distance, and uncertainty—"Some enchanted evening'. You will see a stranger'. . .Across a crowded room." Since married life is anything but mysterious, distant, and uncertain, what happens to romance in the process? As the popular 1940s song put it: "Love was grand when love was new/Birds were singing, skies were blue/. . .The thrill is gone." When romance fades, after all those years or myth and search, all too often the marriage fades with it. Thus, by tooting the horn of romance so loudly we may be simultaneously undermining the very relationships we hope to promote; stable, enduring, child-producing marriages.

Since marriage is a business partnership as well as a romantic fairy tale (it involves among other things, compromises, division of labour, specialisation, communication systems—all the trappings of a bureaucracy), to bill it as a flower-shown paradise is to risk its eventual demise.

Divorce

That American society has been successful in promoting marriage as a way of life is clear from marriage statistics. Nine out of ten people in America get married at least once in their lives (*Population and the American Future,* 1972, p. 67). And, what is more they do it early in life. The median age for marriage among women is slightly over twenty year and for men between twenty-two and twenty-three. But what happens to all of those marriages that start out with so much love and high hope? Unfortunately, it is very difficult to know for certain what *does* happen.

In the first place, it is almost impossible to come up with a satisfactory definition of what constitutes a happy or an unhappy marriage. One couple's happy compromise may be another's insurmountable stumbling block. If we cannot define "good" and "bad" marriages, we can hardly expect to come up with figures about how many of each kind occur. But even if we rely on information that does seem to be measurable, for instance the number of marriages that end in divorce, we soon discover how complicated the task is.

Measuring Divorce

If we were to compare the number of divorces in any one year to the number of marriages in that year, we would come up with a boggling divorce rate, for example, 36 per cent for 1972. (In that year there were 2,269,000 marriages and 839,000 divorces [*Statistical Abstracts,* 1973, p. 51.] But let us look for a moment at the origin of that astronomical rate.

The number of marriages recorded in any one year is a reasonably straightforward statistic. But remember that the population that is eligible or likely to marry in any one year is relatively small. For the most part this population includes people eighteen to twenty-eight years old who are not already married. The number of divorces in any one-year is also a straightforward statistic, derived from court records of divorce proceedings during that year. But when it comes to *comparing* the yearly number of divorces to the yearly number of marriages in order to arrive at a *divorce rate,* the statisticians run into trouble. The population eligible for divorce is many times greater than the population eligible or likely to get married. *Everyone* who is married is a member of the divorce-eligible population. That population includes people married one, five, ten, fifteen, or twenty-five years. Thus, comparing *yearly* marriage data with *yearly* divorce data drastically inflates the rate of divorce because the population from which divorces might come is so much larger than the population from which marriages might come.

Another problem with comparing yearly marriage and divorce data is that those figures reveal nothing about current trends or about changes in divorce patterns. That is, since the same people do not marry and divorce in one year, we cannot know whether marriages today are more or less enduring than those in the past because the increases in divorce proceedings may come from an *older* population married for ten, fifteen, or twenty years; they therefore cannot be included in the population that marries today.

The great difficulty researchers have in calculating divorce rates comes in determining whose divorces should be compared to whose marriages. This dilemma is still unsolved, although attempts are continually made to circumvent the problem. One recent study, for instance, surveyed households throughout the country in an attempt to discover national marriage and divorce patterns. The researchers found that among the population that had been married for the first time twenty or more years before the survey, 80 per cent had been married only once; 17.7 per cent had been married twice, and 2.2 per cent had been married three or more times (Glick and Norton, 1971). In the same study the researchers also found that the highest incidence of divorce occurred among those who married young (below twenty-two for men, below twenty for women) and that young black people have almost twice as many divorces as young white people (46 per cent of black people who had married young had been divorced at least once, compared to 25 per cent of young white people).

Explaining Divorce Rates

Since it is so difficult to calculate current divorce rates, it is also extremely difficult to compare divorce rates over time. But it seems likely that the popular sense of an increase in marital dissolution probably is, in fact, taking place. There would certainly be ample social explanation for such increases in divorces. In the first place, perhaps because of its frequency, divorce is decreasingly stigmatised so that people are more willing to risk the consequences of ending a marriage. In addition, increasing career opportunities for women allow them to consider alternatives to hanging on forever to a failing marriage. What is more, the old saw of staying together for the children is losing its validity as psychologists discover that a divided household is better for children than a household awash with tension (Udry, 1971, p. 458).

Whether the percentage of marriages that end in divorce will increase, decrease, or remain constant is, or course, a matter of speculation. But whatever else divorce does, it doesn't seem to sour people on the institution of marriage. One-fourth of the people who get divorced are remarried within the year, and within nine years of divorce a full 75 per cent are married again. Thus, while marriage may be difficult to sustain, it is certainly not going out of style. Almost everybody does it (and redoes it when necessary).

The Changing American Family

The relative ease with which present-day marriages may be dissolved is only one of the recent changes in American family life. Another involves the amount of time a couple spends in married life and the number of years they devote to raising children. As late as 1920 the average. American lived fifty-four to fifty-five years. Today the average man lives to be sixty-seven and the average woman to be seventy-four. Thus, couples who marry young and stay married can now expect almost fifty years of togetherness—a long stretch of time encompassing many different life-cycle changes. The most crucial of these changes are, perhaps, the ones that revolve around children.

When the first child is born to a couple, drastic life-style changes occur. The couple are no longer free to come and go as they please, but must make arrangements for every outing, excursion, or supermarket trip. The mother, if she has been working, must either quit her job or make complicated arrangements for child care. Usually the couple must move to larger quarters and perhaps a neighbourhood where there are likely to be other young children. In addition, the love, attention and leisure time that were formerly shared between two people must now be spread out among three or more individuals. These changes can be very trying, and with the birth of a first child a couple is launched into a whole new social framework.

Drastic changes also occur at the far end of child-rearing. As grown children leave home, the couple are once again thrown back on their own resources, and after all those years of activity, commotion, demands and scheduling, the new regime may be as unsettling to the couple's equanimity as was the birth of the first child twenty years or so earlier.

While this sequence of events concerning the child-rearing aspects of marriage has not changed much over the decades, the amount of time the sequence takes has. In fact, it has changed markedly. For a variety of reasons the child-oriented years of marriage have been compressed into a shorter time span. One of the reasons for this is that couples now have children earlier in their marriages than they used to. At the turn of the century the average American woman married at twenty-two, had her first child at twenty-three and her last at thirty-two. Today, the average woman marries at twenty, has her first child at twenty-two and her last at twenty-six. This means, of course, that in addition to starting their families earlier, couples also space their children closer together. Thus, as sociologist Arthur Norton has said:

> [There is now] a trend among families toward beginning their childbearing sooner, spacing their children closer, and completing childbearing earlier. These factors, coupled with an increase in the length of time couples survive jointly, show that more "child free" years are or will be spent by couples during middle or old age than ever before (in Winch and Spanier, 1974, p. 168).

When the foreshortened child-oriented years of marriage are linked with the greater longevity for both sexes and the increasingly earlier retirement ages, we can see that one of the crucial changes in married life is the amount of time the couple will spend alone together at the end of their lives (and due to the disparity in mortality rates for men and women, in also increases the amount of time that a women is likely to be a widow). As sociologist Robert Winch notes, "In 1890 the average marriage was broken by death before the marriage of the last child, whereas the average couple now survives about 15 years after the marriage of the last child" (in Winch and Spanier, 1974, p. 481).

These changes in family life-cycle schedules have, of course, provided women with substantially more free time, particularly in their middle years. As the labour market statistics show, women are using this time to enter (or reenter) the occupational world. In 1971, for instance, over 45 per cent of the work force between the ages of thirty-five and forty-four was comprised of women (*Statistical Abstracts*, 1971, table 333).

The more that women work (particularly in satisfying and responsible occupations) the more pressure they will bring to bear on the traditional roles in family life. They will balk at traditional divisions of labour and at traditional patterns of authority. As political scientist Andrew Hacker said recently:

> Put very simply, the major change in the family in recent years, and the problems of the future, are both summed up in one word: women. In the past and until very recently, wives were simply supplementary to their husbands, and not expected to be full human beings. Today, women are involved in much greater expectations and frustrations. . .The trouble comes from the fact that the institution we call marriage can't hold two full human beings—it was only designed for one and a half. (1970, pp. 34-39).

As Hacker's second "half" becomes more of a social and psychological whole, there are likely to be a series of profound reorganisations in that much beleaguered institution called the isolated nuclear family.

Alternative Farms of Marriage

One of the reorganisations, already in its formative stage, may be the attempt to rewrite the marriage script. Instead of expecting a man and woman to be legally linked in a male-oriented, monogamous, isolated household, a new set of expectations and arrangements may arise (as they have already begun to do). Rapid changes have already occurred regarding monogamy and nonmarital sex. With the development of an easy, efficient, accessible, inexpensive contraceptive, these changes are likely to become even more dramatic. As Robert Winch has pointed out:

> The rational basis for a society's prohibition of heterosexual intercourse outside marriage has to do with the consequences of such intercourse because many societies—probably most societies—do not have suitable provisions for raising children born out of wedlock. As unwanted pregnancies. . .become rare to non-existent, the society would lose the basis of its interest in trying to control such behaviour. Then—with some cultural lag—the strength of legal and moral sanctions against extramarital intercourse would weaken. . .The first consequence of the development of an efficient contraceptive and widespread access to it, then, would seem to be a disappearance of moral and legal sanctions against extramarital sex. (in Winch and Spanier, 1974, p. 485)

If, in fact, extramarital sex becomes solely a matter of private conscience and not public taboo, and if sexual relations come to occupy two separate spheres—recreational and procreational—then it is likely that some of the powerful motives for undertaking traditional marriages will lose their force. Clearly, attitudes toward the recreational aspects of sexual relations are changing, as every study on the subject indicates. One such study, which surveyed the readership of *Better Homes and Gardens,* showed that fully 91 per cent of the respondents felt that children should be planned through the use of birth-control procedures; 79 per cent approved of sex education in American schools; and 75 per cent favoured making birth-control information available to everyone—including unmarried teen-agers. This is a far cry from the national attitudes that showed up in a Gallup Poll in 1936. In that study 70 per cent of the American people opposed the legalisation of distribution of birth-control information, even to married people (Wattenberg, 1973).

The effects of such changing attitudes (and of rapidly changing sexual behaviour) may be far reaching. Couples will feel increasingly free to live with each other before marriage, or after a marriage has terminated. As women come increasingly to determine their own child-bearing histories, they will, in all likelihood, make greater demands on their mates for more equal unions, for greater work opportunities, and they will determine for themselves the number of children they wish to raise.

There are already in this country several types of innovative marriages, which are being pursued by substantial numbers of couples. With increasing frequency, for instance, Americans are undertaking *two-career marriages* in which the work requirements of both the male and the female are given serious consideration before such family decisions as geographic location, vacation schedules, and child-births are made.

Another type of innovative marriage that is attracting an increasing number of couples is the *contract marriage* in which the couple design their own marriage contract, specifying rights and obligations of each spouse concerning domestic and economic activities, division of labour in the household, and the number and timing of children (Edmiston, 1972, pp. 66 - 74). Arguing in favour of such marriages, feminist writer Susan Edmiston claims:

> First we thought marriage was when Prince Charming came and took you away with him. Then marriage was orange blossoms and silver. But most of us never suspected the truth. Nobody ever so much as mentioned that what marriage is, at its very heart and essence, is a contract. . .When you say "I do" you are subscribing to a whole system of rights, obligations and responsibilities many of which may be antithetical to your most cherished beliefs. (1972, p. 2).

In the 1960s Margaret Mead began to rekindle interest in an idea first suggested in the 1920s. Marriage would be contracted in two steps. First would be a trial marriage in which young people would live together as long as it suited them but without any permanent commitment. The second step, undertaken once a baby was on the way, would be a legal agreement binding the couple together until the child (or children) reached adulthood. Mead calls the first step *individual marriage* and the second *parental marriage* (Mead, 1966).

While Mead's seemingly revolutionary suggestion is not likely to gain immediate or widespread acceptance, another

Table 11.2
A Pilot Study of the Problems of Unmarried Students Who Live Together[1]

Problem area	*Number Indicating* *No problem*	*Some problem*	*Average rating given by those indicating some problem*
Emotion Problems			
Over involvement (loss of identity, lack of opportunity to participate in other activities or with friends, overdependency)	14	21	2.7
Jealousy of partner's involvement in other activities or relationship	14	15	3.1
Feeling of being trapped	18	15	2.9
Feeling of being used	19	13	2.6
Guilt about living together			
—at beginning of relationship	20	9	3.7
—during relationship	25	5	3.8
—at end of relationship	15	2	4.0
Lack of feeling of "belonging" or of being "at home"	22	9	3.4
Sexual Problems			
Differing degrees of periods of sexual interest	10	23	3.4
Lack of orgasm	11	21	3.6
Fear of pregnancy	15	15	3.1
Impotence of partner	23	6	3.0
Problems Related to Living Situation			
Lack of privacy	15	17	3.4
Lack of adequate space	19	13	3.0
Did not get alongwith apartment or housemates	20	6	2.2
Lack of sufficient money	26	6	3.3
Disagreement over use of money, sharing of money, etc.	27	4	3.5

[1]This table is based on interviews with junior and senior women at Cornell University. Respondents were asked to rate each problem from 1 to 5, with 1: great deal of problem, 5: no problem (no other points defined). The last category (5: no problem) has been separated because it may be qualitatively different from the other rating categories. Average ratings are therefore based on ratings from 1 to 4; thus, the lower the average rating the greater the problem for those experiencing it.

Source : Adapted from Eleano, D. Macklin, "Heterosexual Cohabitation among Unmarried University Students," *Family Coordinator,* vol. 21 (October 1972), p. 42.

marriage-model has gained considerable attention (at least if media coverage is any measure of public interest). This schema is known as the *open marriage.* In a best-selling book about the virtues of open marriage, a husband-wife team of anthropologists contrasted their flexible marriage arrangement with the more traditional or closed marriage. In conventional marriages, claim Nena and George O'Neill (1972), couples feel that they possess each other and conform to rigid marital roles, which include, among other things, absolute fidelity. Open marriage, by contrast, stresses more flexible roles and more consideration of each partner's needs, talents, and desires, and a considerable amount of autonomy and independence for husband and wife.

While the open marriage does not depart drastically in structure from the nuclear marriage, as we know it, other, more radical departures have been attempted. There are, for instance, a variety of plural mating arrangements in which several individuals or couples share the responsibilities of house, child-rearing, financial income, and bed. These arrangements meet with varying degrees of success depending of the personalities of the individuals involved and the attitudes of the surrounding community (Constantine, 1970).

The prevailing force behind most experimental forms of marriage is to maximise security an intimacy while at the same time minimising constraint and imposed obligation. Whether a man and a woman can satisfy the need for variety and safety within the framework of one ongoing relationship is really difficult to predict. As sociological Jessie Bernard notes :

> Human beings want incompatible things. They want excitement and adventure. They also want safety and security. These are difficult to combine in one relationship. Without a commitment, one has freedom but not security; with a commitment, one has security but little freedom, (in Cornish, 1972, p. 3).

The great stumbling block for most experimental forms of marriage seems to center around the issue of fidelity. For individuals raised in a society where sexual possession and exclusiveness are the legal and moral rights of married partners, it is extremely difficult to reformulate the rules so that each partner may go his or her own way while maintaining one central commitment to a spouse. One of the solutions to this enduring dilemma may be to gradually redefine the anticipations concerning the exclusivity of the marriage relationship so that a breach of monogamy will not be interpreted as a breach of love or commitment.

All of these explorations into innovative forms of marriage are earnest attempts to retain commitment and permanence while maximising individual freedom and growth. No one can predict how these experiments will succeed in the long run; what is certain is that traditional marriage is under fire and is likely to display a different profile as future generations arrive at new solutions to the age-old tension between freedom and responsibility.

12
Education

Americans tend to regard education as a panancea. When the Russians launched Sputnik in 1957, how did we respond? By pouring millions of dollars into science education. How can we end prejudice and discrimination against blacks and other minorities? By integrating schools. What can we do to eliminate chronic poverty? Design special programmes to educate the poor. (Nearly every night television stations broadcast such messages as, "Drop out now pay later". "Learn more to earn more.") How can we fight sexism? Again, one answer is education: revise textbooks to show women doing something other than housework and childcare.

In 1972, 61 million Americans (31 per cent of the population) were enrolled in schools. Nearly 80 per cent of Americans between the ages of twenty-five and twenty-nine are high-school graduates, and 18 per cent are college graduates. As the number of Americans attending school has increased, so has the number of years Americans spend in school. In 1972, 42 per cent of Americans between the ages of three and five were in daycare programmes (*Statistical Abstracts*; 1973). At the opposite end of the age spectrum, 180,000 Americans aged fifty and older were attending school (*Current Population Reports,* no. 260, February 1974. p. 20).

Is our faith in education justified? In the first and second sections of this chapter we examine the functions of education and ask whether American schools are performing them. We then look at the social structure of schools and how it affects both students and teachers. In the last part of the charpter, we explore new directions in educational reform.

The Social Functions of Education: Ideals and Questions

In small, nontechnological societies children learn everything they need to know by observing and imitating adults. There is little or no formal schooling. Eskimos, for example, do not hold classes in hunting. Rather, when they kill a bear, they give small children spears and encourage them to stab at the animal as they have seen adults do. By the time children are old and strong enough to hunt, they have thoroughly rehearsed this skill and know, from watching and listening, the legends and magic that surround the hunt (Pettitt, 1946). In modern technological societies, informal education is not enough. There are simply too many things to learn, too many skills to master. In the last fifty years schools have become a vital link between the individual and society.

One of the primary functions of formal education is *cultural and political socialisation:* teaching students what it means to be American, or English, or Russian, or Chinese. In fact, mass education in this country was especifically designed to Americanise the waves of non-English-speaking peoples who emigrated to the United States during the nineteenth century. Cultural and political socialisation is both direct (classes in civics and history, and student government) and indirect. Classes are conducted and students are evaluated in ways that are designed to socialise them to their culture. In the Soviet Union students are divided into "links" or groups, and graded according to how well the group performs, not for individual effort. An exceptionally bright student is only rewarded if he or she helps others in the group who are not as quick (Bronfenbrenner, 1970).

The American grading system, in contrast, stresses individuality. Several students helping one another to solve a math problem during an exam are punished for cheating.

In China government personnel retire to the country for six-week "refresher" courses in communism. The courses include studying the works of communist theorists, farming (to learn "the true feelings of the labouring masses"), and group criticism (to learn "to distinguish right from wrong".) At these schools the individual is under constant group pressure to conform. In the American educational system, teachers are responsible for enforcing conformity. Peers often encourage nonconformity in school—students who let others know they work hard may be labelled "grinds".

The goal of political and cultural socialization directly conflicts with ethnic identity and pride in America. In the effort to achieve cultural integration, our schools have traditionally focused on white history and middle-class culture. Leonard Covello, the first Italian-American principal in the New York City school system, recalls his own school days:

> Throughout my whole elementary school carreer, I do not recall one mention of Italy or the Italian language or what famous Italians had done in the world, with the possible exception of Columbus. . .We soon got the idea tha "Italian" meant something inferior, and a barrier was erected between children of Italian orgin and their parents. . . We were becoming Americans by learning how to be ashamed of our parents. (1958, pp. 57-58)

The demands for classes in black history, and bilingual education for Spanish-speaking children reflect a growing resistance to forced Americanisation.

A second function of formal education is *instruction:* teaching young people the skills and knowledge they will need as adults, and training them to do necessary work. (According to a 1972 Gallup Poll, parents consider job-preparation the primary function of education. See the Box 12.1.) The need for skilled workers in America has grown dramatically over the last fifty years. White-collar workers already out-number blue-collar workers, and profession also and technicians now make up the second largest occupational category, after semiskilled labourers (Bell, 1973, p. 17). However, at present our best schools emphasise intellectual development and theoretical knowledge over practical skills. How "practical," for example, is geometry? How "relevant" is French literature? Does a B. A. in English prepare a student for a carreer as a writer, editor, or teacher? Not really. Career-minded English majors find they need courses in education to teach, a degree in journalism or on-the-job training for minimal pay to write or edit. On the other hand, this country's vocational high schools are usually considered dumping grounds for students who perform poorly in academic programmes. Often the skills they teach are obsolete. In 1973 the President's Science Advisory Committee recommended heavy investments in job training—if necessary at the expense of liberal arts (Reinhold, 1973). The battle between those who believe education should be practical and those who feel education is "learning to think" will be heated.

Box 12.1

The Goals of Education: The Public's Views

A Gallup Poll conducted in 1972 found that most Americans are extremely pragmatic about education. When asked why parents want their children to get an education, respondents answered as follows:

1.	To get better jobs	44%
2.	To get along better with people at all levels of society	43%
3.	To make more money—achieve financial success	38%
4.	To attain self-satisfaction	21%
5.	To stimulate their minds	15%
6.	Miscellaneous reasons	11%

These results show that the majority of Americans emphasise material goals—not intellectual development. (The percentages do not total 100 because respondents were allowed to give more than one answer.) Gallup also found that the public is concerned about discipline. When asked what things schools should pay more attention to respondents ranked the choices as follows:

1. Teaching students to respect law and authority.
2. Teaching students to solve problems and think for themselves.
3. Teaching vocational skills.
4. Teaching students to get along with others.

Respondents considered discipline the number one problem in public schools (followed by lack of money, integration-segregation problems, and the difficulty of getting good teachers). Forty-one per cent thought students had too many rights and privileges.

Source: Gallup Opinion Index, September 1972. Report No. 87.

Selecting and developing talent is a third function of education. In small, nontechnogical societies boys nearly always enter their fathers' occupations, and girls learn the household roles of their mothers. But modern, technological societies cannot afford to rely on sons and daughters pursuing their parents' occupations. The need for skilled personnel is too great. For this reason an open schools system that allows any child with talent and ambition to become a doctor, a lawyer, or the president is not only just, it is necessary. Schools bear primary responsibility for selecting talented children and developing their abilities. At the same time, however, the schools are expected to educate *every child,* whatever his or her talents are Americans regard a high-school education (and, increasingly, a college education) as a basic right.

Finally, schools are called upon to *innovate* for the rest of society—to conduct medical research and to offer solutions for social problems. For example, we expect grade and high schools to accomplish integration and to break the cycle of poverty. These functions, solving technical and social problems, involve schools in political controversies. Should universities accept defence contracts or take a moral position against war? Should children be bused to strange and perhaps hostile neighbourhoods, white or black, because adults decide they must integrate? Are we using children as political pawns, at the expense of their education?

We raise these questions to show that the social functions of education are not simple or clear-cut. To think of schools simply as organisations that dispense knowledge and skills is unrealistic. The conflicts between cultural integration and ethnic pride, intellectual development and job training, mass and quality education and the schools' responsibilities to society and to children point to the relationship between schools and the political and economic needs of society.

The American Educational System: An Evaluation

How well do our schools perform the functions we have outlined? How are conflicts in educational goals resolved?

Schools as Agents of Socialisation

All available evidence suggests that the school system is an effective agent of socialisation. The more education a person has, the more likely he or she is to vote, to participate actively in politics, and to feel he or she has an impact on the political system. In addition, education seems to mute intergroup suspicion and hostility; college-educated people are more tolerant of group differences than high-school graduates or drop-outs.

Whether our schools succeed in creating cultural integration is debatable. Observation of schools in black and Chicano communities and on Indian reservations reveals a policy of forcing Americanisation on minority students. For example, approximately one-third of all Indian youngsters attend boarding schools run by the white-dominated Bureau of Indian Affairs. These schools were first instituted in the nineteenth century—for the express purpose of separating children from their "savage" parents so they might learn to be "Americans". Visits to and from parents are discouraged. As many as sixteen thousand Indian children do not go to school at all because their parents refuse to send them away, and every year hundreds run away from school. The Sherman Institute—named for General William Tecumseh Sherman, whose Indian policy was summed up in the quote, "Give them whisky; it kills them off like flies"—is typical of these schools. In 1969 Sherman had an operating budget of $ 350 per pupil (75 per cent of which was used to provide three meals a day). Eight of the school's buildings had been condemned, so dormitories doubled as classrooms. There were no recreational facilities (no gyms) and no laboratories. The shop was equipped by the Navy with tools donated after they had become obsolete. Sherman did not offer classes in Indian culture or languages, even as electives; only three staff members were Indian. Although the Supreme Court has declared prayers in schools unconstitutional students at Sherman were forced to attend church (Brightman, 1971).

Indians are not the only Americans whose heritage is ignored or denigrated in school. Until the late 1960s Texas law forbade teaching in any language but English. In one school students from extremely poor Mexican-American families were fined a penny any time they used Spanish words; in another they were forced to kneel and beg forgiveness for the same "offense" (Silberman, 1971. p. 94). Most textbooks give only brief attention to Indian, Chicano, and black history—if they mention these peoples at all. The following statement is typical :

> Following both World War I and World War II, millions of Negroes moved to Northern cities. As voters and officeholders there, they were able to wield great political influence. Many Negroes joined organisations whose main purpose was to obtain for Negroes "equal protection of the laws" in all respects. As more and more Negroes got a better education and improved their economic status in both North and South, they demanded an end to all discrimination. Many whites, many of them influential, supported their cause. (quoted in Knowles and Prewitt, 1969, p. 50).

The reality of crowded ghettos, racial inequalities and tensions is thus "whitewashed" for white and black students alike, imagine how unrealistic this description must seem to a young person who lives and attends school in a black ghetto. But the assumption in our schools has always been that minorities must be assimilated—for their own good—and that they will not become "Americanised" unless they abandon their different ways. Until recently books on black history simply did not exist. Busing Cultural integration is one of the issues in the school busing controversy. The 1954 Supreme Curt decision on school desegregation had more impact in the South than in the North. By 1972, 70 per cent of black students in northern and border states attended nearly all-black schools, compared to 54 per cent of black students in the South (Farrell, 1974). School segregation in the North reflects segregated housing patterns, not deliberate policy. To overcome this, the Supreme Court ordered the schools of Charlotte, North Carolina, to bus students out of their neighbourhoods to achieve racial balance in 1971—a decision that would have applied throughout the country.

This decision touched off a furor among parents and educators. Both former President Nixon and Alabama Governor Geroge Wallace, who was campaigning for the presidency, opposed "forced busing," and parents began to resist. Busing, they argued, violated the time-honoured custom of neighbourhood schools under local control. It would be too expensive; it would be physically hazardous (what if a child became sick far from home?); it would be "socially dangerous" (what if a white girl decided to date a black student?). Underlying these public objections was the fear that minority youngsters would lower standards and perhaps disrupt white, middle-class schools.

Some black parents also voiced objections to busing. With complete integration whites might control *all* the schools instead of some of them (Knowles and Prewitt, 1969). Would integrated schools teach black studies? Would they be responsive to the needs of black and other minority children? Although black parents, like all parents, want a better education for their children. Some blacks are not anxious to be assimilated. Complicating this debate, there is little concrete evidence that integration would really helps black students. Irwin Katz found that although black children did well in genuinely integrated schools, they did very poorly where racial tensions ran high (in Hodgson, 1973, p. 40). David Armor insisted that "busing is *not* an effective policy instrument for raising the achievement of blacks or for increasing inter-racial harmony" (1972, p. 93). Whether Katz and Armor were correct or not (schools have not been integrated long enough to say for sure), the Supreme Court reversed itself in 1974. By a majority of five to four, the Court declared that unless it could be proved that school district lines had been deliberately drawn to maintain school segregation, the courts did not have the authority to order busing across district lines to achieve integration. The suburbs, Chief Justice Burger reasoned, cannot be held responsible for the *de fecto* segregation that has created black majorities in the inner city. Justice Thurgood Marshall, who as an NAACP lawyer had argued the *Brown* v. *Board* of *Education of Topeka* case before the Supreme Court twenty years earlier, was among the dissenters. Describing the decision as "a glant step backward." Marshall wrote, "unless our children begin to learn together, there is little hope that our people will ever learn to live together." At this point in history, how schools will be integrated, and indeed whether they will be integrated, are open questions.

One suggested remedy for educational inequality is the voucher system. Instead of giving money directly to schools, communities would divide available funds among parents of school-age children. Using tuition vouchers, parents could send their children to any school, public or private, that met standards of quality and nondiscrimination. Vouchers would provide an escape for children once confined within their own (often poverty-stricken) school districts. Vouchers could also help keep financially troubled parochial schools in operation. And because schools would have to compete for students (land money, they might be forced to improve (Cohen, 1971, pp. 198, 200).

Schools and Learning

Peter W. Doe is suing the San Francisco Unified School District for $1 million. Why? Although he was promoted regularly year after year and received his high-school diploma, he cannot read (*The New York Times,* September 16, 1973, p. 75). Peter Doe is not alone. In 1974 the Department of Health, Education, and Welfare released the results of a survey showing that one in twenty Americans between the ages of twleve and seventeen (about 1 million people) could not read at a fourth-grade level. In these days of written employment applications, complicated government forms, four - and five-page credit contracts, and the like, a fourth-grade reading level amounts to illiteracy. (Indead, 34 per cent of the people Harris polled in 1974 could not complete a Medicaid form.) Reading levels are lowest in inner cities and rural areas. Nationwide, 20.5 per cent of black males, 9.6 per cent of black females, 4.7 per cent of white males and 1.7 per cent of white females are functionally illiterate (Reinhold, 1974).

The obvious conclusion is that blacks attend "bad" schools and learn less. [Christopher Jancks estimates that America spends 15 to 20 per cent more to educate white children than to educate black children (1972, pp. 23 - 29)]. This is what James Coleman and his colleagues assumed when they undertook a massive survey of 645,000 students attending four thousand selected schools (1966). Halfway through the research

Coleman told an interviewer, "The study will show the difference in quality of schools that the average Negro child and the average white child are exposed to. You know yourself that the difference is going to be striking" (in Hodgson, 1973, p. 37).

The results were not at all what Coleman expected. He found relatively little difference between predominantly black and predominantly white schools in expenditure per pupil, building age, library facilities, number of textbooks, teacher characteristics and class size. For example, 98 per cent of the white schools and 94 per cent of the black schools had chemistry laboratories. Even more surprising, Coleman found that modern buildings, up-to-date texts and curricula, and higher expenditures per pupil had *no* discernible effect on achievement-test scores. Neither did the quality of teachers. The government and most educators have always assumed a cause-and-effect relationship between school resources and student performance: the more money you spend on pupils, the better their education. Finally, Coleman found that blacks who attended integrated schools for an extended period did only slightly better on achievement tests than blacks who attended segregated schools. But the difference was negligible.

A study of nearly seven hundred students at selected four-year colleges led to similar conclusions. Alexander W. Astin (1968) found that, after controlling for background characteristics, the quality of a college (measured in terms of average intellectual level of the student body, the level of academic competitiveness, and financial resources) had little effect on student achievement (measured in terms of scores on Graduate Record Examinations and entry into Ph.D. programmes). High-school performance, major, career aspirations, and sex were the best predicters of college achievement.

What, then, explains group differences in achievement? Coleman concludes that socio-economic background is the crucial factor. (See the Box 12.2 for cross-cultural support for this conclusion.)

Box 12.2

In the News

Home, School and Achievement

Stockholm—The home is more important than the school to a child's overall achievement. Mass education does not lower academic standards for gifted students, as is widely held. Elitist school systems create and perpetuate inequality.

These conclusions come from a seven-year study of schools in nineteen countries, which was conducted by the International Association for the Evaluation of International Achievement (I.E.A.) Seeking to understand what accounts for differences in achievement, educators measured the performance of 258,000 students in reading comprehension, literature and science.

In general, the Stockholm report confirmed Coleman's (1966) finding that home background affects academic performance more than the school does. Reading comprehension and achievement in science, in particular, seemed to depend upon home background (see Figure 12.1). In literature and languages, on the other hand, good teaching and school quality proved more important. Specifically, the data showed:

1. Girls lag behind boys in their interest and performance in science, and the gap grows wider the longer they attend schools for girls only; but the gap narrows significantly in coeducational schools.

2. The number of books and magazines in a student's home has a greater effect on achievement in literature than income and education of the student's family.

3. An analysis of the schools' greater success in teaching science than in teaching reading suggests a serious discrepancy in the schools' relative efforts. "The schools appear to do little to mobilise their resources for the improvement of reading beyond the early years," the report said.

Mass education does not appear to penalise the gifted student. In a separate reading comprehension study the top 9 per cent of American students did better than the top 9 per cent in the other fourteen nations in the survey. The same elite group rated seventh out of nineteen countries in science. Moreover, American's mass education system is less class-biased than the more selective systems of countries like West Germany. There, only 1 per cent of lower-class children are still in school at age eighteen; in the United States 14 per cent are.

But what about education payoff? Does education have any effect on economic mobility? The study's answer: a tentative yes:

The Stockholm report challenges directly some claims made recently in the study by Christopher Jenckss at Harvard that the schools fail to reduce social inequality. Although the I.E.A. survey did not examine inequality in income, it concluded that open access to public education is a key factor in allowing lower-class children to rise to the level of the academic elite. This increases their chances of greater economic success.

Source : The New York Times, May 27, 1973, p. 579, based on a survey by the International Association for the Evalution of Educational Achievement.

> Taking all these results together, one implication stands out above all: that schools bring little influence to bear on a child's achievement that is independent of his [or her] background and social context; and that this very lack of an independent effect means that the inequalities imposed on children by their home neighbourhood, and peer environment are carried along to become the inequalities with which they confront adult life at the end of school. (Coleman, in Silberman, 1971, p. 71).

In short, the family, not the school, is the major educational institution—even in modern society. Family differences strongly affect children's chances for equal educational opportunities. Traditionally, equality of opportunities has meant trying to give all children access to the same kinds of educational *inputs*—teachers, facilities, and so on. This is roughly equivalent to giving someone who has never played golf the same set of clubs and balls as an experienced player, and pointing them toward the same green. There is little doubt who will win. Coleman argues that to achieve true equality of opportunity we must treat individuals differently, much as we give a handicap to a beginning golfer. Just as we calculate a fair handicap by counting the average number of strokes it takes a beginner to complete a golf course, so that with his handicap he will come out about the same as the more experienced player, so we should measure educational opportunity by *outcome*. Equal opportunity in education exists when the average scores of graduates from different schools (not per-pupil expenditures, facilities, and the like are about the same.

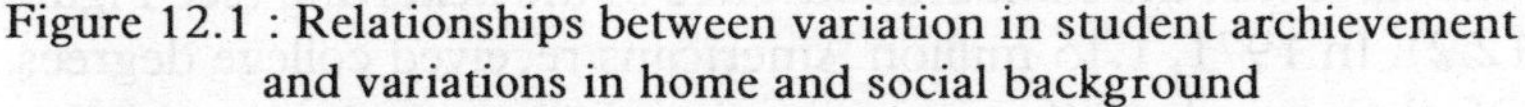

Figure 12.1 : Relationships between variation in student archievement and variations in home and social background

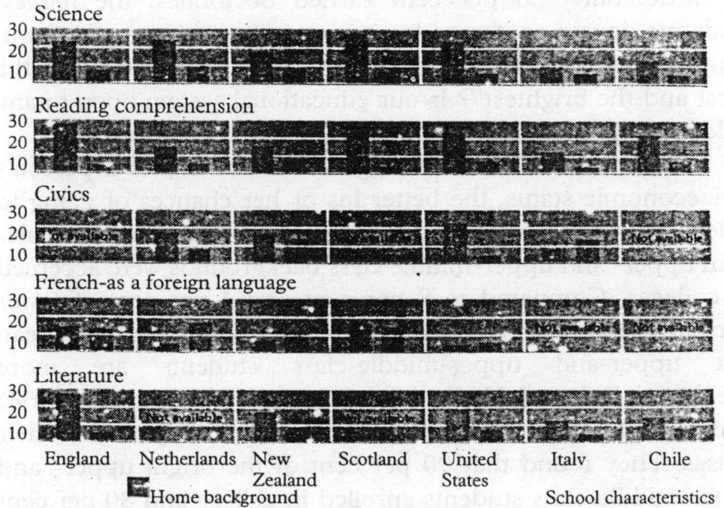

Source: The New York Times, May 27, 1973, p. 74C. Based on data from the International Association for the Evalution of Educational Achievement.

The long simmering debate over value of schooling was heightened by the results of a twenty-one country study by the International Association for the Evaluation of Educational Achievement. As some of the results above show differences in home background were a major factor in explaining variations in reading and science levels.

The Coleman Report is not the final word on educational differences. Only 59 per cent of the schools he and his associates surveyed completed all of the questionnaires. Their calculations reflect school averages, not individual achievement, and may obscure significant individual variations. A number of sociologists have criticised the study and the way data were analyzed. Nevertheless, its conclusions are widely accepted by educational sociologists.

The Screening Function

One way of thinking about educational institutions is as screening systems. At each step up the educational ladder a number of students are excluded or drop out voluntarily. Those who have met the standards advance to the next rung (see Figure 12.2). In 1971, 1.15 million Americans received college degrees. Of those, only 2.8 per cent earned doctorates, the highest academic degree conferred by American universities (*Statistical Abstracts,* 1973, p. 137). Does that 2.8 per cent constitute the "best and the brightest"? Is our educational system open to any child with talent and ambition, as we would like to believe?

The data in Table 12.1 suggest that the higher a person's socioeconomic status, the better his or her chances of going to college. In 1965, 90 per cent of males and 80 per cent of females from upper- and upper-middle class backgrounds were accepted by colleges. Compared to 8 per cent and 4 per cent of lower working-class males and females, respectively. Does this mean that upper-and upper-middle-class students are more intelligent? Robert J. Havighurst and cernice Neugarten (1968) analysed data on students who were all in the top quarter of their classes. They found that 90 per cent of the bright upper- and upper-middle-class students enrolled in college and 80 per cent

Figure 12.2 : School retention rates: 1924 - 1962, from fifth grade to high school graduation

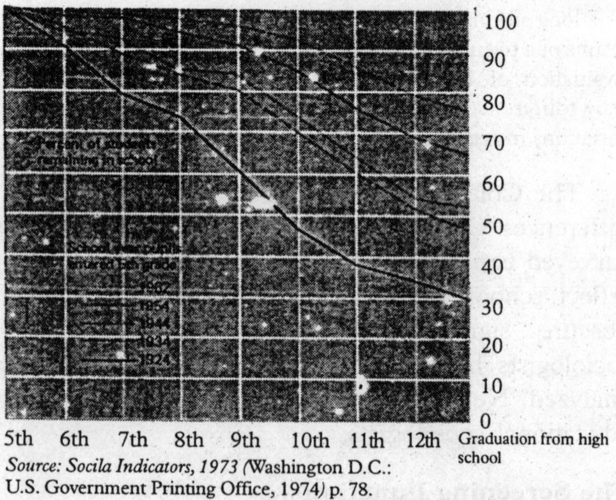

Source: Socila Indicators, 1973 (Washington D.C.: U.S. Government Printing Office, 1974) p. 78.

At each rung of the educational ladder a smaller percentage of students remain in school although the proportion of these completing high school has more than doubled since 1924.

graduated, whereas 63 per cent of the bright working-class students went to college, and only 29 per cent graduated—despite their equal abilities (see Table 12.2). Clearly, social class influences a person's chances for finishing high school, getting into college, completing college, and going on to graduate school. This means that a lot of talent in America is screened out and goes undeveloped.

Table 12.1
Per cent of Given Class who Enter College[1]

Social Class	*1920*	*1940*	*1950*	*1960*	*1965*	
					Males	*Females*
Upper and Upper-middle	40	70	75	80	90	80
Upper-middle	8	20	38	50	62	45
Upper-working	2	5	12	25	35+	24
Lower-working[2]	0	0	2	4	3	4

[1] Note that the percentage of working-class students entering college today is nearly as high as the percentage of upper-and upper-middle-class students entering college in 1920.

[2] Since 1920 college has become increasingly accessible to all but the lower working class.

Source: Robert G. Havighurst and Bernice Neugarten, *Society and Education* (Boston: Allyn & Bacon, 1968).

Table 12.2
Level of Education in Relation to Social Class of Youth in the Upper Quarter of Intellectual Ability (IQ = 110 +) 1965 (By Per cent)

	Social class			
	Upper-and upper middle	*Lower-Middle*	*Working*	*Totals*
Do not finish high school	0	2	10	5
High school graduates. Do not enter college	10	10	24	15
Enter college but do not finish	10	26	37	27
Complete a four-year college programme	80	62	29	53

Source: Robert J. Havighurst and Bernice Neugarten, *Society and Education* (Boston: Allyn & Bacon, 1968), tables 4.1; 3.5.

Tracking

The screening process begins in elementary school, when children are divided into slow, average, and bright groups on the basis of aptitude and achievement tests and teachers' recommendations. *Tracking,* as ability grouping is called, is based on the assumption that students will learn more if they do not have to compete with students who are much brighter than they are or wait for students who are slower. It is designed primarily to accelerate above-average children and give below-average children the extra attention they need.

In practice, tracking tends to segregate students along socioeconomic and racial lines—white, middle-class youngsters being assigned to the advanced track, nonwhite lower-class children to "general" and vocational tracks. According to one study of 467 southern school districts, 60 per cent of racial segregation in elementary schools and 35 per cent in high schools was justified in terms of tracking ("Testing and Tracking," 1973, p. 15).

In Washington, D.C., where over 90 per cent of high-schools students are black, tracking perpetuates economic divisions. In 1966, 85 per cent of students in neighbourhoods where the median income was $ 3,872 a year found themselves in a basic or general track, even though their schools had college preparatory tracks. Where median income reached $ 16,374 a year, 82 per cent of the students were in college preparatory or honours tracks (Lauter and Howe, 1970, p. 318).

Although tracking does seem to improve the performance of good students, it does not appear to help poor students. In fact, Coleman found ghetto youngsters did best in racially; and economically mixed classes. Tracking merely widens the gap between good and poor students, stigmatising those who are placed in the "dummy" programmes. Three researchers (Schaefer, Olexa and Polk, 1972) discovered a relationship between low track placement and delinquency, lack of involvement in school activities, and drop-out rates, as well as low grades. By lowering the students' self-esteem, they conclude, the system alienates young people from school norms. Thrown back on the peer group they may turn to antisocial behaviour.

Tracking also influences teacher expectations. Low expectations tend to become self-fulfilling prophecies.

> A fourth-grade math teacher writes a half-dozen problems on the board for the class to do. "Think I can pick at least four children who can't do them," she tells the class, and proceeds to call four youngsters to the board to demonstrate, for all to see, how correct the teacher's judgment is. Needless to say, the children fulfil the prophecy. (Silberman, 1971, p. 139).

Rosenthal and Jacobson (1968) tested this proposition experimentally. They gave elementary-school teachers a list of students, supposely with very high IQ's, but who were actually selected at random. They told teachers to expect great progress from these students. At the end of the school year the IQ scores of this group had increased significantly more than the scores of students who had not been selected. (The influence of teachers' expectations on student performance is known as the *pygmalion effect.*) A study by Lezcock (1969) confirmed Rosenthal and Jacobson's findings with an added twist. The author studied four kinds of elementary schools: lower-class white, middle-class white, lower-class black, and middle-class black. In the middle-class, schools, teachers treated students better if the children were "supposed" to be bright. But in the lower-class black school, teachers rejected bright children as "smart-alecks" and "wiseguys".

Contest Mobility and "Cooling Out"

Although tracking eliminates some students, a great many complete academic high-school programmes every year, with the expectation of going on to college. Ralph H. Turner (1960) compares our school system to a race in which every effort is made to keep as many students in the running for as long as possible. The race is considered fair so long as everyone has equal footing at the start. The outcome depends on individual effort—on "common sense, craft, enterprise, daring and successful risk-taking: as well as on inteligence and hard work". This is why Turner calls our system "contest mobility."

In contrast, the British eliminate all but the brightest students at an early age, before the race begins. Nearly all of the children selected for college preparatory programmes do obtain university degrees and the high social and economic status that come with them. Education in Britain, Turner argues, means learning to take one's destined place in the elite, under the sponsorship of those already in power (hence his term "sponsored mobility"). Education in America consists largely of learning to complete. In Britain children of eight or nine know more or less where they are headed in life.

In America the "finish" is postponed until late adolescence. Less than a third of the 1 million Americans who start college every year graduate. What happens to the others? Some are dismissed outright and suffer the public failure of returning home at the end of their first semester or freshman year. Some quit; but most who do not meet the standards are eased out gradually. Many who enter colleges are assigned to remedial classes or to "terminal programmes" in junior colleges; counselled to think about noncollege career alternatives; required to take an Orientation to College course that states the "facts of life" in an impersonal way, enlightening overambitious students. If necessary, students are put on probation with two or three semesters' warning—a slow death for those who cannot meet stadards. Burton R. Clark (1960) argues that this gentle, slow dismissal is designed to "cool out" young people who have been led to believe that hard work alone will win them the social and economic rewards that come with college degrees. By letting students down slowly, colleges prevent the build-up of potentially disruptive frustration of discovering that the prizes society promises are available only to a very few.

Education and Income

Everyone "knows" that you need a college education to get ahead in America (that is, to earn more money than your parents did). We tend to assume that a B.A. (or, even better, a medical or law degree or a Ph.D.) is a guarantee to gaining the "good life". Indeed, the government has long assumed that the way to reduce income inequality is to educate the poor. Is this assumption correct?

Statistics on education and income suggest it is (see Table 12.3). An elementary-school drop-out earns only 64 per cent of the average national income; a person with one or more years of graduate school earns 171 per cent of the national average. But does this mean that the elementary-school drop-out would be earning nearly three times as much as he does today if he had gone to graduate school? Christopher Jencks (1972) thinks not. Education is not the only difference between the drop-out and the graduate. In all probability they came from very different socioeconomic backgrounds and had very different experiences while growing up. These differences—not education, says Jencks—may account for the income gap between them. Comparing data on people from similar socioeconomic backgrounds who had similar test scores but different educations, Jencks concludes that an extra year of elementary or high school boosts income less than 4 per cent; a year of college, 7 per cent; a year of graduate school, only about 4 per cent (1972, pp. 221–25).

Table 12.3

Incomes of Full-time, Year-round Workers over 25 with Different Amount of Schooling, as a Percentage of the 1968 Average

Amount of Schooling	*Males*	*Females*	*Total*
Didn't Finish Elementary School	70	40	64
Finished Elementary School, No High School	85	47	76
Entered High School, Didn't Finish	96	51	84
Finished High School, No College	111	61	95
Entered College, Didn't Finish	129	71	115
Finished College, No Graduate School	170	84	150
At Least 1 Year of Graduate Work	188	106	171
All Individuals	114	62	100
Grand Mean			$7,995
Number of Individuals in 1,000s	34,432	12,575	47,008

Source : Table 41 in the U.S. Bureau of the Census, "Income in 1968." "Elementary Schools includes the first 8 years of schooling. "High School" includes grades 9-12. "Finished College" means a 4-year college. "No High School," "No College," and "No Graduate School" includes individuals who entered these institutions but did not complete the first year.

In addition as more and more people obtain high-school, college, and graduate degrees, their values in the job market declines. When only 6 per cent of Americans entered college, college graduates were an elite minority and could command high salaries. Today, about 40 per cent of American students go to college, and a B. A. isn't the badge of distinction it once was. As a result a college degree is now often required for mundane, relatively low-paying jobs.

This is not to say that education is not important, but rather that we cannot expect schools to solve all of our social problems. The way to equalise income, in Jencks's view, is simply to redistribute it through taxation—not to educate the poor. Education is an end in itself, he argues, not a means to individual mobility and social equality. "There is no evidence that building a school playground will affect the students' chances of learning to read, getting into college, or earning $50,000 a year when they are fifty," he writes. "Building a playground may, however, have a considerable effect on the students" chances of having a good time during recess when they are eight" (in Hodgson, 1973, p. 44).

The Social Structure of Schools

Beginning at the age of five or six, children spend about a thousand hours a year in school—next only to the amounts of time they spend sleeping and watching television. In traditional schools they are subjected to a level of regimentation they will not encounter again, unless they enter the military. Where else are people forced to remain silent, to sit still for hours, to line up and march on command, to ask permission to speak or to go to the bathroom? These peculiarities—the amount of time, regimentation, and compulsory attendance—shape the social structure of many schools and the roles of both teacher and student (Jackson, 1968). And as Philip Zimbardo's 1972 study so clearly showed, the social structure of an institution strongly influences the behaviour of people in that institution.

Kindergarten is the child's initiation into the student role. On the surface most kindergarten activities seem purposeless

> [T]he teacher asks, "who wants to be the first one?" One of the noisy girls comes to the center of the room. The voice on the record is

> giving directions for imitating an ostrich and the girl follows them, walking around the center of the room holding her ankles with her hands. . . .This is apparently a familiar game. For a number of children are calling out "can we have the crab?" Edith. . .plays the part of the record with music for imitating crabs by. The children from the first table line up across the room, hands and feet on the floor and faces pointing toward the celling. (Gracey, 1972, p. 248)

But the children are learning—learning to do what the teacher wants, when she wants it. In kindergarten there is a Story Time, a Nap Time, a Pick-up Time—in short, an official routine.

> The record ends at 2:40. Edith says, "Children, down on your blankets. "As the class is lying on blankets now, Edith refuses to answer the various questions individual children put to her because, she tells them, "It's rest time now." (Gracey, 1972), pp. 250–52.

Day after day kindergarten children are shown the rituals of school, including hand-raising and lining-up. They are taught behaviour and attitude teachers believe essential, and drilled in these patterns. Herry L. Gracey compares kindergarten to a boot camp: it is "successful" if youngster learn to follow routines and obey orders without question, even if the order are trivial (1972, p. 251).

The Hidden Curriculum

As this analysis of kindergarten suggests, the official curriculum—reading, arithmetic, and other subjects—does not begin to describe the content of education. In a detailed study of elementary schools, Philip Jackson (1968) found that to advance from grade to grade, to survive academically and socially, youngsters must also learn to be quiet, to line up, to wait, to act interested even if they are not, to please teachers without alienating peers, to come to grips with the inevitability of school, and the host of other skills that comprise the *hidden curriculum.*

By the time they enter first grade, most children have learned the three basic facts of school life that will structure their school experience: crowds, praise and power (Jackson, 1968, p. 6). In school a child's every act is open to public scrutiny, by teachers *and peers;* there is little or no privacy. One of twenty or more in a class, he or she must learn to tolerate delays (waiting to be called on, waiting for the class to line up for reces) and interruptions (children breaking into an other's dialogue with a teacher, teachers in vading daydreams, bells terminating a struggle with a math problem). For much of the day, however, children are expected to act as though they are alone—even though their friends (and perhaps enemies) are just inches away. School teaches youngsters to be alone in a crowd.

The public nature of school activities is made all the more trying by the fact that the child is constantly being evaluated. In one fourth-grade classroom, for example, pupils recorded their math test scores on large bar graphs in red pencil. After a test the teacher would line them up in the front of the room, score cards in hand, in the order of their grades. That way everyone could see who got the highest and lowest scores. From first grade on, children's victories and failures become a matter of semipublic record: IQ, aptitude and achievement test scores, and grades are all duly recorded. Children also begin to earn a reputation as bright or slow, highly motivated or dawdling, helpful in maintaining classroom order or troublesome. These informal teacher evaluations can be as important as grades. How many teachers will fail a student who has behaved beautifully and tried his or her hardest? "Although it offends our sensibilities to admit it, no doubt that bright-eyed little girl [or boy] who stands trembling before the principal on graduation day arrived there at least in part because she [or he] typed her [or his] weekly themes neatly and handed her [or his] homework in on time" (Jackson, 1968, p. 34).

In addition children evaluate each other, often through teacher encouragement: "Who can tell me if George's answer is correct." Children also decide whether their classmates are teacher's pets or good guys, cheats or good sports. In effect, each child plays to two audiences—teachers and peers—whose standards often conflict. In one second grade, for example, a teacher praised a boy for his "creative dancing," but his classmates teased him for being a sissy (Jackson, 1968, pp. 22–25).

Formal and informal evaluation by teachers and peers may have more impact than we like to admit. Educator John Holt contrasts his seventeen-month-old niece to tense, anxious fifth graders. Every object the baby sees she experiments with. Although she usually fails to make things do what she wants them to, she keeps trying. The older children, in contrast, seem defeated before they begin. Why the difference? Holt reasons, the baby "has not yet been made to feel that failure is shame, disgrace a crime" (1964, pp. 62–63).

Finally, the distribution of power in schools is decidedly unequal. School places children under the abolute and sometimes highly insensitive authority of teachers.

> A precocious sixth-grader has become attached to a particular pencil, now down to a small stub. His teacher orders him to use a larger pencil; the youngster politely informs her that so long as his work and penmanship are satisfactory (he is receiving A's on all his work), what pencil he uses is a matter for him to decide. The teacher sends him to see the principal, who summons the boy's parents for a conference to discuss his "disobedience." (Silberman, 1971, p. 88).

Teachers do most of the talking in classrooms (as much as 80 per cent according to one study). Students are confined to answering questions and commenting on the teacher's statements. Teachers decide what students will and will not do.

> All over the United States, that last week of November, 1963, teachers reported the same complaint: "I can't get the children to concentrate on their work; all they want to do is talk about the assassination." The idea that the children might learn more from discussing President Kennedy's assassination—or that, like most adults, they were simply too obsessed with the horrible events to think about anything else—didn't occur to these teachers. It wasn't in that week's lesson plan. (Silberman, 1970, p. 85)

In effect the teacher is the child's first boss, and learning to do what the boss wants you to do is an essential part of the hidden curriculum. This, in Charles Silberman's view, is the basis for the dichotomy between work and play.

> [A] by-product of teacher dominance, one that has profound consequences for children's attitudes towards learning, is the sharp but wholly artificial dichotomy between work and play which schools create and maintain. Young children make no such distinction. They learn through play, and until they have been taught

> to make the distinction ("Let's stop playing now, children; it's time to start our work"), they regard all activities in the same light. But the dichotomy grows out of the assumption that nothing can happen unless the teacher makes it happen. (Silberman, 1971, p. 90).

Critics of the school system argue that this hidden curriculum stifles initiative and creativity, that the obsession with rules and regulations keeps youngsters in a chronic state of dependency, and that the assumption of distrust regarding students is harmful and unfounded. After conducting a national study of public schools, Charles Silberman concluded that :

> The preoccupation with order and control, the slavish adherence to the timetable and lesson plan, the obsession with routine *qua* routine the absence of noise and movement, the joylessness and repression, the universality of the formal lecture or teacher-dominated "discussion" in which the teacher instructs an entire class as a unit, the emphasis of the verbal and de-emphasis of the concrete, the inability of students to work on their own, the dichotomy between work and play—none of these are necessary; all can be eliminated. (Silberman, 1971).

Others reason that young people must learn to accept orders from a boss, to cope with contradictory evaluations from superiors and peers, and to tolerate frustrations, delays, and being in a crowd—if, for example, they are to function effectively on an assembly line or in a large business organisation.

The Teaching Situation

Teachers often start out with high ideals. They like children, remember things they disliked about their own school years, and are determined to do better. All too often, however, the very structure of schools transforms them into the "traffic cop" teachers they vowed never to become. Teachers, unlike other professionals, rarely have offices of their own. Instead they share an open lounge designed primarily for coffee and cigarette breaks. They have little control over curricula, textbooks, and other aspects of teaching that directly concern them. Added to large class enrolments, most teachers must also perform a variety of clerical and menial tasks, such as patrolling the halls and the student cafeteria. They have little time for either private reflection or consultation with colleagues. Often their principals and city employers distrust teachers as much as teachers distrust students: like clerks and factory workers, most punch time clocks. Their salaries are relatively low, and they generally do not enjoy very much prestige. The National Opinion Research Center found that Americans rank teaching thirty-fifth, between building contractors and railroad engineers.

Added to these factors, teachers are usually evaluated on the relative quite in their classrooms and on the stillness of their students. Teachers are rarely fired if their students haven't learned anything. When new teachers ask for advice, more often than not they are given tips on discipline. For example, a National Teachers Association manual recommends, "Plan the lesson. Be ready to use the first minute of class time. If you get Johnny right away, he has no time to cook up *interesting ideas* that do not fit into the class situation" (Silberman, 1970, p. 88, italics added) . It is no wonder, then, that teachers focus on maintaining order. Indeed, this is what most parents want them to do. A Harris Poll showed that two-thirds of parents (but only 27 per cent of teachers) considered discipline more important than learning (Silberman, 1970, pp. 90-92).

With all these problems, some teachers nevertheless manage to do excellent jobs. Philip W. Jackson tried to discover what the best teachers (as rated by colleagues) had in common. His observations surprised him. The "good" teachers were not the most gifted intellectually. Often they appeared irrational, because they reacted intuitively and did not generalise about their experience. Immersed in the ongoing life of the classroom, all tended to offer simple answers to complex questions: "Why is Fred such a troublemaker? Because he comes from a broken Home" (1968, p. 144). Elsewhere, these qualities might be a handicap, but they seemed to work in the classroom. The teacher's close involvement with students can make up for the coldness of schools routines. And in a class of thirty students, oversimplifying may be the only way to get any point across.

Student Society

We have talked about the institution's impact on students, but what about the students' responses and values? These form another part of the hidden curriculum.

In the 1960s Patricia Sexton studied freshmen at twenty-three colleges. Only 19 per cent said their major interest was the "pursuit of ideas". A whooping 51 per cent devoted most of their attention to extracurricular activities such as sports and social life, paralleling Coleman's study of adolescents a decade earlier (1961). Only 27 per cent in Sexton's study concentrated on their future careers (1967).

Social success seems to be even more prized in high school. Good grades are all right, as long as the student is also athletic (boys) or popular (girls). Tannenbaum (1960) created eight imaginary boys and asked other students to rate them in order of acceptability. The highest-rated student was the Brilliant Nonstudious Athlete; the lowest, a Brilliant Studious Nonathlate. In other surveys almost no one wanted to date a brilliant girl; brilliant boys were only slightly more acceptable as dates (Coleman. 1961). College plans improve a student's status, but only for students with no overt intellectual interests (Coleman, 1961).

Why the emphasis on athletics and smooth social skills? Partly, perhaps, because schools isolate students, encouraging them to turn to peers and the mass media for their values (Coleman 1961, p. 9). But aren't these youngsters simply reflecting the values of their elders? Coleman asks: How much do adults value intellectual ability and nonconformity?

Edgar Friendenberg's explanation is more cynical. In a study of student values (1965) he asked students to choose the "ideal" student from a fictitious list. First choice was a neat, helpful, other-directed good student. Last choice was the class nonconformist. Though his description contained no hint of antisocial behaviour, the nonconformist was regarded with suspicion. Why do students reject any suggestion of individuality? Perhaps, Friendberg argues, because schools have taken on the community's task of preparing students for the dull business of living and working in a bureaucratic society. Where nonconformity is feared, people must learn to submit to the judgments of others.

The Future of Education

In the preceding section we focused on problems, but many educators believe there is hope for better schools. In this section we will look at new directions in education: the open classroom, which has captured the imagination of many educators; open admissions to college, which give minority students a second chance; Headstart and "Sesame Street." Both designed to close the gap in school readiness; and research into the infant's learning capacity, which is revolutionising our view of education.

The Open Classroom

> To learn is to change. Education is a process that changes the learner. Learning involves interaction between the learner and his [or her] environment, and its effectiveness relates to the frequency, variety and intensity of interaction. Education, at best is ecstatic. (Leonard, 1968)

> [All children], without exception, [have] an innate and unquenchable drive to understand the world in which [they] live and to gain freedom and competence in it. Whatever truly adds to [their] understanding, [their] capacity for growth and pleasure, [their] sense of [their] own freedom, dignity and worth may be said to be true education. (Holt, 1972).

The *open classroom,* or open education as it is sometimes called, is a direct attack on the distrust and regimentation that underlie traditional education. It is a concerted effort to deinstitutionalise education by letting youngsters learn what they want to learn, when and how they want to learn it. The practice of fighting students' natural inclinations and curiosity and forcing education on them according to an imposed schedule and plan is banished.

In a typical open classroom the uniform rows of desks, all facing front, are eliminated. Instead, seating is flexible, changing as groups come together and move apart for instruction. The room is organised around various interest areas—science, art, reading, and so on. Each area contains a wide variety of appropriate materials, including books, maps, plants and colourful containers. Instead of doling out materials, teachers make sure everything is accessible. Often students bring in their own things—not for the old fashioned "show and tell," but to use and learn from.

In the open classroom teachers do not direct from the front but walk around helping students in their projects. Instead of dividing time into rigid blocks, they base their plans on what children need at a given moment. Sometimes classes move outside the school altogether:

> Very often things can be learned by experiencing them firsthand. Why read about how a port operates when there is one a short bus ride away? Why read a book about how steel is made if there is a steel plant nearby? Does it make sense to study about crime and police protection. . .without ever visiting a real police station? (Wurman, 1972, p. 12)

Outwardly an open classroom may look chaotic: in one corner two children are tending their soybeans; a girl is working with Cuisenaire rods in another spot, while a group sings.a song in the middle of the room. To keep classrooms from degenerating into mere playgrounds, the teacher must plan carefully, maintaining structure and direction. Such a system imposes heavy demands on teachers, but frees them from their usual roles as "timekeeper, traffic cop and disciplinarian" (Silberman, 1971).

What about discipline? Do open classrooms work only with middle-class children who have been taught from babyhood to be neat and obedient? Apparently not. Open education began with working-class British children, and many open classrooms operate in depressed areas here. Silberman visited some of these classes and found poor children from crime-ridden streets working busily at their projects. In one science area two children were rebuilding a washing machine motor and two others were fixing an old radio. In another class a boy excitedly described all held learned dissecting a pig. Equally important, children were enjoying themselves. One child told a visitor, "Last year we had to work all the time. Now we can play all the time." He was "playing" with a difficult mathematical game. Another child's father wrote asking if his son could come to school earlier; he couldn't seem to do everything he wanted during regular hours (Siberman, 1971).

Open education is less common in high schools, where classes are more specialised. However, some schools are taking tentative steps toward giving students greater freedom. Innovations range from doing away with student dress codes to giving credit for work in the community and for individual projects (Silberman, 1973, p. 87). However small, these changes are evidence of a new interest in reducing regimentation in high schools.

Open Admissions

In 1970, under pressure from minority groups, the City University of New York opened its doors to *every* high-school graduate. The programme was extremely controversial, for it went right to the heart of the conflict between the ideals of equal opportunity and selectivity. Minority groups argued that they were not responsible for the poor quality of ghetto schools. They demanded another chance for ghetto children to display their talents. Although they agreed in principle, university officials were fearful that teachers would lower standards, depriving better-prepared students of a quality education. Could mass education *and* quality education coexist on a massive scale?

Researchers were waiting when the first New York City open admissions classes graduated in 1974. The results seem mixed, though accurate figures are hard to obtain. What figures there are seem to indicate higher drop-out rates for open admission students, though not too much higher than for regular students. At City College, for example, 55 per cent of traditional students who entered in 1970 were still enrolled by the fall of 1973. Of the open admissions students, 43 per cent were still in school (Maeroff, March 17, 1974).

Drop-out rates do not tell the whole story, of course. Open admissions have led to over-crowded facilities; remedial programmes are frustratingly inadequate. Some believe that standards have dropped, partly as a result of pressure on teachers not to fail too many open admissions students. Once again the educational community must do battle with an old issue: Should college be only for the talented elite or is it the right of everyone, regardless of formerly displayed talent? In June 1974 some proud students—once considered failures—received diplomas because open admissions had given them a second chance. For them, if for no one else, the answer was clear.

Preschool Education

Many educators are attacking the problem of inequality not from the top, but from the bottom. If poor children come to school already behind, why not solve the problem at its source, by changing their preschool environment?

Headstart

In 1965 the office of Economic Opportunity began a preschool programme for disadvantaged children. Project Headstart aimed at teaching poor children the word and number skills middle-class children learn at home. Though Headstart teachers concentrated on cognitive skills, the children received medical and nutritional attention as well. By 1969 Headstart was spending about $1,400 per child, compared to the public schools' $700 ("Following Up on Headstart," 1969).

What were the effects? A series of tests in 1969 found no significant difference between Headstart children and others once they entered school. But the Headstart children did show superiority in learning readiness. How can we account for these mixed results? Some felt the tests were inadequate; others believed the schools might be undoing all of Headstart's good work ("How Head a Head Start?"1969). Still others faulted Headstart programmes themselves for being too rigid, too "middle-class" to be useful to minority children (Smith, 1969). No one disputes that Headstart provided the opportunity to treat a lot of neglected health problems, however. And it did generate important research in the area of preschool education—research that is continuing.

"Sesame Street"

While the debate on Headstart continued, a new television show, "Sesame Street," began making headlines. The show's creators applied the flashy, fast-paced techniques of advertising to teaching the alphabet, numbers, and other basic skills. With its genial adults and appealing monsters (the voracious Cookie Monster, Oscar the Grouch, who lives in a garbage can, and Big Bird), "Sesame Street" was an immediate hit with its young audience. Parents liked it too. But what about its more serious purpose? Did "Sesame Street" really teach children "recognition of letters, numbers, and simple counting ability"? Did it encourage "reasoning skills, vocabulary and an increased awareness of self and world," as the producers claimed?

In 1970 the Educational Testing Service reported the results of a two-year study of the "Sesame Street" audience. They found that children who watched the show regularly gained significantly over children who watched only occasionally, or not at all (see Figure 12.3). Children from poor homes showed the greatest improvement, particularly those whose mothers watched and discussed the show with them (Ball and Bogatz, 1970; Malcolm, 1970).

"Sesame Street" seemed to affect attitudes as well as skills. Second-year research showed regular watchers were readier for school, had better attitudes towards schools, and were less racist than nonwatchers (Ball and Bogtz, 1971). One starting finding was that three-year olds showed the greatest gains in all cognitive areas. Parents used to worry about "pushing" very young children. The study of "Sesame Street" supported the view that very young children learn quickly.

Infant Education

Recently the Harvard Preschool Project rated a group of three- to six-year-olds according to seventeen specific intellectual and social skills (the ability to plan and carry out projects, the ability to attract and hold adults' attention, etc.). Using teachers' reports and their own observations, the researchers divided the children into two groups: an "A" group of very competent children, and a "C" group of those less able to cope. What made the difference?

Researchers turned their attention to todollers, aged one to three. They found that children with "A skills" had received special attention from their mothers during a critical age period:

from ten months to one and one-half years. Not that these mothers hovered over their infants: some, in fact, worked outside the home. Instead, in a very informal way they created a learning environment for their children. They provided plenty of toys and other objects, and gave children considerable physical freedom. An ordinary event, such as a bath, often became an occasion for

Figure 12.3: Sesame Street: First year report card:
Percentage of items answered correctly by all disadvantaged children at present and posttest

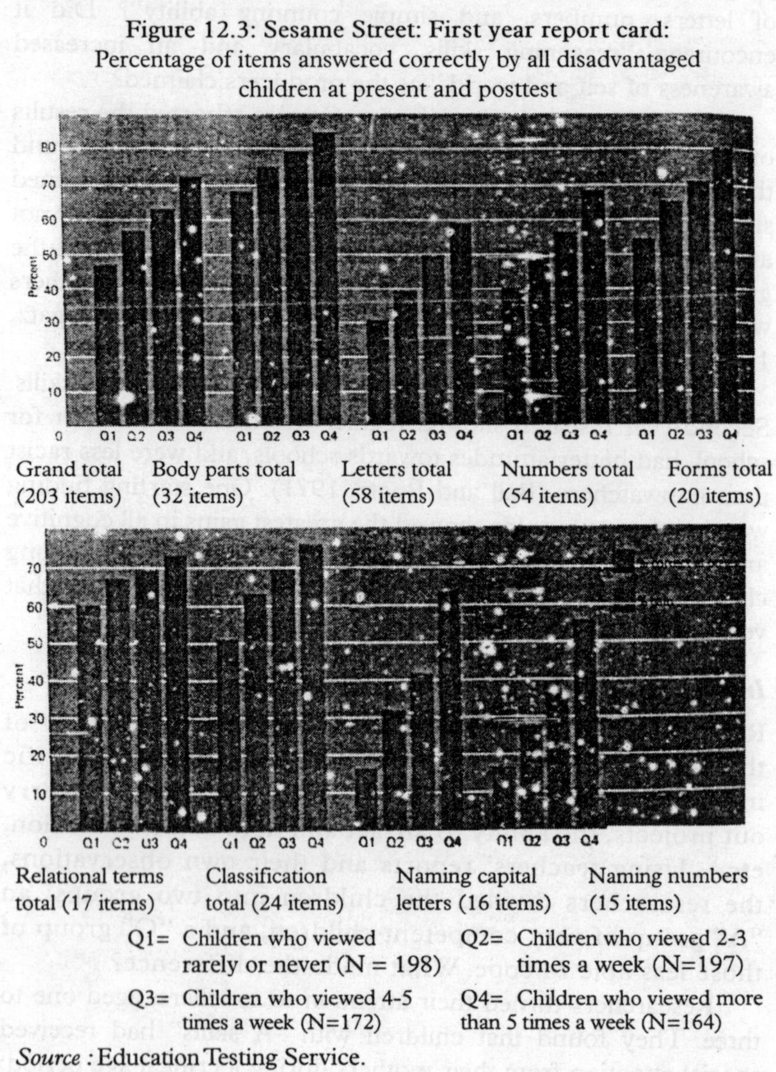

Source : Education Testing Service.

an informal lesson: "Show me your knee. Now where are your toes?" Later, these mothers answered questions and provided information when asked. None had really tried to teach in any formal way (Pines, 1971).

Studies like this remind us again of an important distinction: education is not the same as schooling. The research on schools by educational sociologists suggests that, *as presently constituted,* schools serve mainly to legitimate inequalities and to prepare students for entering an organisational society. Efforts to change this abound. How much difference they will make remains to be seen.

13
Religion

Defining Religion

The remains of flowers found among the skeletons of a Neanderthal burial site, indicating some kind of burial rite, suggest that human religiosity may extend as far back as 60,000 years. The massive slabs of Stonehenge in England, the temple ruins of Greece from Rhodes to Corfu the monumental heads carved from volcanic rock on the slopes of Easter Island all attest to the existence of religious behaviour among different peoples in different times. What can sociologists say about this pervasive human phenomenon?

Emile Durkheim in *The Elementary Forms of Religious Life* (1972), defined *religion* as a "unified system of beliefs and practices" that pertain to "sacred things" and that unite adherents of the system "into one single moral community" (Durkheim, 1965, p. 47). There are four elements of Durkheim's definition that merit our attention : sacred things, religious beliefs, religious practices and the moral community.

Sacred Things

All aspects of human experience, according to Durkheim, can be divided into two radically and diametrically opposed categories: the sacred and the profane. The *sacred* is ideal and transcends everyday existence; it is extraordinary, potentially dangerous, awe-inspiring, fear-inducing. The *profane* is mundane and ordinary. Almost anything can be sacred: a grasshopper, a cross, a stone. These are sacred only because some community has marked them as sacred. Once established as sacred, however, they become symbols of religious beliefs, sentiments and practices.

The sacred may be a supernatural being—god or ghost. Those who believe in one god—the world's 985 million Christians, 14.5 million Jews, and 471 million Muslims—are monotheists. Those who worship more than one god—like yesterday's Greeks and today's Hindus—are polytheists. Some 472 million Hindus, for example, most of them in India, have a pantheon of five great gods—Krishna, Vishnu, Rama, Lakshmi and Siva—all of whom are subordinate to "the One." Gods are not alone among the sacred. Many worship the sacred ghost or ancestor spirit. Such spirits are also imbued with supernatural qualities, but they are of human rather than divine origin. Shintoism, for instance, with its 60 million disciples, mostly in Japan, is based on reverence toward family ancestors.

A moral or philosophical principle can also be sacred. Three Asian religions—Buddhism, Confucianism and Taoism—all focus on the achievement of certain ethical and spiritual ideals. Buddhism, with more than 300 million adherents, is less concerned with the God Buddha than with his message of the "four noble truths," the first being that existence is sorrow, and that for anyone to attain *nirvana*, a state of spiritual detachment, he or she must follow a "noble eightfold path." Some of the steps along the way include right thought, right action, right contemplation and right meditation.

Totems are another example of Durkheim's "sacred things". They are worshipped by primitive people the world over—in North America, Melanesia and Australia. The totemic object may be a sacred animal, such as the kangaroo or the bear, or even a vegetable, such as corn or grass seed. The *totem* is a symbol, a repository of deeps, group based sentiments and feelings. It is worshipped as a god or an ancestor, or both, and it generally possesses some special quality or significance for the religious community—the capacity, for instance, to provide unique benefits or to inflict great harm. Totemist religious rituals often include mimicking the behaviour of the totem or, on very special occasions, eating it. Symbols of the totem are sometimes tatooed on the skin or carved in solid objects, like the grotesque poles of some American Indians.

On certain Islands or Oceania, a warrior successful in battle while using a particular spear will attribute his victory to *mana*—a force that entered his spear. A supernatural force, in other words, is still another example of a sacred thing although it has no shape of its own and inhabits living or inanimate things. Supernatural forces may be good or bad—the good being called *mana*, a word of Melanesian and Polynesian origin. If a farmer high in the Tongan Island mountains should plant a crop next to a large boulder and the crop grows well, he might feel that the boulder has mana. Any good luck charm such as a rabbit's foot is a Western equivalent of that boulder. Objects or beings with mana are to be associated with or stroked or handled so that their good qualities rub off. Evil supernatural forces, on the other hand, also reside in objects and beings and are *taboo*; they are not to be touched or approached because they cause bad luck or trouble. Typical taboos might include animals, often a totem animal, which are not to be killed, or wooded areas that hunters are forbidden to enter.

Be it a force, a god, a ghost, a moral principle, or a totemic object, all are elements or Durkheim's definition of religion. All are forms of the sacred and all bear witness to the existence of religious behaviour.

Religious Beliefs

Religious beliefs explain the sacred and determine and give significance to religious practices. Durkeim defines *religious beliefs* as "the representations which express the nature of sacred things and the relations which they sustain, either with each other or with profane things" (Durkheim, 1965). These beliefs are held not just intellectually but emotionally. The beliefs may appeal to the subconscious as well as the conscious.

Not all who profess a certain religion accept all its beliefs with complete conviction, a point demonstrated by sociologists Charles Glock and Rodney Stark. Gallup Polls have consistently found that about 97 per cent of Americans believe in God, a high level of belief compared with Europeans. But how sure people are of this belief is another matter. To ask churchgoers whether they believe in God might seem silly, but Glock and Stark did so by testing the degree of belief held by members in different churches and social groups, and they came up with some not so ridiculous answers. They found that whereas 99 per cent of the southern Baptists unequivocally believed in God, only 81 per cent of the Catholics and 41 per cent of the Congregationalists were quite so certain. Few of those surveyed absolutely denied the existence of God or professed to being agnostics. They merely expressed some degree of doubt or believed not in God but in a "higher power" Glock and Stark, 1965, pp. 90-91).

Table 13.1
Belief in God (by per cent)[1]

Which of the following Statements comes closest to What you Believe about god?	*Congregationalists*	*Episcopalians*	*Disciples of Christ*	*Presbyterians*	*American Baptists*	*Southern Baptists*	*Sects*	*Total Protestants*	*Catholics*
"I know God really exists and I have no doubts about it."	41	63	76	75	78	99	96	71	81
"While I have doubts, I feel that I do believe in God."	34	19	20	16	18	1	2	17	13
"I find myself believing in God some of the time, but not at other times."	4	2	0	1	0	0	0	2	1
"I don't believe in a personal God, but I do believe in a higher power of some kind."	16	12	0	7	2	0	1	7	3
"I don't know whether there is a God and I don't believe there is any way to find out."	2	2	0	1	0	0	0	1	1
"I don't believe in God."	1	0	0	0	0	0	0	0	0
No answer	2	1	4	0	2	0	1	1	1
Per cent	100	99	100	100	100	100	100	99	100
Number of respondents	(151)	(416)	(50)	(495)	(141)	(79)	(255)	(2326)	(545)

[1]Asterisks indicate fewer than 5 per cent.

Source : Charles Y. Glock and Rodney Stark, *Religion and Society in Tension* (Chicago: Rand McNally. (1965), p. 91.

Religious Practices

Beliefs are the conceptual aspect of religion; practices and rituals are its visible expression. Practices very from the simple gesture of removing a hat upon entering a church to the elaborate festivals, ceremonies and parades of primitive tribes. In a study of primitive religions Anthony Wallace (1966, pp. 53–66) determined that rituals can include anything from the use of drums to the use of drugs. Praying, singing, declaiming, drinking, sacrificing, mimicking, congregating, drugging, feasting, yelling, dancing—all may be ritual activities.

Durkheim defined rites as "the rules of conduct which prescribe how a man should comport himself in the presence of sacred objects." (Durkheim, 1965, p. 56). A ritual can recall an aspect of religious belief, honour the sacred, or establish a relationship between the believer and the sacred. Ritual is usually highly symbolic, often condensing elements of belief into a single activity and touching the deepest responsive chords of the participants. Its power transcends theology.

For example, the Lord's Supper or Eucharist has had many theological interpretations over the centuries, and indeed it is a pre-Christian ritual taken over and retheologised. The theology of the Catholics is not the same as that of the Lutherans or the Reformed or the Orthodox, yet the ritual is age-old and has continuing power.

As with beliefs, people who profess a religion do not necessarily subscribe to all its rituals. Not all Protestants who believe in Christ go to church, and not all others who do go to church take part in the Eucharist. A 1961 study of religious practices in Detroit, for example, found that among members of the three major American faiths, Catholics were the most ritualistic, with 70 per cent attending church regularly (Lenski, 1961, pp. 33 - 36). Nationwide in 1973, with 40 per cent of the populace attending religious services regularly, Catholics again led, with 55 per cent, Protestants came next with 37 per cent, and Jews were last with 19 per cent (Gallup Poll, 1974, p. 3).

Table 13.2
Church Attendance During an Average Week, 1973 (by per cent)
(Projects to 55 million adults)

National	40
Catholic	55
Protestant	37
Jewish	19[1]
Men	35
Women	43
White	40
Nonwhite	41
College	40
High School	38
Grade school	43
18–29 years	28
30–49 years	41
50 and over	46
East	38
Midwest	43
South	44
West	29

[1]Since Jews represent about 3 per cent of the U.S. population, the number included in the 1973 audit (179) is necessarily small.
Source : George Gallup, "Churchgoing Decline of Last Decade Result of Sliding Catholic Attendance." *The Gallup Poll,* January 13, 1974, p. 3, Copyright 1974, Field Enterprises, Inc.

Attendance at church or synagogue is not, of course, an absolute indicator or personal involvement in religion. Those who do not go to church may stay away from services for nonreligious reasons. One former parishioner put it this way, "There's too much dressing up for church these days; he used to go in his overalls just as good as anybody. But now, it won't do for people to go without being all dressed up and we just haven't got the clothes for that" (Lynd in Demerath, 1965, p. 13). Motivations for church attendance vary tremendously. Is it to pay homage to a supreme being or to pay attention to styles? Is it to hear a word of the prophets or to hear a word about profits? Does it fulfil an inner need or is it merely a habit? "Why, it just never occurred to me to question church going!" said one regular attender. "Most of the time I am just plain bored," said another, "but feel I ought to go" (Lynd and Lynd, in Demerath, 1965, p. 13).

Moreover, not all ritual occurs in church or synagogue. Concentrating on synagogue attendance among Jews, for instance, overlooks the importance of home ritual. More than one-third of American Jews perform rituals at home often enough for their household to be categorized as "traditional" (Goldstein and Goldsheider, 1968, p. 196).

The Moral Community

For Durkheim the foundation of religion was the moral community. "The idea of society is the soul of religion," he wrote (Durkheim, 1965, p. 419). He felt community and religion were inseparable for two reasons—because religion celebrates community and because religion creates community.

Durkheim based his theories about religion and the community on studies of preliterate societies. He observed that in such societies each person is highly dependent on his fellow tribesmen for protection and sustenance. To remain a member of such a society, the individual must abide by its mores, work for its preservation, and sacrifice personal desires for the good of the community. Durkheim speculated that the idea of divinity originated from the individual's experience of society as a powerful force transcending human desires and life span. He further speculated that the first gods were anthropomorphised versions of primitive man's view of his community. In short, the worship of gods, Durkheim felt, was the celebration and deification of sentiments of community life, and all societies, not simply primitive ones, feel the need for "upholding and reaffirming at regular intervals the collective sentiments and the collective ideas which make its unity and its personality" (Durkheim, 1965, p. 474).

Durkheim also maintained that religion and community are inseparable because religion sustains community. To him, a religion is born when a number of people worship together in a common faith. Close social contact encourages similar sets of values and thus unites persons in a "moral community," which has its own beliefs and rituals. In addition, participation in the moral community can lead to feelings of belonging and the development of friendships. These ties of *communal involvement* are a significant dimension of religious behaviour (Lenski, 1961).

The variation in communal involvement can be seen in the 1961 Detroit study. Respondents were asked questions that revealed not only how ritualistic they were, but how many of their friends and relatives were members of their religion. Ninety-six per cent of the Jew reported that all or most of their close relatives were Jewish, an extremely high percentage that may be due to discrimination against Jews, which gives them less choice than Catholics and Protestants in their associates or makes them distrust gentiles. Seventy-nine per cent of the Catholics indicated most of their relatives were Catholic, and the corresponding percentage among Protestants was somewhat smaller. "And what about your friends? Are they of your faith?" the Detroiters were asked. Seventy-seven per cent of the Jews said yes whereas only 44 per cent of the Catholics and a slightly smaller percentage of the Protestants answered affirmatively. Though Jews do not attend services regularly, their religion still shapes their personal life (Lenski, 1961, pp. 33 - 36).

The Functions of Religion

Sigmund Freud once wrote that religion was created expressly to reduce neurotic anxiety. He felt that man, torn between Oedipal desires for his mother and anger and fear with regard to his father, created and exalted a fearful good in his father's image so that his sexual and aggressive impulses could be checked. Benjamin Franklin once wrote that "all crimes will be punished and virtue rewarded either here or hereafter," a comforting view that God would indeed see to it that social injustices would never go uncorrected.

Whether one endorses these views or not, they do specify two functions of religion; Freud's relates to the individual, Franklin's relates to the community. These are the two categories under which we will examine the functions of religion.

Not all gods, despite Freud, are fearful. Concepts of gods in past and present religions vary. Zeus had his thunderbolts, true, but there have also been comforting gods, gods that increase fertility, gods that protect the hunter and traveller, gods that heal the sick and still the waters. The images of god, along with religious beliefs and practices, seem to fulfil certain individual and social needs, and their variety suggests that religion serves people in myriad ways.

Human Events in the Cosmic Order

> Friday at sundown. The Sabbath comes in cold and clear during early spring in Minnesota. In the warm shelter of the Chabad House, the young women greet it with flickering Shabbas candles set on glistening white tablecloths. . .Barbara is one of them. She is 20 years old, blue-eyed, blond. She is from Los Angeles, the product of a broken home and a half-dozen private schools.
>
> "I had the whole cycle," she explains, matter-of-factly. "Drugs, sex, alienation, I couldn't stand being alone, or not being high. It was existence by escapism. Until a bitter realisation that I was still alone—and travelling a horrible road."
>
> Barbara surveys her new surroundings. "I've found peace here," she says, "and purpose." (Spiegel, 1974, p. 48).

One of the most important functions of religion is to offer answers and rules about life. Religion explains that human life is part of a divine scheme, and like it or not, that is why we are all here spinning through the universe. By following rules laid down by the gods, believers are assured that they will be at least virtuous and at best successful. If life is fraught with sorrow and hardships, religion again supplies answers—that the believer offended an important god or violated a taboo or failed to live according to the rules. If the offender makes amends but the woes still continue, religious teachings may also suggest that sorrow. and hardship are really not very important after all because a far better existence awaits the believer in the hereafter.

This comfort in times of distress particularly in the face of death—is an especially important function of religion. Many religions reassure their adherents that the soul lives on after death: some even provide detailed descriptions of its progress once it leaves the body.

Religion also serves to interpret and consecrate experience in this life. Most religions have some sort of puberty rites that mark the transition from childhood to adulthood. Many have ceremonies celebrating victory in war and the succession of a new ruler to head the stage or community. All these ceremonies glorify human life and human achievement, and because they invoke supernatural powers they offer assurance that the divine is aware of and gives blessing to human affairs.

Religion can also bestow a sense of identity on its followers. Eric Lincoln, a sociologist who has done participant studies of the Black Muslims, has described the spiritual transformation that sometimes occurs when a black person accepts Islam :

> The true believer. . .casts off at last his old self and takes on a new identity. He changes his name, his religion, his homeland, his "natural" language, his moral and cultural values, his very purpose in living. He is no longer a Negro, so long despised by the white man that he has come almost to despise himself. Now he is a Black Man—divine, ruler of the universe, different only in degree from Allah Himself. . . . . Now he is a Muslim, bearing in himself the power of the Black Nation and its glorious destiny. (Lincoln, 1961, pp. 108-109).

If religion can function to provide a sense of identity, it can also function to provide, in a sense, a loss of identity through dissociation. Anthony F.C. Wallace has pointed out that religion can generate an ecstatic or visionary experience by "crudely and directly manipulating the physiological processes." Such an experience, he says, is often induced by drugs :

> Plains Indians, for instance, eat or drink infusions of *peyote,* a cactus containing a number of alkaloids including mescaline, which is a potent hallucinogen. Ancient Greek celebrants of the great god Pan chewed the intoxicating leaves of ivy to induce ecstatic abandon. The Koryak, Chuckchee, and other Siberian peoples chewed the crimson mushroom fly agaric (*Amanita muscaria*) to bring on episodes of euphoria. Scandinavian *berserkers* ate certain kinds of mushrooms to achieve dissociation. Some modern Americans experiment with such "psychedelic" drugs as lysergic acid dyethylamide (LSD) in the hope of spiritual growth. (Wallace, 1966, p. 55).

The reassurances offered by religion have a powerful effect on the human psyche, and many psychologists have felt that religious behaviour is so prevalent because it alleviates anxiety. Freud, as we have noted, believed that religion was deliberately established to relieve tensions. In a study of primitive culture on the Trobriand Islands in the South-west Pacific, Malinowski found that religion lessened the anxiety of fishermen heading out to the high seas. The Islanders were excellent fishermen who sought their catch both in lagoon and in the open ocean. The lagoon was calm and protected and, when fish were plentiful, fishing there was easy. On the open ocean, however, the seas and winds could be dangerous. Malinowski observed that before fishing in the lagoon, the fishermen made no special preparations, but before going to the open sea, the men invoked the help of their gods through a variety of rituals. He concluded that when the Trobriand islanders knew they were entering a dangerous situation they felt the need for religion and divine aid. When they were confident of their skills and their safety, they felt religion was expendable (Malinowski, 1954).

Can Science Replace Religion?

Malinowski's example raises the possibility that religion might disappear if mankind found other means of coping with the world. Could scientific knowledge and technological skills ever provide human beings with such confidence in their abilities that the functions of religion would become irrelevant, thus causing religion itself to disappear? Could mankind become so self-sufficient and capable that people would no longer need the protection and guidance of a god?

Science does fulfil a vital role for man by providing answers about the universe, says anthropologist Clifford Geertz, but scientific inquiry cannot deal with all the problems that are part of man's experience. Geertz characterises science as rational, objective, restrained, a branch of knowledge that uses conscious doubt and systematic inquiry to disclose the natural laws behind everyday reality. He sees religion as requiring acceptance and commitment in dealing with ultimate truths of the cosmic order. Geertz finds three situations in which science must fail: when people are at the limit of their intellectual capacities and remain completely baffled; when they are faced with prolonged and acute suffering; and when they are confronted with overwhelming and senseless evil. In these instances, Geertz feels, science can offer no insight, no reassurance that man is not "adrift in an absurd world." Only the cosmic vision of religion can cope with these situations, and as long as they continue to be part of human existence, religion will have a place (Geertz, 1968).

Box 13.1

Rimrock and Homestead

Forty miles apart in the vast stretches of western New Mexico lie the towns of Rimrock and Homestead. Both subsist primarily on farming, though both communities also raise some cattle. Both have similar soil, and both are approximately the same size. In fact, the two towns are very similar in any number of ways except for one crucial difference—the religion of their inhabitants. Life in these two small towns, then, shows the extent and nature of religious influence in the public sphere.

Rimrock was founded in the 1870s by a group of Mormons sent out by their church to settle and preach in the West. They arrived with a strong sense of group purpose and unity, and they built their houses together in the town, with their farmlands fanning out from the center. Their original sense of unity persisted through the years, bolstered by Mormon church beliefs and practices. By contrast. Homestead was first settled in the 1930s by migrants, like the uprooted, uncertain wayfarers described in *The Grapes of Wrath*. Of various religions and independent ways, the Homesteaders built their farms quite far from one another.

In the 1940s and 1950s, two parallel events occurred in the towns that reveal the impact religion can have on the life of a community's residents. After World War II, Rimrock had thirty-two veterans who were faced with the choice or remaining underemployed and poor in Rimrock or leaving the community. The Mormons wanted to keep their group together, so when an opportunity arose to buy a tract of land far too expensive for the veterans, the church welfare agency provided the funds and the land was set up as a cooperative ranch with the veteran-owners holding shares in the operation. In Homestead, a similar opportunity arose to acquire some useful land when the federal government offered to sell a sizable track for ranching on a cooperative

Box 13.1 Contd.

basis. The Homesteaders, however, refused the offer. They could not agree to work cooperatively because each wanted his own private building on the land.

The second incident involved a high-school gymnasium. Rimrock was presented with a plan for a gym and after discussing it in church and school meetings, the townspeople decided to build it with each man agreeing to give either fifty hours of his time or $50 in cash toward its construction. Despite some dissent over the plan, the town members contributed their shares and the gym was completed. The same plan for a gymnasium was put before the Homesteaders. At first, the community voted against it because resident did not want to commit themselves to working on the building. Later, when a little money became available, the town hired builders to do the job. When the money ran out, however, construction stopped and the gym remained half completed. In both instances, the Mormons' religious beliefs favoured a political consensus that produced economic and social benefits for the community while the Homesteaders' independence and lack of cooperation bred economic and social weakness. Of course, it must be added that Rimrock and Homestead are isolated, homogeneous communities and that the influence of religion is not always so clear-cut.

Source : Evon Vogt and Thomas F. O'Dea, "A Comparative Study of Values in Social Action in Two Southwestern Communities," in Milton Yinger, ed., *Religion, Society and the Individual: An Introduction to the Sociology of Religion* (New York: Macmillan, 1957), pp. 563-77.

Religion and the Community

Religion offers both norms of "right behaviour" within a community and sanctions against antisocial acts. It can also provide a kind of social cement by offering ways of atoning for infractions through prayers, fasting, or penance (see the Box 13.1).

Religious doctrine may do more than affect social behaviour; it may also help legitimise—for better or worse—the community's social structure. Where wealth is distributed unevenly or one class is decidedly more privileged than another, religious doctrine may sanction the *status quo* and thus allay discontent. In fact, in cultures where wealth is privately rather than communally owned, there are many more reports or myths about divine intervention in human affairs. In these visitations, the gods tend to support the propertied groups and disapprove of social disruption, thereby strengthening the social structure when political institutions are incapable of doing so (Swanson, 1969, pp. 153 - 79). Religion can also encourage social tranquility by assuring that injustices will not go uncertified—as Franklin guarantees in his statement about crime being punished in the hereafter. With such confidence in divine justice, inequities are much easier to accept.

Civil Religion in America

Unlike many countries, America does not have an established religion that buttresses and is buttressed by the power of the state. Separation of church and state was established first by practice and then by law in the Bill of Rights. However, sociologist Robert Bellah sees American civil and political life permeated with religious elements so coherent and of such importance for the American people that they constitute a national or "civil" religion (1970, pp. 168 - 86). To Bellah, a collection of potent beliefs, symbols and rituals, outside the church that pervades and helps legitimise the community is, in effect, *a civil religion.*

At almost every American state or political occasion, says Bellah, God plays an important role. He is mentioned in the pledge of allegiance, in legislative invocations, in an oaths of office, in party conventions, in courtroom procedures, in political speeches, and, inevitably, in presidential inaugural addresses. Even the nation's currency proclaims "In God We Trust". Bellah also points to the traditional feeling in the United States that the nation was established "under God," and that the government derives its legitimacy from its acknowledgment of God-ordained law and from its protection of God-given individual rights.

The God of American civil religion has a number of qualities that make him a unifying figure in a pluralistic society. He is universal rather than sectarian, and he is sufficiently impartial so that no religions group is offended. Also, he is not concerned with personal ends, such as salvation. Instead, the American god devotes his attention to law, justice, order, and other matters of interest to the entire community.

Every religion must have not only its gods but its symbols, its hymns and high priests, its martyrs and rituals. For the American civil religion, the symbols are the flag, the American eagle, and the monuments in Washington, D.C. and in many town squares; the hymns are the "Star-Spangled Banner" and "America, the Beautiful". Among its high priests are George Washington and Thomas Jefferson, and among its martyrs are Abraham Lincoln and John Kennedy. Its rituals commemorating and honouring important events and ideals include the Fourth of July, which, like Christmas, celebrates a significant birth; Memorial Day, which honours the sacrifices of its military men; and Thanks-giving Day, which commemorates the successful voyage across an alien sea and the founding of a new promised land.

Civil religion in America is not merely ceremonial or a matter of myths. A nation of different social, ethnic, religious, and regional groups, America has been bound together largely through a spirit of nationalism and a common dedication to a high political and moral good that its civil religion has inspired. Bellah does not, or course, confuse civil religion with, mindless patriotism. He sees the nation's action judges by a transcendent law: "The concept of civil religion simply points to the fact that some links between [religion, morality and politics] seem to exist in all societies. At its best, civil religion would be realised in a situation where politics and morality are open to transcendent judgement" [Bellah, 1973, p. 20].

Religion and Social Change

Religion is created by society, yet it may also help to shape society. One of the issues in churches today is their degree of involvement in social movements and social change. Should they clergy prod the laity on civil rights, on Women's Liberation, on grape and lettuce boycotts? There are those among the laity who grumble that they are not in church to hear about grapes. Conversely, there are those who ask the church to speak out—on birth control, on political corruption, on minimum wages, on imperialistic wars. How religion views the society at large and its role in changing society depends in part upon its institutional form.

Church and Sect

Studies by Ernst Troeltsch (a sociologist of the early twentieth century) demonstrate the problem of institutionalising religion. To Troeltsch the effectiveness of religion as an ongoing institution is often at odds with its social message. He views religious institutions as being basically either church or sect (Troeltsch, 1957); these, he says, differ from each other in size and in their attitudes toward religiosity and society. (Because church and sect are ideal types, however, any group may not conform to them in every respect.)

Troeltsch describes the *church* as a large, conservative, universalist institution. Most members are born into it, not converted to it. The church promises its members grace, but it makes few demands on them. Because it is large, it tends to acquire a certain amount of social and political power, which it more often than not maintains by becoming associated with government or the ruling classes. Thus, the church accommodates itself to the claims of other powerful social-political institutions and tends to support the *status quo*. The Church of England would come close to fitting this ideal type.

The *sect,* on the other hand, is a small, exclusive, uncompromising fellowship of individuals seeking spiritual perfection. Members are voluntary converts drawn primarily from the lower classes, and their lives are pretty much controlled by the sect. Sects are usually characterised by asceticism, and their attitude toward society tends to be either indifferent or hostile. Most sects are concerned strictly with religious values and withdraw as much as possible from social matters; a few, however are critical of the social order and have positive ideas about how to improve it.

Marx and Weber

Church or sect, Karl Marx believed that all religious institutions inhibited social change and revolution by legitimising the *status quo*. Marx hoped in vain for an uprising among the working classes, and he felt that one reason they did not revolt was because religion defused rebellion against the social order.

Table 13.3
Church and Sect

Characteristic	*Church*	*Sect*
Size	Large	Small
Relationship with other religious groups	Tolerant	Rejects; feels it has sole truth
Wealth	Extensive	Limited
Religious services	Limited congregational participation; formal; intellectual emphasis	Extensive congregational participation; spontaneous; emotional emphasis
Clergy	Specialised; professional	Unspecialised; little training; part time
Doctrines	Liberal interpretation of scriptures; emphasis upon this word	Literal interpretation of scriptures; emphasis upon other world
Membership	By birth or ritual participation; social institution embracing all socially compatible	By conversion; moral community excluding unworthy
Social class of members	Mainly middle class	Mainly lower class
Relationship with Secular world	Endorses prevailing culture and social organization	Renounces or opposes prevailing cultural standards; requires strict adherence to Biblical standards such as tithing, pacificism

Source: Adapted from Glenn M. Vernon, *Sociology of Religion* (New York; McGraw-Hill, 1962), p. 174, supplemented with material from Leonard Broom and Philip Seiznick, *Sociology,* 5th ed. (New York: Harper & Row, 1973), p. 411.

The religion of the lower classes, Marx believed, grows out of their need to understand the reasons for social oppression and their need to cope with it. "Religion is the sign of the oppressed creature," he wrote, "the heart of a heartless world, just as it is the spirit of a spiritless situation. It is the opium of the people"

(Marx, in Aptheker, 1968, p. 33). Although religion ministers to some real needs, it provides false comfort. By promising the working classes a better life in the world to come, it blinds them to the possibilities of creating a better world on earth. In this way it endorses the *status quo* and supports the dominance of the capitalists.

For Marx capitalism shaped religion, but for Marx Weber religion shaped capitalism. Weber thought that religion was capable of inducing social change, and that, specifically, Protestant doctrine created a climate in seventeenth-century Europe that encouraged capitalism to flourish (Weber, 1930).

The influence of religion was not so much through doctrines about economic activity, but more importantly through a set of attitudes about the proper relation between the individual and God (Eisenstadt, 1968). Early Protestantism, and specifically Calvinism, espoused the concept of predestination—the fate of each person was determined at birth. Either the individual was one of the elect or one of the damned. There was no sure way of telling whether one was elected or damned, but the Calvinists believed that anybody who had the good fortune to be successful in his worldly endeavours probably had God's blessing and, consequently, was probably one of the elect. Accordingly, hard work, selfdiscipline, and clean living were seen not only as virtues but as signs of salvation. And because a frivolous, expensive life-style was regarded as sinful, profits from hard labour were traditionally plowed back into the business, thereby compounding success. Every Calvinist also believed that the individual was alone before God, and that he had a direct relationship with the deity. Therefore, because every man was essentially for himself, independence and competition were esteemed and encouraged. The values of hard work, individualism, and competition were readily translated, Weber believed, into capitalism—an economic system that has thrived on individualism, the private ownership of goods, the reinvestment of profits, competition, and the independence of decision.

Of course, Protestantism began as a small secessionist movement and thus originally had the qualities of a sect. However, once it was espoused by the rulers and the upper classes of a number of northern European nations, it became a "church" in Troeltsch's sense Protestantism had its great influence not because it attacked the powerful groups in the social hierachy, but because it was accepted by them and became a part of the *status quo*. Only by becoming a church and generating the force of a church did it produce social change.

Religion and the Individual

Statistically, Americans are a "religious people". Gallup has found that 96 per cent of us profess belief in some kind of formal religion (Gallup, 1971, pp. 70-71). But what effect, a sociologist would ask, does religion have on life in the United States? Does religious affiliation have any noticeable impact on our secular activities, our occupations, our family life?

Gerhard Lenski would answer the latter question with a resounding yes. Religion, he maintains, has about the same influence on personal behaviour, attitudes and ideas as social class. Religion, moreover, is a causal factor, not a correlational factor, he adds. It determines behaviour directly and independently and is not totally the result of other variables like national origin or education. Lenski developed his ideas after an exhaustive study of religion and the individual in metropolitan Detroit (Lenski, 1961); we will discuss some of his findings—and those of other sociologists—in this section to see how religion touches various aspects of an American's life.

Politics

Although religion and politics are formally separated in American life, in actual fact the values of one sphere carry over into the other. Take party affiliation, for example. A Gallup Poll in 1971 pointed out that Jews and Catholics are predominantly Democrats. Protestants show a significantly different pattern. While they have about the same percentage of independents (26 per cent), the balance is more evenly split between the two major parties: 33 per cent are Republicans and 39 per cent Democrats. The figures for Protestants are not particularly meaningful, however, because they lump together different regional and economic groups. Figures analysed by denomination show that other factors besides religion help to determine party affiliation. For example, the Episcopalians and the Presbyterians, the two wealthiest denominations concentrated heavily in the East, have a high proportion of Republicans (44 and 55 per cent, respectively), whereas the Baptists, the largest denomination with the poorest members, most of whom live in the rural South, have a high percentage of Democrats (Gallup, 1971, p. 52).

Table 13.4
Profiles of American Religions (by per cent)

Characteristics	*Protestants*				*Catholics*	*Jews*
	Total	*Methodists*	*Episco-palians*			
Percentage of population	65	14	3	21	26	3
Education						
College	22	24	47	12	21	42
High School	52	55	42	54	57	42
Grade school	26	21	12	34	23	16
Occupation						
Professional and business	20	22	38	14	22	40
Clerical and sales	12	12	12	10	12	22
Farmers	8	8	1	8	3	1
Manual	40	38	25	49	45	16
Income						
$15,000+	12	13	32	6	15	30
$10,000–S14,999	22	23	25	18	27	26
$7,000–S9,999	20	20	15	20	23	16
$5,000–S6,999	17	17	10	20	5	11
$3,000–S4,999	15	14	7	19	10	9
Under S3,000	13	12	10	16	9	7
Community Size						
1,000,000+	12	10	20	11	31	66
500,000–999,999	10	9	18	9	18	14
50,000–499,999	22	21	25	22	26	14
2,500–49,999	18	19	16	18	10	3
Under 2,500 (rural)	37	41	22	39	14	1
Politics						
Republican	33	35	44	21	19	6
Democrat	39	36	32	52	52	63
Independent	26	26	23	25	27	29

Source: Gallup Opinion Index, *Religion in America,* 1971. Report no. 70, April 1971, p. 57.

Income and region are obviously influential in determining political affliction, too.

Education

The religious factor can be found in the area of education. A nationwide Gallup Poll in 1971 showed that Protestants and Catholics had similar educational patterns whereas Jews attained notably higher levels. Forty-two per cent of the Jews had gone to college but only 22 per cent of the Protestants and 21 per cent of the Catholics had done so (Gallup, 1971, pp. 57-58).

Although, unlike the Gallup Poll, Lenski's Detroit study did not find important differences in the educational level among whites of different religions, Lenski did find differences in the drop-out rate. The rate was determined from the number of people who failed to finish a level of education, be it grade school, high school, or college. Black Protestants had the highest drop-out rate with 67 per cent, and Catholics were second at 48 per cent. Among white Protestants, the rate was 39 per cent and among Jews slightly more than 25 per cent. Once started, Jews had the greatest drive to finish their education (Lenski, 1961, pp. 236 - 40). One of the interesting questions, not well understood, is *how* religion asserts its influence on education and whether it is the primary or subsidiary influence on the motivation to stay in school. Religious affiliation is linked with different economic, political and ethnic attitudes, and sorting these out is extremely difficult.

Career

Is a particular religion related in any way to career, to whether its adherents wear a blue collar or a white one? In some cases it is. A 1971 Gallup Poll showed that Catholics have become so integrated into American life that their job choices are quite similar to those of Protestants. Jews, however, offer distinctly from both groups. Jews are concentrated in professional, business, sales and clerical jobs; they are far more likely to wear a white collar than their Christian peers. For example, 20 per cent and 22 per cent of Protestants and Catholics, respectively, are in the professions and business whereas 40 per cent of Jews chose these fields. Twenty-two per cent of Jews are in clerical and sales jobs compared with 11 per cent of Protestants and 12 per cent of Catholics.

That the percentage of Jews in professions and business is so high accounts for their relatively higher incomes. The same 1971 Gallup Poll revealed that 30 per cent of the nation's Jews earned more than $15,000 a year compared with 15 per cent of the Catholics and 12 per cent of the Protestants, black and white. The poll also registered that in the lower-income brackets, those earning less than $5,000 a year were 16 per cent Jews, 19 per cent Catholics, and 28 per cent Protestants. Protestants whose income exceeded $15,000 varied from 32 per cent of the Episcopalians to 6 per cent of the Baptists.

Lenski found that religion also had an effect, and a very substantial one, on career success. Jews had the greatest success, followed by white Protestants. Lenski's study demonstrated that the success of both these groups contrasted rather sharply with that of the Catholics and black Protestants. Jews and white Protestants also shared certain characteristics that appeared to influence their economic behaviour. Both had positive attitudes toward work, believed that ability was more improtant than family connections, emphasised intellectual autonomy, tended to be self-employed, and had small families. As groups, Catholics and black Protestants either did not share these attitudes or had them to a lesser extent.

Lenski argues that his data support Max Weber's thesis that the Protestant ethic inspires earthly success. Lenski found that persons raised in devout white Protestant families were more likely to be successful than persons raised in less devout white Porotestant families. More importantly, he found that economic success correlated with a positive attitude toward work. Highly successful Jews, of course, share this view, and their economic behaviour, alongwith that of white Protestants, may be cited in support of Weber. (For a critique of this view, see Schuman, 1971, pp. 30–48).

Religion and the Family

Studies of religious behaviour demonstrate time and again that a salient relationship exists between religious affiliation and the choice of a marriage partner, the decision on divorce, and the planning of a family.

Religion seems to be particularly important to Americans when they choose a mate Eighty-eight per cent of all marriages occur between members of the same religion. According to a 1957 census report, the only source of reliable national data on this matter, Catholics have the highest proportion of members who marry outside their religion (21.6 per cent). Only 8.6 per cent of the nation's Protestants marry non-Protestants, and only 7.2 per cent of its Jews marry no-Jews. Had the census figures distinguished between blacks and white Protestants, the intermarriage rates for black would have been extremely low; for whites they probably would have approached those for Catholics.

Many factors are involved in intermarriage. A study by Heiss (1960) of marriages in New York City suggests that the close proximity of different religious groups increases the rate of intermarriage. He found that in the religiously mixed society of Manhattan, intermarriage rates were 21.4 per cent among Catholics, 33.9 per cent among Protestants, and 18.4 per cent among Jews. The rate for Catholics in New York City was not surprising; it was the same as their nationwide rate. But the rate among New York Jews was twice the national rate, and for Protestants it was four times the national percentage. People who intermarry are also likely to be older and to have been married before (Barron, 1972, p. 44.)

Those who intermarry are also more likely to get divorced. Several studies have found that the divorce and separation rates for Catholics and Jews with partners of a different religion were three to six times higher than in marriages between members of the same religion (Barron, 1972, p. 44). For those who do not intermarry, the rates of divorce differ by religion. Lenski in his 1958 survey of by Detroit concluded that black Protestants and white Protestants are far more likely to rescind their marriage vows than are Catholics or Jews. (His figures for Jews may be some what misleading because the Jewish sample was very small.) Twenty-two per cent of the black Protestants and 16 per cent of the white Protestants severed their marriage ties, but only

8 per cent of the Catholics and 4 per cent of the Jews did so. (Separation rates for Catholics are far higher of course.) Even more remarkable were the differences in remarriage rates: 86 per cent of the black and 75 per cent of the divorced white Protestants remarried, but among divorced Catholics, who are expressly forbidden to remarry, only 50 per cent again took the vows. Lenski speculated that the low divorce rate among Catholics can be attributed to the pressure exerted by their religion to make their marriage work.

Catholicism also exerts pressure in other ways. Indeed, of the three major religions in the United States, it places the most sanctions upon the lives of its members. The Catholic Church is particularly adamant about birth control all methods are forbidden except rhythm (abstinence from intercourse during fertile periods of the menstrual cycle). Nonetheless, national fertility studies conducted over the last fifteen years reveal considerable erosion of support for church doctrine on birth control. (Westoff and Bumpass, 1973). In a 1967 article in *Newweek*, one Pennsylvania house-wife argued, "The Problem of birth control should be settled by husband and wife—not by the Vatican."

Several trends can be observed in this revolution against the Catholic church. College-educated Catholic women, once the most dutiful followers of birth-control dictates, are now the most rebellious. Among this group, roughly three-quarters use a disapproved method of birth control. "If you take a pill", a Catholic mother has declared, "you are not as conscious of preventing pregnancy." The most important fact in this revolution, however, is that the greatest defection from church doctrine has taken place among religious Catholic women.

Although the influence of religious belief on the American family is still strong is still strong in every aspect of family life—marriage and children and attitudes about divorce—signs such as these indicate the influence is fading. Whether this also means that religion itself is dying requires a broader look at religion in America.

Figure 13.1: Catholics and contraception, 1955–1970

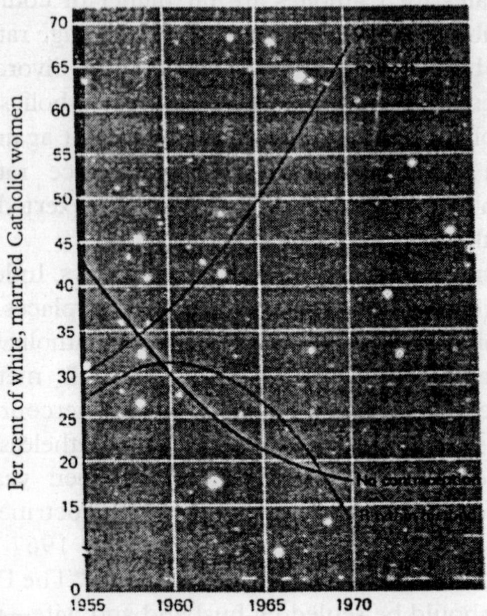

Source : Based on Charles F. Westoff and Larry Bumpass. "The Revolution in Birth Control Practices of U.S. Roman Catholics", *Science* 179, January 5, 1973, table 1, p. 42.

In fifteen years there was a revoluation in birth control practices among Catholic women eighteen to thirty-nine. In 1955 over two-thirds of the white, married Catholic women in these fertile years followed church doctrine by using either no contraception whatever or the approved rhythm method; less than one-third were using disapproved methods. By 1970 the proportions were reversed; over two-thirds were resorting to unsanctioned birth control methods (the pill being the favoured method by a large margin, particularly among younger married Catholic women). Only 18 per cent were using no contraceptive method at all by 1970. Is this falling away from the church simply limited to this area or has the influence of the Catholic church declined more broadly? The last section of the chapter deals with what this trend means.

The Future of Religon

> Times are changing, and some of the most important changes in the religious realm have been of a kind that few would have predicted as recently as the early 1960s. (Lenski, 1971, p. 50).

Secularisation

Formal religion in America is on the decline. About that change there is little question. Church attendance has been creeping downward since 1955. Gallup pollsters found that 49 per cent of Americans attended religious services once a week in 1955; in 1971 the figure declined to 40 per cent, where it remained through 1973 (Gallup, 1974). "Do you think religion is increasing its influence on American life?" they asked. In 1957, 69 per cent of the respondents said yes and only 14 per cent thought religion was losing its influence. In 1967, the percentages were reversed: 57 per cent thought religion was losing ground and only 23 per cent felt it was gaining it (Hadden, 1969, p. 25). By 1970, 75 per cent agreed that religious influences were declining (Hoge, 1974, p. 167).

Who are the disillusioned? The greatest drop in church attendance has been among Catholics. In 1964, 71 per cent of all Catholics attended mass in a given week; by 1973 this figure was down to 55 per cent, a drop of over one-fifth. Belief is waning most among Jews and youth. Between 1952 and 1965 the percentage of Jews who expressed belief in God dropped an extraordinary 31 per cent—from 70 per cent to 39 per cent. In 1965 only 17 per cent of Jews believed that the Old Testament was the revealed word of God or that there was life after death. Over the same thirteen years, belief in God dropped 15 per cent among America's youth—from 87 per cent to 71 per cent (Marty, Rosenberg and Greeley, 1968, pp. 60-61). Other studies have demonstrated that the decline in religious belief among students is an even longer-term trend. Between the late 1940s and the late 1960s, a 13 per cent to 23 per cent drop occurred among students in orthodox beliefs about God and immortality. Similar but lesser declines have been noted among young adults (Hoge, 1974).

Despite the downward trends in religious beliefs, some observers question whether their implications for religion are quite as serious as they appear at first glance. Hoge has noted that American belief in religious orthodoxy has tended to fluctuate—zealous at one time, indifferent the next. Studies of personal belief-commitment systems have indicated that religious orthodoxy is often associated with commitment to family life, to military duty and patriotic wars, to the routing of communism, to dominant social norms. The general acceptance of these values has varied widely during this century—high in the twenties, low in the thirties, high again in the fifties, and low again today. It is a pattern that suggests religious orthodoxy and belief may well increase again in the future (Hoge, 1974).

Trends in the Major Faiths

While disinterest in religion has been spreading among the flock, upheavals have been increasing among the shepherds as well. The voice of the clergy has become increasingly strident over church dogma and church institutional structure. The major faiths are going through a period of critical self-analysis, asking themselves how they can hold onto their membership and make religious practice have greater appeal, meaning and relevance.

During the 1960s the larger Protestant denominations were exploring ways to resolve theological differences in preparation for merger. Such ecumenical fervor has wanted in the seventies. To some Protestant theologians coming to terms with each other has been less crucial than coming to terms with a world in which "God is dead". This debate revolved around the question of whether the traditional concept of God has any meaning in the modern world. Anglican Bishop J.A.T. Robinson, in his book *Honest to God* (1963), answered no. He argued that the traditional concept of a loving father up in heaven was outmoded and must be replaced. Shortly thereafter, Harvey Cox published *The Secular City* (1966), quoted at the beginning of this chapter, which viewed the world as moving into a secularage in which traditional religion is irrelevant.

Questions about doctrine have been only one part of a wider crisis in Protestantism, according to Jeffrey Hadden (1969, pp. 3–33). The Civil Rights Movement unleashed sources of conflict over the purposes of the church and the authority within it, as well as over beliefs. The main cleavage is between the clergy and the laity. To many church members the purpose of the church is to comfort them; to many in the clergy the purpose is to offer challenges. The question of the social gospel has created great divisions within individual churches and whole denominations and has led to a decline in contributions and in the willingness of church members to assent to policies of church leaders when they attack the *status quo*. Protestantism is threatened not simply by secularisation but by the crises of purpose, belief and authority.

Catholicism has been undergoing rapid changes. It is reassessing its views toward other churches and wrestling with the burgeoning spirit of individualism and contemporary ferment within its own ranks. In an effort to achieve greater Christian unity, the church has been renegotiating its differences with certain Protestant groups. Catholic and Anglican theologians, for exemple, have reached agreement on the nature of the priesthood and the ministry; Catholics recognise the legitimacy of the Anglican clergy, and the sharing of communion between the two churches is now possible. Catholics and Lutherans have also reached accord on the issue of papal primacy, a major issue in the Protestant Reformation four centuries ago. A joint study has declared that papal primacy is no longer a "barrier to reconciliation" of the two churches and envisions the day when they will be part of one "larger communion".

All these fraternal moves on the part of the Catholic church are the legacy of Vatican II, the Catholic ecumenical convocation called by Pope John XXIII to reexamine the doctrine and rituals of the Catholic church. The Council, which met from 1962 to 1965, brought sweeping changes within the church, such as the vernacular Mass, but it also led to a crisis of authority. Many among the clergy and the laity are no longer willing to accept the will of the Pope. Laymen are more and more asserting their rights to share in decision-making, and priest, and nuns are questioning the role of celibacy and their own role in the church. The Pope is still extremely influential, but internal changes in the power structure are a foot.

In Judaism there is mounting concern over the decline in Jewish religious beliefs and the possible weakening of Jewish communal ties as the children and grandchildren of Jewish immigrants have become Americanised. Much of the blame for the divisions within the family over the issue of Jewishness lies with the parents, says one editor of a Jewish monthly, because they have failed to impress upon their children the importance of the Nazi holocaust and the creation of the state of Israel. "To most American Jews, being a Jew is like being a stamp collector. It's an avocation," says a student supporter of the Radical Jewish Union, who sees Jewishness as a totality. "Encompasses a political ideology, a set of values, a general philosophy, a religion, customs, diet, language—a whole way of life" (Newsweek, March 1, 1971, pp. 61- 62).

Some Jewish religious leaders are not particularly worried over the decline in orthodox belief because they feel that heterodoxy has always been a part of Jewish tradition. Moreover, though they note a decline in regular synagogue attendance, they are pleased with the stability in synagogue membership. And they have found the increased interest in Jewish education gratifying. Such training through the synagogue and Hebrew schools reinforces the sense of Jewishness that persists in spite of the decrease in formal religious belief.

Is the Secular City at Hand?

The evidence is fairly convincing that traditional Catholic, Protestant and Jewish religiosity is being challenged in this country. But does this mean that institutionalised religion is dead or gasping in the United States? Without question, church membership continues to decline. Even so, 79 per cent of Americans claim membership in a religious group. Obviously, church membership will have to drop a good deal more before the churches can be described as moribund. Reports of their death, to use Mark Twain's description after reading of his own, are "greatly exaggerated". Religion in America is still big business. Its combined assets in the late 1960s were double those of the top five corporations in the United States (Demerath 1968, p. 365).

One way of gauging they vigour of an institution is to compare it with another social institution. Swanson (in Greeley, 1969, pp. 32-33) found that religious participation compared quite favourably with political participation. He found, among other things, that roughly 60 per cent of the American electorate votes in national elections and that approximately 68 per cent of

Box 13.2

In the News

Motel Parish

There is a temptation to confuse religion with church. But people may look to religious leaders without wanting the communal involvement of organized religion. One unlikely place they may now find a minister is at a motel. Over 1, 300 of the 1,638 holiday Inns, for example, now have a chaplain on call. Some hold religious services, but their main purpose is to counsel troubled travellers.

"When people are running away from something, they run to a neutral place. A hotel or a motel is a logical choice of a neutral place," [said Rev. Jack Chellew, founder of a motel chaplain program for Holiday Inns of America, Inc.The chaplains] are often aroused in the middle of the night by callers who may be suicidal, lonely, playfully drunk, having a fight with their wives or anxious to borrow money. . .The average motel chaplain gets about 15 calls a year but some receive many more. [Rev. W. A. Nance, corporate chaplain for Holiday Inns] ascribes the frequency of calls partially to the special loneliness that comes with being isolated in a motel room far from home, where "problems tend to magnify."

Almost 1,000 potential suicides have been prevented by the Holiday inn chaplains, but the larger problem is the drunk.

"I'll go alongwith the guy for a while," says one chaplain, "but eventually we'll get at the reason why he felt the need to get drunk that night. A lot of counselling sessions come from those drunk calls."

One advantage of a motel chaplain is that the person will not have to face him in church the next Sunday.

"Three times this year people have called and said they stayed in a Holiday Inn for the single reason that they had heard of the programme and wanted to talk to an anonymous chaplain rather than their own clergyman." says [a Toronto minister].

A sociologist who concentrated only on what goes on in churches would miss the motel chaplains and much of the religious activity on the contemporary scene.

Source: Ron Cooper, "Room Service? Send 3 Bourbon, 2 Scotch—And One Chaplain, *The Wall Street Journal* (May 21, 1974): 1, 40.

the adult population attends religious services in any given four week period. In the public's eye, then, religion is no less viable than politics.

The Fundamentalist Revival

If formal organised religion is not generating quite the allure it once did, another form of religious experience is again in ascendance in America. The revivalists, the evangelists, the fundamentalists have been back on the religious scene in ever-increasing numbers since the late 1960s. Billy Graham's "old-time religion" continues to rise in popularity, a substantial number of young adults have become Jesus People, and some fundamentalist churches and sects are attracting more and more followers. The Assemblies of God, Pentecostal groups, Evangelicals, Mornons, and Seventh-day Adventists have all had steady increases in membership. The Southern Baptist Convention, a large, relatively conservative denomination, has expanded by more than 2 per cent a year since 1957, and the Jehovah's Witnesses have increased annually by 5 per cent since 1958, more than doubling their membership (Kelley, 1972, p. 21). Even Catholicism has been reached by Pentecostalism; nearly a quarter million of its members "speak in tongues" and regard themselves as "chromatics," or Pentecostal Catholics.

All these groups are essentially evangelical sects, having all the attributes that Troeltsch described. They tend toward extreme orthodoxy and a fairly literal interpretation of the Bible. Their doctrines emanate from a premillennialist tradition in American theology, which holds that the troubles of the world are created by man's sinfulness, and that the human condition cannot be improved until the Second Coming of Jesus. They feel the need for and seek personal salvation in Christ, and they view religious participation as a means of redemption through faith.

Beyond these common doctrines, the groups have other shared characteristics (Kelley, 1972 p. 26). They impose absolute conformity in religious belief on their members through censorship or the threat of expulsion. They believe fervently in the power of faith, with some Protestant Pentecostal groups going so far as to have their followers prove their faith by handling poisonous snakes during services. Jehovah's Witnesses, as another example, refuse to have blood transfusions when there are medically sound reasons requiring them. In short, all fundamentalist groups make strong demands on their members—and all of them turn a fairly cold shoulder toward other religions.

In trying to understand the attraction of these evangelical groups, Kelley has hypothesized that their success rests on the very fact that they make extensive demands on their membership. He believes that everybody has a basic need to find meaning in life, and that people are not satisfied with concepts or theologies. Only when they make personal sacrifices and only when they see others making sacrifices in the name of a belief can they feel they have found something impellingly meaningful. What is free is not worth much. The evangelical movement, therefore, has attracted more and more of a following because it exacts commitment and thereby creates meaning.

The Jesus People are also part of the evangelical revival, though their membership is comprised almost exclusively of middle-class white teenagers, often former drug users. Sometimes tagged as Jesus Freaks, they seek personal salvation through the teachings of Christ. They attend prayer services and go through baptism rituals. Some live and work together in communes, where the life-style is ascetic and a strict code of morality is observed. Emphasis is placed on the experience of religion, the experience of feeling God's will and performing it. Intellectualism and independent thought are not encouraged.

Religion, then, remains a lively object of study. Commitment to religious behaviour has not disappeared; it exists side-by-side with secularisation in America. Although the institutions are changing and the beliefs are changing, leading some to think that religion is dying, the functions of religion endure. They endure because mankind's' basic questions about existence, about the ultimate, about the meaning of life, and about morality persist. "The basic human religious needs and the basic religious functions have not changed very notably since the late Ice Age." Says sociologist and priest Andrew Greeley (1972, p. 1). "What changes have occurred make religious questions more critical rather than less critical in the contemporary world".

14

Urban Life and Technology

Today's Landscape is being changed by two forces: urbanisation and technology. The development of machine technology has within a century and a half loosened the ancient link between man and his crops and has produced what Philip Hauser terms a *population implosion*—the progressive movement of the world's peoples off the fertile lands into increasingly dense arban areas. In 1800 only 2.4 per cent of the world's population lived in settlements larger than 100,000. By 1960, 27.1 per cent were located in settlements larger than 20,000 persons, and 19.9 per cent resided in places large then 100,000. Projections of world population growth indicate that by the end of the century about 42 per cent of the world's peoples will live in places having more than 100,000 inhabitants (Hauser, 1969, pp. 1 - 19). This rapid movement from the land to the cities has been accompanied by a massive disruption of relatively stable social and cultural patterns. For this reason rapid urbanisation contributes to many of the ills that are bemoaned daily in the newspapers and analysed in the textbooks: street crime, poverty, the energy and ecological crises, among others.

Whereas the mechanisation of farm and factory production created an urban, industrialized society, continuing technological advance has produced such widespread change that some sociologists proclaim that we are now moving into a postindustrial society. Whether or not this society will say with the sorcerer's apprentice. "The Spirits I summoned I cannot now dismiss!" is a matter of debate. Has technology helped humanity to overcome nature only to reduce the individual to an appendage of the machine robbing men of all their creativity and possibly even of their homes on this planet? The following pages will address these questions.

The Urban Transformation

The date when humans first appeared as a distinct species is still unclear (it was at least a hundred thousand years ago), but it is certain that they have known cities for a much shorter time. The first permanent settlements were created some eight to ten thousand years ago, and their effect upon social organisation was enormous. Stationary residence encouraged the development of written language, the calendar, organised scientific inquiry, complex stratification systems, an organised priesthood, institutionalised religion, and the state, among many other important social institutions. Indeed, civilisation as we know it is very much a product of urban society; the word *civilisation* itself comes from the Latin, meaning, "culture of cities".

The Birth of the City

For at least the first three-quarters of human history, human beings were nomadic creatures who travelled about in small families or bands, hunting, fishing and foraging for food. Because the bounty of nature in most parts of the world was not plentiful enough to support more than a few persons in any one spot, humans were constantly on the move. Without adequate means of storing supplies, these people were unable to accumulate a surplus and therefore lived a rather precarious existence (Childe, 1952).

The Neolithic Revolution

At the dawn of the neolithic period, some ten thousand years ago, people began to develop techniques of cultivating plants and domesticating animals. Simple tools were invented for gardening and pots were made for storage; these technological innovations were a way of multiplying nature's bounty sufficiently to forego nomadic wandering for a rooted residence. The earliest villages were small by today's standards, housing only two hundred to four hundred residents. Because neolithic farming methods were inefficient and because transportation technologies were undeveloped, a village was limited in the amount of adjacent land that it could profitably bring under cultivation. This placed a limit on the expansion of these villages. Instead of the village expanding as its families grew, colonies were established at a distance to accommodate these growing numbers. This was the prevailing pattern of village organisation for the next four to five thousand years (Childe, 1952).

The First True Cities

In about 6000 to 5000 B. C. in the alluvial plains of the Nile, Tigris-Euphrates, and Indus River valleys there emerged settlements more than ten times the size of any previous ones. Housing between seven thousand and twenty thousand persons, these first true cities developed largely because innovations in agricultural and transportation technologies enabled these societies to take advantage of the valleys' exceptionally fertile soils. Agricultural output increased with the development of the oxdrawn plow, irrigation, newly domesticated plants, and metallurgy. Grain-storage facilities were improved and enough food was produced to support all farming families and a large population of nonfarmers as well. This relative abundance permitted the emergence of a complex division of labour, which has been characteristic of all human societies since. Then, even though the overwhelming proportion of the residents were engaged in farming, some could become specialists in crafts (potters, weavers, blacksmiths) or services (selling, teaching, fighting, governing, or performing rituals). Traders imported goods that were not locally available. To extend their control over all planning and organising of the community's affairs, the governing classes invented systems of record-keeping. Writing and numerical notation, two of mankind's momentous inventions, grew out of these needs. And because the community's survival depended on successful planting and harvesting of the crops, the scribes and clerks of the courts and temples had to develop exact, predictive sciences—including arithmetic, geometry and astronomy. The accuracy with which the early calendars predicted celestial events attests to the intellectual precision achieved by these early city dwellers (Davis, 1970, pp. 121-22).

The first cities reached their zenith about 3000 B. C. and then feded away. The next flowering of urban life occurred in classical Greece and Rome. Roman urban life attained a remarkable degree of sophistication, from magnificent public architecture down to such conveniences as water pipes and stepping stones for crossing muddy streets. But these classical cities declined with the fall of Rome. Urban development did not begin in Europe until the rise of the feudal city during the Middle Ages. Although many of these cities survive today, their preindustrial character was quite different, according to sociologist Gideon Sjoberg (1960).

The Preindustrial Feudal City

Feudal technology was such that about a hundred thousand persons could inhabit a city. Agricultural techniques were productive enough to allow about 10 per cent of an area's total population to live in an urban setting. However, the technological base limited the growth of cities beyond this. Transportation methods were poorly developed and it was therefore difficult to bring in the bulky goods needed for construction and manufacturing. Without large-scale manufacturing, job opportunities were limited. Poor communication methods limited the effective governing of a large adjacent hinterland. And sanitation and medical techniques were so primitive that dense urban settlement bred disease and death.

The social order of these cities was rigidly stratified and there was little mobility from one stratum to another. Contrary to today's American pattern, the rich lived in the center of the city and the poor on the outskirts. People of like class, ethnicity, and occupation lived in strictly defined quarters wherein they carried out most of their work, worship and marketing. The most powerful forces regulating people's behaviour in these cities were traditional folkways and mores (rather than formal law) enforced through the dominant institutions of family and guild. Guilds controlled the economy of the feudal city, regulating the price and quality of goods and services, the number of people in each craft, their training, and the length of the working day and week. Each guild disciplined its own members and assisted its families in times of need. Guild membership was likely to be hereditary, which created a rigid occupational system allowing little choice of work (Sjoberg, 1960).

The Industrial Revolution and the Urban Explosion

The Technological innovations of the Industrial Revolution reduced the constraints on the size and density of the city. The mechanisation of agriculture increased food production dramatically. Chemical and biological advances also produced new ways of raising animals, new insecticides, new herbicides, new fertilisers, and new plants which also stimulated food surpluses. Because of the increased productivity, fewer workers were now needed on the farms. Displaced farmers and their families streamed into the cities in search of jobs, which were increasing as a result of the growing factory production—again the sequence of the revolution in machine technology. Techniques for overcoming the obstacles of space also aided the explosive growth of cities. The spread of the railroads allowed the city to extend its grasp of faraway resources needed for growth. The development of cheap steel and the invention of the elevator made possible skyscrapers, which accommodated the residential and office needs of an increasingly dense urban population. And innovations in medicine and public hygience facilities cut the health risks that had plagued the earlier, preindustrial cities.

Whole nations relocated themselves from the hinterlands to metropolitan areas within a matter of decades. In 1850 only 15 per cent of the population of the United States lived in urban areas; by 1900 the proportion was almost 40 per cent. The turning point came around 1920, when more than half of all Americans were urban dwellers. Fifty years later, more than 70 per cent of the population was urbanised, by which the Census Bureau means living in towns or cities larger than twenty-five hundred persons (Hauser, 1969). Within a generation America shifted from being a rural-based nation to an urban one. (See Figure 14.1.)

This rapid urbanization meant the rise of a new social order. Municipal Fraderic C. Howe declared in 1906:

> The city has become the central feature of modern civilisation and to an ever increasing extent the dominant one. . . Rural civilisation, whose making engaged mankind since the dawn of history, is passing away. The city has erased the landmarks of an earlier society. Man has entered on an urban age. (in Fava, 1968, p. 11).

The traditions of rural society—its customs, habits, and indeed, its very way of life—were strained and often cast aside as the urban society grew more dominant and ultimately penetrated even those remaining rural communities through the institutions of government and the mass-media.

The widespread social disorganisation accompanying the breakup of the old rural order by the machine and the rise of cities was an important stimulus to the development of modern sociology. As the structure of a crystal is best revealed when it is cracked, the structures of human society, which had long been taken for granted and had thus remained "invisible", became apparent in their breakdown and transformation. Social structures and processes were changing at a perceptible rate. Marx Durkheim, Weber, Simmel and Tonnies were among those who developed new intellectual tools for understanding these changes, and these tools have served to construct sociology as we know it today.

Modern Urban Life

Describing the character of the modern city and of its social life has been a persistent challenge to sociologists. Much of the pioneering work was done by sociologists at the University of Chicago in the 1920s and 1930s. One of the early classics in urban sociology is Louis Wirth's "Urbanism as a Way of Life" (1938). Wirth saw the city as the prototype of mass society, in which the traditional bases of social solidarity and control—kinship and the neighbourhood—are undermined, leaving the individual atomised, depersonalised, and subject more frequently to mental break-down, suicide, delinquency, crime, corruption, and disorder. Wirth believed that urbanism fosters sophistication, rationality, and a utilitarian accent in inter-personal relations. This cluster of traits, in turn leads to reserve, indifference, and a blasé outlook and to anonymity and depersonalisation. Wirth understood that the peculiar kind of social relationship fostered by city living is determined by three factors: the *size, density* and *heterogeneity* of the city population. According to his view, larger populations tend to be more diversified and heterogeneous than small ones. Although a city dweller may have an enormous number of encounters with others, these encounters are likely to be segmented and superficial, impersonal and transitory. In place of sustrained and intimate relations with relatives and close neighbours, a person encounters the butcher, the taxi driver, the waitress, the news, vendor, yoga teachers and co-workers on the job. In other words, a person's social relations are secondary rather than primary.

Figure 14.1 : American urbanisation. 1900 - 1970

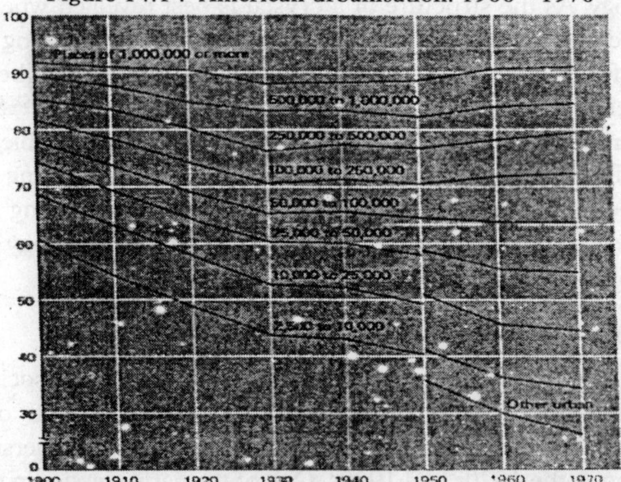

Source: Social Indicators 1973 (Washington, D. C.: Government Printing Office, 1974).

The Census Bureau counts any town of 2500 or more as urban by this measure, America has become increasingly urbanised. Most of its people still live in smaller cities and towns or in rural areas, however. Only a little over a quarter can be found in places larger than 100,000. (Notes The break in the lines at 1950 reflects a change in the Census Bureau's definition of "urban" to include unincorporated areas over 2500, the inclusion of these other urban areas reduced the percentage of rural population even further.)

These impersonal and anonymous social relations give people in the city a sense of increased personal freedom. Freedom is not an unmixed blessing, however, for it can mean that a person is free to prey on others. With the waning of traditional social constrains, the urban society must maintain order through formal mechanisms of control—law and its supporting agencies, the police and the courts. (See Figure 14.2.) But because these mechanisms of control are rarely as constraining as tradition and custom, the urban society is more prone to personal and social disorganisation, more prone to alienation. In Tonnies's terminology the social relations of an earlier rural age have been replaced in the cities and in urban society with *Gesellschaft-like* relations.

Is the city Alienating?

Does the city necessarily destroy intimate social bonds? Marvin Sussman (1959) found in his study that 70 per cent of working-class persons and 45 per cent of middle-class persons have relatives in their neighbourhoods, and that having a car

Figure 14.2 : Violent crime is urban crime

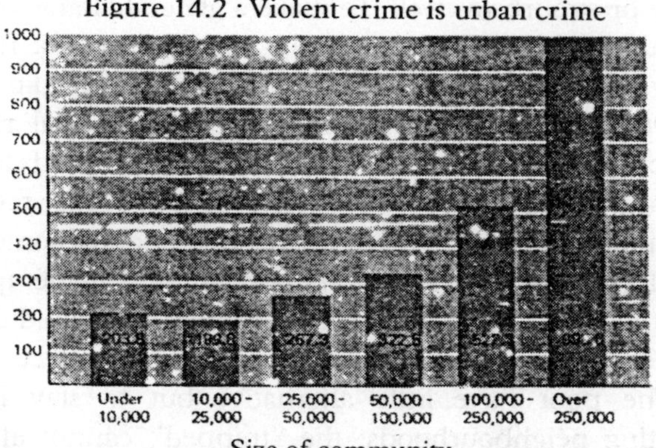

Source: Federal Bureau of Investigation, *Uniform Crime Reports, 1972* (Washington D. C.: Government Printing Office. 1973), p. 4.

The risks of murder, assault forcible rape and robbery are far greater in large cities than in medium-size cities and much greater there than in small towns. The direct relationship between size and violent crime supports Lotus Wirth's contention that size is an important variable in explaining the effects of urban life.

permitted city dwellers to keep in contact with relatives living further away. He also found that urban relatives commonly help one another by giving sick care, financial aid, child care and advice.

And what of Asian cities, which often have a preindustrial structure unlike cities in the industrialised countries of the north Atlantic region? Does Wirth's portrait of pervasive social disorganisation suit them well? Philip Hauser (in Fava, 1968, p. 93) found that Wirth's description did not apply to Rangoon, Bangkok, Djakarta, or Calcutta. Some segmentation, anonymity, and competition can be found, and there are glaring contrasts between neighbourhoods, but these are not the dominant features. And contrary to Wirth's portrait there appears no increased rationality and sophistication on the part of city dwellers as opposed to the country folk, no breakdown of caste barriers, and no especially pronounced loneliness.

Wirth's emphasis possibly stems from the fact that he drew upon studies that had been done by university of Chicago sociologists, studies that usually focused on the inner city. Metropolitan centers consist not only of an inner city but of an outer city or suburbs as well. To make a general characterisation of the entire metropolitan area on the basis of evidence from the inner city is misleading. Herbert Gans, in a well-known paper (in Rose, 1962) argues that the peculiar type of social relations sometimes found in the inner-city are not related to large population size, density, and heterogeneity, but rather to residential instability and the economic condition of some inner-city dwellers. Part of the inner-city population is made up of the poor and the "trapped," who live in sections with rapid resident turnover and who therefore suffer most the ill effects of city living. The poor have little alternative but to stay in their deteriorating neighbourhoods: the "trapped" cannot afford to follow their friends to the suburbs. The situation is quite different for others, such as the cosmopolites, the unmarried or childless young adults, and those ethnic groups who have recently immigrated to the inner city. The way of life of the ethnic villagers, for example, differs sharply from Wirth's portrait because these people place great importance on kinship ties, have little to do with formal organisations wherein secondary relations prevail, and are suspicious of anything and anyone outside their neighbourhood. Gans writes:

> While it is true that a not insignificant proportion of the inner-city population was, and still is, made up of unattached individuals, Wirth's Formulation ignores the fact that this population consists mainly of relatively homogeneous groups, with social and cultural moorings that shield it fairly effectively from the suggested consequences of number, density and heterogeneity. This applies even more to the residents of the outer city, who constitute a majority of the total city population. (Gans, in Rose, 1962, p. 635)

Because the inner-city comprises but a part of the entire modern metropolis, an accurate description of the city must take intò account the suburbs.

Life in the Suburbs

City life in America is increasingly suburban life. Propelled by the nostalgic belief in the values of intimate, neighbourly association, millions have fled the inner-city to the surrounding suburbs. The earliest suburbs grew up on the fringes of New York City in the 1850s and were predominantly havens for the rich. In these formerly rural areas the early city planners tried to develop model communities—"garden cities"—that would preserve the idyllic character of country living. At the turn of the century only one-sixth of the population of the United States was living in the suburbs. This pattern changed rapidly with the technological developments of the automoblie and mass transport and with the advent of mass financing for housing construction. During the post-Second World War years suburbs sprouted up almost overnight to house less affluent families. Many of these were "packaged suburbs," having five or six basic types of houses repeating themselves in a grid like fashion block after block, making a mockeny of the garden-city concept. By 1970, 38 per cent of the total population of the United States lived in the suburbs, comprising 54 per cent of all city dwellers (Commission on the Cities in the 70s, 1972, p. 71).

Many of the portraits of suburban living that are presented to Americans on the silvery screens of television and the movies have been far from attractive. One of the strongest images of the 1950s was James Dean in *Rebel Without a Cause:* The inarticulate misfit in a conformists suburb. The 1960s had Dustin Hoffman in *The Graduate* escaping to the bottom of his swimming pool to get away from his parents' hollow and oppressive suburban neighbours. The suburbs were seen to breed mass-produced Americans in mass-produced houses, driven into a desperate round of group activity governed by strict conformity. Incapable of true friendships, they were seen as bored, longly, alienated, atomised and depersonalised. Wives were supposed to be domineering, husbands absent, children spoiled, marriages on the rocks of adultery and divorce, and everybody drunk or stoned out of their unhappy minds.

The reality is that the suburbs are far from being all alike; life in them differs largely on the basis of the inhabitants' social class and place in the life cycle (Gans, 1968, pp. 132 - 40). Most of the postwar suburbs have been settled by the lower-middle class, often with young families, and consequently their way of life has commonly been identified as the suburban one. But sociologists have found that lower-middle-class life-styles are much the same in the suburb as they are in the city. Painted in broad strokes, a generalised picture of the lower-middle-class style shows that social life focuses on friends and neighbours rather than distant relatives. The major recreation is home and child care; indeed, the home is the vital center of life here. These people swell the membership in churches and others sorts of voluntary organisations—the Elks, P.T.A., and the like.

Much of the conformity found in the suburbs and derided by the critics is a consequence of the lower-middle-class being "on the make". In the fifties, William F. Whyte (in Stein, 1960) studied a Chicago suburb called Park Forest, which was then a home for middle-level "organisation men" and their families. The tone of life there was set by the work ethic of the husbands: if you wanted to get ahead, you had to get along, be a company person, and avoid being too different. Houses there were consequently very similar and were furnished in good but modest taste. The accent was on appearances: adults were supposed to look happy and to be friendly with neighbours, and the kids were supposed to get alongwith one another. Although people were expected to make friends in the community, those friendships were not supposed to interfere with upward mobility.

The image of excessive drinking, wide spread adultery and divorce, and intense social competition comes from an exaggerated version of *upper*-middle-class suburban life. One such suburb studied in the fifties by A. C. Spectorsky (in Stein, 1960) was populated by people in the New York City communications industries who commuted to work from a wealthy "exurbia" far outside the city. Reacting to the frantic pace of radio and T. V. Work, these men and their families sought a countrified haven from the rat race, and a suburban home seemed to provide such a place. But the wives became bored with the childrens conversation and hungry for adult companionship. Husbands had to work even more frantically to meet the increased costs of suburban living. Excessive drinking and extramarital affairs offered an escape from the pressures of their life-style. The suburban idyll thus became a part of rather than an antidote to the hectic life.

Other studies have shown upper-middle-class suburbanites to be quite different from the less affluent suburban dwellers (Gans, 1968). Being better educated and more cosmopolitan in their interests, they put less emphasis on home as the center of life. These people tend to be extensively and intensively involved in community activities, social, cultural and civic. They participate in many shared activities with friends, such as partying, and they are even less likely than lower-middle-class persons to have strong ties with relatives. And again, this life-style is characteristic of the upper-middle class in general, both in the suburb and in the city.

Urban Ecology

The metropolis is divided not only into city and suburb, but into specialised areas of manufacturing, commerce and housing. Major cities typically have areas that correspond to Wall Street, skid row, the Gold Coast, Watts and Broadway. But how does this organisation develop?

During the 1920s and 1930s a number of sociologists, again at the University of Chicago, felt that urban land specialisation could best be explained by analogy to the ecological model in biology. They saw the urban environment as a product of competition and natural selection. The *urban ecologists,* as the group came to the known, hypothesised that established land uses usually resist displacement and since dissimilar uses are usually incompatible with one another, a single area typically harbours one kind of development (factories *or* low-cost housing *or* entertainment). When competition for the limited urban space becomes particularly intense, however, the land use of the greatest economic significance generally winds out.

Ecological Succession

That neighbourhoods go through changes is all too obvious, especially to long-time residents. Some neighbourhoods physically deteriorate while others are reclaimed and renovated. Industries move to the residential suburbs and provoke zoning battles in the councils of city government. Change is visible enough, but is there a pattern to these changes? The urban ecologists described an *invasion cycle,* which they felt constituted a general pattern (Park, Burgess, McKenzie, 1925). The invasion cycle begins before it is recognised by the area's inhabitants. One brownstone or dilapidated urban mansion in a rundown are a is bought and refurbished by an architect, for example. Next, more professionals buy houses nearby and then habitants notice and oppose the invasion. As land values and taxes and rents go up, the older and poorer residents protest that they can no longer afford to live there and have nowhere else to go. If opposition is unsuccessful, a general influx begins. Newcomers flood the area. A "tip point" is reached as the old inhabitants are forced out or no longer wish to remain in the area. The invasion reaches the climax stage when the new inhabitants completely occupy the area. This is how a slum becomes a Georgetown or a Georgetown a slum. The neighbourhood may stabilise in climax or it may undergo further succession.

The Shape of Cities

The urban ecologists thought that not only could the *dynamics of* city growth and change be generalised, but that similar outcomes in the overall *structure* of the city could also be detected.

Certainly St. Louis, New York, Boston, Los Angeles, and Albuquerque are different in many different ways. Each city has its own unique features to be sure, but a number of observers have seen general similarities.

Box 14.1

In the News

The Human Side of Ecological Succession

An area undergoing succession often experiences a good deal of tension, as the views of the new residents clash with those of the old. Take, for example, a Slovak blue-collar neighbourhood on Cleveland's East Side, where blacks who had been financially successful enough to move out of downtown ghetto areas were buying homes, and the invasion cycle had reached the general influex stage. The major issue for most of the older residents was the increase in crime. One woman who sold her house at a $ 4,000 loss spoke of her plans to move to the suburbs.

One of the turing points for me was when I heard people were bying guns. I asked some of the women on the block and found three of them. . . . who carry guns in their purses. Imagine, women who have never fired a gun in their lives carry one to go to the Pick pay.

What do the blacks say?

Everything we have we worked for scrapping together $1,500 for a down payment was the toughest thing we've ever done. So may be blacks are the cause of crime in this area. But it isn't me out there bopping old ladies over the head. Talk about law and order—Yes, Sir, I'm for law and order. You can put me down as in love with the police. All I wanted was place I could live and let live. Down at East 100th where we lived, we were robbed three times. We bought the dog and started looking for a house. Originally, I came from a farm in Lousiana; no electricity, no indoor plumbing. So this house, this neighbourhood. . .well, I love it, I just love it.

Part of the problem is a difference in perspective. While whites thought the crime rate was skyrocketing, blacks thought it was going down. The whites remembered the area when there was virtually no crime, while the blacks, newly arrived from the crime-ridden inner city, fell, far safer that they had before.

Source: Paul Wilkes, "As the Blacks move in, the Ethnics Move Out, " *The New York Times Magazine* (January 24, 1971): 9ff.

On the basis of evidence at hand, Ernest W. Burgess proposed in the 1920s that cities are laid out in a series of *concentric circles* (Park, Burgess, McKenzie, 1925, pp. 47 - 62). At the center is the business district of shops and offices. By day this section is crowded with people, but by night it empties of all but a few souls who inhabit scattered transient hotels in the area. Adjacent and outward from the business district is an area of transition characterised by residential instability, high crime rates, and various forms of vice. Residents of this zone are racial and ethnic minority groups and outcasts. Beyond the transitional ring are the various residential zones. The innermost is inhabited by working-class people, the next by the middle class, and the outermost by the upper class. While concentric zone patterning is by no means typical of all or even most urban areas it can be seen in certain cities like Chicago, which developed very rapidly in the period after the Industrial Revolution and before the development of the automobile. (See Figure 14.3).

In the 1930s Homer Hoyt proposed a theory of urban patterning that emphasised the importance of transportation routes—highways, railroad lines and waterways—in shaping the growth of cities (1943). According to Hoyt's *sector theory,* a business district occupies the center of the city and beyond that, development occurs in sectors that tend to be distributed along major transportation routes, radiating out from the city center. As land uses expend they tend to remain within their respective sectors, but extend outward toward the edge of urban development. Like the concentric zone theory, the sector theory held that lower-class residential area were adjacent to business or manufacturing areas, while middle and upper-class neighbourhoods were successively further away.

A third theory of urban ecological development, the *multiple nuclei theory,* was proposed by Chauncy D. Harris and Edward L. Ullman (1945). These men identified four principles that shape urban development. These are: (1) similar or related land uses are mutually complementary and tend to locate near one another; (2) dissimilar land uses are mutually destructive and tend to locate at a distance from one another; (3) real estate values limit certain types of development because high costs are prohibitive to certain land uses; and (4) certain land uses can locate only in areas with specialised facilities. On the basis of these principles, Harris and Ullman proposed that the city develops in a series of nuclei, each with specialised activities. For example, a car manufacturing nucleus might develop in an area on the outskirts of town with lots of space, low rents, and good transportation facilities. Manufacturing interests requiring less space might cluster in a nucleus closer to the center of the city, while residential centers might develop on the other side of town. As the city grows, nuclei proliferate and become specialised.

Figure 14.3 : Models of urban space

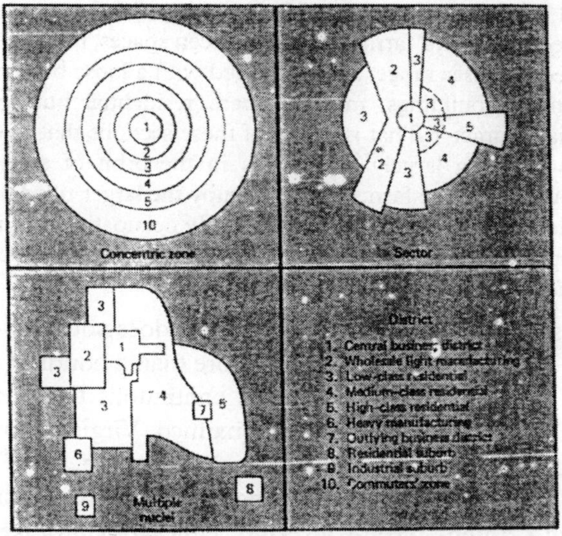

Source: Chauncy D. Harris and Edward L. Ullman, "The Nature of Cities", in Paul K. Hatt and A. J. Reiss, Jr., eds, *Cities and Society* (Glencoe Free Press, 1957). Courtesy of Professor Harris.

Attempts to describe the structure of cities produced the three alternative models shown here. A newer approach to the analysis of urban structure is called *social area analysis*. Analysis, using the census and other social indicators attempt to explain residential patterns by correlating broad social categories such as social rank, family structure and ethnicity. With the advent of the computer even more factors are being taken into account in models of urban land use and social structure.

During the past decade and a half a number of observers have perceived a new pattern of urban development, on that is regional. A number of American metropolises are growing so large that they are growing together, forming what Jean Gottman has called a *megalopolis:*

> As one follows the main highways or railroads between Boston and Washington, D.C., one hardly loses sight of built-up areas, tightly woven residential communities, or powerful concentrations of manufacturing plants. Flying this same route one discovers, on the other hand, that behind the ribons of densely occupied land along the principal arteries of traffic, and in between the clusters of suburbs around the old urban centers, there still remain large areas covered with woods and brush alternating with some carefully cultivated patches of farmland. These green spaces, however, when inspected at closer range, appear stuffed with a loose but immense scattering of buildings, most of them residential but some of industrial character. That is, many of these sections that look rural actually function largely as suburbs in the orbit of some city's downtown. Even the farms, which occupy the larger tilled patches, are seldom worked by people whose onely occupation and income are properly agricultural. And yet these farm areas produce large quantities of farm goods (1961, p. 5).

The distinction between rural and urban does not apply in this area any more. Municipalities having more than a hundred people per square mile are stretched along a continuous five-hundred-mile belt from Kittery, Maine, to Quantico, Virginia. Over 40 million people live in this sprawling belt (Tunnard, 1967). And there are other emerging megalopolises as well: Pittsburgh-Youngstown-Canton-Akron-Cleveland; Chicago-Milwaukee, and a new strip between Chicago and Detroit, Los Angeles-San Diego; Palm Beach-Miami; Dallas-Fort Worth; and perhaps even Seattle-Takoma. Because this trend seems to be the wave of the future, we must give up the idea that a city is a tightly settled and organised territory in which people, activities, and riches are crowded into a small area distinctly separated from its non-urban surroundings. The unplanned growth that has created these megalopolises—called "urban sprawl" by some—continues unabated. Indeed this is an essential part of what is often called the crisis of the cities.

The Urban Crisis

Metropolitan Segregation

The flight of whites to the suburbs has created a pattern of segregation that is increasingly explosive. The deteriorating inner city—the core of the metropolis or megalopolis—has been left to the poor and the black, who can least afford to finance its upkeep. Because the buildings are older and the rents lower in the inner cities, the poor and unskilled migrants from the rural areas take up residence there. The movement of blacks off the southern countryside into the northern cities made ghettos of the inner cities. Even though blacks constitute only one-tenth of the total population in America, nineteen of the nation's thirty largest cities are more than 30 per cent black. Four are more than 50 per cent black. Moreover, four-fifths of all urban blacks live in the inner city, whereas only two-fifths of the urban whites live there. This trend shows no sign of letting up. By the end of the decade it is possible that most of our biggest cities "will be pre-ponderantly black and brown, and totally bankrupt," in the words of the Commission on the Cities in the '70s (1972, pp. 36-37).

The quality of public services and housing in the inner cities is declining because its residents are poor. Cities raise their money for public services—education, mass transportation, hospitals, police, sewers, etc.—through taxes. Poor populations yield smaller taxes. Whereas one in fourteen suburban residents had an income that fell below the poverty line in 1971, one in seven inner-city dwellers was listed as officially poor. And blacks are generally poorer than whites. Non-white income for 1973, averaged only three-fifths of white income that year (*Social Indicators*, 1973, 1974, p. 175).

Unemployment rates are also high in the inner-city slums. In 1966, which was a good year for the national economy (3.7 per cent unemployment nationwide), some slums had as much as five times the national unemployment rate. But unemployment figures are not the best indicators of work and wage deficiency. In a special study the Department of Labour determined the "sub-employment" rates in several inner-city slums throughout the nation. This figure included all those persons who did not show up in the official unemployment statistics but who made wages inadequate to live on. These sub-employment rates were 45 per cent in New Orleans's slums, 24 per cent in Boston's Roxbury section, 31 per cent in New York's Harlem, 47 per cent in San Antonio's East and West Sides, and 34 per cent in North Philadelphia (Matza, 191, p. 605). Unemployment seems to hit black teen-agers the hardest. In 1970 teen-age joblessness in America's black urban ghettos soared to 35 per cent.

One of the reasons for urban poverty is the decline of job opportunities in the inner cities. Industry and commerce once located in the inner cities are moving to the suburbs. This means that fewer jobs are available to the inner-city resident. New York City alone lost a quarter of a million jobs between 1970 and 1974, Stern, 1974, p. 1). Job losses were greatest in manufacturing, which is precisely the kind of work that the inner city needs for its increasing population of unskilled minorities.

Because of the inner cities' deteriorating conditions, there is a strong demand for public services, which cannot be supported by the cities inadequate tax revenues. Widespread unemployment means that more money must be spent on welfare. Because the buildings are older in the inner city, more money must be spent on fire protection. Because crime and poverty are so closely associated, more money must be spent on police services. Health, education, and mass transit get the short end of the budgetary stick. In New York's rich neighbourhoods, there is one private doctor for every two hundred persons; in some poor inner-city neighbourhoods, there is one per ten thousand persons. Inner-city schools spend two-thirds as much per pupil as some suburban schools do. Rural- or sub-urban-dominated state legislatures allocate more money to highway construction than to mass transit. Inner-city buildings are falling apart and being abandoned in some cases. Estimates of abandoned buildings in New York City go as high as a hundred thousand (Commission on the Cities in the '70s, 1972, pp. 43 - 80). And New York City is not alone in its problems; this is the condition of most of America's cities.

City governments cannot reverse this decline because they have no way to make the suburban dweller pay for his use of the city. Suburbanites commute into the city for work and entertainment and thereby use the city's transit, fire, police, and other public services. Increasing toll fees on commuter routes into the cities runs the risk of further losing the commuters' business. Because the suburbanite is getting a good deal, he is not going to put more money into the city's coffers voluntarily. And because the city government seldom encompasses the entire metropolitan region, no unified local government exists that can enforce a more equitable taxation scheme. (The average number of separate governing unites for the typical metropolitan area is ninety-one!)

Unslumming the City

The causes of urban disorganisation and inner-city decline are numerous, and there are numerous proposals for reversing these trends. Some of these concentrate on improving the inner cities, others on coping with sprawling urban growth.

One strategy that has been popular in the past has been to bulldoze slums and build middle-class housing in an attempt to lure the middle-class back into the city. This has merely provided the city's already existing middle class with better places to live—with a subsidy. At the same time it has forced the poor into smaller and smaller areas (Gans, 1968, pp. 261 - 65). The concentration on physical face-lifting has ignored other avenues of renewal.

Another strategy is to upgrade the income of those already in the inner city. Jane Jacobs writes:

> The processes that occur in unslumming depend on the fact that the metropolitan economy, if it is working well, is constantly transforming many poor people into middle-class people, many illiterates into skilled (or even educated) people, many greenhorns into competent citizens. (1961, p. 288)

Raising incomes will in turn stimulates the renovation of neighbourhoods and reduce population density as these people demand better housing.

Some have championed the idea of building *new towns,* carefully and comprehensively planned communities usually near a larger metropolis, which would take care of urban growth in a systematic fashion. Ebenezer Howard began an English new town, Letchworth, back in 1902, and Britain had over 150,000 people living in such developments by their 1966 census. Columbia, Maryland, and Reston, Virginia, in the United States are perhaps the best-known new towns (Schaffer, 1970, pp. 22 - 25). But this strategy offers only a partial and slow solution to the urban crisis.

Some observers see the need for massive federal aid to the cities. They propose a Marshall Plan for the cities comparable to the outlays that the United States spent on rebuilding western Europe after World War II (Commission on the Cities in the '70s, 1972).

The problems of the cities are so massive that a national policy is needed to help solve the crisis. Tinkering separately with transportation, urban renewal, employment, education, health services, and the rest, does not work. Comprehensive plans for monitoring cities and devising strategies for dealing with their problems are imperative.

The Technological Transformation

Technological developments have changed more aspects of society than simply the kinds of cities we live in. The pace at which we live, the kind of recreation we enjoy, the work we do, even the air we breathe, have sometimes been affected by technology. Technology consists of not only machinery but of ways of organising resources, including people. For example, a computer is just a piece of equipment, but it demands that a whole social organisation of engineers, programmers, and service people support it. Moreover, the group or institution that uses it often changes its way of doing things to accommodate it or to implement its results.

Technology is not limited to economic applications, and these new forms of organising life reach into every corner of society. Think, for example, of the impact of television upon our culture. Some commentators have seen in the advent of electronic communication, no less than the transformation of how we see—from serial experience to instantaneous perception. This, in turn, implies a nonrational, tribal way of relating to others (McLuhan, 1964, pp. 36 - 45).

The profound effects of technology are often quite incidental to the original purpose of the invention. The growth of cities was not what the people who invented the reaper or the spinning jenny had in mind. Neither were the destruction of the environment and the changes in work satisfaction and occupational structure, yet technological change has brought these in its wake, too. In the next sections we will look at some of the profound and unanticipated effects of technology upon the environment, work, and the society as a whole.

Technology and Ecology

Man has developed his tools to tame nature and often to tame other men as well. But industrial man has more than tamed nature; he has carved it into his own image. An American Indian woman has said: "When we burn grass for grasshoppers, we don't ruin things. . .But the White people plow up the ground, pull down the trees, kill everything. . . . How can the spirit of the earth like the White man? Everywhere the White man has touched it, it is sore" (in McLuhan, 1971, p. 1).

Zen Buddhist D.T. Suzuki believes that the Judeo-Christian tradition has led the West to desecrate nature on a grand scale; for that tradition has preached that man has a rightful dominion over nature. Microbiologists René Dubos (1972) disputes this by showing that abuses of nature have occurred throughout the history of man and throughout the non-Christian world. Others have pointed to capitalism as an aggravating force in this desecration, but socialist countries have serious environmental problems as well. It is undeniable, however, that the profit motive of capitalism has produced a plethora of manufactured commodities that satisfy needs that have been artificially stimulated through mass media advertising campaigns. And workers who receive little or no intrinsic satisfaction in their work seek compensatory gratification in buying a wide range of consumer products. Whatever factors have created an industrialised consumer economy, one thing is clear industrialised technologies have made a massive assault on the environment and have placed a tremendous drain on the earth's bank of nonrenewable resources.

The scale of this assault has recently been estimated in a study, *The Limits of Growth,* sponsored by the Club of Rome (Meadows et al., 1972). By applying a computerised systems analysis to present trends, this study has explored the earth's capacity to support the human population and economy. The human population has been growing exponentially because the birth rate is increasing and the death rate decreasing. Similarly, the world economy grows exponentially because the means of production increase while their rate of depreciation decreases. The Club of Rome asserts that there are limits in the ability of the planet to support exponential population and economic growth. These limits are the availability of food, raw materials, fossil and nuclear fuels, and the ability of the earth's ecosystem to absorb wastes and to recycle matter. Two factors that are rapidly pushing the earth's ecosystem toward its upper limits of tolerance are the rapid depletion of nonrenewable resources such as metals and fuels, and the rapid increase in pollution. The effects of pollution are particularly unpredictable. There is almost no knowledge about the upper limits to pollution. Many pollutants are distributed globally and their effects may be felt at a distance from their source. Finally, the Club of Rome study sees a natural delay in an ecosystem's response to stress, a fact that makes it possible that the limits of pollution tolerance could be reached and passed inadvertently.

The study's ominous conclusion is that if present growth trends persist in population, industrialisation, food production, resource depletion, and pollution, the earth's upper limits of tolerance will be reached within the next one hundred years. When this occurs, population and industrial capacity will collapse. (See Figure 14.4)

The only possible way to avert world collapse is to halt economic and population growth and establish environmental and economic stability. The authors of the Club of Rome study emphasise that technology alone cannot rescue the world from its predicament. Even if improved technology increased agricultural output, created highly efficient forms of pollution control and of the recycling of natural resources and offered foolproof methods of population control such that only wanted children would be born, there would still be a world collapse from environmental stress. Eventually, overuse of land would cause erosion and a rapid drop in food production, resources would become depleted, and pollution would start to rise sharply, rapidly accelerating the death rate. Reliance on technological solutions is simply not enough.

These conclusions are a matter of debate and not fact, for the Club of Rome study has its critics. Some attack the model, pointing out flaws in its underlying assumptions or its construction ("The Limits of Doomsday Predictions," 1973). Others find that "it is not all that difficult to sketch out a scenario of social catastrophe in a non-growth society to equal, in its

Figure 14.4 : A model of ecological crisis

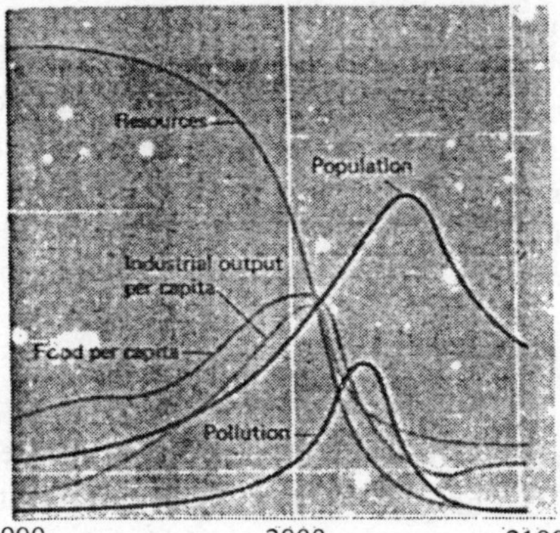

Source : Donella H. Meadows et al. *The Limits to Growth* (New York: Universe, 1972), p. 124.

If present trends continue (based on certain assumptions about the growth of population and industrial capacity), many researchers predict the exhaustion of resources scarcity of food, and industrial collapse within the next hundred years. Pollution and population will continue to grow for a while after this collapse, but they too will peak. Note that after the collapse, population will still be greater than today but food and industrial capacity will be far lower. Because of this living standards will drop dramatically.

horror, the scenario of ecological catastrophe in a growth society" (Klein, 1974, p. 14). No growth could mean that those in poverty will be trapped there. This, in turn, could increase national and international tensions. Furthermore, the problem of arriving at a no-growth society will place stresses on the political structure. Who will cut back on births and on consumption? How will desirable increases in public services be obtained when every increase in one area of society implies a decrease in resources devoted to another area? Collective decision-making will be imperative; whether this will be harmonious or involve coercion is very much an open question.

> This scenario might then suggest that a society which had adopted the values of nongrowth would be introvert rather than extrovert, traditional rather than innovative. Whether it had settled for an egalitarian distribution of wealth or for the perpetuation of inequalities, it would be resistant to change, stressing social control as the inevitable counterpart of social stability. There would be little social mobility, since this tends to be a product of economic growth. There might well evolve a gerontocracy, with power going hand in and with seniority, since it would no longer be open to the young to secede from existing organisations to start their own. The only frontiers that would be open for exploration would be those of artistic or spiritual activity. The resemblance of the picture to medieval society in Western Europe is not accidental. (Klein, 1974, p. 84).

Technology and Work

Alienation

Technology has not only changed the face of the city and natural surroundings but also has affected the organisation of work and the satisfaction people derive from their jobs. There exists a long tradition of sociological thinking that sees people alienated from work under the impact of industrialisation and the division of labour, which industrialization produced. Karl Marx developed this them over a century ago, and it has been a cornerstone to social criticism ever since. In the *Communist Manifesto,* he and Friendrich Engels declared:

> Owing to the extensive use of machinery and to division of labour, the work of proletarians has lost all individual character and, consequently, all charm for the workman. He becomes an

appendage of the machine, and it is only the simplest, most monotonous, and most easily acquired knack that is required of him. (in Feuer, 1959, p. 14)

The propertyless worker is alienated or separated from his work because the ownership of the tools of production and the product itself has been appropriated by another. The worker is not paid to "express himself"; the boss is only interested in getting the work done. The worker is thus reduced to his mere labour power, which has a market value. His lobour power becomes a commodity, a thing to be bought and sold. Man thereby becomes alienated from himself, for his labour power is no longer an inextricable part of his essential self. Work becomes separated from play; work becomes separated from self-expression: work has no intrinsic meaning and is only self-sacrifice undertaken to earn money for leisure-time pursuits. As Sociologist C. W. Mills wrote in 1951:

> [Alienation from work] means that the most alert hours of one's life are sacrificed to the making of money with which to "live". Alienation means boredom and the frustration of potentially creative effort, of the productive sides of personality. It means that while men must seek all values that matter to them outside of work, they must be serious during work: they may not laugh or sing or even talk, they must follow the rules and not violate the fetish of "the enterprise". In short, they must be serious and steady about something that does not mean anything to them, and moreover during the best hours of their day, the best hours of their life. . .Each day men sell little pieces of themselves in order to try to buy them back each night and week end with the coin of "fun". With amusement, with love, with movies, with vicarious intimacy, they pull themselves into some sort of whole again, and now they are different men. (p. 237)

Are Workers Actually Alienated?

Determining worker's satisfaction or alienation is a deceptively simple task. Why not just ask them if they are happy with their work? A number of such studies are reported in *Work in America* (1973), a special task force report for the Department of Health, Education and Welfare. One is a Gallup Poll, which revealed that 80 to 90 per cent of those questioned felt that their work was satisfying. In a representative cross section of American workers, about 80 per cent indicated that they would continue to work even if they inherited enough money to live without working. Another finding was that as people increased their income and wealth, they did not reduce the amount of time and energy expended in work.

There may be more to this than meets the eye, however. Robert Blauner (1960) cautions that statistics on job satisfaction may be misleading for two reasons. First, job satisfaction is a vague concept, hard to define and therefore hard to assess. Second, "Under normal conditions there is a natural tendency for people to identify with, or at least be somewhat positively oriented toward, those social arrangements in which they are implicated" (p. 336). People might have a difficult time articulating their dissatisfaction and might only appear to be satisfied. *Work in America,* therefore, goes on to probe the true feelings of workers. One man who said he had a "pretty good job" replied when pressed to tell what made the job good: "Don't get me wrong. I didn't say it is a good job. It's an O.K. job—about as good a job as a guy like me might expect. The foreman leaves me alone and it pays well. But I would never call it a good job. It doesn't amount to much, but it's not bad." Is this America's happy worker?

Box 14.2

Youth and Work

Because of the postwar baby boom there are more young people than ever before entering the labour force. Young workers, particularly in the auto industry, have not been reluctant to act out their discontent; absenteeism, tardiness, and arguments with foremen have increased significantly. Other youths have withdrawn into the counterculture. Many older people have concluded that the country is in trouble because of lazy self-indulgent attitudes, but research suggests that the attitudes of youth are more complex.

A 1973 Yankelovich Poll surveyed over three thousand youths both in and out of college to discover their career aspirations and their attitudes toward work. It found that a majority of the young accept the necessity of hard work and are seeking challenging jobs that will provide them with the opportunity for self-fulfilment, self-

Box 14.2 Contd.

expression, participation in decision-making, fellowship, and equality. But there exist disparities between college and noncollege youths in their ability to attain intrinsically rewarding jobs.

Among college students there has been a steady increase over the past six years of traditional job aspirations, stressing economic security and the chance to get ahead. College is therefore seen more and more as a training ground for a career. Only about 34 per cent of all college students are unconcerned with the extrinsic rewards of work, largely because they take affluence for granted. But a growing number of students, now comprising 32 per cent feel that they can achieve *both* the economic rewards of a career and the intrinsic rewards of self-fulfilment and self-expression. They feel that they can strike a bargain with society, fulfilling themselves while also getting ahead in the world. Quite conveniently, the chances for economic rewards and self-fulfilment appear to be the greatest in the expanding professional technical, and managerial occupations, which require higher education for entrance. A good "fit" therefore appears possible between what the college students want and what the society has to offer.

Blue-collar youth not in college are increasingly unwilling to accept work that does not offer the possibility of self-fulfilment. In 1969, 79 per cent believed that "hard work would always pay off" in 1973 the proportion of believers had fallen to 56 per cent. And the nature of an acceptable "payoff" is changing; more blue-collar youth are emphasising the need for meaningful and gratifying work. The crucial dilemma, however, is that blue-collar work offers fewer apportunities for gratification. About a third of all questioned blue-collar workers are "just hanging on until something better comes along," whereas only a tenth of all professional and managerial respondents feel this way. But most youths lack the educational certification needed to get these professional and managerial jobs. Only one in four of all youths eighteen to twenty-five years of age finished college. The blue-collor youth without a college education is therefore more likely to be frustrated on his job, unable to fulfil his aspirations.

Source: Yankelovich Youth Study, 1974 by the JDR 3rd Fund, pp. 17-30.

A better indicator of job satisfaction may be whether or not workers would choose their line of work again if they were given the chance to start over. By this measure job satisfaction appears far lower than the 80 to 90 per cent reported by the Gallup Pollup Poll. (See Figure 14.5.) One such study reported in *Work in America* finds that 41 per cent of skilled steel workers and only 16 per cent of unskilled auto workers would choose their jobs again. About twice as many white-collar workers as blue-collar workers are satisfied with their work, but in both groups the percentage satisfied was less than half. Only among professionals

Figure 14.5 Job Satisfaction

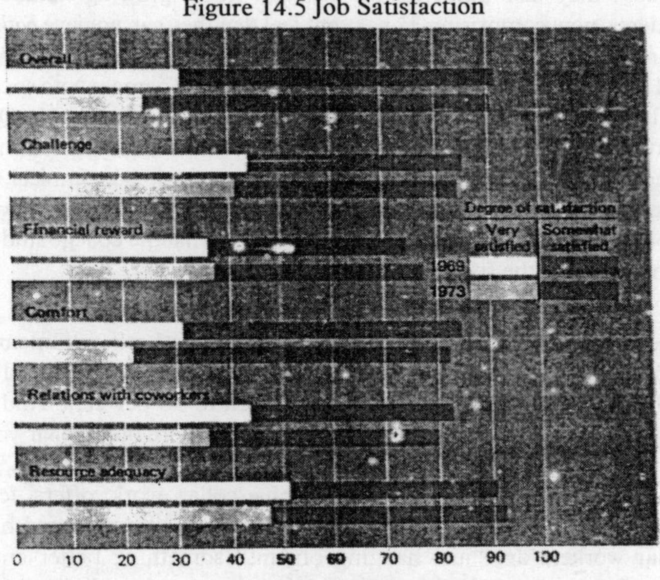

Source: Social Indicators, 1973 (Washigton, D. C: Government Printing Office. 1974) , p. 123.

In 1969 and 1973 the Survey Research Center of the University of Michigan asked a sample of workers to rate twenty-three aspects of their jobs. Analysts then grouped the answers into various demensions. The overwhelming majority of Americans expressed some degree of satisfaction with their jobs but the percentage that were very satisfied was significantly lower. Not surprisingly workers seemed most displeased about their compensation. These findings support the conclusion of *Work in America* that American workers are dissatisfied only if the group "somewhat satisfied" is taken to indicate a large pool of people with reservations about their work.

was satisfaction really high: 83 per cent of the surveyed lawyers, 89 per cent of the physicians and biologists, and 97 per cent of the urban university professors would choose their profession again (*Work in America,* 1973).

What Makes Work Satisfying?

Phil Stallings, a twenty-seven-year-old spot-welder at a Ford assembly plant in Chicago, describes life on the assembly line:

> I stand in one spot, about two- or three-feet area, all night. The only time a person stops is when the line stops. We do about thirty-two jobs per car, per unit. Forty-eight units an hour, eight hours a day. Thirty-two times forty-eight times eight. Figure it out. That's how many times I push that button. . .I don't understand how come more guys don't flip. Because you're nothing more than a machine when you hit this type of thing. They give better care to that machine than they will to you. They'll have more respect, give more attention to that machine. And you *know* this. Somehow you get the feeling that the machine is better than you are. (Laughs). (in Terkel, 1974, pp. 159-60)

Phil Stallings is clearly alienated from his work. The noise where he stands is tremendous and when he opens his mouth, he is liable to get a mouthful of sparks. Needless to say, he has very little contact with others on the assembly line. "You can work next to a guy for months without even knowing his name." And that assembly line—"It don't stop. It just goes and goes and goes. I bet there's men who have lived and died out there, never seen the end of that line. And they never will, because it is endless. It's like a serpent. It's all body, no tail. It can do things to you. "Phil Stallings has to ask the foreman if he can go to the bathroom. "If he doesn't like you, he'll make you hold it, just ignore you," And he certainly does not have pride in his craft. "Whenever we make a mistake, we always say, 'Don't worry about it, some dingaling'll buy it".

One important factor in work satisfaction is the degree to which one's task is fractionated and repetitious. Recall Marx and Engels's assertion that the use of machinery and the division of labour robbed work of its individual character and charm. Phill Stallings's product certainly has no individual character and he does not identify with the product of his labours. But listen to a piercer-dragout worker who works in a steel plant with heavy machines: "There's nothing like working here in this mill. Everybody cooperates. Every man works as a members of a team and every man tries to turn out as much steel as they possibly can. We work hard and get satisfaction out of working here" (in Blauner, 1960, p. 346).

Clearly, an important difference between these work experiences is that working on a team affords workers the chance to develop friendships. The formation of friendships and feelings of group responsibility is apparently a major determinant of job satisfaction. This is supported by a study of factory workers that revealed that 65 per cent of workers integrated into work groups were pleased with the *intrinsic* and ancillary aspects of their work (that is, the pay, working conditions, and the like), while only 28 per cent of isolated workers expressed a similar degree of satisfaction (*Work in America*, 1973).

The degree of control is also important. On the assembly line, the pace is unyielding. But the assembly line employs only 2 per cent of America's work force. Today technology often demands greater responsibility from workers and offers greater freedom. In the automated plant the machines do the work without operators, and the men supervise or repair the machines.

> The case of continuous process industry, particularly the chemical industry, shows that automation increases the worker's control over his work process and checks the further division of labour and growth of large factories. The result is meaningful work in a more cohesive, integrated industrial climate. (Blauner, 1964, p. 169)

Modern technology then, can actually be arranged in such a way as to *reduce* the division of labour, increase the amount of teamwork, and thereby relieve worker alienation. The Volvo automobile plants in Sweden have successfully experimented with abandoning the assembly line. *All* the auto's parts are conveyed to a work space where a small team of workers assemble the entire car. Working as a team, the group decides who will do what, thus allowing for day-to-day variation. Workers have more contact with each other, have a stronger identification with the product of their labours, and apparently receive direct satisfaction from their work. Absenteeism has decreased dramatically and productivity has remained high.

It is important to note that the Volvo team system not only allows a reduced division of labour but also an increase of the workers' decision-making opportunities. Reorganising work to extend the control of employees can pay big dividends. For example, Texas Instruments, a manufacturing company, had contracted out its janitorial services. It found that its plant was only 65 per cent clean and that among the janitorial personnel there was a 100 per cent quarterly turnover rate. To change this situation the company tried an experiment involving 120 maintenance personnel. They divided the personnel into teams of 19 each, involved the teams in planning and goal-setting for the project, trained the teams, and gave them adequate equipment. Scheduling and task assignment were left up to each team, and the teams were held responsible for their performance. As a result of this effort to increase workers' control over their work, the company found that the plant cleanliness rose from 65 to 85 per cent and the quarterly turnover tumbled from 100 to 9.8 per cent. In all, the company saved approximately $ 103,000 per year from the changes. A number of other experiments in work reorganisation have been conducted with equally dramatic results. The findings indicate that job satisfaction and productivity can be increased simultaneously if workers are treated like human beings instead of machines *(Work in America,* 1973, pp. 96 - 100*)*.

Technology and the Occupational Structure

The transformation of the content of work brought about by technological change was accompanied by a transformation in the occupational structure. The advances of the Industrial Revolution turned many a farmer into a machine operator in an urban factory. The statistics show this clearly. In 1820 about 70 per cent of the American population worked the farm. This proportion fell to about 40 per cent in 1900 and is presently less than 5 per cent (Thomlinson, 1965, p. 478).

In time fewer workers were needed for manual labour and more were needed for servicing, distributing and coordinating.

This has meant an enormous rise in paperwork, again reflected in aggregate figures. Whereas clerks constituted only 0.6 per cent of the labour force a hundred years ago (Mayer, 1956), they are now the largest occupational group, comprising one out of every five people (*Statistical Abstract*, 1973, table 373, p. 234). Furthermore, with coordination and administration of work becoming more complex, the proportion of nonfarm managers, officials and proprietors has risen from less than 6 per cent of the 1900 labour force to over 10 per cent in 1972, an increase of about 80 per cent (Thomlinson, 1965, p. 478; *Stastical Abstract*, 1973, table 373, p. 234).

Another significant shift is the increased demands for technical and professional workers. The growth of science and technology during the past few centuries has produced an explosion of knowledge. This in turn has created new occupations that require mastery of a complex body of specialised knowledge and skills. Agricultural societies, with their low level of technological development, needed only a small professional class. Precise figures on the size of this group in preindustrial America are not available, but it must have been small judging from its size in other preindustrial societies. Mexico in the 1940s had only 1 per cent of its work force in the professions, and Greece in the 1920s had only 3 per cent. In contrast, America had 14 per cent of all workers in professional and technical occupations in 1972 (*Statistical Abstract*, 1973, table 373, p. 234).

The point of all these statistics is that Americans are again living in the midst of a radical shift in the occupational structure of our society. Within the past two decades, America has become the first society with a majority of workers engaged in service occupations rather than in the production of foods and goods. A growing service economy also means that there will be a growth in the services of health, education, research and government. The growth of nonmanual service jobs has meant the increasing expansion of job opportunities for women. Whereas women make up less than a fifth of all production workers, they constitute half of the service sector (Fuchs, 1966, pp. 7 - 17). The continuing growth of the service sector and the expanding opportunities for women are bound to have an impact on the structure of the family, on women's views of themselves, and on the general definition of sex roles.

The Postindustrial Society

Some sociologists, notably Daniel Bell (1973) of Harvard, see this shift as evidence of a more profound change—the change from an industrial to *a postindustrial* society. This shift will usher in changes as profound as those produced in the change from an agricultural to an industrial society. Bell argues that it will although it is difficult to define precisely the nature of the changes that loom on the horizon. After all, it is only with the advantage of hindsight that we can begin to comprehend the nature of the extensive changes that industrialisation brought in its train.

Bell traces this momentous shift in the technological revolution that we have experienced since the Second World War. Whereas earlier inventions were typically produced by craftsmen or tinkerers unschooled in the principles of theoretical physics and chemistry, new technologies depend upon such specialised knowledge. The development of the machine was the central force in industrial society. In postindustrial society the central force will be the organisation of theoretical knowledge. Energy production drove industrial society; information production drives the postindustrial society. Economic growth was the goal of industrial society; advancement of theoretical knowledge is the new goal.

The leadership structure of industrial society will be replaced by new figures of dominance. "If the dominant figures of the past hundred years have been the entrepreneur, the businessman, and the industrial executive, the 'new men' are the scientists the mathematicians, the economists, and the engineers of the new intellectual technology" (Bell, 1973, p. 343). The class structure of postindustrial society will be based on access to information and control of decision-making rather than on ownership of property. Thus, the lower class will be defined not by their poverty but by their lack of knowledge that would give access to dominate organisations. The primary value of technological society is efficiency, which means greater output for less costs. In

Table 14.1
Preindustrial, Industrial and Postindustrial Society

	Preindustrial	*Industrial*	*Postindustrial*	
Regions:	Asia	Western Europe	United States	
	Africa	Soviet Union		
	Latin America	Japan		
Econmic	Primary	Secondary	Tertiary	Quaternary
Sector:	Extractive:	Goods producing.	Transportation	Trade
	Agriculture	Manufacturing	Utilities	Finance
	Mining	Processing		Insurance
	Fishing		Quinary	Real estate
	Timber		Health	
			Colucation	
			Research	
			Government	
			Recreation	
Occupational	Farmer	Semiskilled worker	Professional and technical	
Slope:	Miner	Engineer	Scientists	
	Fisherman			
	Unskilled			
	Worker			
Technology:	Raw materials	Energy	Information	
Design:	Game against	Game against	Game between persons	
	nature	fabricated nature		
Methodology:	Common sense	Empiricism	Abstract theory: models,	
	experience	Experimentation	simulation, decision theory,	
			systems analysis	
Time	Orientation	Ad hoc adaptiveness	Future orientation	
Perspective:	the past	Projections	Forecasting	
	Ad hoc			
	responses			
Axial	Traditionalism:	Economic growth:	Centrality of and codification	
Principle:	Land/resource	State or private	of theoretical knowledge	
	limitation	control of		
		investment decisions		

Source: Daniel Bell, *The Coming of the Post-Industrial Society* (New York: Basic Books, 1973). Table 1-1, p. 117.

order to promote efficiency, Bell argues, human activities are likely to be more bureaucratised. Postindustrial society will not be without its conflicts. Bell contends. The political system will stress the values of equality and popular participation, which contradict the values of hierarchy and subordination found in bureaucratic organisations. These two contradicting forces will generate conflict. There will also be contradictions between postindustrial culture and its social structure. Whereas the modern culture has stressed and will continue to stress the values of self-realization and self-fulfilment—the development of the whole person—the demands of a bureaucratised social structure will pressure people to conform to specialised roles. Thus, it is along these cleavages that postindustrial society will experience strain and conflict.

The Technological Society

According to French sociologist Jacques Ellul (1964), technology is like a virus. A virus perpetuates its strain by invading a cell, taking over its chemistry of reproduction, and causing it to stop producing its own kind and begin producing viruses. Similarly, "technique," or technology, takes over society and "dissociates the sociological forms, destroys the moral frame-work. . .explodes social and religious taboos, and reduces the body social to a collection of individual's" (p. 126).

This occurs because technology always seeks the most efficient way of performing tasks, no matter if it makes work less satisfying to the individual or fouls the environment or disrupts the social fabric. Trying to curb pollution with new technology (or correct other defects of technological progress) only compounds the problem since the criterion is still efficiency and the new technology has its own imperatives that may lead to equally unfortunate side effects. One of these imperatives is a tendency toward self-perpetuation and immunity from human control, so technology may proliferate if unchecked.

Technology is monolithic, Ellul argues. Although different techniques operate in the spheres of government economy, and culture, they do not compete with or impede one another because that would be inefficient. When clashes do occur, an efficient solution is worked out. The means of technology become ends. Thus, these spheres form a coordinated whole, dominating society and its mores.

Because of the importance of efficiency in a technological society, Ellul maintains there will be an increasing effort to limit the effects of human error and interference in technological progress. As a result techniques will be developed to manipulate behaviour through education, propaganda and psychology. Ellul suggests that although people will be unhappy about these encroachments on their freedom, they will not revolt, for unhappiness is just another technical problem. Instead, technique will devise one last ignominy, a human technology that will manipulate people into happiness or at least complacency. Thus, technique will become a tyrant, ruling human society with absolute power. "Inside the technical circle, the choice among methods, mechanisms, organisations and formulas is carried out automatically. Man is stripped of his faculty of choice and is satisfied. He accepts the situation when he sides with technique" (p. 82).

Two main perspectives, then, dominate speculation about the future of industrial society. One, represented by the Club of Rome or Ellul, is pessimistic, predicting increased government control, mechanisation, and dehumanisation. The other, represented by Bell, is more optimistic, citing the growth of knowledge, the increase of leisure, and greater diversity and individualism. Obviously, each is looking at somewhat different facts or interpreting some of the facts differently. What is clear is that industrial society is moving toward a new phase in which automation and other technological developments will become far more important and will engender significant social change.

15

Social Change

Ways of Thinking About Change

In order to explain social change we first need to describe it. The English language provides a number of different words to use in talking about change: development, progress, evolution, revolution, reaction, disintegration. Underlying these terms are certain dimensions that help us think about different kinds of social change.

1. *Scale.* Changes differ in the magnitude or scope of their impact. A town mayor might order the desegregation of the towns' public places, but certainly this is on a very small scale compared to a Supreme Court ruling on desegregation.
2. *Duration.* Change, by definition, occurs over a period of time. Some changes occur within a short time; others take centuries to be completed.
3. *Continuity.* Some changes represent a continuation in the basic pattern of activity; others are discontinuous, sharply breaking away from old patterns and establishing new ones. Instituting martial law and suspending electoral politics would mark a discontinuous break from our political traditions, whereas shortening the campaign period or limiting the amount of campaign funds would not.
4. *Direction.* Sometimes what seems like rapid change turns out to be a repeating set of activities that form a cyclical pattern. Many of these correspond to the biological and

astronomical rhythms of nature—the cycles of night and day, of the moon, and of the seasons. Thus, farmers sow in the spring, reap in the fall, and rest in the winter—each season bringing its own pressures and rituals in predictable succession year after year.

Other changes show a linear, or straight line, progression from one stage to the next. Many trend changes are of this type. For example, cities have grown in number, size, and influence over the past several thousand years. Still other changes appear to be random because the direction of change is not always easy to discern. This difficulty is especially pronounced when the changes are long-term and on a large scale. Thus, some observers assert that Western civilisation has been on a decline for the past several centuries; others assert that there has been continuous progress; and still others see history repeating itself in cycles.

Theories of Social Change

Explaining particular events by identifying particular causes or isolating particular features is helpful, but social scientists have tried to develop general theories to explain social change and social stability. We need to understand the forces that produce regularity and persistence in patterns of social behaviour before we can fully understand the dynamic aspects. The past Chapters have shown that sociologists have not yet been able to fomulate their understanding of social stability into an organised set of abstract principles. It is, therefore, impossible to present a single unified theory of social change (Appelbaum, 1970; see Moore, 1963, and Etzioni-Halevy and Etzioni, 1973, for a review of the theories).

Evolutionary Theories

Prior to the eighteenth century, Europeans tended to understand change in religious terms: man is born into his station and occupies it by divine providence. Radical changes come about only by exceptional withdrawals and bestowals of divine grace. With the Industrial Revolution change rather than fixity became the outstanding feature of social life (Lewontin, 1968). The discovery of simpler and seemingly more primitive societies in other parts of the world also challenged people to account for the vast differences in human societies. The earliest popular explanation held that the primitives represented an earlier, evolutionary stage and that the more complex societies of eighteenth- and nineteenth-century Europe were in more advanced stages of development. A natural fact of social life, change had a direction: from simple societies to more complex and differentiated one. And as wealth multiplied it was clear that change must mean progress. Change was seen as good. Much of the earliest social philosophy carried this strong moralistic undercurrent.

In the nineteenth century, social thinking became less philosophical and more empirical. Much of the debate focused on what caused evolutionary change—some arguing for new ideas, inventions, discoveries; others for class struggles or conflict (Service, 1968).

Emile Durkheim identified the cause of societal evolution as a society's increasing "moral density". (Durkheim, 1964). Simple societies have a relatively undifferen-tiated social structure, with minimal division of labour among members of the same society. People share a common set of values, and these values provide the chief source of solidarity among members. Durkheim called this kind of moral cohesion "mechanical solidarity".

As the population grows, resources become scarcer and division of labour increases in order to exploit these scarce resources efficiently. The society becomes differentiated into increasingly specialised units, which are more dependent upon each other—"organic solidarity". Social differentiation multiplies, common values decrease, the fragmented social order then requires more formal means to hold it together. Civil law and a central government are among the institutions that help societies cohere in the face of growing change and diversity. In sum, Durkheim viewed societies as changing in the direction of greater differentiation, interdependence, and formal control under the pressure of an increasing moral density. Durkheim, of course, is but one of a number of evolutionary theorists; E.B. Tylor, L.H. Morgan, Herbert Spencer, Saint-Simon, A. Compte, and Karl Marx offered different explanations for the evolutionary impulse in societies.

Cyclical Theories

With the onslaught of World War I many thinkers were much less sure that societies were in fact advancing. It was perhaps more accurate to view societies and civilisations as passing through inevitable cycles of development and decay. This theme was announced with immediate impact in 1926 by Oswald Spengler in *Decline of the West*. Cultures are destined, in his view, to follow a course of growth and decline in much the same way that individual men's live do. But Spengler's explanation was more poetic than scientific. His appeal was to cosmic destiny rather than finite causes.

Arnold Toynbee's massive, multivolume *A Study of History* (1946) is, on the other hand, a detailed and concrete comparative history of civilisations. While fault has been found with his analyses on many points, Toynbee's significant contribution is his method, which applies key specific questions to each of the twenty-one major civilisations of past and present that he chose for study.

> Toynbee's volumes ask four main questions, each with numerous subquestions. The first concerns the genesis of civilisation: What are the conditions which allow or stimulate the rise of civilisations—the conversion of what had been preliterate, simple, more or less lethargic peoples into the kinds of civilisation of which the classical, the Indian, the Chinese, and the Mayan are notable types? Second, what are the factors involved in the expansion and development, in what Toynbee calls the "growths" of these civilisations? Third, what accounts for the breakdowns of civilisations, that is, the conversion of what had been for centuries a highly dynamic, innovative, intrepid, and enterprising people into one characterised by mere routinisation and repetition of the old? Fourth, what leads to the disintegration of historical civilisations, the passing into nothingness or atavistic primitivism of civilisations? (Nisbet, 1970, p. 353)

In answering these questions for individual cultures, Toynbee developed several partial theories. One key explanation for social change was his concept of challenge and response: a civilisation's accomplishments are its particular responses to the specific physical and social challenges posed by its environment.

When a civilisation can no longer respond to challenges, it rigidifies and atrophies.

Pitirim Sorokin's work (1941) has had a more lasting impact on sociological thinking. Rather than viewing civilisations in terms of development and decline, this exiled Russian scholar proposed that they alternate between two extreme configurations, the sensate and the ideational. In the *sensate* phase everything points to that which can be experienced directly. The emphasis in art is on the representational; in philosophy the emphasis is on rationalism and objectivism. What matters above all for this world view is direct senses. By contrast, *ideational cultures* are typified by the opposite values; truth lies beyond the reach of the senses, inaccessible to human reason. Religion stresses the reality of the other world, as a super rational God, Brahman, Atman, or Tao. Art is abstract and philosophy is oriented to issues of faith and belief. As the culture of a society develops toward one pure type, it is countered by the opposing cultural force. Cultural development is then reversed, moving toward the opposite type of culture. Societies contain both impulses in varying degree, and the tension between them creates long-term instability.

Equilibrium Theories

In the middle decades of the twentieth century many American sociologists shifted their curiosity away from trying to understand social change and focused on how to explain social stability. One of Sorokin's students at Harvard, Talcott Parsons, took over Sorokin's interest in cultural development and stressed the central importance of cultural patterns in controlling the *stability* of a society (1951, 1966). In Parsons's view society has the ability to absorb disruptive forces while maintaining overall stability because it is a dynamic system straining for equilibrium.

The idea of society as a system in equilibrium derives from an analogy made between societies and biological organisms. Each of the specialised parts of an organism is continually active, but all the different changes within the parts are coordinated and integrated so that the total organism is relatively the same from one day to the next. The counterpart of these organs are the specialised structures of society, or its subsystems.

Box 15.1

In the News

Cultural Lag Then and Now

Cars. The material basis of the free and-easy, go-where-you-want character of latterday American culture. Agents of the ordinary citizens' liberation from the structures of geography. Life for most Americans rests as much today on the internal-combustion revolution of the twentieth century as on the political revolutions of the eighteenth.

Yet, when cars were first introduced, the cry was, "get a horse," as people passed the driver of a houseless carriage cranking up his new-fangled machine. The mayor of a major American city officially stated that no woman was physically able to undertake the complicated and strenuous operation of driving an automobile. Such reactions are an example of *cultural lag,* a term coined by William F. Ogburn to describe the problem that arises when one part of a culture changes before the other parts have a chance to adapt. Material culture (inventions, artifacts) are much more apt to change rapidly than nonmaterial culture (beliefs, values, laws) creating a period of disequilibrium. Before we dismiss the quaint ideas of our grandparents and great-grandparents about the auto, we might look at some of our own ideas for symptoms of a new instance of cultural lag. Today the old cry rings again.

"Fight pollution, ride a horse," read a sign noticed by a visitor at a shopping center. . .The sign was affixed to the bumper of a car spewing out hydrocarbons, carbon monoxide and nitrogen oxides. . . Like virtually all technological developments, the automobile has its bad side. . .Destruction and mutilation, measured in the familiar statistics of highway deaths. Choking frustrating traffic jams. Automobile graveyards, the ugly debris of affluence. Freeway spaghetti that disfigures cities. And air pollution.

Now for the first time since Henry Ford began mass-producing Model T's in 1908, the automobile-based way of life is being directly challenged. With the express aim of reducing air pollution, the Federal Government has proposed to restrict automobile traffic in some 30 metropolitan areas across the country.

The reaction to such proposals as banning autos one day a week or reducing the number of parking spaces employers provide has been predictably vehement.

Box 15.1 Contd.

When a Bostor City Councilman heard of the proposed ban on driving, he woved that no one was going to tell him where or when to drive his car. . . "Without a car you're nowhere," they say in Phoenix.

The American love affair with the auto is probably the largest obstacle to the solution of air pollution today—a clear case of cultural lag. Trying to solve environmental problems by removing the center of a highly integrated cultural complex is bound to create disequilibrium and tension.

Source: William K. Stevens, "Nation Dependent on Car is Resentful of Curbs Planned as Pollution Check," *The New York Times* (July 15, 1973): 1, 54.

Parsons asserts that each of the subsystems in a society performs a different function. The economic structures adapt a society to its physical environment. Changes in the environment therefore produce changes in the economic structures. Political structures are the means of setting and attaining the society's goals. The family instils the prevailing cultural patterns into the new members of society. The church and state are the cultural subsystems and ensure the society's integration and coordination. Because cultural patterns (or basic values) change very slowly, the cultural subsystem is the crucial force for ensuring the continuity of society. Changes in the economic or political systems tend to be slowed down as they come up against the more steadfast cultural system. Because cultural systems tend toward stability rather than continual development (as in Sorokin's model), change in the social system must come from forces outside the system—perhaps from its environment. Overall change in the social system must therefore involve cultural change, and this kind of major change is, in Parson's view, infrequent.

Conflict Theories

Whereas the equilibrium theories emphasise the integrative and stabilising processes at work in social systems, the so-called conflict theories highlight the forces producing instability, struggle and social disorganisation. Ralf Dahrendorf, a German sociologist who has become a leading figure in his country's political life, pinpoints the differences between these two broad types of theories of social change (Dahrendorf, 1973, p. 103). According to his view the equilibrium theories assume that:

1. every society is a relatively persisting configuration of elements;
2. every society is a well-integrated configuration of elements;
3. every element in a society contributes to its functioning;
4. every society rests on the consensus of its members.

Conflict theories on the other hand, assume that:

1. every society is subjected at every moment to change; social change; is ubiquitous;
2. every society experiences at every moment social conflict; social conflict is ubiquitous;
3. every element in a society contributes to its change;
4. every society rests on constraint of some of its members by others.

Dahrendorf sees the unequal distribution of power and authority as the fundamental source of conflict in a society. Those persons or groups with power want to preserve the *status quo*. This puts them in conflict with the subordinate groups, whose interest is to change the *status quo*. Organised interest groups emerge in each of the two broad classes, and these interest groups struggle over numerous issues. This conflict can lead to various changes in the society's structure if dominance relations are changed. The nature, speed and depth of the conflict and the resulting change depend on numerous variable conditions.

By far the most famous and influential of the conflict theories is that of Karl Marx. In his extensive writings on sociology, politics, economics, history and philosophy, Marx developed a theory of such complexity and subtlety that it resists summarisation. To outline his theory of social change in the broadest of strokes, Marx (1932) saw all societies up to his time as arenas for class struggles. He understood the source of these struggles not to be power but rather the essential foundation of power—the control of a society's resources and productive facilities. Societies have therefore been split into two main camps—owners and nonowners. In ancient societies the split was between master and slave; in feudal societies, between lord and serf; in capitalist societies, between bourgeoisie (industrial owner) and proletariat (industrial worker). Throughout history those groups of families who have maintained control over a society's productive forces have either created or supported whole political systems, laws, religious beliefs, and philosophies to justify and continue their dominance. Representatives of these two opposing classes struggle against each other in ideological, political and economic battles. In times of economic crisis the struggle becomes more sharply drawn, and the cleavage between classes becomes more apparent. The lower class becomes increasingly impoverished. Activists stimulate their brethren to become aware of their true class interest, of their solidarity with their fellow workers or fellow owners, thereby developing a "class con-sciousness". Acting in a self-conscious fashion members of the oppressed class muster their forces, develop new ideas about how to organise society, and battle the dominant class in the political or military arena. Marx envisioned that these class divisions would disappear after the final socialist victory (coming after the maturing of capitalist society), when control over the resources and the productive forces is socialised—that is, distributed equally among all of the society's members.

Revolution : The American Case

Marx understood a revolution to be a casting off of an established political order and the creation of new forms of government, of new patterns of power-holding. Indeed, most people think of a revolution as a large-scale upheaval creating a discontinuity in the politics of a society. Revolutionaries typically intend not to correct a limited number of specific ills but to make broad and idealistically inspired changes. A true revolution involves mass mobilisation and mass participation. The *crop d'état* (sometimes called a palace revolution), which occurs throughout the Third World in the present day, is not revolutionary unless it involves the masses and radically restructures the forms of government. Neither are "revolutionary" achievements proclaimed by presidents or premiers when they succeed in some new national venture.

The upheaval of revolution is not an entirely disorganised event. Historian Crane Brinton (1966) studied four revolutions–the English of the seventeenth century, the American and French of the eighteenth, and the Russian of the twentieth—and constructed a hypothetical model for other revolutions. He cautions that this model may not apply to *all* revolutions but only to those mass uprisings in the modern period of Western civilisation that have been undertaken in the name of freedom for an oppressed minority, and that have ended in the successful transfer of power.

The revolution begins when the dissatisfied groups press their claims for power and are ineffectively opposed by force. The old regime falls. With the fall of the old regime, moderates rules for a period. Extremists then rise to power and initiate a reign of terror that is coupled with an almost religious fervor and claim to virtue. There then occurs a reaction to extremist rule and a counterrevolution that reinforces the basis principles of the original revolutionaries. This moderating reaction (known as *Thermidor*, from the month of the revolutionary French calendar in which the equivalent reaction stage of that country's revolution was initiated) is typically ushered in by a dictator.

These then are the stages of revolution. We are all familiar with the chronology of the American Revolution but can Brinton help us understand why it happened there and why it happened than?

The Reluctant Revolution

The American Revolution seemed to start quite by accident. Americans had grown accustomed to the sight of the red-jacketed British troops, even though they didn't like their presence. After all, two regiments had been stationed in Boston Harbour for nearly six years. But when the troops were seen setting out from Boston, it was understood that they were heading toward Concord, where the volunteer army of the Massachusetts colony stored their meager supply of guns and ammunition. Paul Revere rode through the night to notify his comrades, and now the Massachusetts militia was gathered in the town of Lexington on the route from Boston to Concord. After several restless hours, the first British troops came in sight. Captain Parker stationed his seventy lightly armed farmers on the green, where they might be seen and heard by the passing soldiers but would not be engaged. The troops on both sides, however, broke ranks and firing began before the commanders regained control (Morgan, 1956).

While the skirmish was an accident, the times had all the ingredients for an outbreak, confirming Brinton's conditions that characterise a pre-revolutionary situation.

1. Revolutionists are not a deprived and oppressed segment of the population; rather, they are relatively well-off, respectable members of society, who recognise the problems and relative deprivations in the situation and have hopes of achieving economic and civil freedoms.
2. The established rulers are, at the same time, disorganised, weak, and divided among themselves. Consequently they are indecisive and contradictory in policy, and lacking in self-confidence. Indecisive policy produces confusion and economic instability, and this creates a noticeable weakness that the revolutionists feel encouraged to take advantage of. Defensive measures taken by the weakened rulers are ineffective, or come too late. And many members of the hitherto ruling class, moreover, recognise their disorganisation and the validity in protest.
3. Since the immediate cause of the crisis is a weakened and ineffectual government, the aim of the revolutionists is to change not only the individuals but the forms of government to protect their interests.
4. Intellectuals desert the cause of the old regime, depriving it of its ideological legitimacy.

This was indeed the pattern that led to the skirmish at Lexington. Middle-class Americans, threatened economically with taxes imposed suddenly by the English Parliament, wanted a return to the period of tax colonial administration. In the decade prior to the revolution, England relaxed, then stiffened its demands in order to bring the colonists into line as these efforts failed, England resorted to even more repressive policies. Each of these measures was received by the Americans as a new imposition, a removal of a freedom they had once enjoyed and were now being deprived of. The colonies, which among themselves had not been able to agree on boundaries or mutual aid during Indian attacks, were able to unite around the principle of "no taxation without representation" in opposition to British policies and government. But centuries of tradition could not be overcome easily, and even after Concord and Lexington leading colonists still hoped to reach an agreement with the king. George III himself forced their hand, declaring the colonies in rebellion. And a recently arrived Englishman, Thomas Paine, in his rapidly circulated pamphlet, Common-sense, established the philosophical justification for revolution. He noted that there was no natural reason for any man to be "so exalted above the rest, and distinguished like some new species," as was the king. He further demonstrated that "nothing but misery has come from kings." Americans, well schooled in English history, recalled that English kings had been deposed twice in the preceding century; here was their precedent. They recalled John Locke's assertions that men band together of their own free will in social and governing groups for the specific purpose of protecting themselves and their property. They recognised the corollary that any government that was neither functioning with the consent of the governed nor fulfilling its intended purpose could, and should, be replaced. The basis for continued allegiance to George III was demolished, and the intellectual validation for revolution was established.

Was There a Thermidor?

Although the events leading up the revolution and even those following the break with England accord well with Brinton's model, scholars still argue about the existence of a period analogous to the French counter-revolution during Thermidor following the excesses of extremist reforms and terror. One school of American historians (called revisionists) see the replacement of the Articles of Confederation by the Constitution as a *coup d'état* by propertied conservatives. Another school, the dominant one, sees the framers of the Constitution not as the betrayers of the revolution but rather as its saviors. This issue largely revolves around the character of the government created by the Articles. Was it an effective government, protecting the rights of individuals against a tyrannical government, or was the government unable to function, threatening the collapse of the Union (Morgen, 1956; Craven, 1973)?

The Critical Period

The Articles of Confederation provided for the unification of the colonies - and then states – under a very weak central government. They protected the power of the states, and did not provide for enforcing any provisions should a state decide not to cooperate.

Following the Revolutionary War the nation was saddled with a war debt, which the Congress successfully reduced through the voluntary contributions of most (though not all) states. The Articles also resolved the problems of disposing of the vast lands to the west, which had previously belonged to the English, by providing that these lands belonged to the national government and not to the individual states they might adjoin, and that new separate states might be created within specific limitations of area, which would have the same rights as other states.

But economic problems abounded, triggered by rampant inflation. In Rhode Island a depreciating paper currency was made legal tender and hordes of happy debtors were paying off their obligations with worthless bills, leaving their creditors bankrupt. As a postwar depression continued, the problems of businessmen became acute. Due to a lack of centralised authority, however, Congress was powerless to come to their aid. In 1986 Virginia suggested a convention to work for a general interstate agreement to regulate commerce. Delegates from five states met that September, and without waiting for other delegates to arrive, they took a giant step and adopted a resolution calling for a general convention to be held at Philadelphia in May of the following year. The purpose of the convention was expressly stated to be a modification of the federal constitution. All states but Rhode Island were represented at the convention in Philadelphia; and the Constitution of the United States was the result.

Thermidor

The revisionist historians agree that there were problems in the political arrangements designed by the Articles but insist that they were not serious enough to warrant its overthrow and replacement by a strong central government. In his classic study entitled *An Economic Interpretation of the Constitution of the United States* (1949). Charles Beard examined the financial holdings of the framers of the Constitution and found that most had invested in public securities of the United States and therefore stood to gain by strengthening public credit. He also examined the political beliefs of the framers and concluded that many were distrustful of the popular masses and therefore designed a political system in the Constitution that safeguarded their property rights.

No Thermidor

Other historians maintain that the Union was on the verge of collapse and that the inflation and depression of the postwar years threatened the ability of the government to protect private property - certainly one of the central principles of the revolution. Moreover, giving the powers of remote corners of the world, people are hungry for the fruits of an industrial economy and are pushing for a rapid – even revolutionary – transformation of their society. Up until the past few centuries there existed hundreds, and perhaps thousands, of local societies that went about their business pretty much the same way day after day. Most were subsistence economies, living either by nomadic hunting and gathering or by sedentary agriculture. But the societies created by the bourgeois revolutions in North America and western Europe have been expansive. In their search for resources to fuel their economic development, they have penetrated these once-traditional and isolated societies and introduced them to the trappings of modern life. Much of the non-Western world was colonised and brought into this worldwide market system – although the colonies (most ex-colonies now) maintained many of their traditional ways while supplying raw materials to the Western industries. From a distance many of these people saw the riches that industrialism produced. And the native elites in these colonies and former colonies often had a chance to see modern capitalist societies from the inside as they came to London, Paris, or New York for their education. Their appetites whetted for manufactured riches and comforts, different peoples all over the world began trying to transform their nations into modern societies. *Modernisation* is usually understood to mean a change toward the type of societies found in the advanced industrial countries. These changes include not only an industrialised economy but a complete transformation of the political, social and psychological spheres.

1. Political modernisation – Modernization means the consolidation of policy-making in a centralised state bureaucracy (Black, 1968). The state expands its activities and absorbs functions once carried out by other traditional structures, such as the family and the church. In America and western Europe political centralisation and the development of democratic traditions went together. Societies that have more recently embarked on a crash course of industrialisation have had a difficult time promoting rapid social transformation within a democratic political structure. But even in those nondemocratic states undergoing modernisation, there is a need for the state to seek popular legitimacy rather than relying on more traditional forms of legitimation (such as appealing to the divine right of kings). Popular legitimation is usually sought and created through the organisation of mass political parties (Eisenstadt, 1966).

2. Social modernisation – Modernisation also means the following changes in social structure: intensive urbanisation; the growth of large-scale and often bureaucratic organisations; levelling of income, education, and opportunity; extension of literacy; extension of communication systems and mass media; improvements in health care; and social mobilisation, which is the process whereby commitments to traditional economic, political, and social roles are loosened. This makes the individual susceptible to new values, new socialisation patterns, and new commitments. In the political sphere this usually means the replacement of local allegiances with an allegiance to the nation as a whole (Deutsch, 1953).

3. Psychological modernisation – People who live in modern societies are change oriented. Less suspicious of novelty, they are more present and future-oriented rather than backward-looking and bound to tradition. Modern men and women have typically cast off the fatalistic attitudes prevalent in more rigid societies and have acquired a faith that they can dominate their environment. They are, therefore, oriented to planning and organising. There is also a tendency to hold opinions over a wide range of issues reaching beyond local matters. Of course, this is associated with expanding mass media and a rising educational and literacy level in the population (Inkeles, 1966).

Box 15.2

Modernisation and IboTraditions

Tradition refers to the customary set of behaviours and symbols of a society. It is not the same as traditionalism, which is a reactionary attitude that involves holding on to some parts of old traditions as a bulwark, or cushion, against new trends. The examples of societies in which traditionalism has hindered change are legion. But it is also possible for a modernizing society to retain strong traditions without this necessarily being traditionalism.

Among the Ibo of Nigeria, for example, tradition *aided* modernisation. The Ibo thronged to urban centers and eagerly entered white-collar and mercantile occupations. They embraced education as a means to advancement. They have been especially active politically, to the extent of establishing their own independent nation. When the Biafran war was lost, the Ibo were reabsorbed into the Nigerian economic and political structure with relative speed. Ibo history and custom account for many of these accomplishments.

Traditionally the Ibo have encouraged individual achievement, and virtually everyone could hope to gain prestige by working diligently and using their abilities effectively. The groupings of Ibo society – villages, familes, and age and secret societies – competed against each other for wealth and prestige. Following colonisation, the Ibo

Box 15.2 Contd.

recognised the value of acquiring British skills, and substituted new forms of prestige – owning European possessions, working for the government, and sending children to school – for the old ones. Villages competed in having better markets and in sending their sons to school. Individuals who achieved wealth, position, and education added to the prestige of the groups to which they belonged. Experience in a verity of societies – age grades, secret societies, men's groups, work groups – prepared the Ibo for trade and labour organisations and political societies. A tradition of leadership by a council of elders laid the foundation for those kills that are required for work in legislative councils and other cooperative units of government.

The Ibo had other important features that aided in modernisation; high population density and, consequently mobility. Groups and families moved to new villages, and communities absorbed newcomers – traditions that facilitated not only movement to the cities but also that key requisite for urban existence; the ability to get along with others. For several centuries and perhaps longer, change itself has been a feature of Ibo culture. This, and the many traditions that aided their adoption of European behaviour and values, has enabled the Ibo to participate successfully in the modernisation of Nigeria.

Source : Ottenberg, 1959, pp. 130–43; Uchendo, 1965.

The changes that occur during the period of modernisation can be grouped into certain general categories. *Structural differentiation* is the reorganisation of family, economic, religious, and other units into more specialised smaller units or substructures. *Integration* refers to the development of interrelationships among the new substructures that replace the now-obsolete network that existed around the old social units. *Social disturbances* of various sorts results from the unevenness of the differentiation and integration processes (Smelser, 1973).

Strains of Rapid Modernisation

The modernisation of America and western Europe took place slowly over the course of two centuries. Leaders of developing countries feel they cannot wait that long; they want to accomplish the transformation within a matter of years. After all, didn't Russia manage to build an industrial economy within a few decades following its 1917 revolution? But rapid social transformation involves great dislocation and strains, and it tends to produce widespread feelings of rootlessness, anomie, outbreaks of mass hysteria and violence (Elsenstadt, 1966).

The sources of *imbalanced* growth and strain are legion. Populations moving into the cities need jobs; the economy must expand correspondingly. Rapid economic growth requires importing at least some technology from the more advanced countries. The labour force must therefore be trained rapidly to operate this imported technology; universities must churn out skilled people. But the graduates coming out of the universities must find work of they tend to become articulate dissenters and even revolutionaries. A new pace of life and new time schedules must be learned. Long training, regular performance, punctuality, and precision in work are things many people just off the farm are not accustomed to. All want the fruits of modernity now, but they must sacrifice for the future because resources must be channelled into building steelworks and highways rather than into manufacturing consumer goods. The expansion of health facilities lowers the death rate, thereby increasing the population size, and this threatens to outstrip any economic gains.

When modernisation occurs slowly over a long period of time, new political systems, new value systems, new economic systems and new personalities have a chance to adjust to one another gradually. These changing patterns reinforce each other, smoothly replacing the traditional ways of life with new and, more importantly, *integrated* patterns of social organisation. In contrast, overnight modernisation is a powerful solvent tending to produce *social disintegration*. The glue that holds traditional society together looses its adhesive powers. Governmental coordination and control of these large-scale changes become all the more necessary. Because the armed forces of these societies are often the most cohesive institutions capable of planning and organising large-scale efforts, many modernising societies experience takeovers by their armies.

Mass Society

Sociologists have characterised this kind of loosely integrated social organisation as *mass society*. Masses are huge numbers of people who are not integrated into any broad social groupings or social classes (Kornnauser, 1959, p. 14). The most significant division of the population is between an organised elite and an unorganised, atomised mass. Elites are susceptible to influence by the masses, and the masses are readily available for mobilisation by the elites. In the name of an abstract concept the masses can be goaded into action – even violent action – by a charismatic leader. Mass behaviour is associated with the separation of symbols from their real meaning and content, and with an increasing reliance on force to resolve social conflicts (Selznick, 1951, p. 329).

> A rather unflattering and ominous picture of mass man was painted by José Ortegay Gasset, a Spanish aristocrat saddened by the loss of traditional European culture and society. Writing in the 1930s, at the time when Germany and Italy were experiencing breakdowns in their modernising efforts (fertilising the ground for fascism), he noted:
>
> The ordinary man, hitherto guided by others, has resolved to govern the world himself. . .The psychological structure of this new type of mass-man. . .is as follows: (1) An inborn, root-impression that life is easy, plentiful, without any grave limitations; consequently, each average man finds within himself a sensation of power and triumph which (2) invites him to stand up for himself as he is, to look upon his moral and intellectual endowment as excellent, complete. This contentment with himself leads him to shut himself off from any external court of appeal; not to listen, not to submit his opinions to judgment not to consider other's existence. His intimate feeling of power urges him always to exercise predominance. He will act then as if he and his like were the only beings existing in the world: and, consequently (3) will intervene in all matters, imposing his own vulgar views without respect or regard for others, without limit or reserve, that is to say, in accordance with a system of "direct action" (1957, p. 97).

An alternative to mass society is the development of a political system that allows for effective participation of the population. One such organisation is that found in the more democratic countries – one in which the people participate in mass political parties, form organised interest groups to express their particular goals, and have a national forum to reconcile these different interests. But such a political system requires that all parties agree to play by the rules of the game. This in turn requires that the various political groups have a reasonably large set of common interests. This kind of consensus is difficult to build in societies undergoing rapid transformation, and it is especially difficult when a society is faced with economic stagnation or breakdown. This is why democratic governments are falling by the wayside throughout Latin America, Africa, Southeast Asia, the Middle East, and even southern Europe.

America Tomorrow

To many of the world's peoples the urban industrial nations are a sort of grand mirror – a mirror in which they can see a reflection of their own future. In this reflection they see darker - skinned people, but the cars, televisions, telephones, flush toilets, and airplanes are essentially the same. But what is the image of America's future? We have no mirrors; nevertheless, we can see forces that are at work shaping our society.

More of the Same? The Affluent Society

One group of analysts looking into the sociological crystal ball foresees a society of continued affluence. "Post-1984 America" has been described by Lee Rainwater (1972) as being more urbanised, suburban-dwelling, educated and affluent. The median family income will be at least $ 16,000 a year, an increase of more than 50 per cent over the 1972 median. However, all classes will share in the increased income in about the same proportions, so there will still be the same class distinctions and social problems that see the poorest 20 per cent of the population earning less than 5 per cent of the money income. The poor and minority group members will still have significantly less of every thing.

Increased urbanisation and communication will expose "the average citizen to a much wider range of information, and a much wider range of perspectives for interpreting that information [and he or she] . . . is therefore likely to be less insulated from national and worldwide trends in taste, style and innovation than has ever been true." Affluence and cosmopolitanism will combine to permit greater pluralism and a multiplicity of life-styles. This will be particularly true for the upper-middle class, who are more affluent and cosmopolitan than the lower classes, and whose "orientation toward living has always been self-sufficiency and the pursuit of self-gratification. . .[along with a] propensity toward elaborate life style innovations" (Rainwater, 1972, p. 28).

Paradoxically, there will not be more leisure. People become busier the more affluent they are. With time limited and goods and services expensive, people will choose "activities that seem to provide more gratification per time unit." Daily life will become "commodity and service intensive" (Rainwater, 1972, p. 25). The individual's time will become so valuable that it will be more efficient to depend on specialised delivery of services by others. The need for services both to the household level and in the public sector will increase.

Less of the Same? The Scarcity Society

Affluence depends upon continued economic growth. The resources needed for that growth are not infinite – a fact that casts a more ominous pall upon predictions of the future. During the past few years we have become increasingly conscious that our environment can absorb only so much waste without seriously threatening our own existence. And the raw materials drawn from the nonindustrial nations are no longer as cheap as before. Seeing their nonreplaceable resources sucked into the industrial machines of the advanced economies, many of the developing nations are beginning to demand a larger return for their contribution. Oil-producing countries have joined together in a producers' alliance to cooperate in raising the price of oil to industrial nations. Other producers of raw materials are following this example and are forging cooperative associations to raise their incomes. The leaders of these nations are motivated by the desire to build their countries into more economically independent and affluent societies. International tensions have increased as the domestic economies of industrial nations have felt the pinch. These developments, coupled with several other economic trends, have aggravated inflation and unemployment, both of which threaten political stability in many of the advanced industrial nations. William Ophuls has written:

> Virtually all the philosophies, values and institutions typical of modern capitalist society – the legitimacy of self-interest, the primacy of the individual and his inalienable rights, economic *laissez-faire,* and democracy as we know it – are the luxuriant fruit of an era of apparently endless abundance. They cannot continue to exist in their current form once we return to the more normal conditions of scarcity. (Ophuls, 1974, p. 47).

Political stability in America depends partly on reducing the inequalities of caste and class, which, in turn, depends on economic growth. Even with the economy operating at full employment (that is, with no more than about 4 per cent unemployment), it would take about thirty years for the disparity of incomes between white and black families to disappear (Guthrie, in Rainwater, 1972, p. 27). Rising unemployment increases this disparity. Blacks tend to be the last hired and the first fired. When jobs are plentiful, blacks make rapid gains; when jobs decline, as they must in a world of scarcity, black unemployment rises much faster than white joblessness. Scarcity could irritate a potentially explosive condition.

Inflation also generates anxieties that undermine confidence in a country's economic and political systems. Rising consumer prices hit hardest at the poor, who spend a greater percentage of their incomes on food and housing. Inflation devalues the worth of retirement pensions and savings, which people depend on for their security in old age. At a 10 per cent annual inflation rate, the value of savings or a pension is halved in a mere seven years. Unable to plan secure futures, people sometimes withdraw support from governments. Referring to the democratic western European societies, Flora Lewis, a *New York Times* reporter wrote in 1974:

> The marked trend has been to turn away from recognised leaders and to call out unhappily for other leadership. It is not yet a crisis of democracy, but it is a sagging of confidence that the systems of government that have fostered prosperity can cope with the new economic problems.

The Counterculture: A Force for Change?

A shift away from overconsumption and unbridled industrialism has been part of the programme of a small but visible minority that arose during the 1960s in opposition to the war in Southeast Asia, to government, and to many of the established values of the society. Radical politics grew up hand in hand with a change in life-styles. Sexual mores were liberalised, respect declined for organised religion, government, law, conventional patriotism, the police, and the boss on the job.

The sudden growth of the counterculture piqued the interest of a number of social scientists, among them Philip Slater (1970). Theodore Roszak (1969) and Charles Reich (1970). The puzzle was how a society could produce what seemed its very antithesis. Among several complex sources of potential conflict within our culture, two stand out in their analyses: the permissive, child-centered family, and the contradictions between worker-consumer roles.

The youth-centered family ill prepares youngsters for the regimentation they will find in the technocratic world. From a home life centered around satisfying juvenile needs and whims, frequently at the subjugation of parents' needs, these sheltered, pampered young people are thrust into lower-echelon positions in enormous, impersonal corporate structures. In the view of Slater, adults are generous, good-natured, indulgent toward their children but "ruthless toward the non-human environment . . . [and] when the child grows up he discovers the fraud" (1970), p. 47). Reich sees the counterculture, which he calls Consciousness III, as "the product of two interacting forces: The promise of life that is made to young Americans by all of our affluence, technology, liberation and ideals and the threat to that promise posed by everything from neon ugliness to boring jobs to the Vietnam war and the shadow of nuclear holocaust" (1970, p. 234). It is the conflict between the ideals they grow up on and the ugly realities they must face at the threshold of adulthood that account for the "turning off" of youth and the development of a distinctive youth culture.

Adult roles also contain an inherent contradiction. The same individual is a worker and a consumer, both of which are crucial to the economy. But as Reich analyses it, "The overpersuaded consumer may no longer be a willing worker. To have consumers for its ever-increasing flow of products, the corporate state must have individuals who live for hedonistic pleasures, constant change, and expanding freedom. To have workers for its system of production, the state must have individuals who are ever more self-denying, self-disciplined, and narrowly confined" (1970, p. 208). For young adults accustomed to life as consumers, the contradiction is heightened. As Reich points out: "When the consumer-worker contradiction . . . hits middle-class youth, it helps to produce a rejection of the whole ethic of the middle class. . . The end product of the overpampered consumer society may well be a person who reacts against pampering, a rootless and truly liberated individual, one who ultimately threatens the corporate state" (1970, pp. 209, 219).

The Impact of the Counterculture

Participants in the counterculture have reacted against society, but was the corporate state ever really threatened? There are some who say the counterculture has already faded away, citing the quiet that now prevails on college campuses and the return to educational commitments. In this view the highly visible and audible youth of a few years past have entered maturity and are tackling the practical problems of adulthood, having learned by experience to accept the majority outlook. But, have they really?

Since the early 1970s the movement's thrust for political change has been blunted (if not completely repressed), but the broader cultural changes have been absorbed by the mainstream of America's youth. A survey by Daniel Yankelovich concluded that:

> Radical political values and life styles, values which travelled together since the mid-1960's, have, in 1971, begun to go their separate ways. Changing cultural values – relationships to marriage, authority, religion, work, money, career, sexual morality, and other aspects of the puritan ethic – have become more marked and dramatic each year since these measurements began, including 1971, while political beliefs have moved in the opposite direction

> away from the 1970 peaks. . . The vast majority of students—the 89 per cent who do not identify with the New Left – have pressed forward in their search for a cultural revolution while taking a step backwards from political revolution. (1971, p. 7).

The manner by which these counterculture values have been absorbed by the larger society is described in Yankelovich's 1974 study as a "case history of cultural diffusion".

> Social change is often initiated by small extremist groups. The mass of the public reacts initially by rejecting the new ideas, and then begins to consider them with tempered selectivity. The proposals of the extremist groups become, in effect, a vast smorgasbord from which people of more moderate temperament pick and choose those ideas that fit best with their own traditional life styles.

But has this diffusion of counterculture or values produced significant *social* changes? What will be the impact of these values upon the crucial patterns of economic and political organisation?

Box 15.3

Late 1960s

The campus rebellion is in full flower.

A central theme on campus: the search for self-fulfilment in place of a conventional career.

Growing criticism of America as a "sick society".

The Women's Movement has virtually no impact on youth values and attitudes.

Violence on campus is condoned and romanticised; there are many acts of violence.

The value of education is severely questioned.

A widening "generation gap" appears in values, morals and outlook, dividing young people (especially college youth) from their parents.

A sharp split in social and moral values is found within the youth generation, between college students and the non-college majority. The gap *within* the generation proves to be larger and more severe than the gap *between* the generations.

The challenge to the traditional work ethic is confined to the campus.
A new code of sexual morality, centering on greater acceptance of

Box 15.3 Contd.

casual premarital sex; abortions, homosexuality, and extramarital relations is confined to a minority of college students.

Harsh criticisms of major institutions, such as political parties, big business, the military, etc., are almost wholly confined to college students.

The universities and the military are major targets of criticism.

The campus is the main locus of youthful discontent; non-college youth are quiescent.

Much youthful energy and idealism is devoted to concern with minorities, and blacks are considered the most oppressed group.

The political center of gravity of college youth: left/liberal.

The New Left is a force on campus: there are growing numbers of radical students.

Concepts of law and order are anathema to college students.

The student mood is angry, embittered, and bewildered by public hostility.

Early 1970s

The campus rebellion is moribund.

A central theme on campus: how to find self-fulfilment *within* a conventional career.

Lessening criticism of America as a "sick society".

Wide and deep penetration of Women's Lib precepts.

Violence-free campuses; the use of violence, even to achieve worthwhile objectives, is rejected.

The value of education is strongly endorsed.

The younger generation and older mainstream America move closer together in values, morals and outlook.

The gap within the generation narrows. Non-college youth have virtually caught up with college students in adopting the new social and moral norms.

The work ethic appears strengthened on campus, but is growing weaker among non-college youth.

The new sexual morality spreads both to mainstream college youth and also to mainstream working-class youth.

Criticism of some major institutions are tempered on campus but are taken up by working-class youth.

Box 15.3 Contd.

Criticisms of universities and the military decrease sharply.

Campuses are quiescent, but many signs of latent discontent and dissatisfaction appear among working-class youth.

Concern with minorities is lower, and American Indians are considered most oppressed.

No clear-cut political center of gravity: pressures in both directions, left and right.

The New Left is a negligible factor on campus; the number of radical students declines sharply.

College students show greater acceptance of law and order requirements.

There are few signs of anger or bitterness and little overt concern with public attitudes toward students.

Source : Daniel Yankelovich, *Changing Youth Values* in the 70s (New York: JDR 3rd Fund, 1974, pp. 7-8.

If the postindustrial society is at hand, the economic system will remain very much as Charles Reich describes it:

> The organisation that make up the corporate state are motivated primarily by the demands of technology and of their own internal structure. . .The essence of the corporate state is that it has just one value, the value of technology as represented by organisation, efficiency, growth, progress. . .In short, industrialism placed man under the rule of laws that were inhuman. (1970, p. 94)

Reich believes that countercultural values can tame this monster without resorting to violence by each person refusing to accept the demands of the industrial society. Such optimism is not widely shared. From the analysis of a number of observers it is probable that many of the cultural values embodied in the counterculture will continue to flourish but that there will be the continuing tension with the demands of a technological economy that Daniel Bell predicts (1973).

Charting out these trends and projecting them into the future affords us only general predictions – or perhaps better said, hunches. The forces of affluence, of scarcity, and of the new values are all at work on American society, but perhaps some other forces, only dimly perceived today, will emerge in the future. Whatever forces have greatest power, however, it is likely that there will be conscious attempts to guide their impact, for social change is increasingly subject to measurement and planning. This active attitude toward social change may itself represent the most fundamental break with the past and the central theme for social development in the future.

Bibliography

Althusser, Louis, *For Marx*, Allen Lane The Penguin Press, 1969, and New York, Random House, 1970, p. 25.

Applebaum, Richard P., *Theories of Social Change*, Chicago: Markham, 1970.

Armor, David, "The Evidence on Busing, "*The Public Interest*, no. 28 (Summer 1972): 90–126.

Astin, Alexander W., "Undergraduate Achievement and Institutional "Excellence," *Science*, vol. 161, no. 3842 (August 16, 1968): 661–68.

——, "A Summary of the Major Findings in 'The Second Year of Sesame Street: An Evaluation", Princeton, N. J.: Educational Testing Service, November 1971.

——, "Equal Schools or Equal Students?" *The Public Interest*, no. 4 (Summer 1966).

Ball, Samuel and Gerry Ann Bogatz, "A Summary of the Major Findings in 'The First Year of Sesame Street: An Evaluation'. 'Princeton, N. J. Educational Testing Service, October 1970.

Bandura, Albert and Richard H. Walters, *Adolescent Aggression*, New York; Ronald, 1959.

Barron, Milton, ed., *The Blending American*, Chicago: Quadrangel, 1972.

Barry, H., Margaret K. Becon, and I.L. Child, "A Cross-Cultural Survey of Some Sex Differences in Socialisation." *Journal of Abnormal Psychology*, vol. 55 (1957): 327–32.

Beard, Charles, *An Economic Interpretation of the Constitution of the United States*, New York: Free Press, 1949.

Becker, Howard S., *Outsiders*, New York: Free Press, 1963.

Becker, Howard S., ed., *The Other Side*, New York: Free Press, 1964.

Bell, Daniel, *The Coming of the Post-Industrial Society*, New York: Basic Book, 1973.

Bell, Daniel, *The Coming of the Post-Industrial Society,* New York: Basic Books; 1973.

Bell, Derrick A., Jr., "Racism in American Courts," *California New Law Review,* vol. 61, no. 1 (January 1973): 165–203.

Bellah, Robert N., "American Civil Religion in the 1970s," unpublished paper given at Drew University, March 1973.

Bellah, Robert N., *Beyond Belief,* New York: Harper & Row, 1970.

Berg, Ivar, *Education and Jobs: The Great Training Robbery,* New, York: Praeger, 1970.

Bettelheim, Bruno, *Children of the Dream,* New York: Avon, 1971.

Black, Cyril, *Dynamics of Modernisation,* New York: Harper & Row, 1968.

Bloch, Albert A., and Gilbert Geis, *Man, Crime and Society,* 2nd ed., New York: Random House, 1970.

Brightman, Lehman L., "Mental Genocide", *Inequality in Education,* no. 7 (February 1971): 15–19.

Brinton, Crane, *The Anatomy of Revolution,* New York: Random House, 1965.

Bronfenbrenner, Urie, "Socialisation and Social Class Through Time and Space," in Eleanor Maccoby. Theodore Newcomb, and Eugene L. Hartley, eds., *Readings in Social Psychology,* New York: Holt, Rinehart and Winston, 1958: 400–25.

Bronfenbrenner, Urie, *Two Worlds of Childhood,* New York: Russell Sage Foundation, 1970.

Bruce, Lenny, *How to Talk Dirty and Influence People,* Chicago: Playboy, 1963.

Chambliss, William J., "The Saints and the Roughnecks," Society, vol. 11 (December 11, 1973): 24-31.

Clark, Burton R., "The 'Cooling-out' Function in Higher Education", *American Journal of Sociology,* vol. 65 (May 1060): 567–76.

Cloward, Richard A., and Lloyd E. Ohlin, *Delinquency and Opportunity,* Glencoe, III: Free Press, 1960.

Cohen, Albert K., *Deviance and Control,* Englewood Cliffs, N.J.: Prentice-Hall, 1966.

Cohen, David K., "Public Schools: The Next Decade", *Dissent* (April 1971).

Coleman, James S., *The Adolescent Society.* New York; Free Press, 1961.

Cornish, Sally Woodhull, "Marriage Has Many Futures," *The Futurist* (June 1972): 103.

Covello, Leonard, *The Heart is the Teacher.* New York: McGraw-Hill, 1958.

Cox, Harvey, *The Secular City,* rev. ed., New York: Macmillan, 1966.

Craven, W. Frank, *The American Revolution, A Guide for Independent Study,* Princeton, N.J.: Princeton University Press, 1973.

Current Population Reports, "Literacy in the United States: November 1969," (series P-20, no. 217 (March 10, 1971).

Dahrendorf, Ralf, "*Toward a Theory of Social Conflict,*" in Etzioni-Halevy and Etzioni, 1973.

Davis, Alan J., "Sexual Assaults in the Philadelphia Prison System," in Wallace, 1971.

Demarath III, N.G., "Trends and Anti-Trends in Religious Change," in Eleanor B. Sheldon and Wilbert E. Moore, eds., *Indicators of Social Change,* New York: Russell Sage, 1968.

Demarath III, N.G., *Social Class in American Protestantism,* Chicago: Rand McNally, 1965.

Deutsch, Karl A., "The Growth of Nations: Some Recurrent Patterns of Political and Social Integration," *World Politics,* vol. 5, no. 2 (January 1953): 160 - 95.

Digest of Educational Statistics, Office of Education, Department of Health, Education, and Welfare. Washington, D. C.: Government Printing Office, 1970.

Dollard, John, et al., *Frustration and Aggression,* New Haven, Conn.: Yale University Press, 1939.

Durham, Michael, "For Swedes a Prison Sentence Can Be Fun," *Smithsonian* (September 1973): 46–52.

Durkheim, Emile, *The Division of Labour in Society,* New York: Free Press, 1964.

Durkheim, Emile, *The Elementary Forms of Religious Life* (1912), trans. by Joseph Ward Swain, New York: Free Press, 1965.

Durkheim, Emile, *The Rules of the Sociological Method* (1895), trans, by S.A. Solovay and J.H. Mueller Glencoe, III.: Free Press, 1964.

Edmiston, Susan "How to Write Your Own Marriage Contract," *Ms.* (Spring 1972): 66–74.

Eisenstadt, S.N., *Modernisation: Protest and Change,* Englewood Cliffs, N.J.: Prentice-Hall, 1966.

Eisenstadt, S.N., "Post Traditional Societies and the Continuity and Reconstruction of Tradition," *Daedalus* (Winter 1973): 1 - 27.

Erikson, Kai T., *Wayward Puritans,* New York: Wiley, 1966.

Etzioni-Halevy, E. and A. Etzioni, eds., *Social Change*, New York: Basic Books, 1973.

Farrell, William E., "School Integration Resisted in Cities of North," *The New York Times* (May 13, 1974): 24.

Findley, Warren G. and Miriam M. Bryan, *Ability Grouping, 1970: Status, Impact, and Alternatives*, Atlanta: University of Georgia, Center for Educational Improvement, 1970.

Friendenberg, Edgar Z., "Status and Role in Education", *The Humanist*, September-October 1968.

Friendenberg, Edgar Z., *Coming of Age in America: Growth and Acquiescence*. New York: Vintage, 1965.

Gasset, Jose Ortegay, *The Revolt of the Masses*, New York: Norton, 1957.

Gibbons, Donald, *Society, Crime, and Criminal Careers*, Englewood Cliffs, N.J. Prentice-Hall, 1968.

Glueck Eleanor and Sheldon, *Physique and Delinquency*, New York: Harper & Row, 1956.

Goffman, Erving, *Behaviour in Public Places*, New York: Free Press, 1963A.

Goffman, Erving, *Stigma : Notes on the Management of Spoiled Identity*, Englewood Cliffs, N.J.: Prentice-Hall, 1963B.

Goring, Charles, *The English Convict*, London: His Majesty's Stationery Office, 1913.

Goslin, David A., *The School in Contemporary Society*. Chicago: Scott, Foresman, 1965.

Gove, Walter R., "Societal Reaction as an Explanation of Mental Illness: An Evaluation," *American Sociological Review*, vol. 55 (October 1970): 873-84.

Gracey, Harry L., "Learning the Student Role: Kindergarten as Academic Boot Camp." In Dennis H. Wong and Harry L. Gracey, eds., *Readings in Introductory Sociology*, New York: Macmillan, 1972.

Hansen, W. Lea, and Burton A. Weisbrod, "The Distribution of Costs and Direct Benefits of Public Higher Education: The Case of California," in Harry G. Johnson and Burton A. Weisbrod, eds., *The Daily Economist*, Englewood Cliffs, N. J. : Prentice-Hall, 1969.

Harris, Marvin, *Culture, Man and Nature*, New York: Crowell, 1971.

Havighurst, Robert J., and Bernice Neugarten, *Society and Education*, Boston: Allyn & Bacon, 1968.

History and Class Consciousness: Studies in Marxist Dialectics, translated by Rodney Livingstone, London, Merlin Press, and Cambridge (Mass.) M.I.T. Press, 1971.

Hodgson, Godfrey, "Do Schools Make a Difference?" *The Atlantic,* vol. 213 (March 1973): 35–46.

Hoebel, E. Adamson, *Anthropology,* 4th ed. New York: McGraw-Hill, 1972.

Hollingshead, August B., and Frederich C. Redlich, *Social Class and Mental Illness,* New York : Wiley, 1958.

Holt, John, *How Children Fail.* New York: Pitman, 1964.

Holt, John, *The Underachieving School,* New York Dell, 1972.

Illich, Ivan, *Deschooling Society.* New York: Harper & Row, 1970.

Inkeles, Alex, "The Modernization of Man," in Myron Weiner, ed., *Modernisation,* New York: Basic Books, 1966.

Jackson, Philip W., *Life in Classrooms.* New York: Holt, Rinehart and Winston, 1968.

Jencks, Christopher, *Inequality: A Reassessment of the Effect of Family and Schooling in America.* New York: Basic Books, 1972.

Kagan, Jerome, "The Poor Are Educable," *The New York Times Annual Education Review* (January 16, 1974): 57ff.

Karnow, Stanley, "China-Journal-IV". *The New Republic* (July 28 and August 4. 1973): 9–21.

Kartz, Michael B., *Class, Bureaucracy and Schools: The Illusion of Educational Change in America.* New York: Praeger, 1971.

Katzenbach, Nicholas de B., Chairman, *The Challenge of Crime in a Free Society,* Washington, D.C.: U.S. Government Printing Office, 1967.

Kitsuse, John I., "Societal Reaction to Deviant Behaviour: Problems in Theory and Method," in Becker, 1964.

Knowles, Louis L. and Kenneth Prewitt, eds., *Institutional Racism in America.* Englewood Cliffs, N. J.: Prentice-Hall, 1969.

Kohl, Herbert R., *The Open Classroom: A Practical Guide to a New Way of Teaching.* New York: Vintage, 1969.

Kornhauser, William, *The Politics of Mass Society,* New York: Free Press, 1959.

Kuhn, James W., "The Misuse of Education. The Problem of Schooling for Employment," in Berg, 1970.

Larry L. and Joan M. Constantine, "Where is Marriage Going?" *The Futurist* (April 1970): 44–46.

Lauter, Paul and Florence Howe, "How the School System is Rigged for Failure." in *The Conspiracy of the Young,* New York, World, 1970.

Lewis, Flora, "Western Europe Falters," *The New York Times* (March 4, 1974): 1,7.

Lewontin, R.C., "Evolution—The Concept," *The International Encyclopaedia of the Social Sciences,* New York: Macmillan 1968.

Lombroso, Cesare, in G.L. Ferrero, *Criminal Man,* New York: Putnam, 1911.

Marx, Karl and Friedrich Engels, *The Manifesto of the Communist Party,* New York: International Publishers, 1932.

Merton, Robert K., *Social Theory and Social Structure,* Glencoe, III. : Free Press, 1957.

Miller, Walter B., "Lower-class Culture as a Generating Milieu of Gang Delinquency," *Journal of Sociological Issues,* vol. 14 (1958): 5–19.

Mitford, Jessica, *Kind and Usual Punishment,* New York: Knopf, 1973.

Moore, Barrington, *Social Origins of Dictatorship and Democracy,* Boston: Beacon Press, 1966.

Moore, Wilbert E., *Social Change,* Englewood Cliffs, N.J.: Prentice Hall, 1963.

Morgan, Edmund S., *The Birth of the Republic, 1763-89,* Chicago: University of Chicago Press, 1956.

Morris, Richard B., *The American Revolution Reconsidered,* New York: Harper & Row, 1967.

Myers, Jerome K., and Lee L. Bean, *A Decade Later:A Follow-Up of Social Class and Mental Illness,* New York: Wiley, 1968.

Nisbet, Robert A., *The Social Bond,* New York: Knopf, 1970.

Ophuls, William, "The Scarcity Society," *Harper's* (April 1974): 47 - 52.

Ottenberg, Simon, "Ibo Receptivity to Change," in William R. Bascom and Melville J. Herskovitz, *Continuity and Change in African Cultures,* Chicago: University of Chicago Press, 1959.

Parsons, Talcott, *Societies: Evolutionary and Comparative Perspectives,* Englewood Cliffs, N.J.: Prentice-Hall, 1966.

Parsons, Talcott, *The Social System,* New York: Free Press, 1951.

Rainwater, Lee, "Post-1984 America," *Society,* vol. 9, no. 4 (February 1972): 18 - 27.

Reich, Charles, *The Greening of America,* New York: Random House, 1970.

Reiss, Albert J., Jr., *The Police and the Public,* New Haven, Conn.: Yale University Press, 1971.

Roszak, Theodore, *The Making of a Counterculture,* New York: Doubleday, 1969.

Schur, Edwin M., *Crimes Without Victims,* Englewood Cliffs, N.J.: Prentice-Hall, 1965.

Schwartz, Barry "Deprivation of Privacy as a Functional Prerequisite' in the Case of Prison," *Journal of Criminal Law, Criminology and Police Science,* vol. 63 (1972): 229–39.

Schwartz, Herman "Prisoners' Rights: Some Hopes and Realities," in *A Programme for Prison Reform,* Cambridge, Mass.: The Roscoe Pound-American Trial Lawyers Foundation, 1972.

Schwartz, Richard D., and Jerome H. Skolnick, "Two Studies of Legal Stigma," in Becker, 1964.

Selznick, Philip, "Institutional Vulnerability in Mass Society," *The American Journal of Sociology,* vol. 56 (January 1951): 320 - 31.

Shaw, Clifford R., and Henry D. McKay, *Delinquency Areas,* Chicago: University of Chicago Press, 1929.

Shaw, George Bernard, *Saint Joan* (1924), Baltimore: Penguin, 1951.

Sheldon, William H., with Emil M. Hart and Eugene McDermott, *Varieties of Delinquent Youth,* New York: Harper & Row, 1949.

Srole, Leo, et al., *Mental Health in the Metropolis : The Midtown Manhattan Study,* New York: McGraw-Hill, 1962.

Sutherland, Edwin H., and Donald R. Cressy, *Principles of Criminology,* 6th ed., Philadelphia: Lippincott, 1960.

Sykes, Gresham, *The Society of Captives,* Princeton, N.J.: Princeton University Press, 1958.

"Following Up on Headstart," *The New Republic* (April 1, 1969): 12-13.

"Goals of the Headstart Program," Letter to the Editor, *The New York Times* (July 10, 1971).

"How Head a Head Start?" *The New Republic* (April 26, 1969): 8-9.